THE SOCIAL PSYCHOLOGY OF PERSONAL RELATIONSHIPS

Edited by

WILLIAM ICKES AND STEVE DUCK

JOHN WILEY & SONS, LTD

Chichester · New York · Weinheim · Brisbane · Singapore · Toronto

Other Wiley Editorial Offices

John Wiley & Sons, Inc., 605 Third Avenue,
New York, NY 10158-0012, USA

WILEY-VCH Verlag GmbH, Pappelallee 3,
D-69469 Weinheim, Germany

Jacaranda Wiley Ltd, 33 Park Road, Milton,
Queensland 4064, Australia

John Wiley & Sons (Asia) Pte Ltd, 2 Clementi Loop #02-01,
Jin Xing Distripark, Singapore 129809

John Wiley & Sons (Canada) Ltd, 22 Worcester Road,
Rexdale, Ontario M9W 1L1, Canada

Library of Congress Cataloging-in-Publication Data

The social psychology of personal relationships / edited by William Ickes and Steve Duck.
     p.   cm.
   Includes bibliographical references and index.
   ISBN 0-471-99881-8 (pbk.)
   1. Interpersonal relations.   2. Social psychology.   I. Ickes, William John.   II. Duck,
Steve.

   HM1106 .S62 1999
   302—dc21

                                                                                   99–048746

British Library Cataloguing in Publication Data

A catalogue record for this book is available from the British Library

ISBN 0-471-99881-8

Typeset in 10/12pt Times by Dorwyn Ltd, Rowlands Castle, Hants
Printed and bound in Great Britain by Bookcraft (Bath) Ltd, Midsomer Norton, Somerset
This book is printed on acid-free paper responsibly manufactured from sustainable forestry, in
which at least two trees are planted for each one used for paper production.

CONTENTS

About the Editors   vi
About the Authors   vii

1   **Personal Relationships and Social Psychology**   1
    William Ickes and Steve Duck
2   **An Evolutionary Perspective on Human Relationships**   9
    Douglas T. Kenrick and Melanie R. Trost
3   **A Process Model of Adult Attachment Formation**   37
    Debra Zeifman and Cindy Hazan
4   **Perspectives on Interracial Relationships**   55
    Stanley O. Gaines and William Ickes
5   **Interdependence in Personal Relationships**   79
    Caryl Rusbult and Ximena Arriaga
6   **Self-expansion Motivation and Including Other in the Self** 109
    Art Aron and Elaine Aron
7   **Self-presentational Perspectives on Personal Relationships** 129
    Mark R. Leary and Rowland S. Miller
8   **Methods of Studying Close Relationships**   157
    William Ickes
9   **On the Statistics of Interdependence: Treating Dyadic Data
    with Respect**   181
    Richard Gonzalez and Dale Griffin
10 **Embracing the *Social* in Personal Relationships and Research** 215
    Linda Acitelli, Steve Duck, and Lee West

    References   229
    Author Index   283
    Subject Index   295

ABOUT THE EDITORS

William Ickes is Professor of Psychology at the University of Texas at Arlington. His early research focused on personality influences on behavior in unstructured dyadic interactions. His current research focuses on empathic accuracy and other aspects of intersubjective cognition. His previous edited books include the three-volume series, *New Directions In Attribution Research* (with John H. Harvey and Robert Kidd), the *Handbook of Personal Relationships* (with Steve Duck et al.), *Compatible and Incompatible Relationships*, and *Empathic Accuracy*. His academic honors include the Berscheid–Hatfield Award for Distinguished Mid-career Achievement (from the International Network on Personal Relationships) and the New Contribution Award (from the International Society for the Study of Personal Relationships).

Steve Duck is the Daniel and Amy Starch Distinguished Research Professor at the University of Iowa and has been a keen promoter of the field of personal relationships research since it was formed. He co-founded the first International Conference on Personal Relationships in 1982, and was founder and first editor of the *Journal of Social and Personal Relationships*, first President of the International Network on Personal Relationships, the professional organization for the research field, and editor of the first edition of the *Handbook of Personal Relationships*. The Steve Duck New Scholar Award was endowed and named in his honor by a group of independent scholars to recognize his promotion of the work of younger professionals and his dedication to developing the field.

ABOUT THE AUTHORS

Linda K. Acitelli is an Associate Professor in the Department of Psychology at the University of Houston. Her research on relationships has been funded by the National Institute of Mental Health. Her major research interests are cognition and communication in relationships, specifically thinking and talking about relationships and the factors that determine their impact on individual and relationship well-being. In 1995, the International Network on Personal Relationships awarded her the Gerald R. Miller Award for her early career achievements.

Arthur Aron received his PhD from the University of Toronto in 1970 in social psychology. His main research interests are in motivation and cognition in personal relationships and the role of personal relationships in intergroup relations. He is currently Associate Editor for the Interpersonal Relations and Group Processes Section of the *Journal of Personality and Social Psychology*. He teaches in the Psychology Department at the State University of New York at Stony Brook.

Elaine N. Aron received her PhD from Pacifica Graduate Institute in 1995 in clinical psychology with a specialization in depth psychology. Her research interests are personal relationships, adult temperament, and the depth psychology of culture. Her most recent book is *The Highly Sensitive Person* (Carol/Birch Lane Press, 1996). Elaine consults and maintains a private practice in San Francisco.

Ximena Arriaga is an Assistant Professor in the Psychology Department at Purdue University. Her research concerns the developmental course of dating relationships (e.g., how variability over time in adherence factors influences the stability of ongoing relationships), interpersonal violence (both basic research and community issues), and subtle forms of prejudice. She has received several funding awards from the National Institute of Mental Health and The Fletcher Jones Foundation.

Stanley O. Gaines, Jr, is Assistant Professor in the Department of Psychology at Pomona College and in the Intercollegiate Department of Black Studies at The Claremont Colleges. His primary research interests include cultural value orientations, ethnicity, personality characteristics, and gender as influences on interpersonal resource exchange, responses to partners' dissatisfaction, and other personal relationship processes. He has published conceptual and empirical articles in a number of journals, including the *Journal of Black Psychology*, the *Journal of Social and Personal Relationships*, *Basic and Applied Social Psychology*, and *American Psychologist*.

Richard Gonzalez was raised in Southern California. He received a BA in Psychology from UCLA and a PhD in Social Psychology from Stanford University. His current research interests include mathematical modeling, interpersonal relations and group decision making.

Dale Griffin was raised in Vancouver, Canada. He received a BA in Psychology from the University of British Columbia and a PhD in Social Psychology from Stanford University. His current research interests include social prediction, interpersonal relations, and medical decision making.

Cindy Hazan received her PhD in Personality and Social Psychology from the University of Denver in 1988, and is currently Associate Professor in the Department of Human Development and Family Studies at Cornell. For more than a decade, she has been investigating romantic relationship phenomena within the framework of ethological attachment theory. Currently, she is PI on a four-year grant from the National Science Foundation to study attachment formation processes.

Douglas T. Kenrick is a Professor of Psychology at Arizona State University. He has conducted research on interpersonal attraction, person-environment interactions, altruism, aggression, and mate selection across human cultures. His main theoretical interest is in integrating evolutionary approaches with traditional social psychological models of behavior and cognition.

Mark R. Leary is Professor of Psychology at Wake Forest University (Winston-Salem, NC). He is the author of six books, including *Self-Presentation: Impression Management and Interpersonal Behavior*, *Social Anxiety* (with R. Kowalski), and *Social Psychology and Dysfunctional Behavior* (with R. Miller).

Rowland S. Miller, a Professor of Psychology at Sam Houston State University in Huntsville, Texas, is the author of *Embarrassment: Poise and Peril in Everyday Life* (Guilford Press, 1996). He is also a co-author (with Sharon Brehm and Dan Perlman) of the 3rd edition of the best-selling text, *Intimate Relationships* (McGraw-Hill, 2000).

Caryl Rusbult is the J. Ross MacDonald Professor in the Department of Psychology at the University of North Carolina at Chapel Hill. Her research concerns commitment processes in close relationships, including the specific maintenance mechanisms by which committed individuals sustain long-term involvements (e.g., accommodation, sacrifice, derogation of tempting alternatives).

Melanie R. Trost is an Associate Professor of Communication at Arizona State University. Her research investigates the evolutionary bases of interpersonal processes such as flirting, rejecting flirtation, expressing and quelling jealousy, and selecting mates. Her other research interests include the communication of minority group messages and influence processes involved in drug use and unwanted sexual activity within high school romantic relationships.

Lee West is a doctoral candidate in the Communication Studies Department at the University of Iowa. Her research interests include how social expectations organize and are reinstantiated through naturally occurring conversations, specifically, in the (re)production of class, gender, and race in both everyday talk and the discourse of academe. She is a co-author of a chapter on cross-sex friendship.

Debra Zeifman received her PhD in Developmental Psychology from Cornell University in 1996 and is currently Assistant Professor of Psychology at Vassar College. She has conducted research on the biological underpinnings, psychological dynamics, and evolutionary history of infant-caregiver and adult pair-bond relationships.

Chapter 1

Personal Relationships and Social Psychology

William Ickes

University of Texas, Arlington, TX, USA

and

Steve Duck

University of Iowa, Iowa City, IA, USA

Imagine that Shakespeare had written *Hamlet* so that Hamlet's soliloquy was the entire play, rather than being limited to lines 57–91 of Act 3, Scene 1. You, as the playgoer, would never see the Ghost of Hamlet's father, nor his mother Gertrude, nor his uncle Claudius, nor Polonius, Ophelia, and Laertes. Hamlet would, of course, describe them to you, tell you about events in his life involving these individuals, and try to explain how—at each point in his narrative—his actions were influenced by the situations and events as he construed them at that time. But what kind of experience would you, as the playgoer, have while watching this completely "interiorized" *Hamlet*?

One possibility is that only the character of Hamlet himself would seem real and vivid in such a production. Perhaps it would be even easier than in the original version of the play to understand and identify with Hamlet's perspective, while the implicit perspectives of the other characters would appear more shadowy and indistinct—and therefore be experienced as less "real". Or perhaps Hamlet's own perspective would itself seem more suspect, as he

The Social Psychology of Personal Relationships.
Edited by William Ickes and Steve Duck. © 2000 John Wiley & Sons Ltd.

begins his account by describing an encounter with the ghost of his dead father without the benefit of this specter appearing on-stage to corroborate his testimony. And once Hamlet has created the unfortunate first impression of being delusional, if not completely insane, how likely is it that you would believe anything further that he had to say?

Neither possibility holds much promise of fulfilling the playgoer's desire for a kind of aesthetic, if not objective, truth. The first possibility gives too much weight to Hamlet's view of social reality and not enough weight to the views of the other "social actors". On the other hand, the second possibility questions the objectivity of Hamlet's perspective to such an extent that we, as observers, would be reluctant to assign much weight to his "self-reports". In either case, it seems unlikely that an interiorized *Hamlet* could ever match the verisimilitude and emotional force of the original version.

We suggest that, just as we should have our doubts about the merits of an interiorized Hamlet, we should entertain corresponding doubts about the merits of a similarly interiorized study of social cognition and social behavior. If there are reasons for being less than satisfied with a theatrical account that presents only a single actor's perspective on his or her social relationships, there are parallel reasons for being less than satisfied with a social psychological account that is also based solely on single actors' self-reports.

It is therefore ironic, and perhaps even paradoxical, that the social psychology of the past 50 years has relied primarily on single-participant research paradigms in which individuals are asked to report their own subjective reactions to nominally "social" stimuli or "social" situations. It is also ironic that these individuals are typically asked to provide such self-reports in complete isolation from those shadowy others—real or imagined—who presumably bestow upon the situation its "social" character. In effect, the research participants in the traditional single-subject paradigms have been cast in the role of soliloquizing Hamlets who must convey their social experience more through reminiscence or anticipated action than through their actual interactions with others (Ickes & Dugosh, in press).

But if the single-subject paradigm has been the major source of this problem, as we and others have argued (Duck, 1994a; Ickes & Dugosh, in press; Ickes & Gonzalez, 1994, 1996), then the primary corrective should be the increasing use of research paradigms in which the unit of analysis is the interacting dyad or small group, as we and others have also argued (Gonzalez & Griffin, 1997; Ickes, Bissonnette, Garcia, & Stinson, 1990; Ickes & Gonzalez, 1996; Kenny, 1994; Wegner, Giuliano, & Hertel, 1985). It is for this reason that the study of personal relationships has, during the past three decades, had such a revolutionary impact on the field of social psychology.

The social psychology of personal relationships, developing out of the early work on interpersonal attraction, has experienced rapid—perhaps even explosive—growth on two related fronts. One the one hand, it has developed into a vibrant, interdisciplinary field of scholarship in its own right (Acitelli, 1995; Berscheid, 1994, 1995). On the other hand, it has emerged as an area increasingly recognized as dealing with central, fundamental social processes that underpin many of the phenomena that have traditionally been studied by social psychologists. These phenomena include (among others) aggression, altruism, intergroup relations, and social influence (Reis, 1998). Moreover, as researchers who study personal relationships have frequently noted, many theoretically interesting social psychological topics such as stress (Hobfoll & deVries, 1995), social support (Sarason, Sarason, & Gurung, 1997), the nature of self (Swann, 1983; Tangney & Fischer, 1995), attribution (Fletcher & Fincham, 1991a), and group/jury decision-making (Duck, 1998) are affected by relational dynamics in ways neither previously recognized nor at this point fully understood.

The chapters in the present volume reflect this dual emphasis, dealing not only with the theoretical bases of the social psychology of personal relationships but also with the ways in which more traditional social psychological topics are illuminated by research on personal relationships. In this volume, we have collected updated versions of the present introductory chapter and the six subsequent chapters that appeared in the Social Psychology section of the second (1997) edition of *The Handbook of Personal Relationships*. We have also included three additional chapters, written or revised especially for this volume, to complement the set of theoretical and meta-theoretical perspectives represented in the original publication. As a context for understanding the place of each of these chapters in a social psychology of personal relationships, we offer the following historical background.

HISTORICAL BACKGROUND

The lack of theoretical diversity in the first wave of social psychological research on personal relationships made the area an easy target for critics. The problem was not a matter of there being no theory at all, as the more misguided of the critics wanted to suggest. Rather, the problem was that a single theoretical perspective—exchange theory—seemed to dominate the work in this newly emerging area. Blau's (1964) exchange theory, the prototype of this research tradition, was an extension into the interpersonal realm of ideas that could be found in Heider's (1958) balance theory. Analogizing from the individual's need for cognitive balance and harmony, Blau focused on power in social life and on the need of relationship partners to achieve a mutually acceptable balance of their respective costs and rewards.

Exchange theory, begotten of balance theory, itself begat equity theory (Adams, 1965; Homans, 1961, 1974; Hatfield, Walster & Berscheid, 1978), the different versions of which aspired to be more precise about the intuitive formulas people use to calculate the returns on their interpersonal and relational investments. Equity theory, in turn, begat interdependence theory (Kelley & Thibaut, 1978), which was premised on the assumption that not all social interactions reflected a mutual desire for equity and fair exchange. Acknowledging both the diversity and the complexity of personal relationships, interdependence theory assumed that the motives of relationship partners can clash as well as converge, leading to a variety of outcomes such as aggression, altruism, competition, capitulation, cooperation, and intransigence (see Rusbult and Arriaga, this volume). In this manner, theory about the subjective harmony or dissonance of a single individual's attitudes, motives, values, or goals was extended and transformed into theory about the intersubjective harmony or dissonance of the attitudes, motives, values, or goals of persons in a variety of social relationships with one another.

The interpersonal exchange approach provided both a guiding metaphor and a theoretical framework for social psychological research on an array of issues ranging from altruism to group functioning. Although its primary contribution has been to amplify our understanding of the variety and intricacy of interpersonal exchange processes, it has also focused theorists' attention on the need to clarify the relational structure on which such processes are based. The development of a social psychology of personal relationships therefore requires researchers to deal directly with the old but persistent question of what is *social* about social psychology (Stroebe, 1980). The answers they are developing should help us to better appreciate and better understand the many perplexing ways in which the subjective and the intersubjective are intertwined in our everyday social lives (Mead, 1934; Schutz, 1970).

Although the ideas generated by exchange-based theories were of central importance to the larger field of social psychology as well as to the emerging field of personal relationships, all of the theories of interpersonal harmony/ disharmony tended to overlook a fundamental question: What are the origins of the conflicting (or complementary) attitudes, motives, values, or goals that generate interpersonal tensions (or symbioses)? The need to answer this question provided the impetus for new theoretical approaches relevant to the study of personal relationships. The answers provided by such approaches focused less on the dynamics of the conflicts/symbioses that occur within relationships (i.e., how they play out, how they are resolved) than on the etiology of these conflicts/symbioses (i.e., how and why they emerge in the first place). In consequence, there are at least two major themes evident in current social psychological theorizing about personal relationships: (1) the traditional theme of how individual motives conflict, converge, and resolve into various individual and joint outcomes within the context of interdependent relationships, and (2) the newer but yet more "precursory" theme of the origins of the personal dispositions that cause such conflicts/symbioses to arise in the first place.

THE PRESENT VOLUME

Both of these themes are evident in the set of chapters that compose the present volume. The precursory theme of the origins of the dispositions that lead to conflicts or symbioses in personal relationships is developed in Kenrick and Trost's chapter on evolutionary approaches to relationships, in Zeifman and Hazan's chapter on the processes underlying adult attachment formation, and in Gaines and Ickes's chapter on interracial relationships. The traditional theme of how individual motives conflict, converge and resolve into various individual and joint outcomes is developed from two distinctly different theoretical perspectives: the perspective of interdependence theory (Rusbult and Arriaga), and the perspective of self-expansion theory (Aron and Aron). This same theme is also developed from a data analytic perspective in Ickes's chapter on methodological options and in Gonzalez and Griffin's chapter on "the statistics of interdependence".

The themes of individual differences and interdependence are also evident in the two remaining chapters. Leary and Miller discuss how the motive to establish and maintain a desired image in the eyes of self and others leads individuals to act toward each other in ways that are sometimes deceptive and sometimes collusive, but are always in the service of "saving face" at the individual, dyadic, or group level(s). Acitelli, Duck, and West encourage researchers to pay as much attention to the variabilities of relational experience as to its constancies, and to be more sensitive to the ways in which traditional social psychological phenomena are underpinned by the relationship between the parties involved. A more detailed overview of these and the other chapters in the volume is provided below.

THE SUBSEQUENT CHAPTERS

The evolutionary origins of the personal dispositions that lead to conflicts or symbioses in close relationships is the topic of Kenrick and Trost's chapter. These authors apply the basic assumptions and principles of evolutionary psychology to the study of human relationships. They begin with the premise that cooperative human relationships are generally adaptive in helping to ensure the inclusive fitness of individuals and their kin. They are careful to qualify this generalization, however, by describing how differences in the evolutionary "payoffs" for the individuals in potential or actual relationships may underlie a range of more competitive and/or conflictive phenomena. These phenomena include jealousy, intrasexual competition, deceptive mating strategies, and family violence. Kenrick and Trost conclude that "the evolutionary perspective provides a comprehensive model of relationships", one in which even apparently anomalous behaviors can be interpreted and explained.

The chapter by Zeifman and Hazan concerns the convergence of individual needs and motives across time that enables adults to develop and maintain romantic relationships. Using Bowlby's (1969/1982, 1973, 1980) ethological attachment theory as their guiding framework, the authors outline a normative model of adult attachment formation. While acknowledging some obvious differences between infant/caregiver attachment and attachment in adult romantic pairs (e.g., attachment bonds in adult romantic partners are typically reciprocal, rather than complementary; adult attachments can serve the function of sexual reproduction), Zeifman and Hazan argue convincingly that the stages in which adult attachment occurs (attraction and flirting, falling

in love, loving, life as usual) are analogous to Bowlby's four phases of infant/
caregiver attachment (pre-attachment, attachment in the making, clear-cut
attachment, goal-corrected partnership). In particular, they suggest that the
needs and emotions evoked in each stage of adult romantic attachment parallel those evoked at the corresponding stage of infant/caregiver interaction,
and that the complementary fulfillment of both partners' needs at each stage
enables their relationship to form, strengthen, and continue.

The topic of the chapter by Gaines and Ickes is the origins of the differences between the perspectives of "insiders" and "outsiders" on interracial
relationships. In this chapter, the authors examine the evolutionary,
perceptual-cognitive, and socio-historical influences that combine to make the
perspective of outside observers of interracial relationships different from
that of the relationship members themselves. The authors argue that tension
between these two perspectives takes characteristically different forms in
different types of interracial relationships (i.e., male–male and female–female
friendships, heterosexual and homosexual romantic relationships). It is therefore important for the members of these relationships to understand the
specific tensions involved in each case so that they can anticipate and attempt
to resolve them—no easy task in the face of anti-"race-mixing" mindsets that
have proved to be extremely resistant to change.

The next chapter addresses and updates the more traditional theme in
theorizing about personal relationships: the theme of how individual motives
conflict, converge, and resolve into various individual and joint outcomes
within the context of these relationships. Rusbult and Arriaga's comprehensive review of the work on interdependence theory provides both a cogent
summary of the theory itself and an informative tour of the different lines of
research it has inspired. Their chapter focuses on how relationship members
perceive and act within the constraints of the interdependence structures that
are the elemental features of their social experience. More specifically, it
examines how individual motives, features of the situation, and features of the
relationship itself define interdependence structures which, as their implications are perceived, can transform the motivation of one or both partners in
ways that can precipitate a wide variety of individual and joint outcomes
(altruism, competition, intransigence, etc.).

The upper limit of interdependence—the blurring of the boundaries between
self and partner—is the topic of the chapter by Aron and Aron. These authors
outline their model of self-expansion motivation, which is based on the notion
that "people seek to expand themselves" (e.g., in their physical and social
influence, in their knowledge and insight, and in their sense of identity and
belongingness) through their relationships with others. Aron and Aron argue
that the desire for self-expansion is a fundamental motive that is expressed not
only in individual exploration, competence, and efficacy, as various other
theorists have noted (e.g., Bandura, 1977; Deci, 1975; Gecas, 1989; White,
1959), but through participation in relationships as well. The research they
describe helps to document two basic processes suggested by the self-expansion
model: "first, that relationship satisfaction is increased through the association

of the relationship with self-expansion and, second, that the relationship means cognitively that each partner has included the other in his or her self." The model is shown to have a special utility in accounting for certain phenomena, such as the motivation for unrequited love and the effects on the self of falling in love, which other theories have rarely addressed.

Leary and Miller offer a self-presentational perspective on personal relationships—one that charts the course of impression management in all stages of personal relationships. Of course, not all of our behavior is self-presentational, and not all of our self-presentational behavior is intended to be deceptive. However, a large portion of our everyday behavior is motivated by the desire to influence the perceptions that others have of us in ways that will promote both our individual and relational goals. Leary and Miller argue that our motivation to engage in such impression management depends upon the extent to which the resulting impressions have the potential to help us attain our goals, the value we place on these goals, and the discrepancies between the images that we wish to convey and the impressions that we appear to be making. They further argue that the nature and content of the self-presentations we attempt are influenced by such factors as the audience's values, the salient social roles and norms, and the self-images and social reputations that we wish to have now and in the future. Self-presentation can take place at the level of the relationship as well, influencing how others might perceive our marriage, our business partnership, or our collaborations with others.

In the first of two chapters dealing with methodological and statistical issues, Ickes reviews the different methods that researchers can use to study close relationships. Essentially, they are the same set of methods that all of us can use to learn more about close relationships in our everyday lives. These methodological options include different types of self-reports that are obtained from the individual relationship members (via questionnaires, interviews, interaction records, diaries and other kinds of accounts). They also include peer reports obtained from knowledgeable respondents, observational data collected in various settings, life-event data collected from archival records, experiments designed to test specific hypotheses, the assessment of relevant physiological responses, and eclectic approaches that combine two or more of these methodological options. Ickes discusses the different trade-offs that researchers must make in deciding which method(s) to use in a given study. He suggests that such trade-offs not only reflect the researcher's perceptions of the relative rewards and costs associated with different methods but the researcher's philosophical and theoretical commitments as well.

In the next chapter, Gonzalez and Griffin address the unique statistical problems that are inherent in the study of personal relationships. They begin by criticizing the "ritualistic mutilation of dyadic data" by generations of researchers who have attempted to circumvent the problems of dyadic interdependence in their data rather than confront these problems directly. To provide researchers with more constructive and appropriate alternatives, Gonzalez and Griffin present an ingenious family of statistical techniques that are based on the intraclass correlation and the pairwise method for computing it. These techniques enable individual-level and dyad-level covariances to be modeled as latent variables in different types of dyadic designs. Both univariate and multivariate applications of these techniques are presented and discussed in a style that is refreshingly "user friendly". Researchers who want to analyze their dyadic data appropriately should start by reading—or re-reading—this chapter, whether their primary interest is in personal relationships specifically or in social interaction more generally.

In the final chapter, Acitelli, Duck, and West focus on two aspects of relational work in social psychology. First, they consider the need to explore the living experience of relationship members, including its contradictions, dilemmas, and difficulties of management. They encourage researchers to pay as much attention to the variabilities of relational experience as to the constancies, and to attempt to characterize relationships by the ways in which partners deal with these variabilities, tensions, conflicting loyalties, and trade-offs between the good and the bad. Second, they assert that relationship experiences and relational states underlie much other social psychological activity. They provide examples illustrating how a number of traditional social psychological phenomena (e.g., group decision making, attitude change, and social psychological conceptions of the self) are grounded in the relationships that exist between the parties involved. They conclude by predicting the growing role of relational studies in the future development of a truly *social* social psychology.

EXEUNT OMNES, CONVERSING

In summary, the chapters in this book not only survey the major social psychological theories about personal relationships but also illustrate the reciprocal influences of this emerging interdisciplinary field of study upon the broader range of processes typically studied by social psychologists. Although the theoretical approaches represented in this volume are, in our opinion, the ones with the strongest claims of being both distinctive and broad in scope, we would hasten to note that many other theoretical and quasi-theoretical traditions have recently emerged within this broad, interdisciplinary field of study. These include taxonomic models of different types of personal relationships, stage and developmental theories concerning the changes in relationships across time, process theories that focus on specific relational phenomena or outcomes, and dialectical or dialogical approaches (Duck, West, & Acitelli, 1997).

Any complaints that critics may have had 30 years ago about the absence of, or lack of diversity in, theories about personal relationships are simply no longer valid as we progress into the next millennium, as the chapters in this volume and its companions in the series should make clear. Moreover, we can safely predict that, in the decades to come, the accelerating theoretical progress in our understanding of personal relationships will be accompanied by a correspondingly greater application of these insights to the entire spectrum of social psychological phenomena.

Chapter 2

An Evolutionary Perspective on Human Relationships

Douglas T. Kenrick

and

Melanie R. Trost

Arizona State University, Tempe, AZ, USA

Evolutionary theory is arguably the most powerful set of ideas in the life sciences. No natural scientist studying the wing of a bat or the flipper of a seal or the long neck of a giraffe would ignore Darwin's theory of evolution by natural selection. Likewise for the behaviors of bats or seals or giraffes— obviously the unique bodies of these animals evolved to do something, and evolutionary theory helps to understand the co-evolution of physical morphology and behavior. Neither would many disagree that an evolutionary perspective is essential to understand the human body, with its upright posture, prehensile grasping hands, and large brain capable of producing complex language. Yet many social scientists have not yet realized that an evolutionary perspective is just as essential for a full understanding of human behavior. Just as bats are designed to survive by flying through the night sky, seals by swimming through the ocean depths, and giraffes by walking through the African plains, so human beings are designed to behave in certain ways in certain environments. To a large extent, humans are designed to live in social groups with other humans, and an evolutionary perspective can enhance our understanding of every aspect of personal relationships considered in this

The Social Psychology of Personal Relationships.
Edited by William Ickes and Steve Duck. © 2000 John Wiley & Sons Ltd.

volume—including love, interdependence, social support, parent–child relationships, and family conflicts. Indeed, an evolutionary perspective can help
us to see how all of these different aspects of human relationships are connected with one another; and, at the next level, how they are connected with
the evolved design of the human body and brain, and ultimately, with the
fundamental principles that underlie the design of all living creatures.

BASIC ASSUMPTIONS OF EVOLUTIONARY PSYCHOLOGY

Evolutionary explanations of life begin with Darwin's (1859) set of simple
assumptions:

1. Organisms reproduce very rapidly, so by normal processes of geometric
   multiplication, even slowly reproducing animals such as elephants could
   cover the globe in a few centuries, if unrestrained. Any given species
   would therefore rapidly exhaust the limited resources available to it, if it
   were not for the fact that other animals are also competing for those same
   resources.
2. Animals vary in ways that influence their ability to survive in competition
   with members of their own and other species (some giraffes have longer
   necks, some have shorter necks).
3. Those organisms whose genetic traits provide an advantage in access to
   resources will survive longer, and be more successful in mating. As a result,
   their genes will increase in the population relative to less well-adapted
   competitors. (Of course, the population growth of even relatively well-
   adapted animals is still limited by resource availability, competition with
   members of other species, predators, parasites, and so on.)

These processes of random variation and selective retention form the basis of
natural selection. Analogous to the artificial selection exercised by animal
breeders, as in selecting for short hair or a peaceful disposition in a dog, the
forces of nature select certain characteristics over others.

As Darwin (1872) spelled out in his classic work on emotion, the process of
natural selection also applies to behavior. Snarling communicates an intention
to attack, and animals who recognize the signal and avoid a snarling adversary
save themselves costly and bloody encounters. The abilities to both transmit
and receive emotional communications are thus selected. Although the pioneering textbooks in social psychology were written from a Darwinian
perspective (James, 1890; McDougall, 1908), later behavioral scientists largely
ignored the implications of natural selection for humans. During the 1970s,
however, stimulated in part by Wilson's *Sociobiology* (1975), social scientists
began to incorporate evolutionary theory into their models of human social
behavior.

   Misunderstandings of the relationship between genetic predispositions and psychological development have led to misguided controversies about the extent to which human behavior is controlled by genes *versus* cultural environment, or by genes *versus* rational thought. The human capacities to create culture and to engage in complex cognition are themselves made possible by our genetic predispositions. These predispositions influence the choice of certain cultural practices over others and the inclination to attend to, think about, and remember certain features of the environment (Lumsden & Wilson, 1981; Tooby & Cosmides, 1992). Genetic predispositions unfold in interaction with experience, resulting in cognitive and behavioral mechanisms that are themselves triggered by, and attuned to, events in the social and physical environment (Buss, 1995; Crawford & Anderson, 1989). Language provides a clear example. As Pinker (1994) notes, language is undoubtedly a species-specific evolved feature of humans: there are brain mechanisms dedicated to its production and understanding; the level of linguistic complexity is the same in all human groups; children acquire it with little effort; sign language shows some of the same deep structure as spoken language; and so on. However, the specific language that a child learns is determined by environmental inputs. No set of genes determines whether a child will say: "Come vanno le cose, signore?" "Hoe gaat het met je, mijnheer?" or "How's it going, man?".

   Depending partly on environmental inputs, genetic predispositions may unfold very differently for different members of a species. Within one fish species, for instance, some males grow into large territorial animals that attract harems; others grow into small animals that look like females and attempt to "sneak-copulate", and still others begin life as females and only turn into males when a large territorial male dies (e.g., Gross, 1984; Warner, 1984). Hence evolutionary theory does not posit static immutable genes working *against* the environment. It proposes a set of general principles that shape the behavioral and cognitive mechanisms underlying human behavior across cultures, some of which may be shared with other species by common ancestry or ecological demands. These general principles may sometimes produce incredibly flexible mechanisms and may sometimes produce more rigid mechanisms. Even so, evolutionary theorists assume that to ignore the general principles underlying the evolutionary design of a behavior is to be blind to the ultimate causal mechanisms underlying that behavior.

SOME IMPORTANT GENERAL PRINCIPLES

In this section, we consider several general principles that have been used to generate evolutionary hypotheses about behavior. Before beginning, it is important to distinguish between ultimate and proximate levels of explanation. A *proximate explanation* considers behavior in terms of immediate determinants, such as the current environment or internal hormonal states. Laboratory experimenters tend to consider proximate causes—events in the immediate environment such as an aggressive prime or a confederate's remark. *Ultimate explanations* consider behavior in terms of more enduring background factors, such as the cultural norms that make a remark an insult, individual differences that make some people more prone to take offense, or an evolutionary past in which males were more concerned than females with challenges to their dominance. Evolutionary theorists are not unconcerned with proximate explanations, they are simply less likely to be satisfied without asking "why" a particular event might or might not elicit a particular response in a particular setting.

Reproduction, Kin Selection, and Inclusive Fitness

The name of the evolutionary game is gene replication. Gene replication is accomplished directly via the production of offspring, hence evolutionary theorists have taken a strong interest in sexuality and heterosexual relationships. However, gene replication can be accomplished indirectly by helping those who share copies of one's genes. Thus, the theory applies not only to sexual behavior, but also to mate attraction and selection, mate retention, and kin relationships. Even forgoing the opportunity to reproduce directly may increase the "ultimate payoff"—more copies of one's genes. For instance, under conditions of resource scarcity and low survival rates for hatchlings, male birds may fare better by helping their brothers to raise a clutch than by mating on their own (Trivers, 1985). Hatchlings receiving the extra resources provided by a helper are more likely to survive than birds raised with only two parents. Because brothers share half of their genes, the net benefit to both is greater if they cooperate than if they go it alone. This is an example of the general process of *kin selection*, which involves sacrificing direct reproductive opportunities to favor the survival and reproduction of relatives. The kin selection model helps to explain the widespread occurrence of altruistic and cooperative behavior in animals. It has replaced the "red in tooth and claw" view of evolution as a process that exclusively involves survival by individual competition.

Before notions such as kin selection were developed, evolutionary biologists evaluated an animal's reproductive potential in terms of individual "fitness." This concept was sometimes operationally defined as the number of offspring that were successfully raised to reproductive age. At its base, however, fitness in an evolutionary sense meant not simply to survive but to successfully reproduce one's genes. *Inclusive fitness* is simply the logical extension of this notion, referring to the net number of one's genes passed on to future generations, a number that includes not only the individuals' direct contribution via personal offspring, but also their indirect contribution to the survival and reproduction of relatives who share copies of their genes (Hamilton, 1964).

Sexual Selection

As we just noted, a characteristic can be naturally selected because it provides a survival advantage to the individual or to kin. Darwin believed, however, that features such as peacock's feathers or large horns on male mammals were selected through a process of *sexual selection*. Sexual selection occurs when a trait provides an advantage in attracting mates, even though it may hinder individual survival. There are two forms of sexual selection—*intersexual choice*, in which a trait gains an advantage because (like the feathers on a male bird) it is attractive to the opposite sex, and *intrasexual competition*, in which a trait gains an advantage because (like the horns on a male mammal) it helps an individual to compete with same-sex rivals. Modern evolutionary theorists believe that sexual selection is just a special case of natural selection, in which the culling force is other members of one's species. The same sex provides obstacles to stop one another from mating; the opposite sex provides tests that must be passed before mating.

Parental Investment

Darwin noted that, when it comes to sexual selection, females are more likely to be the selectors, and males are more likely to be banging their heads against one another to win the females' attentions. Trivers (1972) developed Darwin's insight into the theory of *differential parental investment*. According to this theory, the sex with the initially higher investment in the offspring has more to lose from a poor mating choice and will demand more before agreeing to mate. In general, females have a higher initial investment and should be more selective about choosing mates. There are, however, species in which males make the larger investment (e.g., by caring for the eggs and young offspring, as in seahorses), and in those species males tend to be more selective about their mates (Daly & Wilson, 1983; Trivers, 1985). In mammals, however, the normal discrepancy between males and females is especially pronounced, because females carry the young inside their bodies and nurse them after birth. Male mammals can reproduce with little cost, and, frequently, the male's direct input does not go beyond a single act of copulation. In such species, males tend to be nonselective about their mates, whereas females demand evidence of superior genetic potential before mating and will often mate only with males who have demonstrated superior capabilities. Humans also sometimes have sexual relations within less committed relationships, in the typical mammalian mode. In those circumstances, an evolutionary perspective would predict typical mammalian differences—females high and males low in selectivity (Kenrick, Sadalla, Groth, & Trost, 1990).

Unlike most mammals, however, humans tend to form long-term pairbonds. Human males, therefore, often invest resources such as effort, time, money, and emotional support in their offspring. In those circumstances, men's selectivity is expected to approach that of women. However, to the extent that men and women make different contributions to the offspring, they should select partners along somewhat different dimensions. Women contribute their bodies, through internal gestation and nursing. Men would therefore be expected to value indications of fertility, including a healthy appearance and a waist–hip ratio characteristic of youthful sexual maturity

(Singh, 1993). On the other hand, men primarily contribute their genes and indirect resources such as money and shelter. Presumably, women could appraise a man's genetic potential from physical attractiveness and his position in a dominance hierarchy (Thornhill & Gangestad, 1994; Sadalla, Kenrick, & Vershure, 1987). His ability to provide resources could be gauged indirectly by his ambition and directly by his social status and acquired wealth (Buss & Barnes, 1986; Daly & Wilson, 1983; Symons, 1979). Even with these differential tendencies, humans cooperate in raising their offspring. Hence, a number of characteristics should be (and are) desired by both sexes, such as agreeableness, kindness, and faithfulness (Buss, 1989a; Kenrick, Groth, Trost, & Sadalla, 1993).

Frequency-dependent Strategies and Individual Differences

A trait's fitness value depends on its distribution in the population. A frequency-dependent strategy is one that may or may not enhance fitness, depending on the number of others who possess it. To illustrate this dynamic process, theorists often use the analogy of a population of hawks and doves (e.g., Dawkins, 1976). If most birds in a population played a meek and non-competitive "dove" strategy and ran from conflict, any bird that used an alternative, aggressive "hawk" strategy, fighting for resources, would quickly benefit by easily driving doves away from their resources. Given this advantage, any genetic tendency toward "hawkishness" would increase in the population. If the majority of the population became vicious hawks, however, and were constantly tearing at one another over every scrap of food, the alternative dove strategy of "eat quickly and run" would have an advantage over the "stand and fight" approach. Once doves again gained the majority, however, hawkishness would be less dangerous, and would again increase. In nature, predator–prey relationships tend to remain in a similar state of dynamic equilibrium, with increases in either population quickly becoming self-limiting. This same analogy also applies *within* a species, where different forms designed to play different strategies are maintained in stable equilibrium. This dynamic equilibrium notion has been suggested as one explanation of the persistent coexistence of antisocial and well-socialized human populations (Kenrick & Brown, 1995; Kenrick, Dantchik, & MacFarlane, 1983; Mealey, 1995). The marginal benefits of antisocial behavior decrease as the frequency of antisocial individuals in the population increases.

In line with the notion of differential parental investment, the biggest difference within a species is often related to sex, with females and males adopting different mating strategies. However, there is also evidence of individual differences in mating strategies within each sex for humans, as for other animals. For instance, Gangestad and Simpson (1990) considered differences in *sociosexual orientation* among females. Women adopting a "restricted strategy" prefer exclusive sexual relations within a long-lasting relationship. Other women are more inclined to have multiple partners, and may be willing to have sexual relations with relative strangers. Restricted women appear to

place more value on characteristics indicative of fidelity and long-term investment; unrestricted women appear to place more value on physical attractiveness, which may indicate good "genetic potential" (Buss & Schmitt, 1993;
Thornhill & Gangestad, 1994).

*Evolutionary Hypotheses are Subject to the Same Standards of Empirical
Evidence as any other Hypotheses*

The principles described above have been tested in a number of studies of
animal behavior, and several of them (such as kin selection and differential
parental investment) are very well established (Alcock, 1993; Daly & Wilson,
1983; Trivers, 1985; Wilson, 1975). Nevertheless, their application to any given
instance of human behavior may or may not be appropriate. There is nothing
any less refutable about a hypothesis derived from evolutionary principles than
there is about a hypothesis derived from principles of information processing or
classical conditioning. Some derivations are astute, others are stretched, and
others are dead wrong. Consequently, some derivations receive empirical support, and some are refuted (Buss, 1995; Buss & Kenrick, 1998; Kenrick, 1994).
As we will describe below, evolutionary principles have proven fruitful in explaining gender differences in sexual behavior, mate preferences, and aggressive behavior. In some cases, findings seem to refute alternative explanations
from traditional social science models; in other cases, traditional models and
evolutionary hypotheses have been used to complement one another. In some
areas, such as kinship and friendship, there have been fewer tests of evolutionary hypotheses, and their utility remains to be seen.

THE ADAPTIVE FUNCTIONS OF RELATIONSHIPS

From an evolutionary perspective, the primary question about a physical or
behavioral characteristic is: "What was it designed to do?" In discussing the
functional design of human cognitive and behavioral mechanisms, evolutionary
theorists often discuss the environment of evolutionary adaptedness (EEA).
Although the distribution of alternative genes can change in a few generations,
it is assumed that the redesign of a functional feature (such as the development
of a giraffe's neck) will take, at a minimum, thousands of years (Lumsden &
Wilson, 1981). There is thus considerable "lag time" in evolution, and any
evolved human cognitive mechanisms were not designed for life on the free-
ways or malls of modern Los Angeles, but for coexistence in small hunter–
gatherer groups. The hunting and gathering lifestyle set the stage for human
social arrangements for well over a million years, as agriculture was only introduced within the last few thousand years (and then only for a minority of our
ancestors), and large urban centers only began to predominate within the past
few hundred years. Hence, evolutionary psychologists assume that the human
mind was constructed for life in a small group of closely related individuals, in
which there was a well-established dominance hierarchy, division of labor by

sex (females devoting more time to parenting and gathering, males more to hunting), marriage to someone from a very similar background (usually a cousin from a neighboring group), and so on (Lumsden & Wilson, 1981; Tooby & Cosmides, 1992). Hunter–gatherers everywhere shared some very similar problems as a function of that lifestyle and, as a consequence, evolutionary theorists expect to find a number of human universals beneath the surface diversity of modern cultures (Brown, 1991). Undoubtedly there are psychologically important differences across cultures, and modern life has introduced many new problems for the human mind. However, there is an assumption that we can better understand how humans respond to contemporary cultural variations if we consider the social arrangements within which our ancestors evolved. Evolutionary theorists also assume that modern cultures are not randomly created, but include many customs and institutions actively constructed by organisms designed for a prehistoric lifestyle (Lumsden & Wilson, 1981; Kenrick, 1987; Tooby & Cosmides, 1992). In the following sections, we consider some of the functions that relationships might have served in the human environment of evolutionary adaptedness.

Romantic Relationships

The primary adaptive functions of romantic relationships are assumed to be sexual reproduction and bonding for the care of offspring (Kenrick & Trost, 1987; Mellen, 1981; Morris, 1972). Romantic relationships also provide secondary adaptive benefits such as mutual sharing, social support, and protection. The joint investment in offspring should facilitate such sharing, moving couples into a strong, communal mode with little accounting of individual contributions or resources. Therefore, men and women should have some shared goals, such as finding a cooperative and compatible partner or ensuring the survival of the offspring.

In line with our earlier discussion, however, men and women are also assumed to have some different goals in romantic relationships (Buss, 1995; Kenrick & Trost, 1987, 1989). For instance, women ought to be concerned that the man contributes his part (i.e., resources) to the child-rearing responsibility. A woman should thus be concerned if her partner is possibly squandering resources on outside mating opportunities. Men should be more concerned with ensuring paternal certainty; that is, that the offspring in whom he is investing are indeed his (obviously, maternal certainty is not an issue for women). In addition, a man is more likely to be concerned with gaining access to additional mates—a goal that is not as beneficial for a woman.

Kin Relationships

Relationships with close relatives primarily serve the ultimate goal of gene replication. By helping one's kin, one helps one's own genes. From an evolutionary perspective, one would expect to find, among close relatives, a higher prevalence of Clark and Mills's (1979) communal relationships than tit-for-tat exchange relationships. In fact, explicit accounting of exchanged rewards should be negatively related to r (an index of relatedness, which would be 0.5 for a woman and her sister, 0.25 for a woman and her mother's sister, 0.125 for a woman and her first cousin, and so on). It is expected that one's willingness to benefit one's kin is also a function of their future reproductive potential (Burnstein, Crandall, & Kitayama, 1994). So, whereas a 40-year-old woman has the same degree of relatedness to her 17-year-old daughter and her 70-year-old mother, she would be expected to feel more positively about investing resources in her daughter (whose reproductive potential is quite high) than in her 70-year-old mother (who, although she may still be capable of providing the indirect benefits of grandmothering to the kin group, has a relatively low reproductive potential).

Friendships

Evolutionary theorists have devoted some attention to reciprocal alliances between non-relatives. Vampire bats, for instance, will often share their nightly take of blood with others. Research on this sharing indicates that it occurs between relatives, or between individuals who have forged a reciprocal exchange relationship (Wilkinson, 1988, 1990). The same sort of arrangement is found in human hunter–gatherer groups (Hill & Hurtado, 1989). In traditional hunter–gatherer societies, the likelihood of capturing game may be quite low on any given occasion for any given individual. If one individual catches a large fish or a deer, however, it is often too much to consume alone, and will rot if not shared. By sharing, the individual helps the other members of the group to survive, and accrues credit for the future when his or her own luck may be down.

In most traditional societies even today, one's best friends are usually related in some way (Moghaddam, Taylor, & Wright, 1993). Even in modern urban societies, most women list a close relative when asked to name someone with whom they are intimate. In hunter–gatherer societies like those in which our ancestors evolved, individuals were all closely related. Thus, the immediate selfish obstacles to reciprocal sharing in humans were diminished by potential kin selection. It would be expected, however, that our ancestors would have benefited from sensitivity to differences between close and distant relatives, and that reciprocal alliances with more distant relatives would involve more direct accounting. In addition to the benefits of trading resources, friendships would have served other functions for our ancestors. In chimpanzees, friends protect one another, and also form mating alliances (deWaal, 1989). Although the most dominant male in a group can monopolize the mating attention of the females, he can be toppled by an alliance of less dominant males. In humans, of course, one's social position is also often related to "who one knows", and cooperative alliances often involve large groups of individuals.

Dominance Hierarchies

In addition to cooperating to survive, group members also sometimes compete with one another. Dominance hierarchies serve to reduce continual competition in stable groups—once everyone knows who can defeat whom, there is less need to struggle over every new resource. When a new member is introduced into an existing group, there is often a period of conflict until a new hierarchy is established (e.g., deWaal, 1989). In addition to reducing conflict, male dominance hierarchies also define the most desirable mates for females to choose from. Thus, male mammals tend to be more concerned than females with their status within dominance hierarchies. Note that there is no assumption of altruism here; animals do not take their place within a hierarchy to reduce conflict or to help the other sex make mating decisions. They jockey for the best available position, and will occasionally re-challenge those just above them in line. However, it is in their best interest to recognize those who are far above them in order to avoid unnecessary and costly competition with them. Thus, the group-stabilizing consequences of dominance hierarchies are indirect byproducts of individual selfishness.

Ultimate Goals are Not Necessarily Conscious or "Rational"

It is important to note that evolutionary psychologists do not assume that people, or other organisms, are conscious of the ultimate goals of their behavior. A woman, for instance, does not have to be aware of choosing a dominant man for his genetic potential. In fact, evolutionary theorists have considered a variety of circumstances in which "self-deception" about one's ulterior motives would be adaptive (e.g., Lockard & Paulhus, 1988; Trivers, 1985). Just because humans are capable of some degree of self-awareness, it is no more necessary to assume that humans are fully aware of the ultimate motivations underlying their behaviors than it is to assume that caterpillars or planarians are.

It is also important to note that the evolved mechanisms are not designed to confer omniscience about the adaptive consequences of every choice. Rather, they are blindly calibrated to the average consequences of a given behavior for our ancestors. A good example is the human preference for sugar, which assisted our ancestors in identifying ripe fruit (Lumsden & Wilson, 1981). This preference was helpful for millions of years and is still strong, even in those who are safe from starvation within modern society and those who have stored several months' worth of calories in the form of fat. In the same way, the comment "Our romance is based on a shared interest in Beethoven, and we have no interest in reproducing" may reflect on the depth of human self-awareness, but it does not negate the evolutionary significance of the mate choice mechanisms.

EMPIRICAL FINDINGS FROM EVOLUTIONARY PSYCHOLOGY

Evolutionary hypotheses have generated a number of empirical findings in recent years. We first review findings on universals in interpersonal communication. Next we consider findings on sexuality, mating, and mate preferences, many of which follow directly from evolutionary models of sexual selection and parental investment. These same models have led to predictions regarding intrasexual competition, jealousy, and deception, discussions of which are followed by a review of evolution-inspired research on aggression and child-abuse. Finally, we consider the less extensive literatures on kinship and friendship.

Universals in Communication

The first research in the field of evolutionary psychology was conducted by Charles Darwin (1872), who surveyed early anthropologists and missionaries for evidence of universals in emotional expression. His conclusion that certain aspects of human emotional expression are universal has received corroboration from a series of studies by Ekman and his colleagues (e.g. Ekman, 1992; Ekman & Friesen, 1971; Ekman et al., 1987). In general, they have found that expressions indicating basic emotional states such as anger and happiness are recognized worldwide; and, although they can be suppressed in public or partially masked when necessary, the expressions do not appear to depend on shared cultural exposure.

Eibl-Eibesfeldt unobtrusively filmed women's responses to flirtation across a wide range of Western and non-Western cultures, and found certain universalities in the sequences of their movements. The patterns were too subtle to have been trained, and they agreed in microscopic detail from Samoa to Papua, France, Japan, Africa, and in South American Indian tribes (Eibl-Eibesfeldt, 1975). Women's flirtation gestures include "proceptive" cues (Beach, 1976; Perper & Weis, 1987), such as smiling and maintaining mutual gaze a bit longer than usual, that invite advances from selected men (Givens, 1978; Moore, 1985).

Sexuality

Because of inherent differences in parental investment, males and females face a different matrix of costs and benefits in casual sexual relationships. A male faces an opportunity to replicate genes with relatively low cost. A female faces the danger of impregnation by a male who has made little commitment to invest in the offspring. If she has an existing partner there is much less marginal genetic gain from an additional partner, and the danger of abandonment or intense jealousy from her current partner can be extremely costly.

There is abundant evidence that women are less eager than men to engage in promiscuous sex. Clark and Hatfield (1989) had confederates approach opposite-sex students with one of three invitations, to: "go out tonight?" "come over to my apartment?" or "go to bed with me?" Approximately half of the women said yes to the date, but only 3% were receptive to going to the man's apartment and not one said yes to the invitation to go to bed. When men were approached with the same questions, about half of them also responded favorably to the confederate's invitation for a date, almost 70% were willing to go to her apartment, and over 70% were willing to go to bed with her. Buss and Schmitt (1993) also found that college men desired to have sex much sooner in a relationship than did women.

Besides being more willing to have sex, men also want to have sex with more partners than do women. Buss and Schmitt (1993) asked college students how many sexual partners they would ideally like to have during the rest of their life. Men wanted, on average, over 18 sex partners in their lifetimes, whereas women desired, on average, fewer than 5. Consistent findings are also found in research on erotica, with males generally indicating more interest in erotica, and more fantasies involving strangers (Ellis & Symons, 1990; Kenrick, Stringfield, Wagenhals, Dahl, & Ransdell, 1980). Men have somewhat more extramarital affairs than women. If not for the scarcity of willing women, the sex difference in partners would likely be even more pronounced, as indicated by the very large difference in sexual experience between male and female homosexuals (Daly & Wilson, 1983; Symons, 1979).

Men are also less selective about casual sexual partners. Kenrick et al. (1990) asked male and female college students about their minimum criteria in a member of the opposite sex for a date, a sexual partner, a steady dating relationship, or a marriage. The two sexes differed most noticeably in their criteria for a sexual partner, with males willing to have sex with someone who did not meet their minimum criteria for a date.

Are these gender differences simply a reflection of an American or Western "double standard" of sexual behavior for men and women? Although there are clear cross-cultural variations in the norms involving premarital and extramarital sex, early anthropological reports of societies in which women were as interested in casual sex as men do not bear up under examination (Freeman, 1983). In reviewing the cross-cultural data on gender differences in sexuality, anthropologist Donald Symons concludes: "Everywhere sex is understood to be something females have that males want" (1979, p. 253). One of the unfortunate consequences of the inherent gender differences in selectivity for sexual partners is that males are much more likely to be the perpetrators, and females to be the victims, of sexual harassment (Studd & Gattiker, 1991). As noted by Clark and Hatfield (1989), males are likely to be receptive to, or at worst flattered by, sexual advances, whereas females are more likely to respond with some degree of aversion.

Love and Marriage

Anthropologists have observed cultural variations in mating relationships: some societies allow polyandry, some allow polygyny but not polyandry, and some allow only monogamy. However, the mix of possibilities is neither random nor arbitrary. First, all human societies have some form of marriage (Daly & Wilson, 1983). This is only surprising when one notes that pair-bonding is relatively rare among other mammals. If human mating patterns were completely arbitrary, one would see whole societies in which people were completely promiscuous, as in the Bonobo chimp, or arena mating patterns such as those found in the Uganda kob (in which females select highly dominant males, but males make no investment in the offspring beyond insemination). On the other hand, pair-bonding is more commonly found in bird species that, like ours, have helpless offspring who require intensive parental care. Evolutionary theorists have argued that forming a strong bond serves the same function in humans as it does in birds—to ensure cooperation in caring for their helpless offspring (e.g., Kenrick & Trost, 1987; Mellen, 1981).

If humans are designed to bond together to facilitate caring for their young, one would assume romantic love to be a universal feature of our species. That assumption was seemingly contradicted by social scientists' common wisdom that romantic love is a recent phenomenon, traceable to the idle, courtly classes of Medieval Europe (e.g., Stone, 1988). In a recent review of reports from 166 societies, however, Jankowiak and Fischer (1992) found only one in which the anthropologist explicitly stated that there was no romantic love (and the supplementary evidence was insufficient to confirm or deny the report). There was evidence of sexual affairs in another 18 cultures, but ethnographers had not asked about romantic love, and Jankowiak and Fischer were unable to establish that the participants felt love. For the remaining 147 cultures, however, they found clear, positive evidence of romantic love.

Although romantic love is a prevalent human bonding pattern, most societies do not require that it occur within a monogamous relationship. Daly and Wilson (1983) reviewed evidence from 849 cultures and found that only 137 were supposedly "strictly" monogamous—although even in those societies men were likely to engage in more extra-pair copulations than were women. Most (708) cultures allowed polygyny (one man with several wives), whereas only 4 allowed polyandry (one woman with several husbands). Moreover, whenever polyandry was allowed, so was polygyny. For instance, Pahari brothers in India pool resources to secure a wife, whom they share. If they accumulate more wealth, however, they add wives. The tendency toward polygyny over polyandry is consistent with the parental investment model. Women select men for their resources, and men with great wealth or power, such as Roman emperors, can attract multiple women because the benefits of sharing a wealthy husband may outweigh the advantages of having a poorer man all to oneself (Betzig, 1992). However, the reverse is not true. Because men select women for direct reproductive potential, a man sharing a woman, even a very desirable one, suffers a disadvantage over a man having a less attractive woman to himself. Also, a woman married to multiple husbands gains resources, but does not increase her own reproductive output substantially enough to compensate for the additional costs, such as male jealousy (Daly & Wilson, 1983, 1988a).

Mate Selection Criteria

Studies of characteristics requested and offered in singles' advertisements support predictions from the parental investment model: men seek youth and attractiveness in partners, and promise economic and emotional resources; women are more likely to seek resources and offer attractiveness (e.g., Harrison & Saeed, 1977; Rajecki, Bledsoe, & Rasmussen, 1991; Thiessen, Young, & Burroughs, 1993; Wiederman, 1993). Although one could argue that such criteria reflect norms of American society, an extensive cross-cultural study of marriage preferences (Buss, 1989a) indicated that men in diverse cultures place greater value than do women on youth and beauty in potential spouses, whereas women place greater value on characteristics associated with resource potential. There is also substantial cross-cultural agreement in judgments of female attractiveness, which cannot be explained by exposure to Western standards of beauty through the media (Cunningham, Roberts, Barbee, Druen, & Wu, 1995).

Age Preferences in Mates

Researchers studying singles' advertisements have been struck by a consistent contradiction to the powerful similarity-attraction principle: women generally prefer older men and men prefer younger women (Harrison & Saeed, 1977; Bolig, Stein, & McKenry, 1984; Cameron, Oskamp, & Sparks, 1977). Explanations for this irregularity typically rely upon the influence of cultural norms (Brehm, 1985; Cameron et al., 1977; Deutsch, Zalenski, & Clark, 1986; Presser, 1975), such as the "norm" specifying that a husband should be older and taller so as to appear "mentally and physically superior" to his wife (Presser, 1975). An alternative evolutionary explanation focuses on inherent sex differences in resources that men and women bring to relationships (e.g., Buss, 1989a; Symons, 1979). Men's indirect resources (e.g., food, money, protection, security) may actually increase over the lifespan, whereas the direct reproductive potential contributed by women decreases as they age, and ends with menopause around age 50.

Although both perspectives could predict the average two- to three-year difference in desired ages across all advertisers, their predictions differ if the preferences are broken down across the lifespan. A societal norm should operate the same for everyone in that society, regardless of age. This slavish desire to do what is regarded as societally "normal" should be most pronounced among younger people, who are especially sensitive to gender-role norms (Deutsch et al., 1986). In fact, a difference in ages should be most pronounced among teenaged males, who are most concerned with gender-role-appropriate behavior. An evolutionary perspective, however, suggests that the reproductive value of men and women, not societal norms, underlies gender differences in age preference. Female fertility peaks around age 24, and then declines more rapidly than does male fertility. In fact, men can father children until very late in life. Therefore, a man's preferred age for a partner should, as he ages, get progressively younger than his own age. For a man in his forties, a woman of similar age would have few reproductive years left, but a younger woman would have many.

According to this view, teenage males should also be concerned with their partner's reproductive capabilities. A similarly-aged female would maximize the remaining reproductive years, but her fertility is lower. Contrary to the normative account, this reproductive exchange emphasis would predict that young males should not discriminate against women who are actually a few years older than they. Women, on the other hand, are looking for signs of status and wealth. Even though older males may lose physical resources (such as health and sexual arousability), they may gain indirect resources and social status. In fact, Leonard (1989) argues that a woman can optimize her reproductive potential by choosing a man 10 years older than herself: he will have more resources and status than a similarly-aged male, but will not be so old as to die while the children are young. If age preferences are tied to reproductive mechanisms, any gender differences should exist across cultures, as women in all societies experience child-bearing and menopause.

Kenrick and Keefe (1992) conducted a series of archival analyses of age preferences in mates, and found results consistent with an evolutionary life-history model. Women's preferences, even when broken down by decade, were surprisingly consistent: women of all ages specified men who were, on average, a few years younger to approximately five years older. When men's preferences were broken down by decade, however, they did not reflect the supposed normative pressure to marry someone several years younger. Men in their twenties were equally attracted to older and younger women, and older males expressed increasingly divergent age preferences. Men in their fifties and sixties showed a strong interest in younger partners. This same sex-differentiated pattern was found in singles ads from different regions of the United States (even those placed by relatively wealthy East Coast men and women) and in ads in Holland, Germany, and India. It was also found in marriage records from a Philippine island during the early years of this century (Kenrick & Keefe, 1992), as well as records from several traditional African cultures (Broude, 1992; Harpending, 1992). The body of evidence makes it difficult to argue that these preferences are due to the arbitrary norms of modern American society.

Even more problematic for a normative explanation are the preferences of younger men. Not only are men in their twenties interested in both younger and older women, but adolescent males (aged 12 to 18) indicated a range of ages extending much further above than below their own age (Kenrick, Gabrielidis, Keefe, & Cornelius, 1996). Moreover, their "ideal" partner was several years older than their own age. The norm to prefer slightly younger women is obviously not shaping their preferences; but they are perfectly consistent with the reproductive exchange model, as the most fertile females will be older, not younger, than a teenage male.

Intrasexual Competition

As described earlier, human evolution is also subject to intrasexual selection—competition among members of the same sex for mating opportunities (Darwin, 1859). Within most species, intrasexual competition occurs mainly among males, manifested as (a) aggressive behaviors designed to limit other males' access to females; (b) competition to range more widely in search of females; or (c) competition in courtship for females (Trivers, 1985). Intrasexual selection plays out somewhat differently for humans because both men and women contribute substantial resources to their offspring. Human males, for instance, do not typically engage in direct combat for access to females, as do elephant seals or bighorn sheep; nor do they display anything similar to the bright plumage of the peacock in order to entice discriminating women. In addition, an ill-fated mating is disproportionately costly for women, so women should be just as eager to attract a man who is willing and able to invest in the offspring as men should be to attract a healthy and fertile woman.

Human intrasexual competition is more likely to be waged by both men and women through differential skills at: (a) locating mates; (b) demonstrating interest or availability; (c) acquiring resources desired by the opposite sex; or (d) altering appearance to look more attractive (Buss, 1988a). The most effective tactics for mate attraction should emphasize the characteristics most valued by the opposite sex. Buss asked subjects to describe the behaviors that people use to make themselves attractive to the opposite sex. Men and women expressed a high degree of similarity not only in their alluring behaviors but also in the rated effectiveness of those behaviors. For instance, having a good sense of humor and being sympathetic, well mannered and well groomed were the most effective behaviors for both sexes. Buss also found results consistent with the predictions of a resource exchange perspective. Men were significantly more likely to engage in tactics related to the display of resources (e.g., flashing money to impress a partner), tactics that were also judged to be more effective than a woman's displaying resources. Women, on the other hand, were more likely to engage in tactics related to enhancing their appearance (e.g., wearing flattering make-up or dieting), tactics that were also judged to be more effective than men doing the same. In general, tactics of intrasexual competition are closely linked to characteristics desired in long-term partners (Buss & Barnes, 1986; Kenrick et al., 1990, 1993).

Jealousy

Selecting an appropriate mate is an essential element in successful reproduction. However, maintaining that relationship was also important to our ancestors' reproductive success, because stable relationships would have promoted the survival of any resultant offspring. Evidence suggests that children in traditional societies with two devoted parents are more likely to reach adulthood than are children with only one (Geary, 1998). Although we tend to associate jealousy with a variety of negative personal characteristics (cf., White & Mullen, 1989), it may also have had an adaptive function as a mate retention mechanism (Buss, 1988b; Daly & Wilson, 1983). Jealousy is both a pervasive (Buunk & Hupka, 1987) and potentially lethal reaction (Daly, Wilson, & Weghorst, 1982). Women and men from Hungary, Ireland, Mexico, the Netherlands, the Soviet Union, and the United States all express strong, negative reactions to thoughts that their partner might flirt or have sex with another (Buunk & Hupka, 1987). In addition, anthropological evidence indicates that jealous outbursts result in wife-beating and spousal homicide across a wide variety of cultures (Buss, 1994; Daly et al., 1982). Although jealousy is usually described as undesirable, its adaptiveness for our ancestors may have contributed to its widespread occurrence.

Both sexes can gain genetic fitness if their jealousy prevents a partner from being successfully courted by a rival: women can prevent the loss of resources required to raise children and men can avoid threats to paternal certainty. Because fertilization occurs inside the woman's body, men risk investing valuable resources in another man's offspring, and any behaviors reducing this possibility would have been selected (Daly et al., 1982). Ancestral women were always certain of their genetic relatedness to their offspring, but had difficulty raising their highly dependent children without support. Women who could defend against threats to their relationship would thus be better able to raise their offspring to adulthood (Daly et al., 1982). So, both men and women lose when a relationship is torn apart, and jealousy may be one of the psychological mechanisms that activates mate-guarding strategies (Buss, 1994).

Given the differences in the relational threats experienced by men and women, the circumstances that elicit jealousy should differ between the sexes. Even though both men and women report similar *levels* of jealousy (Wiederman & Allgeier, 1993), men report more intense jealousy to a scenario describing their partners' sexual indiscretions (exaggerating concerns about paternity); and women report more jealousy to a scenario describing their partners' emotional attachment to a rival (which could cause the man to redirect his resources). This pattern was found not only in the United States (Buss, Larsen, Westen, & Semmelroth, 1992; Wiederman & Allgeier, 1993), but also in Holland and Germany (Buunk, Angleitner, Oubaid, & Buss, 1996). Moreover, the sex differences were most dramatic when imagining an infidelity before it had occurred (Wiederman & Allgeier, 1993). Once an infidelity *has* occurred, it may be most adaptive to end the tainted relationship and find a new, potentially monogamous partner, especially for men. Cross-cultural evidence indicates that wives' infidelity is cited more frequently as a cause for divorce than husbands' infidelity (Betzig, 1989), even though men are more likely to have extramarital relationships. Moreover, consistent with the general tendency for men to be more violent, men are significantly more likely to murder their partners during a jealous rage than are women (Daly et al., 1982). Assuming that a couple's offspring were conceived before an infidelity occurred, this tendency to flee an unfaithful partner might be attenuated in couples who have children because, for most of our evolution-ary history, children with both parents would have had a survival advantage over single-parent children.

Deceptive Strategies in Mating and Acquiring Resources

Animals have evolved a variety of elaborate systems of deception (Trivers, 1985). These mechanisms tend to take the form of either deceiving predators or deceiving competitors for valued resources, such as food or mates. As an example of a physical characteristic designed to deceive predators, the brightly colored bands of the non-poisonous shovelnose snake mimic those of the highly poisonous coral snake. Another approach to avoiding predators is to develop deceptive behavioral strategies. For example, female pronghorn antelope routinely distance themselves from their fawns, presumably to de-crease predation by coyotes (Byers & Byers, 1983). Deceiving the competi-tion to gain access to valued resources, such as food or the opposite sex, can also enhance genetic fitness. For instance, male scorpionflies mimic female courtship behaviors in order to lure other males into handing over their nuptial gift of food, intended to woo a real female. This single act has the double benefit of disadvantaging the competitor while increasing the decep-tive male's likelihood of attracting a mate (cf. Trivers, 1985). As these ex-amples illustrate, successful deceit can provide a reproductive advantage.

Although modern humans may not need to "change our stripes" to repel predators, our mating strategies often involve deceiving both competitors and potential partners (Tooke & Camire, 1991). Moreover, the types of deception exhibited in intrasexual competition and intersexual relations take a familiar pattern: men and women deceive others about those characteristics that are most desired by the opposite sex. Women tend to enhance their bodily appearance through behaviors such as wearing perfume, suntanning, and walking with a greater swing than normal when around men. Men exaggerate their dominance or resources (e.g., wearing expensive "label" clothing one can't really afford or misleading the partner about career) and by exaggerat-ing their commitment (e.g., their sincerity, trust, vulnerability, and kindness). Men also engage in more intrasexual deception to create the illusion that they are more desirable to women than their competitors. For example, in their interactions with other men, men tend to elaborate on their superiority (e.g., intelligence, toughness), and to exaggerate their level of sexual activity, sexual intensity, and sexual popularity. Moreover, women use relatively passive de-ceptive techniques whereas men use active deception, in line with the notion that female choice limits male reproductive success and escalates the intensity of male–male competition.

Because hunter–gatherer groups were highly interdependent, the ability to detect violations of reciprocity in social exchange would be highly adaptive (Axelrod & Hamilton, 1981). Cosmides and Tooby (1989) argue that we may have evolved "social contract algorithms" allowing quick and effective detection of cheating. In line with this reasoning, Cosmides and Tooby (1989) found that students had great difficulty with an exercise in formal logic (called the Wason task) unless the content of the problem related to a standard social contract (costs versus benefits). When the problem was framed in terms of "looking for a cheater", people easily solved a traditionally difficult logical problem. Cosmides and Tooby (1989) argue that, rather than having a brain that operates as a "general-purpose learning mechanism", the human brain is equipped with specialized algorithms that facilitate reasoning about social exchange problems with very little learning.

Violence in Relationships

Criminologists have frequently noted the high prevalence of homicide among family members. Gelles and Straus (1985) observed that "With the exception of the police and the military, the family is perhaps the most violent social group, and the home the most violent social setting, in our society" (p. 88). Indeed, one of the classic studies of homicide found that almost one quarter of victims were "relatives" (Wolfgang, 1958). From the standpoint of models of kin selection and inclusive fitness, family violence seemed to pose a puzzle for evolutionary views of human behavior. However, a closer examination of the classic statistics indicated that most homicide victims labeled as "relatives" were not blood relatives, but spouses (Daly & Wilson, 1988b; Kenrick et al., 1983). Many were also step-relatives, who do not share common genes but may compete for common resources. Children living with a step- or foster-parent in two samples were 70 to 100 times more likely to be fatally abused than children living with both natural parents (Daly & Wilson, 1988b, 1994). Relatives also spend more time together, providing more opportunities for conflict; however the risk of homicide for unrelated coresidents is 11 times greater than the risk for related coresidents (Daly & Wilson, 1988b).

Daly and Wilson (1988a, 1989) have criticized prevailing cultural determinist explanations of homicide. The prominent criminologist Marvin Wolfgang, for instance, attributed the enormous gender difference in homicide he found to the "theme of masculinity in American culture" and the cultural expectation that females would not engage in violence. Indeed, an examination of homicide statistics from the FBI's uniformed crime reports indicates that, every year and despite changes in the overall rate of homicide, men commit over 80% of all homicides. However, to attribute any phenomenon to a particular culture requires cross-cultural comparisons (Daly & Wilson, 1989; Kenrick & Trost, 1993). In the case of homicide, Daly and Wilson note that the same gender difference appeared in every culture for which they found records and during every period of history they examined. In fact, the gender difference is somewhat less pronounced in American society than in other cultures—men never commit less than 80% of homicides in any society, and often commit closer to 100%. The universality of the gender difference fits with the parental investment and sexual selection models. Given that humans are mildly polygynous and that women select high status men, it follows that men should be more competitive with one another everywhere. Further, male violence is particularly pronounced among males who are young, unmated, and resource poor (Wilson & Daly, 1985). Homicide case reports show that male–male violence is most often precipitated by an encounter between acquaintances, one of whom challenges the other's position in the local dominance hierarchy by attempting to humiliate him (Wilson & Daly, 1985).

Examination of spousal homicides reveals that they tend to occur when the reproductive interests of men and women conflict. As we noted above, men, not women, face the danger of cuckoldry. Consequently, jealousy is the predominant reason for a man to kill a woman across cultures (Daly & Wilson, 1988a, 1988b). When a woman kills a man, she is less likely to be jealous of another woman and more likely to be protecting herself from the man's jealous threats (Daly & Wilson, 1988a). Daly and Wilson (1994) also found that, in the rare instances in which a father kills his own children, it is likely to be accompanied by suicide and/or uxoricide (wife-killing). Step-fathers who kill children are unlikely to commit suicide or kill their wives, but they are more likely to be brutal (beating the child to death). The authors suggest that step-fathers' murders seem to reflect feelings of antipathy toward their victims, whereas killings by genetic fathers indicate very different underlying motivations (accompanying suicide notes, for instance, often claim the motivation to "rescue" the children from a hopeless situation). Thus, the differential prevalence of step-parental murder, and the different means used, suggest different underlying conflicts that are consistent with inclusive fitness theory.

Rather than viewing homicide in terms of individual psychopathology, evolutionary theorists view it as the tip of the iceberg, revealing evolved coercive impulses in genetically important situations. Presumably, all humans possess the same cognitive mechanisms designed to elicit competitiveness and hostility in situations where survival or reproductive interests are challenged. Kenrick and Sheets (1994) asked people if they had ever had a homicidal fantasy, and, if so, who and what caused it. Most men (75%) and women (62%) reported having had at least one homicidal fantasy. Men's fantasies were more frequent, longer and more detailed. Only 13% of the respondents had lived with a step-parent, and of those who had lived with a step-parent for over six years, 59% had at least one fantasy about killing that parent (compared to 25% for natural fathers and 31% for natural mothers). Thus, per unit of time spent together, homicidal fantasies were more likely to be provoked by step-parents, providing a complement to the statistics on step-parental abuse of children (Daly & Wilson, 1988b; Lenington, 1981).

Kinship, Friendship, and Altruism

Although less work has been conducted on kinship, the theory of inclusive fitness leads to a number of predictions about the preferential treatment of relatives. Rushton (1989a) reviewed human and animal evidence linking genetic similarity with altruism, family relations, and friendship. Experimental research suggests that animals can recognize their kin, and are likely to treat them preferentially (Greenberg, 1979; Holmes & Sherman, 1983). For instance, rhesus monkeys are promiscuous, and it would be difficult for a male to know which offspring are his own. Nevertheless, blood tests matching adult males with the troop's young show that males treat their own offspring better than others (Suomi, 1982). Because of random variation and overlap between parents' genes, it is possible for children to have more genetic similarity to one parent than to another (Rushton, 1989a). There is evidence that human children who share more genes with their parents are perceived to be more similar to the parent than children who share fewer genes; to be seen as "taking after" the genetically-related parent more than the other. When a child dies, parents who perceive that the child "takes after' their side grieve more for the loss (Littlefield & Rushton, 1986). Compared with dizygotic twins, monozygotic twins are more altruistic, and more affectionate, toward one another (Segal, 1988). Finally, there is evidence that people choose friends who are genetically similar to them, and that the similarity cannot be fully explained as due to the tendency to choose friends who look like oneself (Rushton, 1989b).

Burnstein et al. (1994) asked people about their inclination to help others who varied in genetic relatedness, age, and health. People were more inclined to help someone with whom they were more related (e.g., a nephew before a cousin of the same age). Most interestingly, helping genetic kin increased markedly in life-or-death situations and was linked to their reproductive capability. In everyday situations, people did the socially appropriate behavior—helping a grandmother in preference to a teenage sister, or a sick relative in preference to a healthy one. In life-or-death situations, however, helping was more likely to be directed toward those who would pass on shared genes—the teenage sister in preference to grandmother, and the healthy relative in preference to the sick one. These experimental findings, which indicate that kinship has a strong influence on life-or-death helping, are corroborated by studies of actual disasters, in which kin are helped first (e.g., Form & Nosow, 1958).

Shared genetic interests also influence the stability of romantic relationships. For instance, marriages with children from former unions have elevated divorce rates, but marriages in which the couple shares children are less likely to end in divorce (Daly & Wilson, 1988b). The importance of shared genetic interests is underlined by the fact that sharing children increases marital stability even though it decreases marital satisfaction.

THE COHESIVENESS OF THE EVOLUTIONARY APPROACH

The evolutionary approach is appealing for its intellectual cohesiveness and comprehensiveness. Although we have ranged over a wide variety of topics, from jealousy and violence through parenting and love, they are all closely connected. Figure 2.1 depicts some central connections between the concepts we have addressed in this chapter.

The basic concepts of evolutionary psychology can be used to generate empirical questions about many of the topics discussed in this volume. Consider, for instance, community psychology and social support. An evolutionary perspective could make predictions about the role of kinship networks in social support. As people are more likely to help kin in highly threatening situations, it might be hypothesized that, controlling for degree of stress, psychological disorder might be lower for those surrounded by kin as opposed to nonkin. Depression has increased dramatically during this century. Is this increase in depression related to the decrease in contact with kin that accompanies urbanization and the modern work environment? If so, depression would be less prevalent in those who have maintained close relationships with kin. Interesting questions can also be asked about evolutionarily important issues in life stress. For instance, the most stressful life events include events

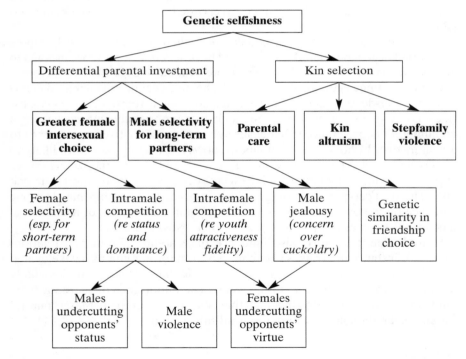

Figure 2.1 Interrelationships between general evolutionary assumptions about relationships. The theory of evolution by natural selection assumes competition between different genes. A number of general principles (such as kin selection and differential parental investment) flow indirectly from that central assumption. Various features of human relationships can in turn be derived from those general principles. This diagram is intended merely to illustrate the cohesiveness of the framework, and not exhaustively list the connections between different processes

such as divorce, death of a spouse, and loss of a job (Holmes & Rahe, 1967), events that are directly connected to reproductive ability. Evolutionary hypotheses could be generated about the influence of gender, kinship networks, and the stage of life cycle on the stressfulness of these events. For example, Thornhill and Thornhill (1989) review evidence and theory on psychological distress from an evolutionary perspective.

Likewise, we might ask about the role of kinship and shared reproductive interests in Aron and Aron's (see Chapter 6 in this volume) measures of overlap between self and others, or the effect of concerns about "face' in dominance hierarchies. For example, Wilson and Daly (1985) noted that "saving face" was a central concern in homicides committed by young males, and Hogan (1982) considered evolutionary constraints on self-presentation in social groups. Several chapters in this volume consider issues of development and aging. The evolutionary life-history perspective assumes changes in reproductive behaviors at different ages that interact with variations in the social and physical environment (Belsky, Steinberg, & Draper, 1991; Kenrick & Keefe, 1992). For instance, we noted that some fish change from a small drab male into a large colorful male if a territory becomes available, and even a female in a harem may change sex if the male dies. Do analogous processes apply to humans? For instance, is the onset of puberty influenced by the availability of attractive members of the opposite sex (signaled by a favorable sex ratio or feedback from the opposite sex about a pre-adolescent's relative attractiveness)? Is the onset of menopause influenced by the existence of nearby healthy children and grandchildren? These questions are not necessarily meant to be exhaustive, and, as noted above, empirical research may indicate that they are ill-conceived. However, all living beings, including contemporary humans, are conglomerations of mechanisms designed by millions of years of natural selection. Our task is to identify those mechanisms and how they interact with the social and physical environment. Humans are in many ways unique as a species, but so are kinkajous, vampire bats, and carpenter ants. An evolutionary perspective does not suggest that we ignore the unique adaptations of our species, only that we consider how they may be elucidated by the light of the most powerful set of principles applying to all living things.

An evolutionary perspective is completely compatible with an interest in cultural determinants of behavior (e.g., Barkow, Cosmides, & Tooby, 1992; Lumsden & Wilson, 1981). However, researchers considering culture should also consider regularities across cultures, in addition to some of the seemingly bizarre differences between "us" and "them". Emerging evidence of cross-cultural universals, such as those regarding love and marriage, flirtation, aggression, and mate criteria, suggest that underneath the surface variability there may be a similar core to human nature. Even cross-cultural differences, as in the case of marriage patterns, may reflect flexible underlying mechanisms. For instance, in cultures where there is a reasonable degree of promiscuity, paternal certainty is more problematic than in cultures with stronger norms of monogamy. In those cultures, maternal uncles may show relatively more interest in their sisters' children and relatively less interest in their wife's children (Daly & Wilson, 1983). This response makes sense from an evolutionary perspective because maternal uncles can be certain they share genes with their sister's children. Considering culture through an evolutionary lens goes beyond cross-cultural universals, then, to consider how cultural practices reflect an interaction between ecological demands and the evolved cognitive and emotional mechanisms of our species.

EVOLUTIONARY PSYCHOLOGY AND EXISTING MODELS OF RELATIONSHIPS

Just as an evolutionary perspective can enrich, and be enriched by, existing empirical evidence on relationships, it can also enrich, and be enriched by, existing theoretical perspectives. For example, traditional social psychological models of relationships have emphasized: (a) the importance of self-evaluation in perceptions of a "fair exchange," (people desire partners who match or exceed their own "market value"); and (b) the importance of considering the phase of a relationship in partner evaluation (relationship expectations depend on the level of commitment). An evolutionary perspective sharpens predictions about how processes of self-evaluation and social exchange will be influenced by not only the level of investment in the relationship but also by the sex of the partner. We noted that men have less to lose from engaging in a casual sexual relationship. Hence, they should be less demanding in their criteria for casual sexual partners, and their criteria should be less tied to their own market value. Women, on the other hand, still risk impregnation in even a casual sexual relationship. They should remain very selective and concerned that the partner matches their own self-appraised "market value". Kenrick et al. (1993) examined subjects' self-ratings and their mate criteria for dating partners, one-night stands, and long-term partners and found clear support for these predictions. For committed, long-term relationships, women and men were equally selective and they both demanded partners matched to their own social value. Women considering partners for one-night stands showed the same self-calibrated standards. Men considering one-night stands, however, were not only willing to accept less desirable partners, but also showed less linkage between their criteria for casual sexual partners and their own self-evaluations.

These findings indicate how evolutionary and traditional social psychological perspectives can complement one another and lead to a more complex understanding of human behavior. Social psychological research on relationship phases was useful in extending previous evolutionary models; in turn, the evolutionary perspective focused attention on important gender differences in the content of the social exchange. The evolutionary perspective is, in essence, a social exchange model, but it differs from other models by making specific assumptions about the contents of social exchange, and rejecting the implicit assumption that what is valued depends arbitrarily on culture.

Cognitive approaches to social behavior can also be enhanced by an evolutionary perspective (Kenrick, Sadalla, & Keefe, 1998). Rather than assuming general cognitive processes that apply across judgment domains, an evolutionary perspective assumes adaptive, domain-specific mechanisms designed to deal effectively with issues important to survival and reproduction (Tooby & Cosmides, 1992). Consider one simple example. Previous research indicated perceptual "contrast effects" on a wide range of judgment tasks, including judgments of attractiveness (Kenrick & Gutierres, 1980): an average looking stranger is rated as less attractive if judged after gorgeous people, and more attractive if rated after unattractive people. Interestingly, men in long-term relationships who looked at attractive female centerfolds not only rated their current partners as less attractive but also rated themselves as less in love with those partners. Women exposed to attractive male centerfolds showed a similar tendency, but it was much weaker (Kenrick, Gutierres, & Goldberg, 1989). From an evolutionary perspective, the sex difference could reflect the gender difference in valuing signs of physical attractiveness; women being less likely to value a sexy, youthful body (as displayed in centerfolds) and more likely to value social dominance (which is not as apparent in centerfolds). A follow-up study varied both the physical attractiveness and social dominance of opposite sex targets (Kenrick, Neuberg, Zierk, & Krones, 1994). Men again rated themselves as less committed to their partners after viewing attractive women, whereas women who viewed attractive men showed no decrement in their relational commitment. Women's commitment was undermined by exposure to a series of highly dominant men, however. Hence, even ongoing cognition can be affected by evolutionarily adaptive mechanisms.

ADAPTIVELY "IRRATIONAL" MATE PREFERENCES

Researchers using an evolutionary framework are often confronted with questions stemming from false assumptions (cf., Buss, 1995; Kenrick, 1994; Kenrick & Trost, 1987; Tooby & Cosmides, 1992). However, one recurring question is still unanswered: What about homosexuality? Homosexuality results in a failure to reproduce, making it appear to be genetically maladaptive. However, the involvement of genetic proclivities, hormones, and neural structures contribute further to the puzzling biological status of homosexuality (e.g. Bailey & Pillard, 1991; Whitam, Diamond, & Martin, 1993; Ellis & Ames, 1987; LeVay, 1993). A variety of hypotheses have addressed the potential adaptiveness of homosexuality (cf., Kenrick, Keefe, Bryan, Barr & Brown, 1995), and it is premature to assume that it is either solely a result of environmental influences or that it is uninformative about evolved adaptive mechanisms.

Bailey, Gaulin, Agyei, and Gladue (1994) suggested that homosexual preference might actually be informative about heterosexual mechanisms. They found that homosexual women, like heterosexual women, were relatively uninterested in casual sex (cf., Buss & Schmidt, 1993; Kenrick et al., 1990, 1993). Obviously, this avoidance is not due to a conscious analysis of the relative costs of pregnancy, or lesbians would be more favorable toward casual sex than heterosexual women. Bailey et al. also found gay men to be as interested in physical attractiveness as heterosexual men, suggesting that heterosexual men's interest in attractiveness may not simply be a byproduct of media emphasis on female beauty. In general, Bailey et al. found the biological sex differences to be stronger than the effects of sexual orientation. In addition, the life-span pattern of age preferences in homosexual males is exactly the same as that shown by heterosexual males: young males want slightly older or younger partners, whereas older males prefer increasingly younger partners (Kenrick et al., 1995). These findings are difficult to explain in terms of either market-based rationality or cultural norms. Older homosexual males are not desirable to their preferred partners, for instance. Moreover, if media projections of the ideal member of the opposite sex determine preferences, homosexual men should, like heterosexual women, prefer relatively older partners. Instead, these data are more consistent with the notion that sexual attraction, like other adaptative systems, is a multifaceted set of proximate mechanisms, each under the control of independent developmental processes (e.g., Buss, 1995; Tooby & Cosmides, 1992).

Modern evolutionary theorists assume that natural selection operates on specific environmentally triggered mechanisms, rather than producing individuals designed to think, feel, and act in ways that are "generally adaptive". A generally adaptive organism is somehow presumed to be omniscient: to have prior knowledge about the particular genetic advantages likely to be gained from using each mechanism in each particular set of circumstances. The fallacy of that assumption can be demonstrated by considering a few mechanisms that appear to have evolved because of their past adaptive consequences. We have already mentioned the evolved preference for sweet tastes, which, in the modern environment of abundant sugary foods, can lead to obesity and diabetes. However, this preference was selected in circumstances where it had, on average, a positive effect on survival. In the arena of sexual attraction, Shepher (1971) found that unrelated children raised in the same family-like kibbutz pods later showed a surprising lack of sexual and romantic attraction. Shepher argued that the unusual conditions of raising children together triggered a mechanism designed to dampen romantic attraction between siblings (thereby decreasing the danger of recessive gene combinations from incest). Again, the incest mechanism seems somewhat "irrational" when considered in isolation and in a novel, modern context.

From the modularity perspective, it becomes easier to understand how homosexual and heterosexual men can be alike in so many ways. By analogy, consider the case of vision, where we do not simply have a mechanism for "seeing" in general but a number of different structures for analyzing color, shape, movement, depth, and other complex features of visual stimuli (Livingstone & Hubel, 1988). Given the central importance of reproduction to evolution, it would be surprising if the human brain had a single mechanism that controlled "reproducing like a male" versus "reproducing like a female." Reproduction involves a series of very different tasks, including choosing a mate (weighing the relative importance of physical health, status, beauty, and faithfulness), evaluating one's ability to attract a mate, making oneself attractive to a potential mate, competing with members of one's own sex for that mate, establishing an ongoing relationship, and so on (Buss, 1995; Kenrick & Trost, 1989). If these different processes, like the processes underlying vision or language, are controlled by independent mechanisms, we would not expect a change in one mechanism to be accompanied by reversals in all related mechanisms. If there is a biological mechanism that controls direction of sexual preference, it need not be accompanied by a complete reversal of other biological sex-typing mechanisms. Homosexual males clearly do not develop physically feminine secondary sex characteristics, such as wider hips and breasts, for instance. Hence, any biological mechanism involved in homosexual choice reflects not a global change in the "general" reproductive biology of the organism, but a much narrower change in one or a few specific cognitive mechanisms. Considered more broadly, this line of research suggests that even behaviors that seem anomalous may lead to interesting insights when considered in light of the emerging interdisciplinary synthesis of cognitive science and evolutionary biology (Kenrick et al., 1995).

CONCLUSION

The evolutionary perspective provides a comprehensive model of relationships, with the potential for elucidating and integrating all areas of relationship research. Beyond that, the model connects our work with cognitive science, anthropology and other areas of social science, as well as ecology, genetics, zoology, and other sciences concerned with living organisms.

Chapter 3

A Process Model of Adult Attachment Formation

Debra Zeifman

Vassar College, Poughkeepsie, NY, USA

and

Cindy Hazan

Cornell University, Ithaca, NY, USA

Imagine that while dining out one evening, you were to observe the interactions of three different couples. One (couple A) is standing at the bar, having a superficial discussion of mundane topics. Nevertheless, each person seems intensely interested in and enthusiastic about everything the other has to say. Their animated conversation is interrupted by frequent laughter and awkward silences. The man reaches for his drink and "accidentally" brushes his arm against the woman's; they lock eyes briefly, smile at each other, and then the woman looks down at her drink and begins stirring it nervously. Across the room, a second couple (B) is seated at a corner table. They seem unaware of the banter and bustle of activity around them. Their eyes are locked in mutual gaze, and their hands mingle playfully atop the table. They are speaking in hushed tones and appear to be totally absorbed in each other. They seem not to notice or care that the soup the waiter had placed in front of them is getting cold. Nearby, a third couple (C) sit across from each other studying their menus. After ordering, they speak in normal tones about the day's events.

The Social Psychology of Personal Relationships.
Edited by William Ickes and Steve Duck. © 2000 John Wiley & Sons Ltd.

When their food arrives, they begin eating immediately and heartily. They appear to be at ease, and spend more time looking at their food and surroundings than at each other.

It doesn't take a trained eye to notice such differences in the way couples interact, nor does it take any knowledge of the empirical literature on personal relationships to make inferences about the nature of their respective relationships. Couple A is obviously engaged in a flirtation, from which one might infer that they just met. Couple B appears to be in love, and have probably been dating for a short time. Couple C is an established pair whose comfort with each other suggests that they have been together for years. Their relationship may well have begun with a flirtation, like that of couple A, and possibly passed through a period during which their behavior toward each other resembled couple B's. Eventually, they ceased to spend long hours completely absorbed in one another. Yet, this couple who, on the surface, appears to be the least emotionally involved would likely be the most profoundly emotionally affected by a prolonged or permanent separation.

Although the many observable differences among couples are obvious to the untrained eye, their meaning and function require explanation. The fact that we can infer something about the length of a relationship from observed differences in couple interactions does not explain why such differences exist or why predictable changes occur. Our thesis is that the processes by which couple A or B may eventually come to look like couple C can be viewed as attachment formation processes.

Our primary goal in this chapter is to outline a normative model of adult attachment formation, using Bowlby's (1969/1982, 1973, 1980) ethological attachment theory as a guiding framework. In recent years, attachment-theoretical approaches to research on adult romantic relationships have proliferated (e.g., Bartholomew & Horowitz, 1991; Collins & Read, 1990; Feeney & Noller, 1990; Hazan & Shaver, 1987, 1990, 1994a, 1994b; Hazan & Zeifman, 1994; Kirkpatrick & Davis, 1993; Kirkpatrick & Hazan, 1994; Kobak & Hazan, 1991; Mikulincer & Nachsohn, 1991, Parkes, Stevenson-Hinde, & Marris, 1991; Simpson, 1990). Virtually all of the work to date has focused on individual differences rather than on normative processes. The findings have enhanced our understanding of the ways in which people differ with respect to their relationship-related thoughts, feelings, and behaviors (See Shaver and Hazan, 1993, for a review). Adult attachment research typically presumes that romantic relationships are, by definition, attachment relationships. The assumption is based on Bowlby's (1979) claim that attachment behavior characterizes humans "from the cradle to the grave" and that, in adulthood, attachments take the form of pair-bonds—i.e., romantic or sexual relationships.

The tendency to presume that two individuals who are romantically involved are also attached to each other is understandable. But, when we began to investigate the processes by which primary attachments are transferred from parents to romantic partners, we found that in adulthood, as in infancy, attachments take time to develop. Infants arrive into the world prepared to form attachments, but the emotional bond between infants and their particular caregivers requires months of interactions to become established. The same appears to be true of adult romantic attachments. However, the evolution of an adult flirtation into an attachment bond may be less predetermined than the attachment of an infant to his or her caregiver. Not every romantic or sexual involvement develops into an enduring emotional bond. Research on adult attachment phenomena should ideally be grounded in an understanding of how adult attachments develop, and anchored to some index of the existence of an attachment bond. Independent of this more practical research concern, adult attachment formation processes are interesting and important in their own right.

The details of our model of adult attachment formation will be explicated in the pages that follow, but the major components can be presented here. The behaviors associated with attraction and infatuation can be viewed as species-typical programs designed to facilitate attachment formation. The observed behaviors, as well as the associated but unobserved processes and mechanisms, presumably evolved because attachment bonds serve unique and essential functions in human adaptation and survival at all ages. Moreover, the processes of attachment formation evident in the hypothetical couples described above are assumed to be similar in important respects to the processes by which each of the six individuals became attached to their respective primary caregivers during infancy.

ETHOLOGICAL ATTACHMENT THEORY

Attachment theory (Bowlby, 1969/1982, 1973, 1980) grew out of the following observations: Infants and young children manifest profound and lasting distress if separated from their primary caregivers—even when their nutritional and hygienic needs are being met by surrogates—and reactions to such separations take the form of a predictable and universal sequence of stages. The first stage, *protest*, is characterized by obsessive search for the absent caregiver, disrupted sleeping and eating, inconsolable crying, and resistance to others' offers of comfort. This stage is reliably followed by *despair*, a period of passivity, lethargy, and depressed mood. The duration of the reactions and the timing of the transition from the first stage to the second has been found to vary as a function of age and other individual difference factors, but their appearance and ordering appears invariant across individuals, with one exception: Infants younger than 7 months of age show little distress and accept surrogate caregiving without protest.

Initially, only the first two stages—protest and despair—were identified. Eventually, the youngsters resumed their normal, pre-separation activities and appeared to be fully recovered. It was only when "recovered" youngsters were reunited with their caregivers that the third stage became evident. Rather than exhibiting the expected response to reunion, they ignored their primary caregivers and avoided contact with them. Their behavior suggested that a kind of emotional *detachment* had taken place. The reunions provided evidence of long-term effects of even brief separations. So did the fact that, when previously separated youngsters were visited by hospital staff several months after returning home, they exhibited an exaggerated fear response to what they thought signalled another separation.

Bowlby documented additional evidence that protracted separations result in long-term deleterious effects on psychological development. Retrospective examination of the life histories of 44 juvenile delinquents revealed that a disproportionate number of them suffered episodes of maternal separation during infancy and early childhood (Bowlby, 1944). And, while the effects of attachment disruption qualified as a significant developmental risk factor, the total absence of attachment seemed to be even more costly. Abandoned infants reared in institutions, where basic nutritional and hygienic needs were met collectively by nursing staff, failed to thrive and often suffered alarming health decrements (Robertson, 1953; Spitz, 1946). Thus, the establishment and maintenance of an emotional bond with a caregiver appeared to be essential for normal physical and psychological development. Psychoanalytic secondary drive theory, in which Bowlby had been trained, was inadequate to account for these observations.

The search for an explanation of the reactions to and long-term effects of separation led Bowlby to examine the work of ethologists such as Lorenz and Harlow. Based on careful observation and experimental manipulation, ethologists had demonstrated that the young of many altricial species possess an innate tendency to become attached to a caregiver. In species who bear immature young, the establishment of a strong and enduring bond between infant and caregiver is adaptive in that it greatly enhances the infant's chances for survival. Bowlby concluded that in our own altricial species, unlearned behaviors such as clinging, sucking, smiling and crying serve to promote contact with a caregiver and ensure that an attachment bond develops and that the infant receives the care it requires in order to survive. Within this framework, the extreme reactions to separation made sense. An innate need had been thwarted.

The reactions to separation from an attachment figure—protest, despair, and detachment—were thus comprehensible in terms of evolution and adaptation. Were the infant to be accidentally separated from its mother in the environment in which humans evolved, there would be a tremendous risk of death by starvation and predation. To avoid its demise, first the infant would let out a stream of loud calls attempting to attract the attention of its mother and guide her path to it (protest). Loud cries would only be adaptive if the mother was nearby, however, and as time passed this would become less and less likely. Because continued calling would attract predators, passivity should soon set in (despair). Finally, when little hope of the mother's return remains, the youngster must let go of the emotional bond completely (detachment), and attempt to survive on its own and/or be open to establishing a new attachment.

Whereas the work of ethologists was helpful in explaining the importance of attachment bonds and providing support for the notion that the tendency to develop emotional bonds is a species-typical behavior, it was control systems theory (Miller, Gallanter, & Pribram, 1960) that Bowlby found useful in explaining the dynamics of attachment behavior and in identifying the features that distinguish attachment bonds from other types of social relationships. All normal human infants exhibit a common pattern of behavior in relation to their primary caregiver: They tend to seek and maintain relatively close proximity to this person, retreat to her or him for comfort and reassurance in the face of perceived or real danger, be distressed by and resist separations and, in her or his presence (and in the absence of threat), engage in exploration and play.

From this universally-observed dynamic, Bowlby postulated the existence of an inborn behavioral system. Just as physiological systems serve to maintain set-goals for body temperature and blood pressure, for example, the existence of an attachment system to regulate proximity to a protector was postulated. The set-goal of the attachment system is a sufficient degree of physical proximity to the attachment figure to ensure safety—a goal that would necessarily vary as a function of endogenous (e.g., state, age) and exogenous (e.g., novelty, threat) factors, as well as individual differences in prior experience. According to Bowlby, such a system is inborn and remains functional throughout the entire human life span. Thus, although the degree and duration of physical distance from an attachment figure that is judged to be tolerable would be expected to change from situation to situation and from one developmental period to the next, and although the attachment figure would expect to change in the course of normative development, once an emotional attachment has developed, prolonged involuntary separations would be distressing.

Implicit in the dynamic functioning of the attachment system are the features or relational components that distinguish attachment bonds from other types of social relationships. Specifically, the defining features of attachment are: *proximity seeking* (the tendency to seek and maintain relatively close proximity), *safe haven* (the tendency to seek comfort and reassurance, especially in the face of perceived or real threat), *separation distress* (the tendency to resist and be distressed by separations), and *secure base* (the tendency to derive security from and be emboldened by the availability of the attachment figure, which facilitates such non-attachment activities as exploration and play). A relationship in which these four components are present qualifies as an attachment bond.

Whereas the attachment system itself—with its inherent dynamic and relational components—is hypothesized to be innate, the target of attachment behavior (i.e., the attachment figure) must be selected. Infants do not emerge from the womb emotionally bonded to any particular individual. Attachment to a specific caregiver develops gradually over the course of the first years of life. Although the processes by which one individual comes to assume this position of lasting and pervasive influence is a continuous one, four relatively distinct phases can be discerned (Bowlby, 1969/1982).

At birth, infants are prepared in a variety of ways to engage in social interaction (e.g., Trevarthen, 1979) and, when distressed, will seek and accept comfort indiscriminately. Bowlby called this the *pre-attachment* phase. Gradually, and beginning at around 3–4 months of age, the infant comes to preferentially direct signals (bids for interaction and contact) toward familiar adults, and especially the primary caregiver. Bowlby called this phase of differential signalling *attachment-in-the-making*. Sometime later, typically around the age of 6 or 7 months, a major transformation occurs. Infants not only become capable of self-produced locomotion but also begin to exhibit two new fears: strangers are treated with increasing caution and sometimes alarm, and separations from the primary caregiver are vociferously resisted.

Separation distress/protest has traditionally been considered the marker of attachment formation (Ainsworth, Blehar, Waters, & Wall, 1978; Bowlby, 1969/1982; Sroufe & Waters, 1977), and the associated phase is accordingly labeled *clear-cut attachment*. A final transformation in the attachment relationship occurs sometime during the second year of life. Increased representational and other cognitive capacities make brief separations more tolerable and delays in caregiver availability more understandable. In addition, children of this age show decreasing interest in their primary caregivers (and less frequent need for contact comfort), and increasing interest in exploratory activities and affiliative contact with peers. Bowlby called this final phase in attachment formation *goal-corrected partnership*.

ADULT ATTACHMENT

Bowlby believed that adults retain a strong tendency toward forming enduring emotional attachments. Whereas the infant becomes attached to a parent, prototypical adult attachments are formed with an opposite-sex peer. Weiss (1973, 1982, 1988) was the first to investigate adult attachment phenomena and, like Bowlby, he began with the responses of individuals to separation and loss. In his now-seminal work, Weiss noted that the ways in which his divorced and widowed subjects responded to separation were remarkably similar to the way children respond to separations from attachment figures. Initial reactions tended to be ones of heightened arousal and anxiety. Subjects reported disruptions in their normal patterns of sleeping and eating, and also experienced what appeared to be a form of search behavior. Widows and widowers hallucinated their lost spouses; newly-divorced or separated individuals experienced a compulsion to reconnect with their former partners. Eventually, both separated and bereaved subjects grew listless and exhibited signs of depression. In time, most recovered through a process of gradual emotional detachment from the former beloved. Thus the sequence of reactions closely resembled the protest-despair-detachment pattern that Bowlby observed among infants and children (see also Lofland, 1982).

Interestingly, the anguish of adult separation was not contingent on relationship quality. Even the most dissatisfied, embittered individuals yearned for their former partners. In addition to their psychological costs, broken attachments have been linked to such negative outcomes as increased risk for cardiovascular disease (e.g., Kiecolt-Glaser, Garner, et al., 1984; Kiecolt-Glaser, Ricker, et al., 1984; Lynch, 1977), cancer (Goodwin, Hurt, Key, & Sarret, 1987), and automobile accidents (Bloom, Asher, & White, 1978).

From an evolutionary perspective, attachment bonds between procreative partners are not as essential for individual survival as those between caregiver and infant. Nevertheless, they would have greatly enhanced the survival of offspring. The trend among mammals (and primates in particular) to bear increasingly immature offspring and nurse them for several years imposed a heavy metabolic cost and increased predation risk for a female parenting on her own. As this burden raised the incidence of infant mortality, parental partnership and male parental care became a necessary adaptation. Several authors have suggested that male-female romantic/sexual emotions were exploited for the purpose of keeping parents together in order to care for their offspring (Eibl-Eibesfeldt, 1975; Short, 1979).

Traditionally, the bond between adult partners has been viewed as having the primary purpose of shared parental caregiving. However, for the bond to effectively serve that purpose, it would have to precede the birth of offspring, and be relatively enduring. The human female shows no outward signs of fertility, and may be sexually receptive at any point in her menstrual cycle. To ensure paternity, the human male would have had to guard his mate constantly until conception, which he could not reliably detect until months after it had occurred. In order to provide care for offspring, the male would have to remain during the lengthy gestation period. These facts all suggest that the attachment bond between adult lovers needed to be enduring and operative, independent of offspring.

The similarities between infant-caregiver and pair-bond relationships are not limited to their adaptive significance. Both engage the emotion we call love, and are subserved by many of the same physiological and neurobiological mechanisms. The similarity in the conspicuous behavior of adult lovers and mother-infant pairs has been noted elsewhere (Shaver, Hazan, & Bradshaw, 1988). Suffice it to say here that the two relationships stand out not only because they are widely perceived as the "closest" (Berscheid & Graziano, 1979) but also because they allow for the expression of numerous behaviors that are non-normative in other social relationships, such as prolonged ventral-ventral contact and protracted mutual gazing. Attachment relationships are a distinct subset of social relationships, distinguished by their characteristics features (e.g., separation distress) as well as their enduring and intimate nature.

Despite the many similarities between infant-caregiver dyads and romantic pairs, there are several noteworthy differences. The attachment bond between infant and caregiver is complementary; the infant solicits comfort, and the caregiver provides it. Attachment bonds betweeen adult lovers are typically reciprocal; partners give as well as receive nurturance and care. In addition to mutual protection and caregiving, adult attachments also serve the function of sexual reproduction.

Adult attachment bonds thus involve the integration of three behavioral systems: attachment, parenting, and sexual mating (Shaver et al., 1988). From a psychological perspective, it is not unexpected that these systems would become integrated to some extent in adulthood. In fact, many studies have demonstrated the importance of mother-infant attachment for the subsequent development of normal parenting and sexual behavior. Harlow's isolation-reared monkeys who did not form an attachment during infancy provide an example of the subsequent adult effects of infant attachment deprivation (Harlow & Harlow, 1962, 1965). Although isolated monkeys were capable of being rehabilitated in their affiliative relations with peers, they later exhibited dysfunctional parenting and sexual behaviors. Likewise, Lorenz's experimental subjects showed enduring effects of early attachment experiences (Lorenz, 1970). Ducklings who imprinted on him during infancy persisted in their attempts to mate with him when they reached sexual maturity, rather than appropriately mating with members of their own species. Such findings suggest that attachment experiences in infancy can influence adult parenting behavior as well as sexual mate choice. In the prototypical case, all three systems are operative in adult pair-bonds.

As noted above, in tracking the development of attachment bonds during infancy, Bowlby identified four phases (although he acknowledged that the boundaries between phases are "fuzzy"). In light of the evidence that infant-caregiver and adult pair-bonds are characterized by similar dynamics and share many featural similarities, it seems reasonable to assume that both types of relationships are regulated by the same behavioral system—the attachment system. If the same system is operative in both cases, the processes by which attachment bonds are formed would likely be similar as well. Starting from these assumptions, we propose a parallel four-phase process model to integrate and explain the behavior and phenomenology of adult romantic relationship development. We will restrict our discussion of relationship processes to the prototypical relationship, acknowledging in advance that each relationship is unique and idiosyncratic, and reserving a discussion of individual differences for later.

Pre-attachment: Attraction and Flirting

The distinguishing features of the pre-attachment phase during infancy are a preparedness for and inherent interest in social interaction, and relatively indiscriminant social signalling. This combination of preparedness for certain types of social exchange and fairly promiscuous but distinctive signalling captures the essence of adult flirting. Eibl-Eibesfeldt (1989) called this unique and distinctive pattern of behavior the "proceptive program." The defining characteristics of the program are: establishing eye contact and holding the gaze briefly; talking inconsequentially but animatedly (by reason of vocal inflection, exclamation, exaggeration, laughing, heightened pitch and volume, and accelerated speed); progressively rotating to an en-face position; being brushed or lightly touched, as if inadvertently, without recoiling; and synchronizing postures, gestures and facial expressions. Typically, flirtatious displays are ambiguous, and hence deniable (Denzin, 1970), and their composition and meaning may vary as a function of gender (Montgomery, 1986).

Similar to the interactions of caregivers and infants, adult flirtations involve an exaggerated sense of excitement and regard for the other. Even relatively trivial information is met with great enthusiasm. This sends the message of interest and, by highlighting the emotional content of speech and gesture, may also serve to facilitate conversational synchronization. Flirtatious interactions are thus emotionally charged and have an arousing effect on the individuals involved.

Unlike mother-infant pairs, lovers are not given to one another by birthright, and certainly their relationship begins on more precarious terms, and with more limited intimacy. In contrast to the protracted gazing present almost from birth in caregiver-infant pairs (Stern, 1977), adult flirtations often begin with an accidental "catch of the eyes," and then a turning away, or with a seemingly "accidental" touch. Any presumption of intimacy is unwarranted at this stage and would likely be met with distancing by the receiving party. For example, premature self-disclosure of highly personal information places a developing relationship in jeopardy (Berg, 1984; Taylor, Altman, & Wheeler, 1972). Disclosures designed to elicit care or emotional support would violate social norms and likely preempt further progress of the pair. Rather, disclosure at this point is typically limited to superficial, often self-enhancing information (Altman & Taylor, 1973). Flirting, like the indiscriminant signalling of a young infant in the first months of life, is not restricted to one partner. Rather, it signifies a general readiness for social engagement. As such, the only component of attachment present during this phase is a strong motivation for seeking proximity.

Is there any reason to believe that a typical flirtation involves the attachment system at all? Isn't it more likely that the excitement and arousal are due to activation of the sexual mating system? We readily acknowledge that the sexual system is implicated in flirtatious behavior. And, as we have argued elsewhere (Hazan & Zeifman, 1994), sexual attraction is likely what fuels the proximity seeking that could eventually lead to attachment formation. However, there is evidence that flirting individuals are also responsive to attachment-relevant cues.

As noted earlier, infants come equipped with an attachment behavioral system, but the target of their attachment behaviors—the individual who will become their preferred partner—has to be selected. How does an infant "decide" whom to become attached to? Familiarity and responsiveness are key factors (Ainsworth et al., 1978). Likewise, these factors play a major role in adult mate selection (Aron, Dutton, Aron, & Iverson, 1989; Zajonc, 1968). When flirtations are initiated with more than immediate sexual gratification as the goal and, more specifically, with the hope or possibility that such engagement might lead to a lasting association, attachment-relevant cues like warmth, responsiveness, and reciprocal liking will be particularly important (Aron et al., 1989; Backman & Secord, 1959; Curtis & Miller, 1986). Sexual attraction ensures that we will seek and maintain proximity to individuals to

might become attached, but their attachment-worthiness is a con-
in and has an effect on the sexual attraction itself. The prepared-
gage and the relatively indiscriminant signalling that typify flirtation
sine qua non of attachment formation.

Attachment-in-the-making: Falling in Love

Some time between 2 and 3 months of age, the indiscriminant signaling of infants becomes more selective. Infants begin to preferentially direct social signals (cries, smiles, gaze, and vocalizations) toward the person who has been their primary caregiver. The movements of mother-infant dyads during this phase begin to have the appearance of synchrony and attunement. Increasingly, they engage in intimate verbal exchanges, close bodily contact, and prolonged mutual gazing. In adulthood, the same types of behavior are evident when two people are "falling in love." Even from the perspective of outside observers, their behavior appears more intimate as it becomes exclusively directed toward the one person who is the object of their affections.

Attachment-in-the-making is similar to the pre-attachment phase in the sense that social exchanges tend to be arousing. However, the arousal that accompanies infatuation is protracted and extends beyond the interaction. For example, adults in love experience sleeplessness and reduced food intake and, paradoxically, unbounded energy (Tennov, 1979). Leibowitz (1983) has hypothesized that this phase is mediated by the neurochemical phenylethylamine (PEA), similar in its effects to the amphetamines. In addition to stimulating increased arousal, amphetamines are known to act as mild hallucinogens, perhaps helping to account for the idealization of the other known to accompany infatuation (Brehm, 1988; Tennov, 1979).

While couples who are in love find each other's presence stimulating, they also begin during this phase to find it comforting to be together, an effect that may be due in part to concomitant neurochemical and hormonal changes. The chemical basis for the desire to remain in close physical contact with the partner (i.e., cuddle), may be the same for mothers-infant pairs and lovers. Oxytocin, a substance released during suckling-nursing interactions, and thought to induce maternal caregiving, is also released at sexual climax and has been implicated in the cuddling that often follows sexual intercourse (i.e., "afterplay") (Carter, 1992). Cuddling, or "contact comfort" as was demonstrated by Harlow, is important in establishing emotional bonds.

In the adult case, the trend toward increasingly comforting interactions is not limited to physical contact. Changes in voice quality can be noted, including soothing whispers and reassurring "babytalk." Further, whereas in the pre-attachment stage, self-disclosures may be usually limited to positive or neutral facts, as couples fall in love they begin to exchange more personal information, including stories of painful experiences, fears, family secrets, and detailed accounts of previous relationships (Altman & Taylor, 1973). The exchange of this type of information constitutes a test of commitment, as well as a bid for acceptance and care. Hence, couples begin to serve as sources of mutual emotional support. Their relationship takes on an additional feature of attachment—namely, safe haven. The partner, who at first is a source of excitement and arousal, comes increasingly to be a source of comfort.

A couple in love engages in the kinds of behaviors known to facilitate attachment formation, at least in infancy. Prolonged mutual gazing, protracted mutually ventral contact, nuzzling, and cuddling are typical and distinguishing features of infant-caregiver exchanges; significantly, they are also typical of lovers' exchanges, but not of friendships or other social bonds. There appears to be a need during the falling-in-love phase to maintain nearly continuous physical contact. We also find it noteworthy that adults who are falling in love engage in physical contact that is "reassuring" in nature—as evidenced by "parental" gestures such as hand holding or placing an arm around the other's shoulder or waist. These behaviors can be contrasted with the less intimate and arousal-inducing ones that typify flirtations or purely sexual encounters. We suspect that the prolonged mutual gazing typical of this phase facilitates the development of a mental representation of the new partner—or what Bowlby referred to as the internal working model.

If a relationship ends during this phase (which, according to Leibowitz, is dominated by endogenous amphetamines), the individuals will probably experience feelings that are the opposite of energized, perhaps even mild sadness or depression, but they are unlikely to experience the intense anxiety or severe disruption of daily functioning characteristic of attachment dissolution. Needs for emotional support (safe haven) can be almost as easily satisfied by family and friends, and stimulation can be found elsewhere.

In comparing the data on premarital break-ups in college samples with the data on divorce and widowhood, our expectations are confirmed. College students who break up after a brief love affair report experiencing a period of disappointment and depression, but rarely suffer from debilitating anxiety (e.g., Hill, Rubin, & Peplau, 1976). The strategies for coping with premarital break-ups also tell us something about what has been lost; individuals increase time spent with friends, and often immediately begin dating someone else. These strategies differ markedly from those which Weiss (1975) documented for people who have lost a marriage partner. Recent widows and widowers can hardly imagine dating anyone, and recently divorced individuals are often unsuccessful in their initial attempts. In these cases, the company of strangers and friends cannot replace the needs fulfilled by an attachment figure.

Clear-cut Attachment: Loving

At what point does a relationship partner become an attachment figure? The answer is revealed in the sorts of changes that occur as couples make the transition from being in love to loving each other. In the course of a developing romantic relationship, several predictable changes occur. As couple members become increasingly familiar with each other, simply being together is no longer as arousal-inducing. Idealization, which so common among new couples, is eventually replaced by a more realistic view of partners' imperfections and limitations (Hatfield, Traupmann, & Sprecher, 1984). The ratio of positive to negative exchanges shifts in a negative direction (Huston & Vangelisti, 1991). The frequency of sexual activity declines (Fisher, 1992; Traupmann & Hatfield, 1981), and the importance of emotional supportiveness and nurturance relative to sexual satisfaction increases (Kotler, 1985; Reedy, Birren, & Schaie, 1981). Couples spend less and less time locked in mutual gaze and, having already shared the intimate details of their lives, begin to spend their time together discussing decreasingly personal and less relationship-focused issues (Brehm, 1992). And, when they talk to each other, they spend less time whispering and more time speaking in normal tones. In contrast to the euphoria, extraordinary energy, and the diminished interest in food and sleep that dominated their first days and weeks together, they now relish shared meals, and long hours of joint slumber.

What explains these predictable changes, and how do they relate to attachment? Recall the 7-month transition in infancy—a qualitative shift between enjoying social closeness and needing the closeness of a specific individual. Although infants of this age typically approach (seek proximity to) as well as solicit and accept care from a number of familiar people (i.e., use them as havens of safety), displays of separation protest and distress are usually exclusive to the primary caregiver. The main function of an attachment bond is to provide a sense of security. Thus, it follows that individuals would experience feelings of anxiety and distress in the absence of their primary source of comfort and security.

The separation distress reactions of infants have been related to a class of brain chemicals known as the endogenous opioids. Panksepp (Panksepp, Siviy, & Normansell, 1985) noted that separation distress reactions are similar to the drug withdrawal reactions of narcotics addicts. Both "withdrawal" syndromes are characterized by tearfulness and distress vocalizations, anxiety and trembling, stereotypies (e.g., rocking) and other self-soothing behaviors. Based on these similarities, Panksepp began an exploration of the role of endogenous opioids in infant attachment formation. In diverse species, opioid administration ameliorates the disorganizing effects of separation, whereas opioid blockage exacerbates it (Panksepp et al., 1985). These findings have led many scientists to the conclusion that opioids are implicated in the formation of attachment bonds.

According to Leibowitz's model, the shift from the amphetamine-like rush of the initial stages of a romance to the calm and contentment of a more established pair reflects a change in neurochemistry (Leibowitz, 1983). As noted earlier, PEA is one source of the feelings of boundless energy and invinceability that individuals often experience when they are in love. If things "go right," Leibowitz predicted, the amphetamine-like feelings mediated by PEA gradually give way to the contentment and subjective sense of well-being associated with endogenous opioids.

In addition to alleviating anxiety, opioids are powerful conditioning agents. Through classical conditioning, stimuli paired with opioid drugs rapidly become associated with their calming effects, and become strongly preferred. Moreover, such preferences are extremely difficult to extinguish. A typical intimate encounter between romantic partners involves an initial increase in stimulation and arousal, followed by relief, satisfaction, and calm. The similarity in symptoms of an addict being weaned from a narcotic drug and a person suffering from a broken heart lends further support to the hypothesis of opioid involvement in the formation of affectional bonds. It also suggests that attachment may be defined as the conditioning of an individual's opioid system to the stimulus of a particular other. As such, separation distress would be an appropriate marker of attachment formation.

If attachment involves conditioning of the opioid system, such effects would be expected to result from repeated anxiety- and/or tension-alleviating interactions. Exchanges of this type are a common feature of both parent-child and adult romantic relationships. When a parent comforts a crying infant, the parent becomes associated (in the infant's mind) with the alleviation of distress. Similarly, a lover comes to be associated with the tension reduction following sexual climax. In summary, relationships that develop into attachment bonds are those in which heightened physiological arousal—even stress—is repeatedly attenuated by the partner.

Leibowitz's description of the phenomenology of the attraction and attachment phases leads to predictions about the sensations that would be experienced were a relationship to end during each of these two phases. Because PEA is a stimulant, withdrawal would resemble caffeine withdrawal. Break-ups during the PEA-mediated phase of arousal and excitement would therefore lead to mild depression and lethargy. Former partners might, for example, eat and/or sleep more than usual, and be generally less active. If, on the other hand, the break-up occurred during the opioid-mediated phase (i.e., after an attachment had formed), the resulting symptoms would likely be quite different. Dissolution would be expected to cause heightened anxiety and even panic, increased activity, dysregulation of bodily functions, reduced appetite, and insomnia.

Bowlby claimed that relationships characterized by the four defining features of attachment would tend to be those between children and their parents, and between adult romantic partners. We developed measures of these components of attachment and administered them to a large group of individuals representing the age range from late adolescence to late adulthood (Hazan & Zeifman, 1994). We found that full-blown attachments—that is, relationships in which all four components were present—were almost exclusively limited to bonds with parents or sexual partners. In addition, we found that adults who either had no partner or who had partners for less than two years reported experiencing separation distress only in relation to their parents—and, interestingly, not in relation to best friends, siblings, or others with whom they might be expected to have close relationships.

Pending the results of our ongoing research, we hypothesize that separation distress is as plausible and reasonable a criterion of attachment formation in adulthood as it is in infancy. However, documenting adult separation distress, except in such extreme circumstances as divorce and death, is far more challenging than documenting it during infancy, when the attachment figure's mere departure from the room reliably elicits agonizing cries (Ainsworth et al., 1978). Adults are more adept at regulating and inhibiting negative emotional reactions, and more capable of employing cognitive strategies to cope with otherwise painful and disruptive experiences. Nevertheless, studies of the prolonged involuntary separations associated with military service and work-related travel provide evidence that adults, like infants and children, are distressed and disrupted by separations from their attachment figures (Vrombeck, 1993).

Goal-corrected Partnership: Life as Usual

Couples eventually resume their pre-romance activities. Friendships, work, and other real-world obligations that are often neglected by individuals in the midst of a courtship gradually reassume their status in the hierarchy of commitments. In a sense, life-as-usual returns.

A similar transformation occurs sometime between the second and third years of life in the way infants (now toddlers) relate to their primary caregivers. The frequency of attachment behaviors decreases and the need for close physical contact is somewhat attenuated. The reliability of the caregiver is well-established, and the resulting confidence and security provide support for non-attachment activities. The child exhibits increased interest in exploratory activity, especially social contact with peers. The final component of attachment—secure base—is now in place.

For adult pairs, there is a noticeable decrease in the frequency and duration of mutual gazing and physical contact—of the sexual as well as the parental variety. And, there is a reorientation of attention and stimulation-seeking to sources outside the relationship. Conversations reflect an outward focus, in contrast to the personal, partner- and relationship-focused exchanges predominant during earlier phases. At this point, the strong emotional connection between partners is not readily apparent, but beneath the surface there may be a profound interdependence—a phenomenon described by Berscheid (1983).

Hofer (1984) has proposed that this deeper interdependence involves the co-regulation of physiological systems. In essence, each partner comes to serve as one of the external cues or stimuli that provide regulatory input to internal systems (just as light-dark cycles influence sleep). Hofer refers to this physiological interdependence as "entrainment." The removal of the cues explain in part the disorganization that accompanies bereavement.

Examples of entrainment abound in the animal and human infant literatures. For example, in one monogamous species of bird, the ring dove, elaborate interwoven behavioral and physiological changes associated with pair-bonding have been elucidated (Silver, 1978). The male sings, and the female's ovaries begin to develop; "she" displays signs of receptivity, and "he" begins to gather materials and build a nest for them. The relationship between human infants and their caregivers are also characterized by a high degree of physiological interdependence. For example, when a human infant cries, the temperature of mother's breasts rises (Vuorenkowski, Wasz-Hockert, Koivisto, & Lind, 1969); as the infant suckles, milk is let down (Brake, Shair, & Hofer, 1988).

Entrainment in human pair-bonds has not been as thoroughly investigated, although a few examples can be found in the literature. For instance, women ovulate more regularly if they are in a sexual relationship than if they have only sporadic sexual contact, or are celibate (Cutler, Preti, Huggins, Erickson, & Garcia, 1985; Veith, Buck, Getzlaf, Van Dalfsen, & Slade, 1983). Likewise, they are more likely to continue having menstrual periods in their middle years, that is to reach menopause later, if they engage in regular sexual activity (Cutler, Garcia, Huggins, & Preti, 1986). Clearly, entrainment of the type described by Hofer does exist in human pair-bonds. Systematic study may reveal other physiological co-adjustments between couples that could help to explain the devastating and pervasive effects of separation and attachment loss.

Another telling sign of couples' dependence on each other as stimuli is the tendency among grieving individuals to report hallucinations and illusions of the bereavement object following death (Lindemann, 1942). This may be a remnant of a mechanism whereby the image is used to derive security during periods of separation. Mourners sometimes express the fear that the image, the face, of the loved one will be forgotten; hallucinations are a meager attempt to hold the image "on line."

INDIVIDUAL DIFFERENCES IN ATTACHMENT

Up to this point, we have said little about individual differences in attachment, except to mention that they have been the focus of most adult attachment research to date. In the first empirical tests of Bowlby's theory, Ainsworth identified three major patterns of individual differences (Ainsworth et al., 1978). Similarly, Hazan and Shaver (1987, 1990) documented three analogous patterns of adult romantic attachment. The *secure* pattern is characterized by the enjoyment of closeness with partners, and confidence that partners will be reliable and responsive. In contrast, *ambivalent* attachment involves a strong desire for closeness coupled with a lack of confidence in partner responsiveness. This tension between desire and doubt leads to frequent and intense feelings of anger and fear. The *avoidant* pattern is also based on a lack of confidence in partners, but results in avoidance rather than intensified approach. In both infancy and adulthood, the normative pattern is secure attachment (Campos, Barrett, Lamb, Goldsmith, & Stenberg, 1983; Shaver & Hazan, 1992).

The present model summarizes attachment formation processes and phases from a normative perspective. We would predict some variations in the

Table 3.1 A process model of adult attachment formation

Phase	Non-attached		Attached	
	Pre-attachment	Attachment-in-the-making	Clear-cut attachment	Goal-corrected partnership
Attachment component*	Proximity seeking	Safe haven	Separation distress	Secure base
Physical contact	Incidental/"accidental"	Frequent, prolonged, arousing, "parental"	Frequent, less prolonged, comforting	Less frequent, deliberate, context-specific
Eye contact	"Stolen" glances, intermittent gazing	Frequent, protracted mutual gazing	Frequent, less protracted mutual gazing	Less frequent, context-specific mutual gazing
Conversational content	Emotionally neutral, superficial, self-enhancing	Care-eliciting, emotional disclosure	Less emotional, care-eliciting, more mundane	Predominantly mundane
Voice quality	Animated, higher pitched, emotionally aroused	Hushed tones, whispers, soothing	Context-specific soothing, more normal tones and pitch	Predominantly normal
Eating/sleeping	Normal	Decreased	Near-normal	Normal
Mental representation of other	Generalized "template", expectations	Under construction	Beginning to stabilize	Well established, easily conjured up
Neurochemistry/hormones	Pheromonal cues, PEA	PEA, oxytocin	(PEA), oxytocin, opioids	Oxytocin, opioids
Reactions to termination	None, minor disappointment	Lethargy, mild depression	Anxiety, disruption of activities	Extreme anxiety, pervasive physical and psychological disorganization

* Entries on this row represent the component of attachment that is added during each phase, such that all four components are present by the final phase.

processes, and perhaps even the phases, as a result of individual differences in attachment, and there is empirical evidence to support such predictions. For example, we found attachment style differences in the types of physical contact that individuals seek and enjoy or try to avoid (Hazan, Zeifman, & Middleton, 1994). Avoidant adults reported enjoying purely sexual contact (e.g., oral and anal sex) but found more emotionally intimate contact (e.g., kissing, cuddling, nuzzling) to be aversive. Ambivalents reported the opposite pattern of preferences, and viewed sexual activity primarily as a means for gratifying intimacy and comfort needs. The secure group found pleasure in both types of physical contact, especially within the context of an ongoing relationship (as opposed to one-night stands, for example).

The physical contact preferences associated with each attachment style may help to explain their relative rates of success when it comes to establishing an enduring relationship. The secures, who are relatively more successful and significantly less likely to experience relationship dissolution (Hazan & Shaver, 1987; Kirkpatrick & Hazan, 1994), engage in the kinds of physical contact necessary to satisfy their own and their partners' attachment (and sexual) needs. Avoidants, in contrast, have an expressed aversion to the type of contact thought to foster an attachment. The preferences of ambivalents suggest that they have somewhat excessive attachment needs and a marked lack of interest in sex, both of which could jeopardize their relationships. Thus, insecure attachment—through its effects on physical contact—appears to interfere with attachment formation.

The effects of attachment style differences are not limited to the arena of physical contact. Existing evidence suggests not only that attachment style influences behavior in several domains relevant to our process model, but that the pattern of influences is consistent across domains. In general, avoidants distance themselves from their partner and ambivalents make inappropriate and premature bids for intimacy. These patterns are revealed in such relevant behaviors as the frequency and selectiveness of self-disclosures (Mikulincer & Nachsohn, 1991), the tendency to solicit comfort from a partner in response to stress (Simpson & Gangestad, 1992), and willingness to engage in uncommitted sex (Brennan, Shaver, & Tobey, 1991; Simpson, 1990). Such findings, together with our normative model, suggest that avoidant adults might be reluctant to engage in the kinds of behavior that facilitate attachment formation, whereas ambivalents might attempt to rush the process and, in doing so, behave in ways that violate norms governing each phase. In both cases, the probability that a stable bond will develop is diminished.

Despite individual differences and their effects on relationship processes, insecure attachment does not preclude the development of strong and enduring emotional bonds. Just as infants who are abused or neglected nevertheless become attached to their caregivers (Crittenden, 1988), so too adults in dysfunctional relationships become attached to their partners. As Bowlby argued, attachment motivation is sufficiently powerful across the life span that attachment bonds will develop even under grossly nonoptimal circumstances.

CONCLUSIONS AND FUTURE DIRECTIONS

We have presented a four-phase normative model of adult attachment form-ation. At this point, we are hypothesizing an invariant sequence of phases, as well as coherence of features within each phase. For instance, a certain level of self-disclosure would coincide with a corresponding level of eye contact; intimate physical contact would accompany a correspondingly intimate de-gree of psychological closeness. However, the timing of progress from one phase to the next would vary widely as a function of individual differences—e.g., in age, attachment style, gender, culture and values.

We are currently testing several different components and implications of the model. An overarching goal is to identify an index of the existence of an adult attachment bond. As we have argued, during the transition from non-attached to attached, a shift occurs in the balance of the arousal-inducing and arousal-moderating effects of the partner's presence. At the same time that the partner's presence becomes more calming than exciting, his or her ab-sence elicits anxiety and distress. Thus, separation distress—the marker of attachment in infancy—is the prime candidate for an index of adult attachment.

Documenting adult separation distress has proved challenging. Unlike in-fants, adults are adept at inhibiting expressions of negative affect. Further-more, they can utilize cognitive strategies to cope with separations and regulate their own negative emotional responses. And, while reactions to such extreme circumstances as death of or separation from a partner provide un-mistakable evidence of separation distress, documenting the negative effects of temporary or short-term separations requires examination of more subtle indices, such as disruptions in routine patterns of sleep, activity, and food intake.

We began with a description of three hypothetical couples whose interac-tions revealed differences in the nature of their respective relationships. Our goal was to move beyond observables to the underlying function and meaning of the differences. Doing so has required that we draw on work from a number of different disciplines and sub-areas within our own discipline of psychology. By adopting a comparative and multidisciplinary approach, we have elucidated several important but unexplored issues. With a full appracia-tion for the challenges that lie ahead, we invite the next generation of attach-ment researchers to join us in exploring this uncharted territory.

Acknowledgments

We thank Richard L. Canfield, Francesco Del Vecchio, Steve Duck, William Ickes, Elizabeth Leff, and David Sbarra for their helpful comments on earlier drafts of this chapter.

Chapter 4

Perspectives on Interracial Relationships

Stanley O. Gaines, Jr

Pomona College, Claremont, CA, USA

and

William Ickes

University of Texas, Arlington, TX, USA

Because interracial relationships are different from other kinds of relationships, they warrant a special accounting. Providing such an accounting—or, at least, a first approximation of one—is the major goal of this chapter. Starting from the premise that interracial relationships are different from other types of interethnic relationships, we will explore the nature of these differences and their implications for the perceptions by "outsiders" and "insiders" of various subtypes of interracial relationships (same-sex vs mixed-sex, romantic vs platonic).

We begin by reviewing evidence that interracial relationships are indeed different from other kinds of relationships. We then examine interracial relationships from two general perspectives: (1) the "outside" perspective of individuals who are observers of these relationships; and (2) the "inside" perspective of individuals who are the members of these relationships. To help illustrate and explain the processes that are presumed to underlie each of these perspectives, several relevant theoretical principles from the field of

The Social Psychology of Personal Relationships.
Edited by William Ickes and Steve Duck. © 2000 John Wiley & Sons Ltd.

social psychology are invoked. Our discussion of these issues leads us to examine six types of interracial relationships (i.e., male–male friendships, female–female friendships, male–female friendships, male–female romantic relationships, male–male romantic relationships, and female–female romantic relationships) in terms of the two contrasting perspectives. From the tensions implicated by the interplay of the "outside" and "inside" perspectives, dynamic elements characteristic of each of these six types of interracial relationships are then proposed.

INTERRACIAL RELATIONSHIPS ARE DIFFERENT FROM OTHER KINDS OF RELATIONSHIPS

Evidence that interracial relationships are indeed different from other kinds of relationships is not hard to find. Two types of evidence are especially relevant: (1) the statistical infrequency of interracial relationships; and (2) evidence that interracial relationships are different in distinctive ways from the larger class of interethnic relationships.

Interracial Relationships are Statistically Infrequent

Interracial relationships are statistically infrequent, occurring much less often than actuarial projections would predict. Even in this ostensibly post-civil rights era, interracial friendships remain the exception rather than the norm (Blieszner & Adams, 1992; Furman, 1985; Todd, McKinney, Harris, Chadderton, & Small, 1992), as do interracial marriages (Levinger & Rands, 1985; Todd et al., 1992; Zweigenhaft & Domhoff, 1991). Statistics regarding the incidence of interracial friendships and dating relationships are, of course, substantially harder to find than are corresponding statistics regarding interracial marriages (see Zweigenhaft & Domhoff, 1991). However, if we assume that marital relationships are the most intimate (and, by extension, most difficult to establish and maintain; Levinger & Rands, 1985) of all interracial relationships, we may regard the incidence of interracial marriages as a lower limit on the incidence of interracial relationships as a whole.

As of March 1993, interracial couples composed 2.2% of all married couples (US Bureau of the Census, 1994). Among interracial couples in 1993, 20.3% consisted of Black/White pairs. Furthermore, among Black/White pairs, 75% consisted of Black male/White female pairs. Interestingly, Latinas/Latinos and Asian Americans are much more likely to marry Anglos than are African Americans (Sanjek, 1994). Also, persons of color rarely marry other persons of color who do not share the same ethnicity.

How do individuals decide which ingroups and outgroups are to be regarded as essential to their self-concept and self-esteem? Clearly, society provides us (via socializing agents such as parents, teachers, religious leaders, and media figures) with the relevant information (Allport, 1954/1979; Samovar & Porter, 1995); we are not born knowing which ingroup–outgroup distinctions are supposed to be most important. In the United States, the enslavement of African Americans until the Civil War, the seizure of land previously settled by Native Americans and Latinas/os during the colonial era, and the incarceration of Asian Americans during World War II (especially those of known or suspected Japanese ancestry) all serve as vivid historical reminders that, as Cornel West (1993) put it, "Race matters".

Interracial Relationships are Different from Other Interethnic Relationships

Further evidence for the distinctiveness of interracial relationships is that they represent a distinct subset within the larger class of *interethnic relationships*. A comparison of interracial and interreligious marriages is informative because both represent different types of interethnic marriages (i.e., marriages involving persons from dissimilar racial, language, religious, and/or national groups; Ho, 1984; Yinger, 1994). Nevertheless, the relatively low rates of interracial marriage contrast sharply with those of interreligious marriages in the United States (Ho, 1984; Levinger & Rands, 1985). If Ho's (1984) estimate of interethnic marriages accounting for one-third of all marriages in the United States is correct, then even after taking marriages among "White ethnics" into consideration, interreligious marriages greatly outnumber (and are greatly more probable than) interracial marriages. Thus, Allport's (1954/1979) assessment that racial differences were markedly more salient than religious differences in American society is just as true at the close of this century as it was during the middle portion.

Of course, the categories of interracial and interreligious marriage are not mutually exclusive. For instance, Black Protestant/White Jewish marriages would qualify as interracial *and* interreligious (see Zweigenhaft & Domhoff, 1991). Nevertheless, the fact that interracial marriages are so infrequent and improbable in comparison to interreligious marriages is *prima facie* evidence for important differences between the two. It is important to note, however, that any consideration of such differences must begin with the recognition of a fundamental similarity: both interracial and interreligious marriages involve at least one partner who is stigmatized by society. Goffman (1963) classified stigma pertaining to (1) race/ethnicity, (2) nation of origin, and (3) religion as "*tribal stigma . . .* that can be transmitted through lineages and equally contaminate all members of a family" (p. 49, italics added). Thus, marriages involving persons from different racial groups as well as persons from different religious groups both have the potential to draw unwanted attention toward the "stigmatized" (i.e., racial or religious minority) partner, toward the "normal" (i.e., racial or religious majority) partner, and toward their offspring as well.

Given that both interracial and interreligious marriages are stigmatized, what factors might account for the contrasting trends in their statistical infrequency? Levinger and Rands (1985) have suggested the following answers:

> An explanation may invoke slow-changing norms concerning race and fast-changing norms for religion. Racial discrimination, even though it has lessened greatly in the legal system, strongly resists change. Not only do people remain suspicious of others who look different physically, but racial differences are linked historically to differences in social class, residence, education, and economic opportunities and resources. One's racial features are determined genetically and do not change over time. In contrast, one's religious affiliation is independent of one's genetic features and is susceptible to alteration. Although some persons hold their religious beliefs throughout their lifetime, others hold them so weakly that they may undergo dramatic change.

> Given the fixity of race and the plasticity of religion, intermarrying racially versus religiously has quite different implications: Interracial partners retain their public skin differences, whereas interreligious partners either can privately deemphasize their religious beliefs or change toward a common orientation. Further, whereas the offspring of interracial unions are marked visibly by their parents' genetic makeup, children from interreligious marriages can develop their personal faith in their own unique fashion. (pp. 315–316)

Levinger and Rands (1985) propose that the greater stigmatization of interracial versus interreligious marriages derives from a number of interrelated factors. These include (a) *xenophobia*—being "suspicious of others who look different physically", (b) *negative social stereotyping* based on historical linkages "to differences in social class, residence, education, and economic opportunities and resources", and (c) the origin of interracial differences in *genetic factors*, which, unlike the different beliefs that underlie religious differences, are highly visible and cannot be readily altered or ignored. We suggest that the analysis by Levinger and Rands (1985) neatly captures the essential features of what we term the "outsiders' perspective" on interracial relationships in general, including—but not limited to—interracial marriages. We further suggest that although this perspective is crucial to understanding interracial relationships, the understanding it provides is necessarily incomplete. A more complete understanding requires that the "outsiders' perspective" be complemented with an "insiders' perspective" that represents the view of an interracial relationship that is held by its members. Moreover, because the dynamic tensions between these two perspectives can influence the nature and course of interracial relationships, the interaction of these two perspectives must be considered as well.

Why should the insider–outsider difference regarding interracial relationships matter to relationship researchers? As Duck (1994b) has noted, relationship researchers commonly assume that one "true" account of relationship processes is to be found and that they (rather than the relationship members) are uniquely equipped to construct that account. Such a rationale implies that, when—as often happens—the insiders construct accounts of their shared lives that are at odds with relationship researchers' accounts of those same relationships, the outsiders (i.e., relationship researchers) are likely to privilege their own accounts over those of the relationship members (Olson, 1977; see also Duck, 1990; Duck & Sants, 1983; Kelley, 1979; Surra & Ridley, 1991). Such a danger is real even when researchers and their participants belong to the same racial group (usually Anglos), and becomes all the more imminent when at least one of the members of each dyad belongs to a racial group that is dissimilar to that of the researchers.

How does the elucidation of this insider–outsider difference in perspective help us to understand interracial relationship processes in particular? Furthermore, what does an examination of the tension between the two perspectives add to our ability to understand and explain interracial relationships? In answering these questions, we note that (a) acknowledging the insider–outsider difference allows us to make explicit and to evaluate critically the oft-implicit, oft-unscrutinized theories characterizing outsiders' accounts of such seemingly anomalous relationships; and (b) examining the potential impact of the tension between insider and outsider accounts *upon the relational lives of insiders* allows us to identify the overt and covert behavioral strategies that insiders employ in order to minimize that tension. Accordingly, in the remaining sections of this chapter we consider both the perspectives of the "outsiders" and the "insiders" regarding interracial relationships. We then examine some implications of the tension between these two perspectives for the various subtypes of interracial relationships.

THE "OUTSIDERS' PERSPECTIVE" ON INTERRACIAL RELATIONSHIPS

Levinger and Rands' (1985) analysis suggests that both genetic and environmental (i.e., social learning) factors contribute to the "outsiders' perspective", and thus in combination help to explain the low incidence of interracial marriage. Unfortunately, a comprehensive review of all the genetic and social-learning factors that might be implicated by such an analysis is beyond the scope of this chapter. Our more modest goal, therefore, is to suggest that *genetic predispositions* provide a deep-rooted and essentially noncognitive basis for the "outsiders' view" of interracial relationships, a view which—in humans, at least—is further modified, refined, and complicated by a *cognitive overlay* that derives from a variety of perceptual and cognitive inputs. In discussing both the genetic predispositions and the cognitive overlay that presumably define the "outsider's view" of interracial relationships, we offer a few illustrative examples instead of an exhaustive list of all of the potentially relevant factors.

Xenophobia as an Unlearned Genetic Predisposition

Writing within an evolutionary framework, Rajecki (1985) proposed that *xenophobia* is a genetically determined phenomenon that explains human as well as infrahuman patterns of within-group cooperation and between-group competition. Rajecki's (1985) evolutionary approach provides a relatively noncognitive account of what he assumes to be primary, deep-rooted reactions to interracial relationships.

To ensure both their personal survival and the survival of their genes in subsequent generations, humans—like other social animals—must to be able to position themselves within status hierarchies. Ingroups such as family, tribe, and nation provide individuals with unique niches within the prevailing social order. By maintaining harmonious relations with ingroup members toward whom individuals adopt either a dominant or a submissive stance, individuals attempt to ensure that their physical and social environments will remain relatively stable and, thus, conducive to their survival as well as the survival of their progeny (Krebs & Miller, 1985).

Whereas interactions with ingroup members tend to promote social stability, interactions with outgroup members may portend social change. With social change comes an implicit or explicit threat to individuals' sense of security. Especially when tangible resources are scarce, outgroup members may serve as visible reminders that individuals' control over their own physical and social environments and, hence, over their own survival (and the survival of their offspring) is tenuous at best. According to Rajecki (1985), xenophobia is evoked as an unlearned, genetically based predisposition when an outgroup member intentionally or unintentionally enters territory demarcated by the ingroup in question. If the outgroup member is outnumbered by the ingroup members, the ingroup members generally will retaliate against the interloper (see also Krebs & Miller, 1985).

Why do ingroup members experience the xenophobia that leads them to retaliate against interlopers (i.e., outgroup members) who are in the minority? Rajecki (1985) proposed that when a preexisting group is left to its own devices, each member of the ingroup is given the opportunity to mate and thus contribute to the "blood line" of the species. In order to minimize within-group conflict *vis-á-vis* acquisition of tangible resources that are crucial to the survival of individual ingroup members (e.g., food) and to the survival of the ingroup's genes from generation to generation (e.g., sex), ingroup members collectively construct dominance hierarchies in which each individual is granted at least minimal access to tangible resources—including opportunities to mate. Once an outgroup member of the same species, biological sex, and approximate age as one or more of the ingroup members actually infiltrates the group, direct ingroup–outgroup competition ensues:

> . . . The [key idea is] that more or less amicable relations between group members are due to their mutual control and predictability . . . . [W]hen [an individual] encounters and confronts a stranger of the same age and sex, it neither knows for certainty what behavior to expect nor what dominance relationship exists between itself and the other. Assuming that the sheer ambiguity is intolerable and further that most gregarious organisms continuously strive for dominance and exercise it when they have it, the issue of the status relationship between the two strangers should not remain unsettled for long. If the two

remain in contact, attempts to establish predictability and control should be made manifest quickly, and perhaps dramatically. (p. 17)

According to Rajecki's account of xenophobia, retaliation toward an outgroup member becomes more likely to the extent that, relative to ingroup members, the outgroup member is (a) physically dissimilar (physical dissimilarity being a probable marker of genetic dissimilarity), (b) unfamiliar and behaviorally unpredictable (thus heightening anxiety and uncertainty about the dominance relationship that might exist), and (c) in a numerical minority (outnumbered). Because inclusive genetic fitness should be enhanced for ingroup members who retaliate against outgroup members when these conditions are met, evidence for outgroup retaliation of this type should be—and is—evident across a wide range of species (see Rajecki, 1985, for a review).

Interestingly, some of the most consistent and compelling evidence for this account comes from field studies of nonhuman primate species, including free-ranging Barbary macaques (Deag, 1977), pigtail macaques (Bernstein, 1969), mangabeys (Bernstein, 1971), and rhesus monkeys (Bernstein, 1964). For example, when outgroup members were introduced into natural ingroups of rhesus monkeys:

> [E]xcept for some infant strangers, all the rest of the introduced animals were met with intense aggression that included threats, chases, and direct physical attacks . . . Overall, aggression in natural groups such as these increased over baseline by from 42% to 822% as a consequence of the release of strangers in the vicinity. Of the 18 strangers released in the study (again, excluding infants) 100% were either killed or driven completely away! (Rajecki, 1985, p. 20)

Rajecki's account of xenophobic aggression toward physically dissimilar outgroup members might provide at least a partial explanation of some of the more tragic and brutal instances of interracial violence in the history of the United States (Allport, 1954/1979; Du Bois, 1986; Rosenblatt, Karis, & Powell, 1995). For example, a once-common lynching scenario in Southern states involved one or more young White males overhearing a rumor (whether verified or not) that a young Black male had entered a predominantly White community and made unwanted sexual advances toward a young White female. Such a scenario often ended with a mob of angry White men accosting the Black man, hanging him, and then mutilating his genitals as the final symbolic act of retaliation.

Rajecki's (1985) view of xenophobia as a biologically adaptive response to strangers of the same species conforms to commonly held beliefs that ingroup–outgroup bias, overt prejudice, and the miscegenation taboo are inevitable aspects of the human condition (Gaines & Reed, 1994, 1995). Returning to our original theme of interracial relationships, this view of xenophobia is also consistent with the relatively low incidence of relationships among those persons who phenotypically are most dissimilar (and, thus, likely to share the fewest number of genes), namely Blacks and Whites (Todd et al., 1992). An important irony should be noted, however. Given that (a) many, if not most, persons designated as Black have one or more White ancestors (Allport, 1954/1979; Porterfield, 1978; Zack, 1993) and that (b) the genes responsible for group differences in physical features such as eye color, hair texture, and skin pigmentation collectively represent no more than 5% of humans' genetic inheritance (Allport, 1954/1979), Rajecki's (1985) account implies that xenophobia leads individuals to ignore the overwhelming genetic similarities in favor of the relatively few genetic differences among human beings.

Perceptual and Cognitive Aspects of the "Outsiders' Perspective"

If xenophobia is an unlearned, reflexive response to the intrusion of outgroup members, interracial relationships may not even be recognized as such by fellow ingroup members who are "outsiders" with respect to those relationships. The prepotent response of these observers may simply be to view the outgroup member as an unwelcome intruder and to "help" the intruded-upon ingroup member drive the intruder off! Recognizing that a genuine relationship exists between their fellow ingroup member and the outgroup member may be beyond the capacity of many infrahuman species, but it is an insight that humans will usually—though not always—achieve. When such insight *is* achieved, interracial relationships will typically present fellow ingroup members with a puzzling attributional problem. Why, given the influence of xenophobia and the psychological barriers created by various perceptual and cognitive processes (some of which are described below), should such a relationship form at all? And why, once it has formed, should such a relationship persist?

The "outsider" may be resistant to even recognizing that an interracial relationship exists because a number of perceptual and cognitive processes militate against such a conclusion. In the following section, some representative examples of these processes are briefly discussed. They include (a) similarity as a gestalt organizing principle in perception, (b) the cognitive linkage of racial markers with negative characteristics, (c) the implications of such linkages for Heiderian models of the interracial relationship as cognitively and affectively imbalanced, and (d) the attributional consequences for the "outsider" of perceiving such imbalance.

Similarity as a Perceptual Organizing Principle

According to principles of gestalt psychology (Köhler, 1947), individuals tend to perceive objects that share salient surface characteristics as "belonging" together, in what Heider (1958) termed a *unit relation*. Although gestalt psychology initially was applied to object perception, the principle of sensory organization may be applied to person perception as well (Fiske & Taylor, 1984). Thus, persons whose skin pigmentation is similar are more likely to be perceived by outsiders as a social unit (as friends, dating partners, etc.) than are persons whose skin pigmentation is dissimilar (see Rosenblatt et al., 1995).

Moreover, given that racial segregation persists across a range variety of societal institutions (e.g., religious, educational, social) throughout the United States (National Research Council, 1989; Pinkney, 1993), the Black person who befriends a White person in a predominantly White setting or the White person who marries a Black person in a predominantly Black setting is likely to be regarded as a social anomaly.

Particularly when the target person is Black, the stigmatization that accompanies "standing out" by being conspicuously different from others (Goffman, 1963) may isolate an outgroup member perceptually and discourage the perception that he or she is a member of an interracial relationship. A double standard seems to be at work here, such that the question is not whether a White person "belongs" with a Black partner but whether a Black person "belongs" with a White partner. Thus, even though perceptual similarity may function as a general organizing principle, the fact that Blacks are singled out (at least by White perceivers; Stephan, 1985) as the targets who "don't belong" suggests that the perceptual process is accompanied by a cognitive bias that implicates more than the response of retinal cells to dissimilarities in skin color. Clearly, some degree of accompanying cognitive bias is required for such a nonrandom tendency to be expressed so often.

Linkage of Racial Markers with Negative Characteristics

The negative stereotyping of the outgroup member can clearly add this type of cognitive overlay to the outside observer's more reflexive xenophobic response. In some instances, racial markers such as skin color may be associated with negative characteristics because a genuine association exists (e.g., African Americans having a slave ancestry and a higher rate of out-of-wedlock births than their European American counterparts). In other instances, however, the association of racial markers with negative characteristics may be spurious. For example, although Kelly's (1955) psychology of personal constructs did not address race *per se*, a construct referring to a racial marker (e.g., the Black/White dichotomy) may be cognitively linked with a host of other dichotomies in a way that can lead to negative stereotyping (e.g., evil/virtuous, unenlightened/enlightened, dirty/clean). To the extent that individuals fail to acknowledge physical or social objects that contradict such global categorization (e.g., Black *and* virtuous, White *and* dirty), these linkages can provide one source of societal stereotypes. Similarly, through a process characterized as "illusory correlation" (Chapman & Chapman, 1969; Hamilton & Rose, 1980), negative behaviors or characteristics that are distinctive by virtue of their low frequency of occurrence in the general population can be spuriously linked with outgroup members who are also distinctive by virtue of their minority status.

Cognitive and Affective Imbalance

The association of racial markers with negative characteristics has direct implications for the outsider's reaction to an interracial relationship when it becomes one of the sentiment relations in a Heiderian p-o-x triad. Heider's (1958) balance theory proposed that such triads are cognitive structures that are evaluated with respect to their logical consistency, with inconsistency being experienced as psychologically aversive. Regarding the consistency of sentiment relations (i.e., feelings directed toward a particular person, place, or thing) within the context of p-o-x triads representing interracial or interethnic encounters, several propositions can be derived. For example, consistent with Rajecki's (1985) view of xenophobia, (1) individuals should tend to dislike persons who are dissimilar to themselves, and (2) individuals should tend to dislike persons who are unfamiliar. From the perspective of the outside observer of an interracial relationship, the ingroup member's apparent unit relation with the outgroup member sets the stage for considerable cognitive inconsistency, being inconsistent not only with the logic of both of the above propositions but also by virtue of linking the fellow ingroup member with an outgroup member whose racial markers are associated with negative characteristics. Thus, in addition to being a threat to the inclusive fitness of the ingroup as a potential competitor for their physical resources and opportunities to reproduce, the intruding outgroup member is a threat to the ingroup's cognitive consistency (i.e., "peace of mind") as well.

Outsiders who can apply p-o-x reasoning to interracial relationships are capable of generating a wider and more sophisticated range of reactions to them than outsiders who cannot. Their options can therefore extend beyond the simple, reflexive xenophobic reaction (i.e., to retaliate against—and either repel or destroy—the outgroup member) to include many additional options. For example, they can (1) deny that the unit relation (i.e., the interracial relationship) really exists; (2) acknowledge the unit relation but view it as momentary, transient, unstable; (3) redefine the ingroup in such a way that it can include the outgroup member; or (4) deny that the particular outgroup member involved in the interracial relationship has the negative characteristics that have been linked to the outgroup's racial markers. They can also (5) acknowledge the unit relation, but attempt to set limits on its strength and implications:

> The relations between sentiment and spatial or interaction closeness underlies the concept known as "social distance." By *social distance* is meant the degree of interpersonal closeness one accepts. For example, one might not mind living in the same city with a particular person, race, or class but would object to being neighbors. Or, one might accept neighborhood association, but resist membership in the same club. Acceptance of the marriage relation represents a minimal degree of social distance, community ostracism the other extreme. (Heider, 1958, p. 191; our italics)

Application of Kelley's Augmentation Principle

In cases in which the outsider cannot readily deny or minimize the unit relation (i.e., the interracial relationship), the outsider is confronted with a puzzling attributional problem. Why, given the influence of xenophobia and the psychological barriers created by various perceptual and cognitive processes of the types we have just described, should such a relationship form at all? And why, once it has formed, should such a relationship persist?

Responses to this attributional problem should vary greatly, depending on such factors as the outsider's intelligence, level of cognitive development, level of motivation (and patience) to solve the problem, willingness to accept a "satisficing" solution (Kahneman, Slovik, & Tversky, 1982; Nisbett & Ross, 1980) to it, and so on. In response to such factors, some observers of the interracial relationship will not attempt to solve the attributional problem the relationship poses, reverting instead to either a primitive xenophobic response or to a minimally effortful attempt to simply restore cognitive balance (e.g., by denying that the interracial relationship exists at all). However, more motivated and cognitively sophisticated outsiders will attempt to account for the interracial relationship, and their typical response will be to invoke Kelley's (1972) *augmentation principle* to assist them in this regard.

Given the various factors ("instinctual", perceptual, and cognitive) that militate against the interracial relationship having been formed at all, the logical inference of the outside observer must be that some other factor(s) augmented the participants' desire to form the relationship to such an extent that this desire overrode the "natural" barriers to such a relationship. The observer's need to postulate the existence and operation of such augmenting factors should be greater to the extent that the barriers to the relationship itself are great—and the barriers to interracial relationships can be great indeed. They include not only the "instinctual", perceptual, and cognitive reactions we have described above, but can include intense societal sanctions (verbal and physical attacks, ostracism, loss of employment, incarceration, etc.) as well. A reasonable inference for the outsider to make, then, is that if something holds an interracial pair together, "it must be something strong".

What is that *something* that causes an interracial relationship to form, and continues to hold its members together? In the lyric by John Sebastian quoted above, the singer's complete response was "I don't know what it is, but it must be something strong". And, just as in the lyric, outside observers are not always able to specify the augmenting factor(s) that would help them to account for the interracial relationship, but can only assume that such factors must exist. In many cases, however, additional cues to the nature of the augmenting factor(s) are available in the subtype of interracial relationship that they are attempting to "explain". By using these cues to refine their inferences, outside observers can logically (though not always accurately) identify at least one augmenting factor that might account for the interracial relationship in question.

Once again, conditional elements such as the observer's intelligence, cognitive resources, motivation, etc., will combine to determine the cognitive sophistication of the inference that is made. The simplest, least effortful, least sophisticated inference would likely be the ascription of a generic disposition to the renegade ingroup member (e.g., "He's a nigger lover"). Such an inference might reflect the upper limit of cognitive sophistication for a group of men with limited educations who are wearing white hoods and are "cognitively busy" (Gilbert, Pelham, & Krull, 1988) with the competing demands of trying to smash the victim's windows and set fire to a cross in his front yard.

On the other hand, for outside observers with more cognitive resources to invest, more differentiated inferences about the augmenting factor(s) that underlie the interracial relationship are often suggested by whether the relationship (a) involves same-sex or mixed-sex members, and (b) appears to be romantic or platonic. For example, to account for heterosexual interracial relationships, outside observers are likely to infer that the major augmenting factor is either an unusually powerful sexual attraction or the lure of "forbidden fruit". They are likely to make a similar inference in the case of homosexual interracial relationships if the corresponding sexual orientation of one or both members is known. However, because augmenting factors that might underlie interracial platonic relationships are not as readily "available" (Kahneman et al., 1982; Nisbett & Ross, 1980), these relationships present a greater puzzle to the outside observer, who may be likely to infer a sexual motive in *any* mixed-sex interracial relationship—even when no such motive exists.

Of course, given more extensive information about the respective histories, personal dispositions, and current circumstances of the members of an interracial relationship, the outside observer is in a position to make an even more refined inference about why the relationship exists and "what's in it?" for each of the members (see Triandis, 1988). We will return to the attributional puzzles posed by the different subtypes of interracial relationships in the final section of this chapter, after first considering the insiders' view of interracial relationships and how this view contrasts with that of outsiders.

THE "INSIDERS' PERSPECTIVE" ON INTERRACIAL RELATIONSHIPS

Some attribution theorists have rightly criticized personality theorists in general (Ross, 1977) and Freudian psychoanalytic theorists in particular (Nisbett & Ross, 1980) for tending to privilege their status as outsiders (instead of privileging their subjects' status as insiders) when attempting to account for their subjects' behavior (see Harvey, Ickes, & Kidd, 1976). It is therefore ironic that both attribution theorists and personality theorists have tended to depict the sexual motive as being the major factor accounting for interracial romantic relationships—as if (a) no factor other than sex could explain the formation and persistence of *interracial* romantic relationships, and (b) any number of factors other than sex could explain the formation and persistence of *intraracial* romantic relationships (see Aldridge, 1978, 1991). All too often, the untested assumption that the partners in interracial relationships harbor an irrational yearning for "forbidden fruit" has been treated as incontestable within the social science literature (Aldridge, 1978; Davidson, 1992; Hernton,

1965/1988; Kouri & Lasswell, 1993; Porterfield, 1978; Rosenblatt et al., 1995; Spickard, 1989; Staples, 1994). Another judgment commonly expressed by outside observers—whether they are lay observers or social scientists—is that interracial relationships are highly volatile and unstable in comparison to intraracial relationships.

Rarely, however, do outside observers—even social scientists—check to see if these attributions are shared by "insiders"—the members of interracial relationships (Olson, 1977; see also Duck, 1990, 1994a; Duck & Sants, 1983; Kelley, 1979; Surra & Ridley, 1991). Rarely are the partners in interracial relationships (and, within families, their offspring as well) given the opportunity to describe their social-psychological experiences *in their own words* (for exceptions, see Funderberg, 1994; Terkel, 1991). Is it any wonder, then, that the relationship processes between persons from different racial backgrounds often are depicted and interpreted in unflattering terms?

For example, would insiders agree with outsiders that xenophobia is the primary barrier to interracial relationship development? Until the abolition of anti-miscegenation laws by the US Supreme Court in 1967, individual states (especially in the South) singled out Black–White marriages as being illegal, and penalized offenders most severely, particularly when the groom was Black and the bride was White (Porterfield, 1978; Spickard, 1989). For decades (and, in some instances, centuries), state legislation stoked the fires of racial animosity more directly than did those presumably innate tendencies that were used to justify such legislation. As Allport (1954/1979) observed near the beginning of the modern Civil Rights Movement, only after anti-miscegenation laws were overturned would social scientists be able to determine whether interracial marriages were held in check by xenophobia *per se*. In contrast to the consistent xenophobia implied by the outsiders' perspective, the overturning of state anti-miscegenation statutes was followed by a dramatic increase in the frequency of interracial marriages (with the notable exception of Black–White marriages; Sanjek, 1994).

As this example suggests, an insiders' perspective that calls attention to such societal barriers to the formation and maintenance of interracial relationships can provide a valuable complement to the perspective of outside observers (Duck, 1994a; McCall & Simmons, 1991; Surra & Ridley, 1991). It enables researchers to gain the kinds of insights that, in many cases, can only be found in relationship members' accounts of their own experiences. With regard to interracial relationships, the "insiders' perspective" could potentially clarify whether partners' stated motives for entering, maintaining, or even leaving such relationships are as simplistic as the "outsiders' perspective" traditionally has maintained. Consider, for example, the following e-mail conversation among individuals subscribing to an Internet newsgroup devoted to intercultural couples[1]:

---

[1] All references to electronic mail correspondence as "personal communications" are in accordance with recommendations set forth in the *Publication Manual of the American Psychological Association*, 4th edn. (Washington, DC: APA, 1994).

. . . I agree with you here. "Other races are exciting" sounds like conditioning to me. (Of course, a given person could find his *own* race "exotic and exciting" if he happened to have grown up differently.) (B. Saunders, Apr. 25, 1995, personal communication)

This was the point I made about, after being married to a black woman for nearly nine years, I "see" her more than I "see" myself (because I only "see" myself when passing a mirror). Although I am white, being with anyone who was not black would have that "exotic and exciting" sort of thing about it— regardless if she was white or something other than black or white. (C. Henry-Cotran, Apr. 27, 1995, personal communication)

Exactly the way I feel. My wife is Chinese—at this point, any non-Asian woman would seem more "exotic" than another Asian woman—but even a near-lookalike for my wife would seem awfully strange. Then again, I'm not after "exotic and strange"—if anything, I find my wife more attractive after [more than 13] years than I did when I first met her. After all this time, racial differences are not what registers when I see her—I see *Alice*, accept no substitutes. (D. Crom, Apr. 30, 1995, personal communication)

As these examples illustrate, the "insiders' perspective" on interracial relationships may assign little weight or credence to the desire for "forbidden fruit" *per se*. Are there, then, other motives that might explain the prevalence of romantic interracial relationships *from the perspective of individuals within those relationships*? One possibility is that certain differences between the partners may be valued because they help to satisfy the partners' motives for self-expansion, novelty, and sensation seeking in areas that may include—but are in no way limited to—their sexuality. A second possibility is that the psychological similarity between the partners might be valued—despite their physical and cultural differences—because it helps to satisfy the partners' motive to have a congenial, supportive relationship with a compatible partner (Rosenblatt et al., 1995).

Valued Differences Contributing to Novelty and Self-Expansion

Cultural differences between the partners might help to satisfy their *needs for self-expansion* (see the chapter by Aron & Aron in this volume). Through their interracial relationship, both partners can gain direct access to another culture or subculture—the one that shaped their partner's attitudes, values, habits, speech, dress, food preferences, and esthetic sensibilities. Because the potential for self-expansion is great in interracial relationships, realizing this potential is likely to be one of the motives that underlie such relationships.

A related motive is the *need for novelty* (Berlyne, 1960). Interracial relationships are particularly likely to offer surprises—elements of novelty that may be highly valued by the partners (though this same novelty may be relatively unacknowledged and unappreciated by the outside observers). For example, a European American man whose cultural heritage emphasizes individualism might find it stimulating to meet an African American woman whose cultural heritage emphasizes collectivism (Penn, Gaines, & Phillips,

1993; Phillips, Penn, & Gaines, 1993). Part of the budding attraction between such culturally disparate persons might be due to precisely that disparity, which represents an opportunity for exploring value orientations other than one's own. Because people with a *high sensation-seeking* motive should be especially likely to value such novelty (again, including but not limited to having a novel sexual partner), we might expect them to find their participation in such relationships to be significantly above an actuarial baseline.

Valued Similarities Contributing to Compatibility and Rapport

On the other hand, perhaps it is the *similarity* between interracial partners' personal and social characteristics that, *despite their phenotypic differences*, serves as the basis for their mutual attraction. If so, interracial relationships would resemble intraracial relationships (whether romantic or platonic) in terms of factors underlying attraction (Byrne, 1971; see also Berscheid, 1985). The uncertainty that interracial partners themselves experience regarding these competing versions of the "insiders' perspective" is manifested in the following e-mail conversation:

> I think my husband and I have much more in common mentally and personality-wise than my co-worker and her spouse. So maybe people [like my co-worker and her husband] are looking for more external similarities such as race, religion, etc. While . . . people [like my husband and I] are more into inner compatibilities, so that the externals are not so important. (D. Smith, Apr. 28, 1995, personal communication, brackets ours)

> The difficulty is, what constitutes opposites? As you note . . . is it the visible externals or the interior emotional/intellectual viewpoint that is opposite, or alike? (R. Brown, Apr. 29, 1995, personal communication)

> Yep, I share lots of political/social opinions with my white [significant other]. However, we are of different race, religion, and (in some ways) cultural background. So are we similar or different? (J. Starkey, Apr. 30, 1995, personal communication)

A key point to be made here is that the association between physical and psychological attributes, no matter how absurd the physical indicator (e.g., number of bumps on one's head, body size, cranial size), has enjoyed a long, if not particularly honorable, history in psychology (White & Parham, 1990). Throughout most of the twentieth century, scores of mainstream psychologists have earnestly believed (but have never demonstrated) that the same gene(s) responsible for skin pigmentation, eye color, and hair texture somehow are responsible for intellectual capacity and personality endowment (Du Bois, 1947/1965; Fairchild, 1991; Howitt & Owusu-Bempah, 1994; van Dijk, 1993; Yee, Fairchild, Weizmann, & Wyatt, 1993). Even some scholars within the relatively new field of Black psychology have contended that racial differences in personality are due in part to unspecified "biogenetic" factors (Penn et al., 1993; Phillips et al., 1993). With regard to interracial relationships, many psychologists and other relationship researchers have been so willing to accept such assertions as a matter of faith that they have not stopped to ask whether the members of interracial relationships evaluate their own points of "similarity" and "difference" using equally crude criteria.

Research Bearing on the "Insiders' Perspective"

Unfortunately, there is relatively little available research that bears directly on the "insiders' perspective." However, a number of findings provide at least indirect support for the conclusion that interracial relationships may be less "deviant" or "unstable" than the "outsiders' perspective" might suggest. For example, divorce rates for interracial couples do not appear to be as deviant from intraracial divorce rates as one might assume (Aldridge, 1978; Clulow, 1993; Durodoye, 1994; Ho, 1990). And even if we were to accept the premise that interracial couples are particularly at risk for divorce, a primary reason may be that spouses in interracial marriages are more likely to be in their second or subsequent marriages (Aldridge, 1978; Durodoye, 1994)—a factor which itself is associated with a greater likelihood of divorce (Cherlin, 1989).

Moreover, when social scientists do make the effort to collect information from African American as well as Anglo participants, a common result is that the ingroup–outgroup bias that usually is presumed to determine the outcome of interracial encounters (Duckitt, 1994; Stephan, 1985) simply is not as pronounced (especially among African Americans) as attribution theory would lead one to believe (see Ickes, 1984; Korolewicz & Korolewicz, 1985; McClelland & Auster, 1991; Tucker & Mitchell-Kernan, 1995; but see also Todd et al., 1992). In addition, ever since Gunnar Myrdal's classic *An American Dilemma* (1944) was published, African Americans in particular have proven less preoccupied with the issue of interracial intimacy than most Anglos (whether social scientists or laypersons) have tended to expect (Allport, 1954/1979; Hernton, 1965/1988; National Research Council, 1989; Rosenblatt et al., 1995). Finally, the United States historically has recorded some of the lowest rates of Black–White intermarriage in the Western world (Pettigrew, 1988), thus indicating that the supposedly "universal" phenomenon of ingroup–outgroup bias in reality is historically and situationally based (Gaines & Reed, 1994, 1995; Penn et al., 1993; Phillips et al., 1993).

As might be expected, the study of interracial relationships is not well differentiated by subtype. For example, *male–male* or *female–female friendships* between African Americans and Anglos rarely have been examined in the personal relationship literature (for an exception, see Messner, 1992). And judging from the available social-psychological literature, the phrase *interracial male–female friendships*, when applied to pairings of African Americans and Anglos, would seem to be a contradiction in terms. Because the socioeconomic disparity between Black males and White females is generally smaller than that between White males and Black females (French, 1985; Hernton, 1965/1988), we might expect that Black male–White female friendships would be more likely to develop than would be White male–Black female friendships. However, societal taboos against any type of Black male–White female relationship often lead White parents to express unusually strong disapproval of their daughters' friendships with Black males (Essed, 1991; Hernton, 1965/1988; Rosenblatt et al., 1995; Zweigenhaft & Domhoff, 1994).

Male–female romantic relationships between African Americans and Anglos are the only cross-race romantic relationships to receive at least minimal attention in the social science literature—interracial *same-sex romantic relationships* (gay or lesbian) have essentially been ignored (see M. Huston & Schwartz, 1995). Porterfield's (1978) qualitative and quantitative research on 40 interracial married couples was crucial in challenging stereotypes regarding interracial romantic relationships as motivated primarily by dysfunctional and/or dishonorable motives. It revealed that interracial couples—like intraracial couples—usually marry because the partners are in love and hope to spend the rest of their lives together (see also Aldridge, 1978; Davidson, 1992; Hernton, 1965/1988; Kouri & Lasswell, 1993; Spickard, 1989; Staples, 1994). Complementary findings indicate that socioemotional intimacy in these relationships not only is high but involves reciprocity of affection *and* respect (thus resembling male–female romantic relationships in general; Gaines, 1996; see also Porterfield, 1978; Rosenblatt et al., 1995). The results of a study of cultural value orientations and interpersonal resource exchange among interracial (and primarily married) couples (Gaines et al., 1999) indicate that reciprocity of affection and respect is rooted in partners' shared orientations toward the welfare of romantic relationship or dyad and toward the welfare of each other as individuals (i.e., *romanticism*; see Doherty, Hatfield, Thompson, & Chao, 1994; Sprecher et al., 1994).

Theoretical Approaches Conducive to the "Insiders' Perspective"

Despite the lack of emphasis on the "insiders' perspective" in the research conducted to date, there is reason to hope that it will be better represented in future research. We suggest that a number of theoretical approaches may be particularly conducive to studying interracial relationships from the "insiders' perspective". Consider, as just three possible examples, how research on the contact hypothesis, filter theory, and social identity theory could be reframed for this purpose. All three approaches are unbiased in the sense that they view interracial relationships as nondeviant. In addition, they tend to privilege the relationship partners themselves (instead of objective or subjective observers) as the ultimate "experts" on the dynamics of interracial relationships.

The Contact Hypothesis

One approach that seems applicable to friendships as well as to romantic relationships is Allport's (1954/1979) *contact hypothesis*, which proposes that the social distance between African Americans and Anglos should decrease as a function of societal dismantling of social, political, educational, and economic barriers to integration (Gudykunst, 1992; Hernton, 1965/1988; Sigelman & Welch, 1994). To better capture the perspective of "insiders," research on the contact hypothesis might be reframed so that the members of different types of interracial relationships can report on whether and how such barriers are perceived as being obstacles to the formation and persistence of their relationships. Such research might help to explain why the rate of increase in interracial relationships lags far behind other indicators of societal change, such as desegregation in schools, neighborhoods, and businesses (see also Brewer & Miller, 1988; Katz & Taylor, 1988; Pettigrew, 1988; Taylor & Katz, 1988). It might also help to explain why the rates of Latino–Anglo and Asian American–Anglo marriages have risen dramatically since the 1960s, whereas the rate of African American–Anglo marriages (which traditionally were the primary target of state anti-miscegenation laws; Spickard, 1989) has remained static (Johnson, 1992; Sanjek, 1994; Spigner, 1994).

Filter Theory

According to filter theory (Kerckhoff & Davis, 1962), mate selection (and, by extension, friendship selection) proceeds in two stages. In the first stage, potential partners limit their field of eligibles by pairing off on the basis of those external characteristics that are meaningful to them as individuals (e.g., race might be the determining factor for some persons whereas socioeconomic status might be the determining factor for others). In the second stage, partners pair off on the basis of those internal characteristics that matter to them individually (e.g., liberalism might be the determining factor for some persons whereas religiosity might be the determining factor for others). Thus, filter theory allows for the possibility that partners will choose each other on the basis of internal as well as external characteristics other than race. However, it is unclear whether real-life partners actually choose each other in the linear sequence that filter theory implies (T. Huston & Ashmore, 1986; Kephart & Jedlicka, 1988). Research seeking the "insiders' perspective" on this question could help to clarify the extent to which the members of interracial relationships considered race as a filter in their selection of a partner, and—if they did—how soon it was considered (early, later) and what type of valence (positive, neutral, negative) and priority weight (high, moderate, low) it was assigned.

Social Identity Theory

The question of which external characteristics and which internal characteristics ultimately serve as the bases for interracial attraction is particularly relevant to Tajfel's (1979) social identity theory, which is based on the assumption that self-esteem is a manifestation of both personal and social identities (Brown, 1986; Phinney, 1995; Taylor & Moghaddam, 1994). The theory postulates that self-esteem is not simply a byproduct of *intrapersonal* attributes, but also reflects a multitude of *interpersonal* attributes (all of which are defined jointly by self and others). From this standpoint, asking "insiders" to report on how their interracial relationship affects their self-perceived identity (and vice versa) could offer important insights about the formation, maintenance, internal dynamics, and dissolution of these relationships (see also Penn et al., 1993; Phillips et al., 1993).

RESOLVING THE TENSIONS BETWEEN "INSIDER" AND "OUTSIDER" VIEWS OF INTERRACIAL RELATIONSHIPS

The likely positivity/negativity of outsiders' attributions regarding interracial pairs as a function of the pair's level of involvement and gender composition suggests the sophistication that insiders must have in order to navigate through potentially treacherous social situations relatively unscathed. We hypothesize that outsiders generally will assume that an interracial same-sex pair is platonic, and thus will react to the pair with moderately positive affect and benign attributions about the reasons for their relationship, unless the partners make it known that they are gay or lesbian, in which case outsiders' attributions will become markedly negative (Frable, Blackstone, & Scherbaum, 1990; Goffman, 1963). We further hypothesize that outsiders generally will assume that an interracial opposite-sex pair is romantically involved, and thus will react to the pair negatively, with accompanying disparaging attributions, unless the partners make it known that they are not married or dating, in which case outsiders' negative feelings and attributions will become somewhat attenuated. In addition, a couple of more subtle interaction effects are proposed. First, regarding same-sex interracial relationships, outsiders' change from positive to negative reactions when a romantic involvement is attributed is likely to be greater when the partners are gay men (e.g., Black male–White male) than when they are lesbians (e.g., Black female–White female). Second, regarding opposite-sex interracial relationships, outsiders' change from negative to more positive reactions when a platonic interest is attributed is likely to be greater when pairing is between White men and women of color (e.g., White male–Black female) than when pairing is between men of color and White women (e.g., Black male/White female). Both of these more subtle interaction effects are consistent with the notion that Black male sexuality—whether real or imagined—poses the greatest threat to outsiders' sensibilities.

In each of the six subtypes of interracial relationships that we have considered, the members are likely to have an "insider" view of themselves and their relationships that differs dramatically from the "outsider" view that is imposed (or, perhaps more accurately, superimposed) by both lay and scientific psychology. That is, "insiders" are aware of many factors (e.g., seeing each other as individuals rather than as representatives of outgroups, being more aware of complementary and noncomplementary attitudes, values, interests, and personality traits) affecting their relationships that "outsiders" frequently do not take into account. Porterfield's (1978) study of 40 Black–White married couples provides considerable support for the ability of insiders to identify those psychological dimensions along which they and their partners are most similar or dissimilar.

At the same time, however, the relationship members as "insiders" are not immune to the implications of the ways in which their relationships are viewed from the "outside". On any given day, virtually all interracial pairs—whether same-sex or mixed-sex, romantic or platonic—may be subjected to a variety of stares, disapproving murmurs, or even verbal and/or physical attacks (Hernton, 1965/1988; Simpson & Yinger, 1985). Such unrestrained reactions by outsiders serve as constant reminders to insiders that, regardless of their implicit or explicit commitment to each other (Johnson, 1991a, 1991b; Levinger, 1991; Rusbult, 1991), outsiders often take it upon themselves to challenge that commitment.

To some extent, outsiders might have a valid point regarding the potential for miscommunication and subsequent undermining of commitment in interracial relationships (see Andersen, 1993). Even though no single racial or ethnic group can claim sole ownership of any particular cultural value orientation, it nonetheless is possible that, in some interracial relationships, the partners do not embrace a given cultural value orientation to the same degree. For example, a highly individualistic Anglo might be chagrined to find that his or her Latina/o partner equates individualism with selfishness (see Mirande, 1977). Or, a highly familistic Asian American might feel disillusioned upon discovering that his or her African American partner views traditional nuclear families as relics of a bygone era (see Fine, McKenry, Donnelly, & Voydonoff, 1992; Staples & Mirande, 1980).

Ironically, however, even when partners in interracial relationships are virtually identical in their expressed cultural value orientations, they still might find themselves ostracized by outsiders who ostensibly share the cultural value orientation in question (Penn et al., 1993; Phillips et al., 1993). For instance, even though collectivism frequently is identified as part and parcel of an Afrocentric world view (Asante, 1987; Fine, Schwebel, & James-Myers, 1987; Kambon & Hopkins, 1993; White & Parham, 1990), some Afrocentrists (e.g., Kambon & Hopkins, 1993) contend that any heterosexual interracial relationship is "odious", no matter how strongly the partners share collectivistic beliefs. Similarly, some Afrocentrists (e.g., Asante, 1987) argue that any homosexual interracial relationship is "misguided", regardless of how deeply the partners are committed to collectivism as a predominant cultural value orientation. This is not to say that all (or even most) Afrocentrists are xenophobic (for an excellent counterexample, see Parham, 1993). We simply wish to point out that although it is easy to understand how outsiders can construe differences between partners' endorsement of specific cultural value orientations as "proof" that interracial relationships are prone to conflict, even the lack of such differences cannot alter the anti-"race-mixing" mindset of certain outsiders. "Damned if we do, damned if we don't" might be the conclusion of some insiders.

If either of the partners in an interracial relationship has engaged in refencing (i.e., maintaining negative outgroup stereotypes despite positive interactions with one or more members of that outgroup; Allport, 1954/1979), the insiders themselves might end up espousing the same racist views that certain outsiders (e.g., neo-Nazis, Black separatists) have endorsed all along (Porterfield, 1978). As we mentioned earlier, some insiders might believe the sexual myths concerning, say, the presumed submissiveness of Asian American women or the hypersexuality of African American men. It is not difficult to imagine the disappointment or even outrage that an Asian American woman or an African American man might feel if her or his interracial relationship partner were to reveal that part of the impetus for the relationship derived from the partner's internalized stereotypes rather than from a genuine appreciation of the individual's unique qualities.

For partners in interracial relationships, the task of resolving "insider" and "outsider" perspectives is not easy. On the one hand, the "insider" view is legitimate in its own right and should be regarded as such by laypersons and social scientists alike Olson, 1977; see also Duck, 1990, 1994a; McCall & Simmons, 1991; Surra & Ridley, 1991). On the other hand, social perceivers' reactions to interracial pairs always threaten to impinge upon their jointly constructed lives. Furthermore, even "subjective" outsiders such as family and friends—normally the network of individuals whose counsel is sought in times of need (see Johnson, Huston, Gaines, & Levinger, 1992)—often are just as skeptical as "objective" outsiders (e.g., passersby, academicians). The resulting dilemma faced by partners in interracial relationships is essentially the social equivalent of the "double consciousness" or "two souls" of African Americans that W.E.B. Du Bois (1903/1969; see also Early, 1993; Gaines & Reed, 1994, 1995; Jones, 1988; Walters, 1993) described so eloquently as an individual-level phenomenon (Rosenblatt et al., 1995).

How do partners in interracial relationships deal with this double consciousness or discrepancy between the "insider" and "outsider" perspectives, feeling that they are—at the same time—not only members of a viable, rewarding relationship but also people who are stigmatized and even scorned by outsiders for their membership in that relationship? This task might be easiest for the partners in male–male and female–female friendships, but only in those cases in which the partners are not presumed by most outsiders to be sexually attracted to each other (i.e., when they pose the least threat to outsiders' sensibilities). Thus, partners in same-sex interracial friendships might be in the best position to react to outsiders' attempts at ingroup–outgroup polarization (e.g., taunting the partners as "traitors" to their respective races) by shrugging off such unsolicited commentary and rededicating themselves to their friendship.

The task of resolving the insider–outsider discrepancy is considerably more difficult for partners in male–female interracial friendships and romantic relationships. To many (if not most) outside observers, both types of male–female relationship will be presumed—through invocation of the augmentation principle—to be sexual rather than platonic in nature (see Rubin, 1985). Given what many regard as a deep-rooted, biologically based taboo against miscegenation, the antipathy of outsiders toward partners in interracial mixed-sex relationships may be intense, immediate, and unthinking. Thus, whereas epithets such as "nigger" and "nigger-lover" occasionally may be hurled at partners in same-sex interracial friendships, such slurs are likely to be experienced more frequently and virulently by partners in male–female interracial relationships (especially by women in those relationships; Porterfield, 1978). Unlike same-sex interracial friendships, male–female interracial relationships often trigger outrage in outsiders who feel that potential mates have been stolen from their grasp by disliked outgroup members (rather than simply other ingroup competitors; Allport, 1954/1979).

In the face of such daily challenges to their right to be together, partners in male–female interracial relationships must do more than simply proclaim anew their commitment to each other. Instead, in public settings they might deem it necessary to try to reduce outsiders' anxieties by placing greater physical and psychological distance between each other than normally would be expected of a heterosexual romantic couple. This strategy might be relatively effective for platonic male–female interracial pairs (who, after all, are simply letting outside observers know they are "just friends"). However, for romantic male–female interracial pairs, such a strategy may prove countereffective in that the partners are, in effect, forced to deny publicly the love that they share privately. Alternatively, then, partners in romantic male–female interracial relationships might opt to return the stares that they receive and thus place outsiders (rather than allow themselves to be placed) on the defensive—a risky tactic that could backfire and result in an even more hostile outsider response (Hernton, 1965/1988).

Perhaps the most vexing dilemma of resolving the insider–outsider dilemma involves partners in male–male and female–female romantic relationships. These individuals are vulnerable to being doubly stigmatized, in that both the interracial and the sexual aspects of their relationship are repugnant to most outsiders. Because theirs is a visible stigma (Frable et al., 1990), members of racial minorities typically cannot avoid being discredited by majority (i.e., White) observers on the basis of their phenotype (Goffman, 1963). Thus, members of racial minorities (as well as their Anglo relationship partners) cannot escape being tagged and, perhaps, targeted by hostile observers for the interracial aspect of their relationship. However, gay and lesbian partners in interracial relationships have to decide whether they also want to be vulnerable to the hostility that might be evoked by the sexual aspect of their relationship as well. Because their sexual preference, unlike their race, is not betrayed by their skin color or hair texture but potentially can be betrayed by their overt behavior, partners in gay or lesbian relationships might try to mask or conceal signs of their sexual orientation when in public. Male partners in gay interracial relationships might be particularly sensitive to the dangers of "coming out" in public settings because society places enormous importance upon male heterosexuality as normative (M. Huston & Schwartz, 1995).

The path of least resistance for same-sex romantic interracial partners might be to display a socially acceptable degree of physical and psychological distance between each other (like male–female romantic and platonic interracial partners). Another response might be to exercise extreme caution in selecting the neighborhoods in which they live and the social settings in which they express their sexuality (a strategy that also is adopted by many interracial married couples; see Porterfield, 1978). This latter approach might be especially useful in avoiding sexual epithets like "fag" or "dyke" along with racial epithets like "nigger" and "nigger-lover".

Above all else, though, all interracial pairs will find it difficult to minimize the ubiquity of the "outsiders' perspective" and the many ways that it impinges on their interpersonal lives. Therefore, partners in interracial relationships might, in relatively supportive social contexts, find it useful to discuss racism, sexism, and homophobia openly; and condition themselves to anticipate outsiders' physical and psychological attacks, as well as to practice those responses that were most successful at lessening danger in the past and/or promise to be most successful in the future. Such proactive strategies illustrate perhaps the most important point in this chapter, namely, that just as individuals of color must acknowledge the potential for insider–outsider conflict and prepare themselves mentally and physically to minimize that conflict, so too must partners in interracial relationships (whether Anglos or persons of color) anticipate insider–outsider conflict and respond accordingly. Unfortunately, society has not changed sufficiently to avoid stigmatizing or persecuting interracial pairs, making it necessary for those pairs to shield themselves from recurring assaults upon their minds and bodies.

In a qualitative study of 21 married/cohabiting couples, Rosenblatt et al. (1995) concluded that many interracial couples continually remind themselves that they are "right" and racist elements in society are "wrong". African American partners in particular are likely to perceive current overt or covert racist behaviors toward them as members of interracial couples as entirely consistent with past as well as present racist behaviors toward them as individuals (see also Goffman, 1963). Although European American partners are not as likely to have experienced past racism as individuals, they nonetheless are especially likely to have rejected racist ideology prior to entering interracial unions. Moreover, for those unions that produce offspring, parents typically make considerable efforts to buffer their children against the behaviors of individual racists as well as the negative messages from media and other societal institutions. Rather than allow themselves or their children to internalize racist messages, partners in interracial relationships frequently learn to anticipate and respond to verbal and physical assaults so as to defuse conflicts and thus place the onus of change upon hostile outsiders (if not society as a whole).

FINAL THOUGHTS

Social myths encourage us to believe that American culture is either a true "melting pot" in which racial and cultural differences are completely assimilated or a "colorful mosaic" in which these differences are both recognized and valued. Members of interracial relationships know better. They know that they do not fit within the mainstream of society and, hence, that they may experience profound loneliness even when in each other's company. In order to let other interracial pairs know that they are not alone, some partners in interracial relationships share their trials and tribulations with others via social support groups, magazines devoted specifically to interracial couples and their progeny, and electronic mail newsgroups (Gaines et al., 1999). Further research on interracial relationships could benefit greatly from examining these and other broadly cast social networks that often help to sustain interracial pairs even when more tightly knit social networks of family and friends fail to do so.

But we cannot afford to be naive. The lasting strength of societal taboos in keeping many persons of African descent from establishing relationships with persons of European descent should not be underestimated—whatever the biological, psychological, and sociological origins of these taboos might be. What is most amazing, perhaps, is the fact that any of us manage to cross the color line and maintain such relationships (not to mention our sanity) in the process.

Chapter 5

Interdependence in Personal Relationships*

Caryl E. Rusbult

University of North Carolina, Chapel Hill, NC, USA

and

Ximena B. Arriaga

Purdue University, West Lafayette, IN, USA

If we wish to understand behavior in close relationships, should we examine the relationship *per se* or should we examine the individuals who comprise the relationship? Should we consider how relationships differ from one another, or should we consider how individuals differ from one another? Most social psychological theories explain behavior in relationships by reference to *intra*-personal processes—by reference to individual-level cognitive processes (Baldwin, 1992), personal dispositions (Hazan & Shaver, 1994a), motivational tendencies (Aron & Aron, 1997), or genetic make-up (Kenrick & Trost, 1997). In contrast, interdependence theory explains behavior in relationships

* Preparation of this chapter was supported in part by a grant to the first author from the National Science Foundation (No. BNS-9023817). Correspondence should be addressed to Caryl E. Rusbult, Department of Psychology, University of North Carolina, Chapel Hill, North Carolina 27599–3270.

The Social Psychology of Personal Relationships.
Edited by William Ickes and Steve Duck. © 2000 John Wiley & Sons Ltd.

by reference to *inter*personal processes, suggesting that experience in a relationship is inseparable from the fabric of interdependence characterizing the relationship (Kelley & Thibaut, 1978; Thibaut & Kelley, 1959). Thus, interdependence theory provides a uniquely interpersonal analysis of close relationships.

Interdependence describes the strength and quality of the effects interacting individuals exert on one another's preferences, motives, and behavior. Interdependence is an elemental feature of experience in at least three respects. First, interdependence shapes the self—relatively stable dispositions, motives, and behavioral tendencies develop as a consequence of adaptation to frequently encountered interdependence situations. Second, interdependence shapes mental events—cognition, perception, and affect reflect our attempts to understand the meaning of interdependence situations, toward identifying appropriate action in such situations. Third, interdependence shapes interaction—interdependence structure describes the opportunities and constraints that characterize everyday interaction, defining the potential in a given interaction for phenomena such as conflict, power, and dependence.

This chapter outlines the basic concepts of interdependence theory, citing illustrative empirical evidence where appropriate. First, we consider the manner in which individuals experience interactions and relationships, distinguishing between the concepts of satisfaction and dependence. Second, we describe the structure of outcome interdependence, suggesting that relationships differ with regard to four key properties—level of dependence, mutuality of dependence, basis of dependence, and correspondence of outcomes. Third, we discuss transformation of motivation, or the tendency to react to interdependence situations not only on the basis of their structural properties *but also* on the basis of broader considerations—long-term goals, personal values, and concern for the well-being of interaction partners. Fourth, we introduce the concept of habitual transformation tendencies, discussing the role of dispositions, motives, and norms in shaping reactions to specific patterns of interdependence. Finally, we describe the role of meaning analysis in guiding reactions to specific interdependence situations.

The theoretical principles reviewed in this chapter are based on the work of Harold Kelley and John Thibaut. These authors initially introduced their model for analyzing interdependence structure in *The Social Psychology of Groups* (Thibaut & Kelley, 1959), developing an analysis framework that was later expanded to deal with informational interdependence (Kelley & Thibaut, 1969). They enlarged their early theoretical framework in *Interpersonal Relations: A Theory of Interdependence*, presenting a formal analysis of interdependence structure and introducing the concept of transformation of motivation (Kelley & Thibaut, 1978). More recent work by Kelley provided detailed analyses of specific components of the theory, including stable transformation tendencies (Kelley, 1983b), cognition and meaning analysis (Kelley, 1984a, 1997), and temporal features of interdependence (Kelley, 1984c).

EXPERIENCING INTERACTIONS AND RELATIONSHIPS

Fundamentals of Interaction

Interdependence theory describes *interaction* as the central feature of all interpersonal relationships (Thibaut & Kelley, 1959). Interacting individuals engage in independent or shared activities, they speak to one another, and they create products for one another—in short, they influence one another's preferences and options. Interaction yields outcomes for interacting individuals. Outcomes can be described in terms of overall "goodness", or can be conceptualized in terms of rewards and costs. The term *reward* refers to the positive consequences of interaction (e.g., contentment, joy, success) whereas the term *cost* refers to the negative consequences of interaction (e.g., pain, frustration, anger).

Humans are assumed to be goal-oriented, implicitly seeking to obtain good outcomes and avoid bad outcomes. Does this mean that we myopically pursue self-interest? No. Although direct self-interest is assumed to be the baseline, "default option" in human motivation, preferences are only partially shaped by immediate outcomes. Preferences are also shaped by the broader considerations that typically are at stake in interaction—considerations such as the well-being of an interaction partner or the impact of current choices on long-term goals. Departures from self-interest are argued to be highly contingent, resting on the specifics of the particular situation encountered with a given partner.

Are preferences shaped by *nature* or *nurture*? Some interpersonal preferences may rest largely on biological make-up whereas others may be learned; most preferences presumably reflect a combination of influences. Interdependence theory does not seek to identify a single preference-defining "engine" that drives social behavior (e.g., genetic fitness, attachment concerns; Bowlby, 1969/1982; Wilson, 1975). Instead, the theory assumes that humans possess a blend of inborn and acquired preferences, and seeks to understand the implications of those preferences for interaction.

Matrix Representation of Interaction Outcomes

Interdependence theory employs the *outcome matrix* to analyze interaction (Kelley & Thibaut, 1978). The matrix is a theoretical tool, not a literal portrayal of lay cognition. (Humans do not experience interaction as an analysis of 2×2 matrices.) Any interpersonal situation can be represented in matrix form, and a single, abstract pattern may represent a rather large class of concrete situations with dissimilar superficial features. The importance of the matrix lies not in the concrete behaviors and outcomes that are depicted, but in the pattern of outcomes the matrix representation reveals. The columns in a matrix represent

Person A's behavioral options and the rows represent Person B's options. Each cell in the matrix is associated with two outcome values, representing the joint occurrence of A's behavior and B's behavior; the two values in each cell represent the impact of each joint event on each individual.

For example, Figure 5.1 depicts a possible interaction for Andy and Betty. Neither Andy nor Betty has done any housecleaning for two weeks. Neither partner likes housecleaning, but neither finds their current sordid circumstances to be congenial. If both Andy and Betty clean the house, both enjoy the moderate pleasure of an improved environment (4 and 4). Of course, both individuals would prefer that the partner clean the house (8), but each is irritated by the prospect of cleaning the house while the partner takes a free ride (–4). The cooperative choice would be to commence cleaning. At the same time, both Andy and Betty dislike housecleaning, so each individual feels tempted to "defect" and let the partner do the cleaning. If both Andy and Betty defect and pursue their immediate self-interest by failing to clean the house, both suffer poor outcomes (0 and 0).

Of course, interaction situations frequently are more intricate than symmetrical 2 × 2 matrices: the partners may possess more than two behavioral options, each individual may possess unique options not shared by the partner, and the partners may hold differing preferences for specific joint events. Interaction may involve more than two individuals, requiring the addition of a dimension to the matrix for each interacting partner. Also, the behavioral repertoires of the individuals may change over time, their preferences may

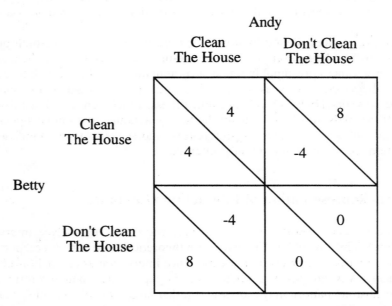

Figure 5.1 The outcome matrix: matrix representation of outcomes resulting from joint decision to clean the house or not clean the house (A Prisoner's Dilemma pattern of interdependence)

change, and behaviors enacted on earlier occasions may modify either the range of options or the preferences attached to the options on future occasions. In essence, the matrix is a snapshot of an interdependence situation as it exists at one time. Although this simple tool ignores the dynamic continuity of actions and reactions in ongoing relationships, the static quality of the matrix allows for a rich analysis of the abstract qualities representing classes of interdependence pattern.

Relationship Standards

Two standards are relevant to understanding how individuals experience interaction outcomes (Thibaut & Kelley, 1959). *Comparison level* (CL) refers to the quality of outcomes an individual has come to expect. CL is influenced by previous experiences in relationships and by social comparison (Festinger, 1954). *Comparison level for alternatives* (CL-alt) refers to the lowest level of outcomes an individual finds acceptable in light of outcomes that could be enjoyed elsewhere. CL-alt is influenced not only by the attractiveness of specific alternative relationships, but also by the desirability of the field of eligibles and the option of noninvolvement. CL affects satisfaction, whereas CL-alt affects dependence.

Satisfaction level refers to the degree to which a relationship is experienced as gratifying. Individuals experience greater satisfaction when the outcomes experienced in a given interaction exceed CL; outcomes falling short of CL are dissatisfying (Thibaut & Kelley, 1959). Diverse literatures support the assertion that satisfaction is influenced not only by the objective quality of outcomes but also by internal, subjective standards: Individuals are happier with their close partners to the extent that the partner matches or exceeds the individual's internal standard (Sabatelli, 1984; Sternberg & Barnes, 1985; Wetzel & Insko, 1982). Also, research regarding interaction in nonromantic involvements reveals that when objective conditions compare unfavorably to individuals' internal standards, they experience dissatisfaction, dejection, and discontent (Crosby, 1976; Davies, 1962; Higgins, 1989).

Dependence level refers to the degree to which an individual relies on a partner for the fulfillment of important needs (i.e., the individual needs a relationship). To the extent that obtained outcomes exceed CL-alt the individual is increasingly dependent and increasingly likely to persist in a relationship; when outcomes fall below CL-alt the individual is more independent and more inclined to abandon a partner for the best available alternative (Thibaut & Kelley, 1959). Indeed, existing research reveals that dependence on a relationship is lower—and the probabililty of voluntary break-up is greater— among individuals who experience poor outcomes in the current relationship and regard their alternatives as attractive (Drigotas & Rusbult, 1992; Felmlee, Sprecher, & Bassin, 1990; Rusbult, 1983; Simpson, 1987).

Satisfaction with a relationship ("am I happy?") and dependence on a relationship ("shall I stay?") to some degree are independent (Thibaut & Kelley,

1959). Figure 5.2 displays three relationships with equivalent outcomes. In Relationship A outcomes are much higher than CL and somewhat higher than CL-alt. Relationship A will produce very high satisfaction yet involves only moderate dependence. In Relationship B outcomes are somewhat higher than CL and much higher than CL-alt. Relationship B will produce moderate satisfaction and involves very high dependence. In Relationship C outcomes are lower than CL yet much higher than CL-alt. This configuration of outcomes and standards is termed a *nonvoluntary relationship*—the relationship will produce *dis*satisfaction but involves high dependence.

Nonvoluntary involvement is tragically illustrated by the plight of the abused woman (Gelles, 1979). Although some researchers have explained the decision to remain with a battering partner by reference to the abused individual's personal dispositions (e.g., learned helplessness), the decision to remain may be governed at least in part by dependence. Indeed, the empirical literature reveals that although an abused woman's outcomes may be poor, her alternatives—especially her economic alternatives—may be even worse. In comparison to women who exit abusive relationships, women who remain with their abusive partners tend to have less job training, less work experience, and fewer employment opportunities (Rusbult & Martz, 1995; Strube, 1988). Thus, abused individuals do not necessarily remain with their partners

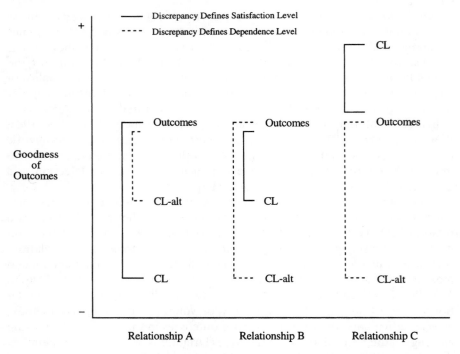

Figure 5.2 Satisfaction level and dependence level as a function of goodness of outcomes, comparison level (CL), and comparison level for alternatives (CL-alt): three illustrative patterns

because they are governed by abnormal personal dispositions—sometimes abused individuals remain with their partners because they are dependent on their relationships and have nowhere else to go.

Implications for Long-term Interdependence

Although we have described CL and CL-alt as fixed standards, over the course of an ongoing relationship these standards may change. Given that CL-alt influences the decision to persist in a relationship, good alternatives threaten the stability of long-term involvements. Interestingly, over the course of long-term involvement, individuals describe their alternatives as increasingly poor (Rusbult, 1983). This decline in the perceived attractiveness of alternatives might occur because (a) alternatives take themselves out of the running, or because (b) involved individuals act in such a manner as to drive away tempting alternatives (e.g., wearing a wedding ring; Kelley, 1983a). In addition to virtual declines in the availability of alternatives, involved individuals may engage in cognitive maneuvers that serve to lower CL-alt, thereby eliminating threats to the stability of their relationships. Indeed, the existing literature reveals that, in comparison to less involved partners, highly involved partners (a) actively avoid attending to tempting alternatives, and (b) cognitively derogate tempting alternatives, presumably as a means of protecting the ongoing relationship from threat (Johnson & Rusbult, 1989; Miller, 1997a; Simpson, Gangestad, & Lerma, 1990).

CL and satisfaction level, too, may change over time. Given that CL is shaped partly by outcomes experienced in the current relationship, "the more satisfactory [a] relationship has been found to be, the higher will be the comparison level" (Thibaut & Kelley, 1959, p. 95). That is, CL may rise to match experienced outcomes—we may come to expect that which we routinely experience. This rise in CL should yield a corresponding decline in satisfaction level. In ongoing relationships additional forces toward dissatisfaction derive from (a) satiation and declining marginal utility (Brickman, Dunkel-Schetter, & Abbey, 1987; Frijda, 1988; Solomon, 1980), and (b) the greater salience and potency of negative outcomes in relation to positive outcomes (Kahneman & Tversky, 1979; Taylor, 1991). Indeed, the empirical literature reveals that over time, the subjective costs of involvement tend to increase and satisfaction level tends to decline (Campbell, Converse, & Rodgers, 1976; Huston, McHale, & Crouter, 1986; Rusbult, 1983). Thus, over the course of long-term involvement partners may come to take their relationships for granted and experience declining satisfaction.

How do partners resist pressures toward rising expectations and declining satisfaction? The extant literature identifies several countervailing forces toward "positive illusion" (Taylor & Brown, 1988)—forces that serve to lower CL, enhance the perceived quality of obtained outcomes, or both. Partners in ongoing relationships frequently: (a) engage in downward social comparison, thereby lowering CL; (b) cognitively transform their partners' faults into virtues; and (c) exaggerate the positive qualities of their partners and relationships (Buunk & Van Yperen, 1991; Murray & Holmes, 1993; Murray, Holmes, & Griffin, 1996a, 1996b; Van Lange & Rusbult, 1995). Thus, involved individuals engage in a variety of cognitive maneuvers that serve to lower CL and exaggerate the attractiveness of their relationships, thereby counteracting tendencies toward rising expectations and declining satisfaction.

STRUCTURE OF OUTCOME INTERDEPENDENCE

The utility of the matrix representation of interdependence resides in the fact that this analytic tool provides a basis for exploring the *structure of outcome interdependence*. What is the meaning of the numeric values displayed in matrices? "The numbers entered in the outcome matrix [are] scaled from CL-alt as the zero point. The entries in the matrix indicate the degree to which each person is dependent on the dyad, and the pattern of entries [represents] their pattern of interdependence" (Kelley & Thibaut, 1978, p. 10). Thus, just as the Lewinian life space served as a tool for understanding individual experience (Lewin, 1936), the matrix is a tool for understanding interpersonal experience. The matrix provides a means of conceptualizing situations so as to identify their structural features.

All patterns of interdependence stem from three sources of control over outcomes (Cook, 1993): *Reflexive control* (RC, or "actor control") reflects the degree to which the individual controls the quality of his or her outcomes (i.e., a main effect of Person A's actions on A's outcomes), *fate control* (FC, or "partner control") reflects the degree to which the individual's outcomes are influenced by the actions of the partner (i.e., a main effect of B's actions on A's outcomes), and *behavior control* (BC, or "dyadic control") reflects the degree to which the individual's outcomes are jointly influenced by his or her own actions in concert with the partner's actions (i.e., an interaction of A's and B's actions).

Kelley and Thibaut (1978) present a logical analysis of the domain of 2×2 matrices—an analysis in which all possible patterns of interdependence are examined, based on the relative contributions to each individual's outcomes of reflexive control, fate control, and behavior control. This analysis yields a comprehensive typology of the domain of interdependence patterns, demonstrating that the possible patterns differ with respect to four properties—degree of dependence, mutuality of dependence, basis of dependence, and correspondence of outcomes. Indeed, these properties align well with the properties that have been identified using inductive empirical techniques (Wish, Deutsch, & Kaplan, 1976).

Degree of Dependence

Degree of dependence describes the extent to which each individual's outcomes are influenced by the partner's actions and by the two partners' joint actions. To the degree that Betty has little control over her outcomes and Andy has high control over her outcomes, Betty is more *dependent* (i.e., her RC is low and Andy has high FC and BC over her outcomes); to the degree that Betty has high control over her outcomes and Andy has little control over her outcomes, Betty is more *independent* (i.e., her RC is high and Andy has little FC or BC over her outcomes). This definition expands on a definition based on CL-alt: individuals are dependent when they cannot unilaterally guarantee themselves good outcomes—either in an alternative relationship or through independent action—and accordingly rely on the partner for the fulfillment of important needs. For example, if Betty is Andy's main source of companionship—and if Betty unilaterally can accord or deny Andy companionship—Andy is dependent on Betty.

Is level of dependence a psychologically meaningful feature of interdependence? As suggested earlier, dependence exerts profound effects on a variety of interpersonal phenomena. For example, to the extent that an individual is highly dependent on a close partner, the individual is tied to the relationship and becomes increasingly unlikely to end it (Felmlee et al., 1990; Rusbult, 1983; Simpson, 1987). Individuals who are dependent tend to develop strong feelings of commitment, including intentions to persist, long-term orientation, and psychological attachment (Rusbult, 1983; Rusbult & Buunk, 1993). Dependence and commitment promote a variety of behaviors that serve to sustain ongoing relationships, including (a) derogation of tempting alternatives (Johnson & Rusbult, 1989; Simpson et al., 1990), (b) accommodating rather than retaliating when a partner behaves poorly (Rusbult, Verette, Whitney, Slovik, & Lipkus, 1991), (c) willingness to sacrifice one's immediate self-interest for the good of a relationship (Van Lange et al., 1997), and (d) positive illusion, or the inclination to perceive one's partner and relationship as better than (and not as bad as) other relationships (Murray & Holmes, 1993; Van Lange & Rusbult, 1995).

Dependence also has its down side: dependent individuals experience greater distress when the continuation of a relationship is threatened. For example, they experience jealousy and feel threatened by the partner's good alternatives (Buunk, 1991; Strachan & Dutton, 1992; White & Mullen, 1989). Also, research concerning entrapment reveals that when dependence is strengthened through increases in the costs of ending an involvement—for example, through committing resources to a previously chosen course of action—persistence at a course of action is more likely, even when that course of action is costly or ineffective (Becker, 1960; Blau, 1964; Brockner & Rubin, 1985; Teger, 1980).

It is instructive to note that individual dependence is the converse of partner power (Huston, 1983). Dependence is greater to the degree that a partner possesses the power to bring about a wide range of outcomes for the individual. A partner's power is limited by (a) the individual's ability to obtain good outcomes elsewhere (i.e., the individual's CL-alt defines a lower limit on the partner's usable power), and (b) the degree to which utilizing power harms the partner (i.e., the partner is unlikely to use available power if doing so yields poor outcomes for the self; Molm, 1985). It is notable that whereas low-power individuals attend to relevant information in a careful and differentiated manner, high-power individuals engage in "quick and dirty" processing of information—that is, highly dependent individuals appear to pay particular attention to interaction-relevant information (Fiske, 1993; Johnson & Ewens, 1971).

Mutuality of Dependence

Mutuality of dependence describes the degree to which partners are mutually rather than unilaterally dependent on one another for attaining desirable outcomes. When just one individual is dependent a relationship involves *unilateral dependence*; when both individuals are dependent a relationship involves *mutual dependence*. It is instructive to discuss this property not only in terms of symmetric versus asymmetric dependence, but also in terms of symmetric versus asymmetric power: Andy's power is relatively greater than Betty's to the degree that (a) Andy possesses the power to provide (or not provide) Betty with outcomes of higher quality than Betty can provide for Andy, (b) Andy has the power to provide (or not provide) Betty with outcomes of poorer quality than Betty can provide for Andy, and (c) Andy has more attractive alternatives than Betty (i.e., Andy has a higher CL-alt).

Is mutuality of dependence a psychologically meaningful feature of interdependence? Mutuality yields benefits that parallel those accruing from balance of power. Given that mutually dependent partners possess equal control over one another's outcomes, there is reduced potential for exploitation. Research concerning the "principle of least interest" demonstrates that the partner receiving higher outcomes in a relationship tends to exhibit enhanced dependence and reduced ability to control events in the relationship (Scanzoni & Scanzoni, 1981; Sprecher, 1985; Waller, 1938). Also, because mutually dependent partners are equally motivated to behave in such a manner as to sustain their involvement, there is less potential for negative emotions that may undermine relationships, including insecurity or guilt. Indeed, the existing literature reveals that mutuality of dependence is associated with enhanced couple functioning (Drigotas, Rusbult, & Verette, in press; Stafford & Canary, 1991).

Patterns of mutuality may originate in broad features of the environment, such as the field of eligibles. Imbalanced sex ratios—circumstances where the ratio of men to women in the "mating market" deviates from 1.0—appear to "dramatically influence the gender roles of men and women, shape the forms taken by relationships between men and women, and in turn produce changes in family structures and stimulate new kinds of association along gender lines" (Secord, 1983, p. 525). A high ratio of men to women is associated with valuing young women, norms of commitment, traditional division of labor, and sexual morality; a low ratio of men to women is associated with sexual libertarianism, brief liaisons, and tendencies for women to establish themselves as independent persons (Guttentag & Secord, 1983).

It is easy to imagine that differential dependence typically would yield abuse, in that low-power individuals can do little but appease high-power individuals, who possess the wherewithal to use (or abuse) their power as they wish. Indeed, when partners' preferences are incompatible, nonmutuality produces suspicion and insecurity, abuse of power, and avoidance of interaction (Tjosvold, 1981). However, given moderate to high compatibility of preferences, nonmutual dependence activates norms of social responsibility; in such circumstances, high-power persons are likely to provide assistance to low-power persons (Berkowitz & Daniels, 1963). Also, in situations of nonmutual dependence low power partners may develop tactics for encouraging formal agreements through which exploitation may be curtailed or prevented (Thibaut & Faucheux, 1965; Thibaut & Gruder, 1969).

Basis of Dependence

Basis of dependence describes the degree to which dependence rests on individual control versus joint control—that is, whether dependence derives from the partner's actions (FC) or from the partners' joint actions (BC). Generally, situations of high fate control are governed by exchange; situations of high behavior control are governed by coordination. Relationships with high fate control are experienced as other-controlled ("my well-being is in my partner's hands"); relationships with high behavior control are experienced as jointly controlled ("together, my partner and I control what will transpire").

Achieving good outcomes in situations involving high fate control requires extended time perspective, in combination with norms of reciprocity ("I'll scratch your back this time if you'll scratch mine next time"; Axelrod, 1984). Given that the possibility of freeloading is a chronic problem in such situations, high fate control frequently engenders threats, promises, or other forms of agreement that enhance the predictability of interaction (Orbell, Van de Kragt, & Dawes, 1988). In contrast, situations involving high behavior control are less complex, in that they do not necessarily require long-term strategies—the coordination issues characteristic of behavior control frequently can be resolved in the context of a single interaction.

Correspondence of Outcomes

Correspondence of outcomes describes the extent to which partners similarly evaluate the joint behavioral events that are available in their relationship—the degree to which events are mutually beneficial or mutually aversive. Note that correspondence does *not* imply similarity in the desirability of discrete behaviors. Partners may have correspondent preferences involving enactment of the same behavior (e.g., both Andy and Betty enjoy playing golf together), but they might also have correspondent preferences involving the enactment of different behaviors (e.g., a mutually congenial division of labor wherein

Andy prepares meals and Betty cleans the house). Degree of correspondence defines a continuum ranging from perfectly correspondent outcomes (i.e., situations of pure coordination) through moderately correspondent outcomes (i.e., mixed-motive situations), to perfectly noncorrespondent outcomes (i.e., zero-sum situations).

Why does correspondence influence the course of interaction? First, given that this property identifies the possibilities for congenial versus conflictual interaction, degree of correspondence exerts reliable effects on cognitive and perceptual processes, determining whether interacting individuals feel that they are working with one another or against one another, whether their relationship is experienced as one of congeniality or war. Relationships characterized by noncorrespondence are stormy, with partners developing suspicious, distrustful, or even hostile attitudes toward one another (Blumstein & Schwartz, 1983; Gottman, 1979; Holmes & Murray, 1996; Surra & Longstreth, 1990).

Second, correspondence is relevant to ease of decision making, in that decision difficulty is greatest under conditions of intermediate correspondence. Decisions are easy in correspondent situations, in that the obviously rational choice is to behave in such a manner as to maximize both one's own and a partner's outcomes ("what's good for me is good for you"). Decisions are easy in noncorrespondent situations, in that the rational choice is to pursue self-interest (e.g., partners seldom worry about whether to compete in a tennis game). Moderately correspondent situations are maximally ambiguous with respect to the appropriateness of cooperation versus competition (Blumstein & Schwartz, 1983).

Third, correspondence sets the stage for the elicitation of key motives, constraining the ability to act on the basis of some motives and providing opportunities for expressing others (Peterson, 1983). Given that it is not possible for both partners to achieve good outcomes in perfectly noncorrespondent situations, as correspondence decreases, competitive motives are activated; as correspondence increases, cooperative motives are activated (Kelley & Grzelak, 1972). Situations of moderate correspondence are highly ambiguous, and therefore activate a wider range of motives, including both (a) fear, derived from the possibililty that a partner may not cooperate, and (b) greed, derived from the temptation to compete in response to a partner's cooperation (Insko, Schopler, Hoyle, Dardis, & Graetz, 1990; Rapoport, 1966).

Transition Lists and Interdependence

Kelley (1984c) expanded the analysis of interdependence through the use of *transition lists*—a "set of lists, each of which specifies each person's options . . . and the consequences for each person of each combination of their respective selections among their options" (p. 960). The transition list overcomes several limitations inherent in the static outcome matrix and addresses the temporal features of interdependence by specifying how current actions enlarge or constrain subsequent outcomes or options. This means of representing interdependence structure allows us to conceptualize interaction in terms of both (a) patterns of outcome interdependence and (b) changes over time in patterns. In addition to characterizing *outcome control*, the transition list also characterizes *transition control*, or control over movement from one situation to another.

Table 5.1 displays an interdependence situation involving Andy and Betty (Kelley, 1984c). List L represents the partners' initial options (A_1 vs A_2 for Andy, B_1 vs B_2 for Betty), along with the outcomes resulting from their joint actions. In List L each individual's outcomes are controlled by the individual's own actions (RC; +5 vs 0 for Andy, +10 vs +5 for Betty). In addition to representing the information traditionally displayed in a matrix, List L represents the future situations that will come to pass as a consequence of each set of joint actions. In List L transition control rests in Betty's hands—B_2 leaves the two in the safe List L, whereas B_1 moves the partners to the perilous List M. If Betty pursues her self-interest in List L by enacting B_1, yielding outcomes for Betty of +10 (rather than +5 for B_2), the partners move to a situation in which all of Betty's outcomes are poor (–20 or 0). Also, in List M outcome control and transition control shift to Andy's hands. Rescuing Betty from List M requires a heroic act: by enacting A_3 and suffering poor outcomes (–5) Andy (a) ensures that Betty does not suffer catastrophic outcomes (0 rather than –20) and (b) restores both partners to the safe List L. Despite its simplicity, this example conveys the sophistication of the transition list representation, illustrating (a) how immediate choices can influence options and outcomes that unfold in the future, and (b) how patterns of outcome control and transition control can shift over the course of extended interaction.

Table 5.1 The transition list: Andy can rescue Betty from the consequences of an unwise action

| | | | Consequences | | |
| | | | Outcomes | | Transition |
List	Option sets	Option pairs	Andy	Betty	(Next list)
L	(A_1/A_2)	A_1 and B_1	+5	+10	M
	(B_1/B_2)	A_1 and B_2	+5	+5	L
		A_2 and B_1	0	+10	M
		A_2 and B_2	0	+5	L
M	($A_1/A_2/A_3$)	A_1 and B_3	+5	–20	M
	(B_3/B_4)	A_1 and B_4	+5	–20	M
		A_2 and B_3	0	–20	M
		A_2 and B_4	0	–20	M
		A_3 and B_3	–5	0	L
		A_3 and B_4	–5	0	L

Parallel to the bases of outcome control, transition control differs in (a) reflexive control, or actor control over transitions across situations, (b) fate control, or partner control over transitions, and (c) behavior control, or dyadic control. In extended involvements, partners' behavioral choices may be based not only on the options and outcomes that presently are available, but also on the future situations that will be made available (or eliminated) as a consequence of present choices. Indeed, preferences and choices at one point in time may be influenced by the desire to enhance future transition control, and conflict between partners may center as much on transition control as on outcome control.

Implications for Long-term Interdependence

Given that long-term partners not only affect the immediate outcomes experienced by each person, but also affect the options and outcomes that will be available in future interactions, long-term partners can exert considerable influence over one another's lives. Through an extended process of behavioral confirmation, long-term partners can even shape one another's dispositions (Snyder, 1984; Snyder, Tanke, & Berscheid, 1977): A partner may (a) hold expectations about the individual, (b) behave in an expectation-consistent manner, and thereby (c) elicit expectation-consistent behavior from the individual, such that over the long run the partner (d) partially shapes the individual's personal dispositions. Depending on the nature of the partner's expectations, such influence can be constructive or destructive.

Partner affirmation refers to circumstances in which the partner's beliefs about and behavior toward the individual are congruent with the individual's ideal self. Through deliberate choice or as an automatic consequence of Andy's expectations about Betty, Andy may constrain interaction in such a manner as to elicit the expression of Betty's best self. Over time, this process should lead Betty to become closer to the person she ideally would like to be. Indeed, the existing literature suggests that partner affirmation promotes individual movement toward the ideal self, enhances couple well-being, and maximizes the odds of persistence in relationships (Drigotas, Rusbult, Wieselquist, & Whitton, in press).

TRANSFORMATION OF MOTIVATION

Given Situation versus Effective Situation

Why do different individuals react in different ways to the same pattern of interdependence? If behavior were wholly determined by the pursuit of self-interest, all individuals should react identically to the same situation (barring perceptual bias, random error, and the like). The interdependence theory distinction between the given situation and the effective situation provides a partial answer to this question. The *given situation* reflects the structure of interdependence based upon immediate, self-interested preferences. Given outcomes are "gut-level" preferences: "The outcome in each cell of the matrix . . . is *given* for the relationship by virtue of the specifications of the social and physical environment and the relevant properties of the two persons" (Kelley & Thibaut, 1978, pp. 16–17).

Behavioral choices frequently reflect more than the pursuit of gut-level, given preferences. Behavior is also shaped by broader considerations, including strategic concerns, desire to affect both one's own and a partner's outcomes, or long-term goals. A process termed *transformation of motivation* accounts for the fact that individuals often respond in ways that depart from given preferences, instead behaving in such a manner as to promote broader interaction goals. "Transformation generally requires freeing behavior from control by the proximal situation and thereby enabling it to be responsive to more distal features, including the partner's outcomes . . . and one's remote outcomes" (Kelley, 1984a, p. 104). The preferences resulting from the transformation process are represented in the *effective situation*, which summarizes the reconceptualized preferences that directly guide behavior.

The Transformation Process

How does transformation of motivation come about? A schematic representation of this process is displayed in Figure 5.3. Given that humans are social animals, human intelligence is highly interpersonal in character (Cosmides & Tooby, 1989)—humans can identify key features of interactions insofar as such features are relevant to personal well-being, recognizing that some situations resemble previously encountered situations. Thus, individuals respond to situations as instances of general patterns rather than perceiving and responding to each situation *de novo* (Kelley, 1984a). The transformation process begins when the individual recognizes the given situation as either (a) a novel, unfamiliar situation or (b) a situation similar to previous interactions sharing the same basic structure.

Given that the successes and failures of previous interactions direct behavior in current situations, the transformation process is partially shaped by categorizing the given situation as one pattern rather than another. When the perceived pattern is a simple one for which no broader considerations are relevant, the individual responds on the basis of immediate, given preferences. But when the given pattern involves more complex constraints or opportunities, further events ensue. The contingencies of the given situation may activate relevant dispositions, motives, or norms—that is, the nature of the given situation may bring to mind relevant broader considerations. These distal variables color the proximal events accompanying an interaction by influencing event-specific cognition and emotion, leading the individual toward one of several possible transformations (e.g., desire to maximize joint

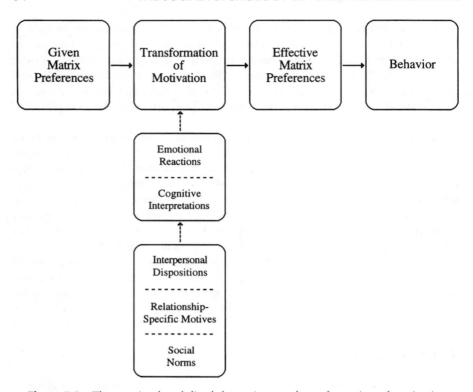

Figure 5.3 The proximal and distal determinants of transformation of motivation

outcomes). The resulting transformation process in turn yields a new set of preferences. These new preferences—represented in the effective situation—direct behavior.

Does the transformation process necessarily involve elaborate mental activity? Through adaptation to repeatedly encountered patterns, individuals may develop habitual tendencies to react to specific patterns in specific ways, such that the transformation process occurs quite rapidly, with little or no conscious thought. At critical choice points individuals may continue to engage in transformation-relevant information-seeking and rational decision-making, but just as often, habits reflecting prior adaptation may guide behavior in a rather automatic manner (Scott, Fuhrman, & Wyer, 1991). Indeed, the existing literature demonstrates that novel patterns involving ambiguous structures tend to yield more deliberate, piecemeal processing of transformation-relevant information (Neuberg & Fiske, 1987).

Functional Value of Transformation of Motivation

Why does transformation of motivation occur, especially in light of the fact that such preference shifts frequently involve forgoing immediate self-interest? First, sometimes it is beneficial to behave in ways other than that which is dictated by immediate self-interest, in that behavior guided by the transformation process yields superior outcomes even in the short run. For example, in situations involving moderate noncorrespondence, if both partners act on the basis of immediate self-interest, both suffer poor outcomes; if both partners engage in prosocial transformation, both receive better outcomes.

Second, as the transformation process becomes relatively more automatic, interactions shaped by such transformations tend to proceed in a smooth and predictable manner—that is, the transformation process provides a clear basis for choice, thereby reducing uncertainty. For example, in interactions characterized by high levels of fate control or behavior control with little reflexive control, self-interest provides no clear choice of action. In situations of this sort, the transformed, effective situation may reveal a desirable course of action, where no such clarity existed in the given situation.

Third, departing from immediate self-interest sometimes facilitates coordination. For example, research regarding conflicted interaction reveals that if, in reacting to a partner's potentially destructive act, the individual follows gut-level impulses and responds in a destructive manner, couple conflict escalates (Gottman, Markman, & Notarius, 1977; Margolin & Wampold, 1981). If the individual instead seeks to maximize own outcomes *and* those of the partner, the odds of escalating conflict are reduced. Such conciliatory behavior not only (a) provides fairly good outcomes for both parties in the short run, but also (b) allows partners to avoid the costs of conflict, (c) minimizes the odds that the partner will behave destructively, (d) promotes the individual's long-term well-being by increasing the probability that the partner will reciprocate this cooperative act, and (e) communicates to the partner that the individual is trustworthy (i.e., cooperatively oriented). Thus, departing from direct self-interest not only solves the problem at hand, but also promotes long-term coordination and harmony (Axelrod, 1984).

Types of Transformations

That transformation of motivation occurs in everyday interaction belies the simple-minded notion that behavior is governed by direct self-interest. But exactly what does transformation of motivation entail? Three types of transformation can be identified (Kelley & Thibaut, 1978). *Outcome transformations* are based on degree of concern with one's own outcomes in relation to a partners' outcomes. That is, outcome transformations can be expressed in terms of the weights individuals assign to their own and the partners' outcomes, as represented in Figure 5.4 (Griesinger & Livingston, 1973).

The simplest way to approach interaction is to act upon direct self-interest by maximizing one's own outcomes (MaxOwn, or individualism; see Figure 5.4); no transformation is involved, in that this orientation is consistent with self-interested preferences in the given situation. However, individuals may

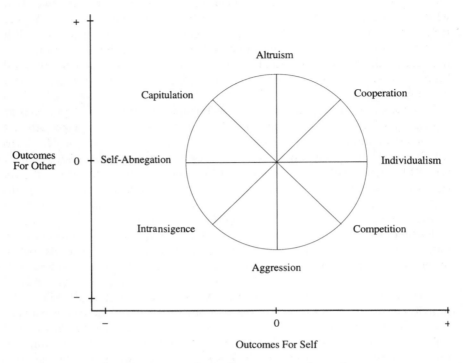

Figure 5.4   A typology of outcome transformations

also enact a number of specific outcome transformations. For example, individuals frequently seek to promote good outcomes for themselves *and* their partners (MaxJoint, or cooperation). Also, individuals may engage in transformations that are completely other-oriented (MaxOther, or altruism), especially with close partners or with individuals who desperately need assistance. Another prosocial transformation—one typically motivated by justice concerns—involves attempts to ensure that partners obtain equal outcomes (MinDiff; this does not follow from Figure 5.4 because it does not involve maximizing one's own or the partner's outcomes—the goal is equality, not outcome maximization).

Sometimes individuals seek good outcomes *in relation to* others (MaxRel, or competition)—a transformation that necessarily involves social comparison (e.g., siblings compete for parental attention). Other outcome transformations are possible, including assigning negative weights to the partner's outcomes (MinOther, or aggression), to one's own outcomes (MinOwn, or self-abnegation), or to both individuals' outcomes (MinJoint, or intransigence). Although such negative transformations can be observed in reaction to unusual patterns of interdependence, tendencies of this sort presumably are rare. Finally, more complex transformations are possible, including MaxiMin (i.e., enhancing the well-being of the person with the poorest outcomes) or MinCost (i.e., avoiding the most aversive outcome for oneself).

Transpositional transformations take account of the microtemporal features of interdependence. This type of transformation involves reconceptualizing the situation so as to act first and preempt the partner; the partner who acts second is confronted with the decision to match or not match the initiator's choice. For example, Andy and Betty may be involved in a task for which each needs the other's help. If Andy acts first and helps Betty, the decision confronting Betty is whether to reciprocate by helping Andy. Transpositional transformations are particularly relevant to situations involving high behavior control, where matching frequently yields coordination. Alternating interdependence situations provide good opportunities for coordination, in that (a) the partner who acts first does so in recognition of how the partner is likely to respond, and (b) the partner who acts second does so in full knowledge of the initiator's choice. Often, the dilemma in such situations centers *not* on which of several possible responses to enact, but on whether to be the first or the second to act.

Sequential transformations take account of the macrotemporal implications of interdependence, involving successive choices over the course of extended interaction. For example, individuals may adopt strategies such as tit-for-tat ("I'll cooperate as long as you do"; Axelrod, 1984) or may develop a pattern of turn-taking ("let's do it your way this time, my way next time"). Sequential transformations typically are responsive to the partner's probable transformation. For example, the individual who approaches a situation cooperatively may change this strategy if the partner is consistently selfish. Sequential transformations may also serve communicative purposes. For example, individuals may enact prosocial choices as a means of expressing their loyalty, or may behave destructively in response to a hostile partner as a means of signaling the boundaries of willingness to accommodate.

Empirical Demonstrations of Transformation of Motivation

Do individuals in fact depart from their immediate self-interest, taking account of broader considerations? It is not easy to document the transformation process, in that transformation is quite routine and may occur in a relatively automatic manner. Nevertheless, existing research provides evidence that is consistent with the transformation concept. For example, individuals behaving in accord with the given situation exhibit shorter response latencies than do those who transform that pattern: individualists (who respond based on self-interest) exhibit shorter latencies when allocating funds to themselves and others than do competitors (who enact MaxRel transformation) or cooperators (who enact MaxJoint or MinDiff transformation; Dehue, McClintock, & Liebrand, 1993). Also, participants in games research (a) describe transformation-relevant reasons for their choices (e.g., "to help the partner obtain more points"), (b) assign different meaning to identical situations depending on the transformation applied to the situation, (c) engage in transformation-relevant information-seeking, and (d) exhibit more prosocial choices when interacting for extended periods of time (Pruitt & Kimmel, 1977).

It might be argued that the motives governing deviations from self-interest are thoroughly defined by the nature of a specific relationship. For example, close partners might automatically take one another's interests into account; in intimate relationships, self-interest and partner-interest might be inextricably merged (Aron & Aron, 1997; Clark, Mills, & Powell, 1986). However, even close partners distinguish between personal well-being and partner well-being. In describing previous conflicts, the responses individuals actually enact (effective situation) are considerably more constructive than are the responses they entertained prior to acting (given situation; Yovetich & Rusbult, 1994). Also, when the broader considerations that might induce pro-relationship transformation are eliminated (e.g., concern for partner well-being, public image), individuals' preferences are less constructive than are those of individuals operating on the basis of normal social concern (Rusbult et al., 1991). Moreover, in reacting to a partner's destructive acts, behavior is more constructive given plentiful response time; when time for transformational activity is limited, prosocial behavior is less probable (Yovetich & Rusbult, 1994).

Implications for Long-term Interdependence

Individuals frequently act on the basis of broader goals rather than in the service of immediate self-interest. At the same time, departures from self-interest tend to be highly contingent, applying to specific situations with specific partners (Huston & Vangelisti, 1991; Miller & Kenny, 1986): "The advantages of acting in ways other than those indicated by short-term self-interest . . . [are] conditional" (Kelley, 1984b, p. 4). In recognition of the diverse features of interdependence that may affect motivation and behavior, it is instructive to address the issue of *altruistic motivation* (Kelley & Thibaut, 1985).

Interdependence theory has been criticized for "sanctioning selfishness" (Wallach & Wallach, 1983). This critique is misplaced, in that interdependence theory argues that behavior frequently is shaped by considerations extending beyond immediate self-interest. For example, prosocial transformation may be guided by desire to enhance a partner's well-being or by desire to achieve a fair distribution of outcomes. But in a more general sense, is it possible that prosocial transformation simply reflects the pursuit of long-term self-interest (rather than immediate self-interest)? Is it possible that prosocial transformation occurs because we know that we will enjoy superior long-term outcomes if we cooperate, or because we will enjoy superior long-term outcomes if others perceive us as well-intentioned?

Interdependence theory *does* suggest that individuals acquire relatively stable transformation tendencies as a result of adaptation. We assume that transformation tendencies reflect prior experiences in interdependence situations, and we assume that specific tendencies persist because they have long-term functional value. However, this is not to argue against the existence of altruistic motives. Repeatedly experiencing situations in which prosocial acts yield good consequences may give rise to relatively more stable prosocial tendencies, but the fact that adaptation underlies such tendencies is not to suggest that self-interest mediates current behavior. Such logic places interdependence theory inside the head of the interactant, suggesting that (a) we are aware of prior adaptations, (b) prior adaptations are labeled as self-interested, and (c) current prosocial acts are interpreted as parallel self-interested adaptations (Kelley & Thibaut, 1985). Once a transformation tendency is established, such a motive may achieve considerable autonomy, taking on value and acquiring the power to guide behavior in its own right. Frequently, when we exhibit prosocial transformation, the goal foremost in our minds is desire to help another person.

More generally, it is unfortunate that the altruism debate frequently decays into a categorization exercise, pitting (a) selfish behavior, or acts including any element of self-interest, against (b) altruistic behavior, or acts that are completely free of such contamination (Batson, 1987). Such an exercise ignores the multifaceted nature of motivation, in that frequently the smart thing to do is also the good thing to do. The existence of an element of self-interest does not preclude genuinely altruistic impulses.

HABITUAL TRANSFORMATION TENDENCIES

When individuals initially encounter specific interdependence patterns, such patterns are experienced as unique events—as specific problems and opportunities to which they must react. In reacting to such situations, the individual may (a) behave in an impulsive manner or (b) deliberately review the options, consider the consequences, and consciously decide how to behave. If the reaction to a given pattern yields poor outcomes, the individual will behave differently in future situations with similar patterns; if the reaction yields good outcomes, the individual will react similarly in future situations with similar patterns (win–stay, lose–change). Over time, some patterns will be regularly encountered and a stable orientation to those patterns may emerge (Kelley, 1983b; Rusbult & Van Lange, 1996).

Interpersonal orientations are pattern-contingent transformation tendencies—reactions to repeatedly-encountered interdependence situations that on average yield desirable outcomes. Typically, interpersonal orientations do not operate as a function of conscious calculation. Individuals sometimes studiously decide how to behave, but just as often such "decisions" are the automatic product of established habits. Once an orientation is established, the individual routinely engages in the activities that are set into motion by the orientation, only occasionally (if ever) being aware of such habitual processes, and only occasionally (if ever) experiencing the behavior as antithetical to self-interest. As illustrated in Figure 5.3, interpersonal orientations exert their effects by (a) coloring cognitive activities and emotional experiences, and (b) giving rise to stable, pattern-contingent transformation tendencies.

Interpersonal Dispositions

Interpersonal dispositions are actor-specific inclinations to respond to particular interdependence patterns in a specific manner across numerous partners (Kelley, 1983b). How do dispositions emerge? Over the course of development different individuals experience different interdependence histories, undergoing different experiences with parents and siblings, and confronting different opportunities and constraints in peer interaction. As a result of their unique histories individuals acquire dispositions, reflected in the manner in which they approach specific interdependence patterns—they develop tendencies to perceive patterns in predictable ways, and to apply transformations to those patterns with greater or lesser probability (Halberstadt, 1986; Reis & Patrick, 1996).

It is instructive to illustrate this process using the example of attachment style (Bowlby, 1969/1982; Hazan & Shaver, 1994a). From the outset, it is important to note that dependence makes one vulnerable, in that dependence reflects a partner's ability to provide one with exceptionally good *or* exceptionally poor outcomes (e.g., affirmation vs betrayal; Reis & Shaver, 1988). Individuals develop avoidant styles as a consequence of seeking intimacy and repeatedly experiencing rejection or betrayal. Accordingly, avoidant individuals come to perceive intimacy situations as dangerous, and resolve such dilemmas by exploiting their partners or by avoiding intimacy patterns. Just as competitors elicit competition from others and create a distrustful world for themselves (Kelley & Stahelski, 1970), avoidant individuals elicit avoidance, and thus create a cold and barren world for themselves (Simpson, Rholes, & Nelligan, 1992). In contrast, secure individuals experience interdependence histories in which attempts at intimacy yield good outcomes. Accordingly, secure individuals perceive intimacy situations as safe, behave in a trusting manner, and create opportunities for partners to safely seek intimacy in return. Presumably, anxious-ambivalent individuals experience inconsistent intimacy histories and therefore come to behave in an erratic manner, alternating between (a) desperately grasping at that which they most desire (intimacy, closeness) and (b) cautiously avoiding the risks of dependence.

The functioning of dispositions is also illustrated in research regarding social value orientations (Messick & McClintock, 1968; Van Lange, Agnew, Harinck, & Steemers, 1997). When presented with opportunities to distribute outcomes to themselves and others, some people consistently select options in which own outcomes are greatest (individualism), whereas others are oriented toward distributions of the MaxJoint (cooperation) or MaxRel variety (competition; Liebrand & Van Run, 1985). Social value orientations (a) influence behavior in a variety of situations, (b) are associated with distinct patterns of belief regarding others' orientations, and (c) are reflected in the probability with which specific transformations are applied to given patterns (McClintock & Liebrand, 1988). For example, prosocials approach interaction cooperatively, and continue to do so as long as the partner behaves cooperatively in return. Individualists are susceptible to the temptation to exploit a partner's cooperation, but cooperate when it is advantageous to do so. Competitors are unwilling to cooperate even when doing so would maximize their outcomes.

The orientations embodied in such dispositions exert their effects by shaping the emotions and cognitions that are activated by specific patterns of interdependence. For example, competitive individuals perceive a wide range of patterns as competitive, believe that others are competitive, and interpret cooperative acts as "stupid" or "sneaky". Given that interaction partners frequently compete in response to competition from others, the competitive individual's assumptions about others' goals and motives are more likely to be confirmed than disconfirmed (Kelley & Stahelski, 1970; Snyder, 1984).

Relationship-specific Motives

Relationship-specific motives are inclinations to respond to particular patterns in a specific manner within the context of a given relationship (Holmes, 1981). Relationship-specific motives are especially evident in situations involving dilemmas between personal well-being and the well-being of the partner or relationship. Holmes and Rempel (1989) term such patterns *diagnostic situations*, in reference to the fact that behavior in such situations is diagnostic of the individual's motives. One important motive concerns trust, which reflects a partner's confidence in the individual's benevolent intentions (Rempel, Holmes, & Zanna, 1985). When an individual enacts prosocial behavior in a diagnostic situation, departing from direct self-interest for the good of the relationship, the prosocial act communicates concern for the partner's well-being. Such behavior has been shown to (a) increase the partner's trust in the individual's benevolent intentions, (b) strengthen the partner's commitment, and (c) increase the odds that the partner will exhibit prosocial transformation in the future (Wieselquist, Rusbult, Foster, & Agnew, in press). Thus, to the extent that Andy trusts Betty, he experiences more benign emotions and forms more benevolent interpretations of Betty's actions, which in turn enhances his tendencies toward prosocial transformation of motivation and prosocial behavior.

Commitment is another important relationship-specific motive (Johnson, 1989; Levinger, 1979; Rusbult, 1983). Commitment emerges as a consequence of dependence upon a partner, and includes intent to persist, long-term orientation, and psychological attachment. Commitment is strengthened when satisfaction level is high (the individual loves the partner), when the quality of available alternatives is poor (alternative partners are unappealing), and when investment size is large (important resources are linked to a relationship). Commitment is the strongest predictor of voluntary decisions to persist (Rusbult, 1983), and promotes prosocial maintenance mechanisms such as derogation of tempting alternatives (Johnson & Rusbult, 1989), accommodation (Rusbult et al., 1991), willingness to sacrifice (Van Lange et al., 1997), and positive illusion (Rusbult, Van Lange, Yovetich, Wildschut, & Verette, 1999). Commitment colors emotional reactions to specific interdependence patterns (e.g., feeling affection rather than anger when a partner is neglectful) and gives rise to patterns of thought that support the decision to persist (e.g., cognitive interdependence; Agnew, Van Lange, Rusbult, & Langston, 1998). In turn, benevolent thoughts and feelings promote prosocial transformation, especially in situations of moderate to high correspondence (e.g., accommodating rather than retaliating when a partner behaves badly; Rusbult & Buunk, 1993).

Social Norms

Social norms are rule-based inclinations to respond to particular interdependence patterns in a specific manner, either with people in general (e.g., "never be the first to defect") or in the context of a given relationship (e.g., "never betray your best friend"; Campbell, 1975; Simon, 1990). Norms are manifested in (a) observed regularity of behavior, (b) attempts to regain control by appealing to the norm in situations where regularity has been interrupted, and (c) feelings of indignation or guilt occasioned by violations of the norm (Thibaut & Kelley, 1959).

For example, most societies develop rules regarding the expression of anger; such rules help groups to avoid the chaos that would ensue if individuals were freely to give rein to hostile emotions. Likewise, etiquette and everyday rules of civility regulate behavior so as to yield more harmonious interaction—"good manners" represent efficient solutions to everyday interdependence dilemmas. For example, in the absence of normative prescriptions, Betty might feel irritated when Andy offers his mother the front seat of the car when driving to a restaurant. But in light of norms regarding suitable behavior toward one's elders, the potential for conflict in such situations is reduced.

Long-term partners may develop relationship-specific rules to solve problems of interdependence. For example, although the temptation to become involved with alternative partners can be acute, the costs of doing so can be equally acute. Therefore, most couples either comply with existing norms or develop their own norms to govern such behavior and minimize the negative impact of extra-relationship involvements. Such norms typically specify the circumstances in which extra-relationship involvement is acceptable (e.g., marriage primacy), as well as the conditions under which such behavior is unacceptable (e.g., high visibility). Couples who adhere to the "ground rules" of their marriage tend to exhibit lower levels of jealousy regarding a spouse's infidelity (Buunk, 1987).

In like manner, partners frequently adopt rules governing the distribution of resources in their relationship (Mikula, 1983; Walster, Berscheid, & Walster, 1976). Allocation rules minimize conflict and enhance couple functioning. Thus, it is not surprising that (a) partners adhere to distribution rules such as equity, equality, or need, and that (b) individuals experience discomfort when normative standards are violated. Also, allocation rules frequently are

relationship-specific. For example, in parent–child or other communal relationships, the norms guiding behavior are need-based rather than
contributions-based (Clark & Mills, 1979; Deutsch, 1975). Moreover, rules
governing conflict resolution frequently center as much on the procedure by
which conflicts should be resolved as on the outcome distribution *per se* (Lind
& Tyler, 1988; Thibaut & Walker, 1975).

Implications for Long-term Interdependence

Over the course of extended interaction partners are interdependent not only
(a) in the patterns of interdependence that are implicit in given matrix preferences, but also at a higher level, (b) in the transformations the partners routinely apply to given patterns. When Andy's orientations lead him toward
prosocial transformation, Betty's options and outcomes are enhanced; when
Andy is inclined toward self-centered or antisocial behavior, Betty's options
and outcomes are degraded. Thus, just as we can characterize outcome interdependence in terms of control, dependence, and correspondence, we can characterize the interdependence of interpersonal orientations in parallel manner.

To the extent that a partner's transformation tendencies are firmly
established, the individual's own transformation task is simplified. For example, in some respects it is easier to be involved with a partner who is
reliably self-centered than to be involved with a partner who is *un*reliably
prosocial, in that the tasks of prediction and coordination are more difficult in
the latter instance. Moreover, to the extent that partners possess knowledge
of one another's orientations, uncertainty is reduced and the odds of achieving congenial and mutually gratifying outcomes are enhanced (Sorrentino,
Holmes, Zanna, & Sharp, 1995). Given that such knowledge rests on abilities
and traits such as empathy and perspective-taking, long-term functioning in
relationships should be enhanced to the extent that one or both partners excel
at the sorts of social-cognitive and social-emotional dispositions that increase
sensitivity and awareness of a partner's preferences and motives (Arriaga &
Rusbult, 1998; Davis & Oathout, 1987; Ickes, Stinson, Bissonnette, & Garcia,
1990; Rusbult et al., 1991).

MEANING ANALYSIS AND SELF-PRESENTATION

Meaning Analysis

As displayed in Figure 5.3, (a) proximal mental events such as cognitions and
emotions represent the individual's internal construal of the meaning of a
given interdependence pattern, and (b) proximal mental events are colored by
the orientations that have developed over the course of repeated exposure to
specific instances of general patterns. Kelley (1984a) used the phrase *interest-*

relevant situation in reference to the fact that interdependence situations have implications for the individual's personal well-being. No two situations are identical, but the properties characterizing situations possess sufficient regularity that classifications are possible. Scanning a situation for its meaning plays a critical role in adaptation, in that such activity provides the material for "marking and recording the pattern (and type of pattern) of the interest-relevant features of each just-experienced situation and of identifying and orienting oneself to each forthcoming situation in terms of its pattern of such features" (Kelley, 1984a, p. 91).

Meaning analysis involves reflecting on a given situation, noting its interest-relevant features and discerning its broader implications (Arriaga & Rusbult, 1998; Frijda, 1988; Mandler, 1975). Meaning analysis is oriented toward rendering the social world predictable, and therefore controllable. As Fiske (1992) suggests, "thinking is for doing"; we suggest that "feeling is for doing" as well. Cognitions *and* emotions both prompt and direct action in such a manner as to adapt to interdependence patterns that will be encountered in the immediate or more distant future. In particular, cognitions and emotions guide interaction via their role in (a) interpreting the direct significance and broader implications of an event, (b) relating the implications of this knowledge to one's own needs and preferences, and (c) directing reactions to the event. Retrospectively, internal events denote a change in the individual's welfare and serve as summaries of the causal factors that are relevant to that event. Prospectively, internal events prompt and direct behavior with respect to the particular causal structure inherent in a given event.

Cognitive interpretations are relevant to interaction in at least three ways. First, individuals scan situations for their interest-relevant features; responding effectively depends on detecting key properties of the situation at hand (Kelley, 1984a). Second, individuals form inferences regarding the motives underlying behavior, attending in particular to departures from given preferences—deviations from self-centered choice reveal the individual's unique goals and motives (Holmes, 1981). In new relationships expectations are probabilistic, in that they are based on assumptions about how the average person would react; in longer-term relationships individuals also employ idiographic expectations based on knowledge of how the partner has behaved across a variety of situations (Kelley, 1991). Third, cognition is central to understanding behavior in novel situations for which stable tendencies have not yet emerged. Individuals are in a position to engage in informed transformation to the extent that they can predict the partner's preferences, motives, and behavior. Such prediction involves abstracting general rules from knowledge of a partner's behavior in previous situations (Weiner, 1986). More generally, cognition is shaped by the interpersonal orientations embodied in dispositions (e.g., anxious-ambivalent individuals interpret a busy partner's neglect as rejection), relationship-specific motives (e.g., committed individuals generously ignore a partner's rude remark, attributing it to work-related stress), and social norms (e.g., during conflict, the injunction to "count to ten" before reacting yields calm and cooperative behavior).

Emotional reactions, too, guide the course of interaction. Prevailing theories suggest that emotions signal (a) interruptions to the flow of interaction (Berscheid, 1983) or (b) changes in action readiness caused by appraising events as relevant to personal well-being (Frijda, 1988; Kelley, 1984a). The prototype approach asserts that emotion prototypes are formed as a result of repeated experience with particular interaction patterns (Shaver, Schwartz, Kirson, & O'Connor, 1987). Emotions vividly and efficiently summarize the meaning of an interdependence pattern, directing attention to key features and identifying the interest-relevant aspects of the situation. Moreover, emotions are colored by dispositions, motives, and norms. For example, attraction to an alternative partner arouses guilt among committed individuals and among individuals who adhere to the normative prescription that adultery is wrong. In turn, feelings of guilt lead the individual to respond effectively, either by behaving in a cool manner so as to drive away the alternative or by cognitively derogating the alternative so as to eliminate the temptation.

Self-presentation

Just as individuals examine one another's behavior for information regarding preferences and motives, they attempt to communicate their own preferences and motives via *self-presentation* (Baumeister, 1982a; DePaulo, 1992; Leary & Kowalski, 1990). Sometimes individuals engage in deceptive self-presentation and sometimes self-presentation is oriented toward making true motives and preferences evident. In either event, self-presentation has the goal of shaping or controlling observers' emotions, cognitions, preferences, motives, or behavior.

Much self-presentational activity involves creating a context in which departures from self-interest are highlighted—revealing one's given preferences so as to make higher-order motives apparent. For example, while serving dinner Andy may comment on the techniques involved in making fresh pasta versus fresh bread, thereby hinting at the effort involved in preparing the meal. Individuals may also distort given patterns of interdependence, manipulating the context within which their actions are judged. For example, when Bobby ends up with a black eye as a consequence of a fight he initiated, he must decide whether to confess to his mother that he started the fight (a given matrix representation that would elicit anger) or to "reconstruct" the situation by convincing his mother that he was the hapless victim of a bully's violent eruption (a representation that would elicit sympathy).

Thus, self-presentation involves conveying disparities between situational demands and behavioral choices, thereby presenting one's preferences and motives in the desired light (Jones & Davis, 1965). Ultimately, the possibilities for conveying self-relevant information are limited by the inherent qualities of a given pattern. For example, it is difficult to convey considerateness in a perfectly correspondent situation because when partners' preferences are in perfect agreement, "considerate" behavior aligns with "self-interested" behavior (i.e., what's good for the partner is also good for the self). Ironically, to effectively communicate one's prosocial motives, partners must encounter difficult, noncorrespondent patterns of interdependence.

Implications for Long-term Interdependence

Cognition, emotion, and self-presentation are exceptionally important in ongoing relationships. To the extent that partners form benign interpretations of one another's actions, couple interaction becomes more congenial and the quality of couple functioning is enhanced (Baldwin, 1992; Bradbury & Fincham, 1990; Fletcher & Fincham, 1991a). Why so? Evaluations of interaction in part are attribution-mediated—that is, experiences are evaluated not only in terms of the direct outcomes experienced in interaction, but also in terms of the orientations that are revealed as a result of interaction (e.g., commitment, self-centeredness; Kelley, 1984b). The added-value of attribution-mediated evaluation appears to exert strong effects on partners' long-term beliefs about one another's interpersonal orientations.

Attribution-mediated evaluation is central to the development of trust, in that trust emerges as a consequence of observing the partner engage in prosocial behavior even when doing so is antithetical to the partner's immediate self-interest (Holmes & Rempel, 1989). Trust represents the individual's inference that the partner's motives are benevolent, and reflects conviction that the partner can be relied upon to behave in such a manner as to promote one's well-being. In turn, trust reduces the risks associated with increasing dependence, and enhances the individual's willingness to enact reciprocal prosocial departures from self-interest (Wieselquist et al., in press). Thus, while relationship-specific motives color the emotions and cognitions partners experience over the course of interaction, these affective and cognitive processes also reaffirm relationship-specific motives, and consequently play a central role in accounting for growth and vitality in an ongoing relationship.

DIRECTIONS FOR FUTURE WORK AND CONCLUSIONS

Directions for Future Work

It is important to comment on some of the strengths and limitations of interdependence theory as it is currently conceptualized. We will begin by noting three strengths of the theory. First, Kelley and Thibaut's (1978) comprehensive analysis of the domain of interdependence patterns provides the field with a much-needed typology of interpersonal situations—a typology that emphasizes the relationships between individuals rather than emphasizing individuals *per se*. To fully understand the meaning of interaction—including

the thoughts and emotions that accompany interaction as well as the dispositions, motives, and norms that may be relevant to interaction—we must begin
with an analysis of the structure of interdependence characterizing a given
interaction.

The concept of transformation of motivation stands as a second notable
strength of the theory, illuminating the significance of departures from direct
self-interest. Why are departures from given preferences so meaningful? Because interdependence structure is *real*, and exerts meaningful effects on
interaction—interdependence structure ultimately "makes itself known". As
noted earlier, departures from that which is dictated by given interdependence structure forms the basis for self-presentation, for attributions regarding motives, and for other meaningful events in ongoing relationships.

A third strength of the theory lies in its potential for integrating such
diverse subfields as close relationships, prosocial behavior, and intergroup
behavior. Across subfields, researchers tend to employ differing methodologies (e.g., experimental games, coding of videotaped interaction), although they frequently examine common interdependence properties.
Unfortunately, at present there is little integration across subfields—for example, textbooks devote separate chapters to specific domains, as though the
superficial character of a behavior defined its essential meaning. Interdependence theory can eliminate such artificial distinctions via its emphasis on the
fundamental properties of interdependence.

What are the primary limitations of the theory as it is currently conceptualized and employed? One limitation centers on the proximal mechanisms
underlying transformation of motivation. Kelley's (1984a) discussion of the
role played by affect takes important steps toward analyzing the internal
events accompanying transformation. At the same time, a good deal remains
to be accomplished in understanding the roles of cognition and emotion in the
transformation process (Duck & Miell, 1986). A related limitation concerns
the distal mechanisms underlying stable transformation tendencies. Earlier,
we noted that interpersonal orientations can be understood as adaptations to
repeatedly encountered interdependence patterns. Based on Kelley's (1983b)
analysis we distinguished among three types of orientation—dispositions,
relationship-specific motives, and social norms (Rusbult & Van Lange, 1996).
Future research might seek to analyze important differences among the several embodiments of stable transformation tendencies.

A second limitation centers on the fact that interdependence theory been
underutilized in the study of interaction and relationships. Why so? First, for
the past few decades the prevailing orientation in the social sciences has
centered on the study of internal events. Such an orientation makes it easy to
(unwisely) ignore the broader context in which such events emerge and function. Second, the theory is difficult—it includes quantitative representations
of interdependence patterns, processes are described using mathematical for-
mulae . . . the theory cannot easily be communicated in a soundbite. Third,
the theory's key constructs were not developed hand in hand with operational
definitions. Translation of abstract concepts into specific empirical procedures

is left to the researcher—a task which can be daunting. It is to be hoped that increasing numbers of scientists will adopt the interdependence approach over the coming decade, and that this orientation will become an increasingly accessible means of understanding interpersonal phenomena.

CONCLUSIONS

Interdependence theory presents a logical taxonomy of interdependence patterns, thereby offering a conceptual framework in which all possible forms of interdependence can be analyzed using four key properties—degree of dependence, mutuality of dependence, basis of dependence, and correspondence of outcomes. By extending the traditional matrix representation through the use of transition lists, we are able to understand important temporal and sequential features of interdependence. Via the concept of transformation of motivation, the theory explains how behavior is shaped by broader considerations, such as long-term goals and strategic concerns. In addition to identifying the themes and properties that define the interpersonal world, the theory also discusses the process of adaptation to repeatedly encountered patterns of interdependence. We have examined the embodiment of such habitual tendencies in dispositions, relationship-specific motives, and norms. The theory also provides a framework for understanding social-cognitive phenomena such as attribution, emotion, and self-presentation. Our hope is that this chapter helps to convey the comprehensiveness of interdependence theory, as well as its status as a truly *interpersonal* account of the nature and consequences of interdependence.

Chapter 6

Self-expansion Motivation and Including Other in the Self

Arthur Aron

and

Elaine N. Aron

State University of New York at Stony Brook, NY, USA

In this chapter we examine thinking and research relevant to what has come to be known as the self-expansion model of motivation and cognition in close relationships. We begin with an explanation of the key elements of the model, followed by a comment on the utility of a model of this kind in terms of the role of metaphor in science. The second and third sections of the chapter consider in some detail two key processes suggested by the model, discussing the theoretical foundation and research relevant to each. These two processes are, first, that relationship satisfaction is increased through the association of the relationship with self-expansion and, second, that the relationship means cognitively that each partner has included the other in his or her self. The fourth section considers more briefly some implications of the model for three other relationship-relevant issues: selectivity in attraction, motivations for unrequited love, and the effects on the self of falling in love. We conclude with a brief consideration of other relationship-relevant ramifications of the model.

The Social Psychology of Personal Relationships.
Edited by William Ickes and Steve Duck. © 2000 John Wiley & Sons Ltd.

THE SELF-EXPANSION MODEL

The self-expansion model proposes that a central human motivation is self-expansion and that one way people seek such expansion is through close relationships in which each includes the other in the self.

Self-expansion Motivation

The original formulation of the self-expansion model (Aron & Aron, 1986) arose directly from an examination of motivation. We began with the question of why people enter and maintain close relationships, which required thinking long and hard about why people do anything, assuming that their basic motivations also influence their desires regarding relationships. We realize that social animals such as primates may simply have a predilection, genetic or cultural, for a social rather than solitary life. Yet there is something different about humans in the way they elaborate everything, be it eating, sex, communication, or social relationships.

It seemed that one way of understanding much of human motivation, including the elaboration of biological drives, is to say that people seek to expand themselves. At least four areas of expansion seem to interest humans in varying degrees (according to temperament, experience, subculture, and so forth): (a) physical and social influence (through territoriality, power relationships, possessions, etc.), (b) cognitive complexity (differentiation, the discovery of linkages, and general knowledge, insight, and wisdom), (c) social and bodily identity (by identifying with other individuals, groups such as family or nation, and nonhumans ranging from animals to gods), and (d) their awareness of their position in the universe (that unique human interest in metaphysics, the meaning of life, ritual, religion, mythology, etc.).

Most of the time this self-expansion serves the cause of individual exploration, competence, and efficacy (e.g., Bandura, 1977; Deci, 1975; Gecas, 1989; White, 1959). But there are seeming exceptions, as when parents sacrifice opportunities to experience personal self-efficacy for the sake of their offspring. However, if one emphasizes *perceived* self-efficacy, which we do, and assumes that a self can be expanded to include another, which the research discussed below suggests, then one can imagine someone experiencing a very self-expanding efficacy through another's accomplishments (as demonstrated, for example, by Tesser's, 1988, work on "reflection"). This is one more example of the elaboration of a biological "given," parental self-sacrifice, but an important one because it allows for sacrifice of the self not merely for the sake of an offspring but for the sake of other relationship partners and for the group and the culture.

There are, of course, specialties or preferences for modes of expansion, and these may also change over the course of a day or a lifetime. There are exceptions to expansion motivation as well, when individuals seem to evidence little desire to expand, explore, or even think due to extensive experiences of failure or punishment for their efforts. We have also emphasized (Aron & Aron, 1986) that there is a correspondingly strong desire to integrate expansion experiences and make sense of them, a desire for wholeness or coherence which sometimes preempts the desire for expansion until it is satisfied to some degree. But expansion and integration are two steps in a general pattern of movement toward self-expansion (much as Piaget, 1963, saw the growth of intelligence as involving steps of accommodating to new experience alternating with the assimilation of the new experiences into existing schemata). Finally, once one has integrated new material into the self, there is a motivation to resist de-expansion or deintegration of self, a motive consistent with processes described by Greenwald (1980) and Swann (1983).

Including Each Other in Each Other's Self

Having assumed a general motivation to expand the self, we then proposed that the desire to enter and maintain a particular relationship can be seen as one especially satisfying, useful, and human means to this self-expansion. Cognitively, the self is expanded through including the other in the self, a process which in a close relationship becomes mutual, so that each person is including the other in his or her self.

People seek relationships in order to gain what they anticipate as self-expansion. When faced with a potential relationship, one compares one's self as it is prior to the relationship—lacking the other's perspectives, resources, identities, and so forth—to the self as prospectively imagined after it has entered the relationship, a self now with full access both to self's own perspectives and so forth *plus* the other's perspectives and so forth. Metaphorically, I will have the use of all my house plus gain the use of all of yours. Thus before one enters a relationship the motive of self-expansion may have a decidedly self-centered air to it. But after entering the relationship, the effect of including each other in each other's self is an overlapping of selves. Now I must protect and maintain my house *and* your house, as *both* are "mine" (as both are now "yours"). This post-inclusion, larger self creates (and explains) the remarkably unselfish nature of close relationships.

Self-Expansion Processes as Metaphors

We have come to think of an important aspect of any theory to be the metaphors or analogies it embodies (Lakoff, 1987; Lakoff & Turner, 1989; Langer, 1948; also see Duck, 1994, for a review of the literature on the metaphors or lay theories; Kovecses, 1986, 1991, employed by those in close relationships, as well as a discussion of some of the metaphors currently used in close relationships research.) Metaphor maps onto confusing phenomena or the "target domain" a schema that is already familiar from the "source domain," generally a bodily experience (Lakoff, 1987). The better the theory's metaphor, the more a phenomenon's intricacies are captured in it. Much of a theory's heuristic value comes from the richness of the parallels between its guiding metaphor and the target phenomenon. In addition to the parallels that are consciously recognized, the metaphor in a model often engenders creative new ideas by opening us up to semi-conscious images that we otherwise would not have considered as aspects of the phenomenon. (For example, to speak of "branches of science" might also activate connections to science's growth, pruning, fruit, roots, and so forth.) Further, when theories or metaphors already explored in other fields, such as market exchanges as a metaphor in economics, are applied to a new field, such as the study of close relationships, all insights already gained in the original application of the metaphor can be tested in the new field.

All metaphors, however, have limits (Duck, 1994). The images they generate direct attention in one direction, tending to close off interest in another. They may mislead as well as lead, be aesthetically jarring rather than pleasing. For example, theories with metaphors rooted in economic exchange will capture important aspects of relationships, yet will also have their limits in that they connote materialism or self-centeredness. They direct attention away from, for example, intimacy. Another example, attachment theory, has its own inherent limits because its core metaphor is parent and child, and one of its images is the primate infant clinging to its mother. The metaphor of attachment directs attention away from, for example, sexuality and adult cognitive processes.

A reason for the growing interest in the self-expansion model seems to be that it captures new aspects of the target domain of close relationships, perhaps because its metaphors are so close to basic bodily experiences and images of expansion and merger. For example, a sense of expansion in the heart or chest is a common bodily experience associated with deeply felt positive experiences, such as when people first fall in love, or looking at their sleeping child. A bodily experience of having the other included in the self can occur when one's own muscles move while watching a beloved partner perform, or when one receives news that would please or upset the other were she or he there, and one feels the physical signs of joy or grief that the other would feel. Most striking, perhaps, are descriptions of losing a partner being like having a part of one's body ripped out or die. Indeed, the common term for the end of a close relationship, "break up," seems to refer to the end of a physical oneness.

Obviously an emphasis on self, expansion, and inclusion directs attention away from important other aspects of relationships, but for now we leave that to other models and metaphors to correct. A greater concern for communicating about this relatively new model of self-expansion is that metaphors have different associations and emotional connotations for different people. When metaphors become the framework for research models, the associations they engender tend, over time, to become shared by all those working in the field. For example, whereas the general public may associate learning theory with metal Skinner boxes and callous treatment of animals, psychologists have more neutral or positive images of the theory as useful and enlightening. With a new model, however—one that is neither shared nor borrowed from another field—personal connotations constitute more of a difficulty. In the case of our model, we have found that self-expansion connotes for some people the acquiring of scarce resources (food, space, money, attention) at the expense of others. For others, ourselves included, self-expansion primarily connotes a broadened identity or awareness, so that expansion can be virtually unlimited and usually leads to greater altruism, not less. We hope that in time the latter connotations will be the more universally shared meaning of the metaphor.

Likewise, the metaphor of including each other in each other's self is one that can connote for some a loss of individual identity, following the issues raised, for example, by family systems theorists (e.g., Olson, Rusell, & Sprenkle, 1983). Such a loss of individual identity would seem to be an appropriate description of the situation for a relationship partner whose individual identity has not been well developed (this kind of analysis is suggested by Erikson's, 1950, model). (An analogy might be the unequal merging of my one goldfish with your aquarium of twenty species, so that the result would feel to me like your aquarium, not mine or ours.) But when each partner's identity is well developed, our assumption is that individual identity is *not* lost, but rather is enriched and expanded, by each including aspects of the other into her or his self. Indeed, there is some evidence that this latter understanding corresponds to the way most individuals understand this metaphor (Aron, Aron, & Smollan, 1992).

THE FIRST OF THE TWO KEY PROCESSES: INCREASED RELATIONSHIP SATISFACTION THROUGH ASSOCIATING THE RELATIONSHIP WITH SELF-EXPANSION

The Autonomous Desirability of Whatever Is Associated with Expansion and the Decline of Relationship Satisfaction over Time

If a basic human motive is self-expansion, then situations and persons present during, or associated with, self-expansion experiences should—through classical conditioning—become secondarily reinforcing or desirable in themselves (Dollard & Miller, 1950). In the case of human relationships, when two people first enter a relationship, typically there is an initial, exhilarating period in which the couple spends hours talking, engaging in intense risk-taking and self-disclosure. The partners are expanding their selves at a rapid rate by virtue of the intense exchange. Once the two know each other fairly well, however, opportunities for further rapid expansion of this sort inevitably decrease. For a time, satisfaction may remain through the association of the other and of the relationship with the just-completed period of breathtakingly rapid self-expansion. But once self-expansion slows to the point it becomes negligible or nonexistent, there is little emotion, or perhaps boredom. Hence we see the well-documented typical decline in relationship satisfaction after the "honeymoon period" in a romantic relationship which is maintained over subsequent years (e.g., Blood & Wolfe, 1960; Glenn, 1990; Locke & Wallace, 1959; Rollins & Feldman, 1970; Tucker & Aron, 1993).

The major theoretical approaches to close relationships (interdependence, attachment, symbolic interaction, family systems theories) say surprisingly little about the reasons for the decline in relationship satisfaction. They seem to assume that a relationship will be satisfying so long as one sees one's own outcomes as interdependent on the other's, investments are high, alternatives low, the partners have secure attachment styles, adequate nonconflictual role enactment is achieved, meaning is shared, individual personal growth is supported, and so forth.

Those who have commented most on the decline are those who have applied learning theories to marital relationships (e.g., Huesmann, 1980; Jacobson & Margolin, 1979). They see such a decline as a special case of habituation—adaptation to a stimulus through repeated exposure (Peeke & Herz, 1973) which occurs at every level, neuron to whole organism. Formerly-valued reinforcement becomes less intensely rewarding as it becomes predictable or familiar. An ongoing relationship is almost by definition repetitious in some ways, increasingly predictable, and therefore subject to becoming less reinforcing. Plutchik's (1967) model also makes "lack of novelty" a prominent force for marital instability. Cognitive theories have re-defined habituation as a loss of uncertainty of informational uncertainty for decision-making processes. Too much uncertainty is overarousing, aversive, and its loss is desired. This is the main emphasis of Berger's (1988) application of uncertainty reduction theory to personal relationships. But too little uncertainty leaves one underaroused, which is also aversive. Berger also makes the point—emphasizing a kind of dialectical relationship between levels of predictability sufficiently high for comfortable interpersonal coordination, but with levels of novelty (perhaps in less central relationship domains) sufficient to maintain some level of excitement. Altman, Vinsel, and Brown (1981) also proposed a similar dialectical relation between what they described as "stability" and "change."

Uncertainty undoubtedly stimulates some of the arousal surrounding the initial phase of a relationship. "Since uncertainties must either be reduced or not, it is inevitable that these cumulative probabilities will eventually stabilize, making nearly inevitable the end of the romantic phase of the relationship". (Livingston, 1980, p. 145–146)

Other psychological explanations have expanded in particular ways on the habituation notion. For example, Aronson and Linder (1965) argued that satisfaction declines in long-term relationships because we habituate to the other's positive evaluation of self, so that the net gain in self-esteem that other can provide decreases over time. Another habituation-type explanation comes from psychodynamic theories of idealization, which discuss the decline in terms of increasing familiarity, making it more difficult to project an all-loving parent (Bergler, 1946), ego-ideal (Reik, 1944), or anima/animus (Jung, 1959) onto the other in the relationship.

The Self-Expansion View of the Decline in Satisfaction

The self-expansion model builds on the basic habituation idea by specifying what about the other and the relationship become decreasingly novel (the loss of new information to be included in the self) and why habituation leads to dissatisfaction (the decline in the highly desired rapid rate of self-expansion, in this case associated with the relationship). Thus, the model provides a more precise and motivationally-based explanation for the role of habituation in relationships. Further, it has made an important and successful prediction: after the initial relationship period, increased time spent together, which ought to increase habituation and decrease satisfaction, will *increase* satisfaction if the time is spent doing self-expanding activities together. The reason is that once the other is familiar (so that further inclusion of other is not a major source of new expansion), then if the couple engages together in self-expanding activities (which are now activities other than getting to know each other), the highly desired self-expansion experience remains associated with the relationship.

The self-expansion model is still consistent with the more elaborated versions of the habituation idea just discussed. For example, idealization is made possible, Aron and Aron (1986) argued, because a particular other is seen as offering a potential for very great expansion (see also, Brehm, 1988, who expressed a similar view). We would emphasize, however, that the self-expansion model implies limits to the idealization and self-esteem explanations. When couples engage in self-expanding activities together, while this enhances relationship satisfaction, it probably does not usually make the other highly idealized again or provide new gains in self-esteem, suggesting that simple association of the relationship with self-expansion is the basis of or acts in addition to these other processes during the original attraction process.

Because of the theoretical importance of the hypothesized consequences of sharing exciting activities, we will discuss this process in some detail.

The Effect of Shared Participation in Activities that Are Associated with Self-Expansion: The General Principle

Studies consistently find wide variation in marital satisfaction, even after the initial phase, with some couples even reporting very high levels of passionate love after 25 or more years of marriage (Traupmann & Hatfield, 1981; Tucker

& Aron, 1993). As we read the literature, it seems that at least some among the more satisfied couples have found ways to associate their relationship with self-expansion by participating in more expanding activities together.

North American couples clearly consider spending time together, regardless of the type of activity, to be an important maintenance strategy (Baxter & Dindia, 1990; Dindia & Baxter, 1987). Further, intuition suggests that couples often do adopt this strategy of engaging jointly in expanding activities—traditionally they build a home and a family (although in U.S. culture these goals are not always shared or central, or may be a source of stress and too much expansion, as suggested by the apparently negative typical impact of the birth of the first child; e.g., Tucker & Aron, 1993). Other examples are causes taken on jointly, businesses run together, and shared professional or recreational activities. Presumably, these shared self-expanding experiences provide relationship satisfaction because the experience or feeling of self-expansion becomes associated with the partner and the relationship, an idea borrowed from learning theory. If self-expanding activities are reinforcing, then through stimulus generalization, when couples engage in such activities together, they experience reinforcement of both the behaviors involved in that activity and also the behavior of staying near the other and any other behaviors that maintain the relationship. The point is that the self-expansion model contributes an explanation for why certain kinds of activities would be especially rewarding: They arise as a result of or are associated with expansion of the self.

What distinguishes an activity that is self-expanding? We think that there are two key aspects, novelty and arousal. Participating in a novel activity expands the self by providing new information and experiences. In general, novel experiences are also arousing (Berlyne, 1960), but arousing experiences that are not novel, such as physical exertion or high sensory stimulation loads, are probably also self-expanding to some extent in that high but tolerable arousal of any kind seems to create a sense of alert expansion and competence. In terms of how self-expanding activities are recognized, we have assumed that the most likely ordinary-language label is "exciting," since this term covers both arousal and novelty. And, as noted in the research below, it is precisely novel and/or arousing activities that couples report when asked about the kinds of exciting activities in which they engage.

Survey Studies Linking Shared Expanding Activities with Satisfaction

There is substantial evidence that, in general, time spent together is correlated with marital satisfaction. For example, significant associations were found in five separate U.S. studies conducted in the last 30 years employing probability samples (Kilbourne, Howell, & England, 1990; Kingston & Nock, 1987; Orden & Bradburn, 1968; Orthner, 1975; White, 1983). None of these studies on time together and marital satisfaction looked specifically at participation in activities that would be classified as self-expanding. However, findings regarding different categories of activities suggest that the important ones may be those that are self-expanding. Several studies (Holman & Jacquart, 1988; Kingston & Nock, 1987; Orden & Bradburn, 1968; Orthner, 1975) reported substantially stronger correlations with marital satisfaction for activities that were intensely interactive versus passive, parallel, or merely in the company of others. Hill (1988), in finding a strong overall link between shared activities and marital stability, reported the strongest effects for shared "recreational activities," all of which were comparatively active or involved some novelty (such as "outdoor activities, active sports, card games, and travel," p. 447).

There are also some correlational data focusing directly on the link between "exciting" activities and satisfaction. McKenna (1989), in a study of respondents to a questionnaire printed in a newspaper, found a strong positive correlation ($r = 0.52$) between scores on a standard marital satisfaction scale and responses to the item "How exciting are the things you do together with your partner?" Further, the link between satisfaction and exciting activities was mediated by reported boredom with the relationship. Finally, there was a clear interaction between exciting activities and length of marriage in predicting marital satisfaction, such that those together more than 3 years had a correlation of .27, while those together a longer period had a correlation of .62. This interaction is important theoretically since in the early phases the relationship's development by itself should provide the partners all the self-expansion each needs or can tolerate. Thus, it is only after this initial phase that one would expect any substantial impact from participating together in self-expanding activities.

In another study (McNeal & Aron, 1995), members of dating and married couples attending night classes completed a standard relationship satisfaction scale and responded to an extensive rating of the activities in which they had participated with their partner in the last 30 days. Over all subjects, there was a moderate correlation of .29 between number of exciting activities engaged in with partner and relationship satisfaction. However, once again there was the interaction such that the correlation for married couples was .48; for dating couples, .08. Also once again, the exciting-activities-satisfaction link was clearly mediated by reported relationship boredom. All of the above results remained essentially unchanged when controlling for overall number of activities (of all kinds) participated in with partner. This study also included some items assessing opportunities to participate in shared exciting activities with the partner. Analyses of the pattern of results involving these measures was consistent with the hypothesized causal direction of exciting activities affecting satisfaction (and inconsistent with the reverse).

Finally, this study provided an indication of the types of shared activities perceived to be exciting. Consistent with our association of self-expansion with arousal and novelty, the exciting activities tend to be of two types—those with high levels of physical activity (e.g., bicycling, dancing, riding horses, roller skating, hiking) and those emphasizing newness or exoticness (e.g., attending musical concerts and plays; studying nature and bird watching).

Studies of Arousal/Unusualness and Attraction

Another relevant line of research focuses on the link between initial attraction to a potential romantic partner and arousal, or being together under unusual or challenging circumstances (Aron, 1970). Research in this area has mainly been inspired by a study (Dutton & Aron, 1974) in which subjects met an attractive confederate in a novel and arousing versus a more common and non-arousing situation (a suspension bridge vs a footbridge). The results were that there was greater attraction in the novel/arousing situation. A number of further experiments have examined the connection between arousal and romantic attraction (Allen, Kenrick, Linder, & McCall, 1989; Dutton & Aron, 1989; Riordan & Tedeschi, 1983; White, Fishbein, & Rutstein, 1981; White & Kight, 1984), generally with subjects meeting an attractive stranger in arousing versus non-arousing circumstances and a measure being taken of their attraction to the stranger. The arousing situations have included humorous or violent films and physical exertion. In most studies, romantic attraction is significantly greater under arousal conditions. Further, Aron, Dutton, Aron, and Iverson (1989) found that one-third to two-thirds of college students' accounts of falling in love included prominent mentions of circumstances that could be coded as either "arousing" or "unusual".

Researchers have suggested a variety of processes underlying the arousal/attraction connection: (a) misattribution of the arousal from its true source to the attractive stranger (Dutton & Aron, 1974, 1989; White et al., 1981, White & Kight, 1984), (b) the object of attraction being associated with a decrease of aversive overarousal (Kenrick & Cialdini, 1977; Riordan & Tedeschi, 1983), and (c) arousal facilitating the most available response in a person's hierarchy (Allen et al., 1989). The self-expansion model argues that arousal is associated with the highly desired state of self-expansion, as are attractive others, and in this case all three are present at once and so all these elements are associated with each other. Further, the model suggests that even if the experience is not highly arousing but is nevertheless novel, the effect should still occur. (This latter idea, though not yet tested directly in the experimental research, is consistent with the studies examining reports of falling-in-love experiences.)

Experimental Studies with Ongoing Relationships

Reissman, Aron, and Bergen (1993) randomly assigned volunteer married couples to one of three groups. Those in the first group, the Exciting-Activities Group, were instructed to spend 1–1/2 hours each week, over a period of 10 weeks, doing one activity from a list of activities both partners had rated as exciting on independently completed prestudy questionnaires. Couples in the second group, the Pleasant-Activities Group, were assigned activities both had rated as pleasant. A third group of couples served as a waiting-list, no-activity control group. The Exciting-Activities Group, compared to the Pleasant-Activity Group, showed a significantly greater increase, of moderate effect size, in relationship satisfaction over the 10 weeks. There was no significant difference for the other planned orthogonal contrast, comparing the control group that spent no extra time together to the two experimental groups taken together. In other words, just spending time together did not increase satisfaction. But doing something exciting, and therefore presumably self-expanding, did increase satisfaction.

Because there are other possible interpretations of the Reissman et al. findings, Norman and Aron (1995) developed a laboratory paradigm for studying the phenomenon. The paradigm enables various aspects of the situation to be systematically manipulated, thereby permitting tests of potential mediating mechanisms. The approach is basically an extension of the arousal-and-romantic-attraction paradigm (e.g., Dutton & Aron, 1974). In the Norman and Aron paradigm, couples in ongoing relationships participate in what they believe is a laboratory evaluation that involves completing some questionnaires, taking part together in a task in which their interaction is videotaped, and then completing more questionnaires. In actuality, the questionnaires are pretest and posttest measures of relationship satisfaction and the task is the experimentally manipulated independent variable of arousal and novelty.

In the first study to use this approach, the experimental task was manipulated to be either arousing and novel or to be sedate and boring. The results were consistent with predictions—significantly greater increases in satisfaction for the arousing/novel-activities group—and this increase was significantly greater for those who had been together a longer period of time. Subsequent studies (which are now in progress) use this paradigm to sort out systematically the possible alternative explanations for the effect, such as reattribution of arousal, cooperation, success, negative effects of boredom, and so forth.

THE SECOND OF THE TWO KEY PROCESSES: PERSONAL RELATIONSHIPS AS INCLUDING EACH OTHER IN EACH OTHER'S SELF

Related Theorizing

The notion that in a relationship each is included in each other's self is consistent with a wide variety of current social psychological ideas about relationships. For example, Reis and Shaver (1988) identified intimacy as mainly a process of an escalating reciprocity of self-disclosure in which each individual feels his or her innermost self validated, understood, and cared for by the other. Wegner (1980) suggested that empathy may "stem in part from a basic confusion between ourselves and others" (p. 133), which he proposed may arise from an initial lack of differentiation between self and caregiver in infancy (Hoffman, 1976). Indeed, perhaps the most prominent idea in social psychology directly related to the present theme is the "unit relation," a fundamental concept in Heider's (1958) influential cognitive account of inter-personal relations. This idea is also related to Ickes, Tooke, Stinson, Baker, and Bissonnette's (1988) idea of "intersubjectivity"—which Ickes and his colleagues made vivid by citing Merleau-Ponty's (1945) description of a close relationship as a "double being" and Schutz' (1970) reference to two people "living in each other's subjective contexts of meaning" (p. 167).

Several currently active lines of theory-based social psychology research focus on closely related themes. For example, in a series of experimental and correlational studies, Tesser (1988) has shown that a relationship partner's achievement, so long as it is not in a domain that threatens the self by creating a negative social comparison, is "reflected" by the self (i.e., the self feels pride in the achievement as if it were the self's). Another relevant line of work focuses on what is called "fraternal relative deprivation" (Runciman, 1966), in which the relative disadvantage of the group to which self belongs affects the self as if it were the self's own deprivation. Yet another example is work arising from social identity theory (Tajfel & Turner, 1979) which posits that our identity is structured from membership in various social groups. In a related line of thinking, Brewer (1991) presents arguments and evidence that people seek an optimal level of distinctiveness from others: They identify with groups to some extent, but are uncomfortable when too closely identified with that group (though the seeking of differentiation from one group typically involves identification with a different group).

In the field of marketing, Belk (1988) has proposed a notion of ownership in which "we regard our possessions as part of ourselves" (p. 139), an idea that has been the subject of considerable theoretical discussion and several studies. For example, Sivadas and Machleit (1994) found that items measuring an object's "incorporation into self" (items such as "helps me achieve my iden-tity" and "is part of who I am") form a separate factor from items assessing the object's importance or relevance to the self. Ahuvia (1993) has attempted to integrate Belk's self-extension approach with the self-expansion model and has proposed that processes hypothesized in the domain of personal relation-ships also apply to relations to physical objects and experiences. In a series of interviews, Ahuvia showed that people sometimes describe their "love" of things in much the same way as they describe their love of relationship part-ners, that they often consider this "real" love, and that they treat these love objects as very much a part of their identity. At the same time, as with human relationships, there is often a sense of autonomous value to the object and even a sense of being controlled by or at the mercy of the object. These ideas about including the owned object in the self are also related to the notion of relationship as each "possessing" the other (e.g., Reik, 1944).

The notion of relationship as an overlap of selves has been popular more generally among psychologists and sociologists, starting at least with James (1890). For example, Bakan (1966) wrote about "communion" in the context of his expansion on Buber's (1937) "I–Thou" relationship. Jung (1959) em-phasized the role of relationship partners as providing or developing otherwise unavailable aspects of the psyche, so leading to greater wholeness. Maslow took it for granted that "beloved people can be incorporated into the self" (1967, p. 103). And from a symbolic interactionist perspective, McCall (1974) described "attachment" as "incorporation of . . . [the other's] actions and reactions . . . into the content of one's various conceptions of the self" (p. 219).

Research on the Perception of Including Other in the Self

One line of relevant research focuses on the extent to which people *view* relationships as connected or overlapping selves. In one recent study, Sedikides, Olsen, and Reis (1993) found that people spontaneously encode information about other people in terms of their relationships with each other, grouping them together by their relationships. This suggests that cognitive representations of other individuals are in a sense overlapped or at least tied together as a function of these others being perceived as being in close relationships with each other.

Focusing on the issue of the perceived overlap of one's self with a relationship partner, Aron et al. (1992) asked subjects to describe their closest relationship using the Inclusion of Other in the Self (IOS) Scale (see Figure 6.1), which consists of a series of overlapping circles from which one is asked to select the pair that best describes one's relationship with a particular person. The scale appears to have levels of reliability, as well as of discriminant, convergent, and predictive validity, that match or exceed other measures of closeness—measures which are typically more complex and lengthy. (For example, the correlation between a score on this test and whether the subject remained in a romantic relationship 3 months later was .46.) Further, most measures of closeness seem to fall into one of two factors: they measure either *feelings of closeness* or *behaviors associated with closeness*. The IOS Scale, however, loads, to some extent, on both of these factors. This suggests that the IOS Scale may be tapping the core meaning of closeness and not merely a particular aspect of it.

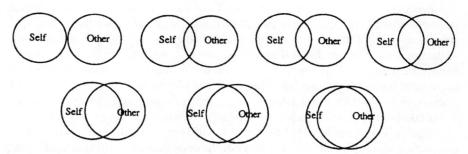

Figure 6.1   The inclusion of Other in the Self (IOS) Scale. Respondents are instructed to select the picture that best describes their relationship. (From Aron, Aron, & Smollan, 1992. Reproduced with permission)

Agnew, Van Lange, Rusbult and Langston (1998), in a study of dating couples, found that scores on the IOS Scale correlated highly with a variety of relationship measures, such as satisfaction, commitment, investment in the relationship, and centrality of the relationship. Most interesting, the IOS Scale correlated moderately with proportion of first-person plural pronouns ("we" and "us") the dating partners used when speaking about their relationship, a finding that Agnew et al. took as an indication of what they called "cognitive interdependence."

Finally, Pipp, Shaver, Jennings, Lamborn, and Fischer (1985) also used overlapping circle diagrams as part of a measure of closeness. They had adolescents draw a picture of two circles, one representing the self and one a parent, "in relation to each other as you believe best illustrates your relationship with that parent . . ." (p. 993). Among other findings, Pipp et al. reported that perceived closeness and the amount of overlap of the circles were both strongly related to scale ratings of love and friendship.

Research on Including Other's Perspective in the Self

A significant body of social psychology research over the last 25 years has focused on differences in actor versus observer perspectives in attributional processes, beginning with the pioneering work of Jones and Nisbett (1971). In the context of the self-expansion model, to the extent a particular person is included in the self, the difference between self's and that particular person's perspective should be reduced. Several studies support this conclusion. Using methods adapted from the original Jones and Nisbett (1971) work, Nisbett, Caputo, Legant, and Marecek (1973, Study 3) found that the longer people had been in a relationship with a close friend the less willing they were to make dispositional attributions about the friend. Similarly, Goldberg (1981) found that subjects made fewer dispositional attributions for people they have spent more time with, compared to people they have spent less time with.

Other research has followed this same theme of examining actor-observer differences in attribution but using different approaches. Prentice (1990) had subjects describe various persons in specific situations and found least overlap between situations for descriptions of self, next least for a familiar other, and most for an unfamiliar other. This finding suggests that people are making situational attributions for self and those close to self but regard less familiar others in terms that are not differentiated by situation. Using yet another approach, Sande, Goethals, and Radloff (1988) found that self, and then liked friends, and then disliked friends were progressively less likely to be attributed *both* poles of pairs of opposite traits (for example, "serious-carefree"). The point here is that for self—and those liked by self—behaviors can vary, even to the extent of representing opposites, according to the situation. But for those distant from self, a single-sided trait description (that is, a dispositional attribution) is quite adequate. Aron, Aron, Tudor, and Nelson (1991, introduction to Study 2) replicated Sande et al's procedure, but compared different degrees of *closeness* (as opposed to liking versus disliking). They found choices of both traits were most frequent for self, next for best friend, and least for a friendly acquaintance.

Yet another approach relevant to including the other's perspective in the self is based on an adaptation of a research paradigm developed by Lord (1980, 1987). Lord presented subjects with a series of concrete nouns, for each of which they were instructed to form as vivid and interesting a mental image as possible of a target person *interacting* with whatever the noun referred to. The target person was sometimes self and sometimes someone else, such as Johnny Carson. On a free recall task afterwards, Lord found *fewer* words were recalled which were imaged with self than which were imaged with the other target person. He interpreted these results in terms of a figure-ground difference between one's experience of self and other when acting in the world. Because self, being ground, is less vivid than other, imaging things interacting with the self is less enhancing to memory than imaging them interacting with someone other than self.

From the perspective of the self-expansion model, if this figure-ground difference represents a different way of understanding and appreciating the world, then if other is included in one's inner world, other should become more like ground and less like figure—that is, more like the self. Based on this reasoning, Aron, Aron, Tudor, and Nelson (1991, Experiment 2) replicated Lord's procedures, again using as target persons self and a prominent entertainment personality, but also added a third target, a close other, the subject's mother. Consistent with predictions, recall was greatest for words imaged with the entertainment personality and much less for both those imaged with self and those imaged with mother. This result was also replicated in a new sample, substituting friend of mother for the entertainment personality (to deal with the possibility that entertainment personalities are simply especially vivid images). In the replication, subjects were also asked to rate their similarity, closeness, and familiarity with their mother. The difference of recall for words imaged with mother's friend minus recall for words imaged with mother (presumably indicating the degree to which other is included in the self) correlated .56 with ratings of closeness to mother, but only .13 with similarity and .16 with familiarity.

Research on Processing Information about Other as if Other Were One's Self

Another influential general body of research in social cognition has focused on the unique role of self-representations, going back to the pioneering articles by Markus (1977) and Rogers, Kuiper, and Kirker (1977). For example, consider the issue of self-relevant information processing (the so-called "self-reference effect," that information processing and memory is enhanced for information related to the self). If, in a close relationship, each includes other in the self, then any advantage for self-relevant information over other-relevant information should be lessened when other is in a close relationship with self—a pattern supported by several studies. In one such study, Bower and Gilligan (1979) found little difference in incidental memory for adjectives which subjects had earlier judged for their relevance to their own life or their mother's life. In another study, Keenan and Baillet (1980) had subjects indicate whether trait adjectives were true of a particular person. The persons were self, best friend, parent, friend, teacher, favorite TV character, and the U.S. president. They found a clear linear trend from self through president for time to make decision and number of adjectives recognized later. Similarly, Prentice (1990) showed that both the content and organization of self-descriptions and other-descriptions tended to follow a pattern in which familiar others were intermediate between self and unfamiliar others.

A related approach focuses on the idea that if being in a close relationship means other is included in the self, then to the extent one is in a close relationships with a person there should be a tendency to confuse traits of self with traits of that person. To test this idea, Aron et al. (1991, Experiment 3) had married subjects first rate a series of trait adjectives for their descriptiveness of themselves and their spouse. After a distracting intermediate task they made a series of "me–not-me" reaction time choices to these trait words. The prediction was that there would be most confusion—and thus longer response latencies—for trait words that were different between self and spouse. (That is, the confusion is hypothesized to arise because one is asked here to rate these traits as true or false for *self*; but if other is part of self, when self and other differ on a trait, the difference is a discrepancy between two parts of "self.") The results were as predicted—longer response times when the trait was different between self and spouse. The same pattern was obtained in a follow-up study. Also, in the follow-up study, subjects completed the IOS Scale, which correlated .59 with the difference between the average response time to spouse-different words minus the average response time to spouse-similar words.

Smith and Henry (1996) have successfully applied this method to demonstrate that even members of ingroups with which we only moderately identify are included in the self. In their study subjects were consistently faster at deciding whether a trait was true or false of self when the trait had been previously rated as similarly true or false of a typical ingroup person (students with like majors) as compared to the situation when the trait had been rated differently than self. However, decision time was unrelated to whether the trait had been rated as similarly true or false to a typical outgroup member (students with different majors).

Finally, Omoto and Gunn (1994), found a self-other confusion effect for episodic memory. In their study, subjects paired with friends versus subjects paired with strangers were more likely to mix up whether they or their partner had earlier solved particular anagram tasks. Although the focus of their study was on other issues, these data would seem to suggest that in a personal relationship identities are sufficiently intermixed that we can actually confuse biographical memories of self and other.

SOME ADDITIONAL IMPLICATIONS OF THE SELF-EXPANSION MODEL RELEVANT TO RELATIONSHIPS

In this section we consider the implications of the self-expansion model for three other relationship-relevant issues: selectivity in initial attraction, motivations for unrequited love, and the effects of falling in love on the self.

Initial Attraction

Presuming that self-expansion is a major motivator in general, then it is reasonable to suppose that, other things being equal, when selecting among potential close relationship partners, one will be most attracted to the person who offers the greatest potential for self-expansion via a relationship with that person. Thus, following a kind of value-expectancy approach, we have reasoned that attraction to a particular other should be affected by two key factors:

1. The perceived degree of potential expansion of self that is possible through a close relationship with a particular other.
2. The perceived probability of actually obtaining that expansion with the other—that is, the probability that one could actually form and maintain a close relationship with this particular other.

The first factor can be summarized as "desirability" (or reward value); the second, as "probability" (or likelihood of achieving that reward value). As noted, this analysis is basically an application of classic value-expectancy analysis (e.g., Rotter, 1954) to our notion that relationships provide rewards by enhancing self through including other in self.

The delineation of these two factors has been useful (Aron & Aron, 1986) in making sense of longstanding findings in the attraction literature that had previously seemed paradoxical. For example, based on the extensive work of Byrne (1971) and others (e.g., Newcomb, 1956), a fundamental tenet of the social psychology of attraction had been that similarity leads to attraction. However, Walster and Walster (1963) found that under conditions in which self is led to believe that other likes self, there is actually a preference for dissimilar partners. In the same vein, Jones, Bell, and Aronson (1972) found that when self is led to believe other likes self, the preference for those with similar attitudes is eliminated.

Although this exception to the general rule that similars attract was long known, there was no general explanation for it. (Murstein's, 1971, commentary on the attraction literature at that time did hint at a process similar to that described here, but it was not elaborated in any detail.) Applying the self-expansion model of attraction, these results make sense. Perceived similarity serves as an indication that a relationship could develop and be maintained.

But if, as in the studies just cited, the probability of forming a relationship is made highly likely by knowing other likes self, then further probability information (provided by similarity information) adds no incremental benefit. Rather, it is now dissimilarity that enhances attraction, by increasing the potential for self-expansion—the more different a person is, the more new perspectives the person can add to the self.

Using a variety of methods and samples, researchers (Aron et al., 1989; Aron & Rodriguez, 1992; Sprecher, Aron, Hatfield, Cortese, Potapova, & Levitskaya, 1994) have consistently found the same two near-universal precursors to falling in love—physical and personal attractiveness and discovering other likes the self. These precursors, which are consistent with the self-expansion model (i.e., they represent desirability and probability), are also consistent with other theoretical perspectives. However, an important contribution of the self-expansion model is its metaphor of expansion, which does seem to explain well the counter-intuitive appeal of opposites in combination with similarity.

Unrequited Love

Thinking about unrequited love in the context of the self-expansion framework, Aron, Aron, and Allen (1998) postulated a three-factor motivational model for unrequited love. The first two factors are the same as in the general attraction model: desirability (perceived potential expansion of self through a close relationship with this particular person) and probability (perceived probability of forming and maintaining a close relationship with this person). Desirability is probably the main element, in the sense that if a relationship with other is seen as extremely valuable, then one might be attracted even if the probability is low. It is a bit like betting on the lottery—small odds but big winnings. An emphasis on probability suggests a second way that unrequited love might arise: Sometimes individuals may initially feel quite certain that their love is reciprocated but then later discover it is not; however, by then they are already in love with the other.

A third path to this state is more specifically inspired by the self-expansion model, and involves wanting the expansion associated with enacting the culturally scripted role of lover, but *not* necessarily wanting a relationship. When this factor of desiring the state of being in love is foremost, unrequited love can be highly rewarding, but only from the viewpoint of self-expansion.

To test this three-factor motivational model, Aron et al. (1995) developed a psychometrically adequate questionnaire measure of the three key motivational variables, then administered this questionnaire to a new large sample. The first and most important prediction in this research was that each of these three motivational factors would significantly and independently predict the intensity of unrequited love. This prediction was supported.

This same research also examined a set of subsidiary hypotheses having to do with the interaction of the different motivational factors with attachment styles (Hazan & Shaver, 1987). In the context of the self-expansion model, we interpreted the attachment-theory work as suggesting that early experiences shape one of the more important channels through which people seek to expand—through relationships. Those who were regularly successful in their early attempts to expand through interpersonal closeness become "securely attached," those who were regularly unsuccessful become "avoidants," and those who had inconsistent experiences become "anxious/ambivalents." Two key predictions, which were supported, were (a) that there would be an interaction in which desirability was most important in predicting intensity for anxious ambivalents compared to its importance among the other two styles, and (b) that the desirability of the state of unrequited love would be most important for avoidants, compared to its importance for the other two styles. (A third prediction, which did not reach significance, was that probability would be most important for the secures.)

Effect of a Close Relationship on Expanding the Self

Yet another implication of the model is that developing a relationship expands the self by including other in the self (as well as in other ways associated with being in a relationship). If in a close relationship other is included in the self, then when one enters a close relationship the self should be expanded to include aspects of the other.

In one relevant study, Sedikides (personal communication, October, 1992) collected self-descriptions of subjects who were or were not currently in a close relationship. These self-descriptions were analyzed to determine the number of different domains of the self they included. Consistent with this prediction (based on the self-expansion model), Sedikides found that the self-descriptions of people in relationships included terms representing significantly more domains of the self.

Following up on this idea, in a longitudinal study Aron, Paris, and Aron (1995) tested 325 students five times, once every 2–1/2 weeks over a 10-week period. At each testing, the subjects listed as many self-descriptive words or phrases as came to mind during a 3-minute period in response to the question, "Who are you today?" and answered a number of other questions which included items indicating whether the subject had fallen in love since the last testing. As predicted, there was a significantly greater increase in the diversity of self-content domains in the self-descriptions from before to after falling in love than was found for average changes from before to after other testing sessions and also when compared to typical testing-to-testing changes for subjects who did not fall in love. A second study, with a new sample of 529 subjects, assessed the subjects' self-esteem and self-efficacy every 2–1/2 weeks. As predicted, there was a significantly greater increase in these variables from before to after falling in love than was found for average changes from before to after other testing sessions and also when compared to typical testing-to-testing changes for subjects who did not fall in love. In both of these studies, the effects on the self were maintained when measures of mood change were controlled statistically.

ADDITIONAL IMPLICATIONS AND CONCLUSION

The self-expansion model offers ways of looking at relationship phenomena that have only begun to be examined with the lines of research discussed here. For example, the model has implications for breakups and loss: The degree of psychological distress should be predictable from the degree of previously existing overlap of self and other. Similarly, commitment may be enhanced by fear of de-expansion (or experienced de-expansion when some moves toward separation are tried), a process related to Rusbult's (1983) investment model of commitment. That is, one can consider inclusion of each other in each other's self an investment that would be lost in a relationship breakup. Another set of implications relates to effects on relationships of the interaction between self-expansion processes and *individual differences* in such variables as boredom susceptibility and desired level of arousal, or *situational differences* such as degree of expansion experienced in other domains of life or whether there needs to be the predicted alternations in expansion and integration. Another potentially fruitful application would be to other types of relationships, such as therapist-client. Yet another is the possibility of applying findings in this area to other areas of social psychology such as intergroup relations, altruism, or aggression.

On the other hand, even in the areas in which there have been a number of relevant studies, in most cases data are preliminary in the sense that some alternative explanations have not been ruled out and only limited populations have been studied. Perhaps what we have at this point can best be described as a demonstration of the potential of the model's metaphors for inspiring an interest in relationship phenomena that might not otherwise have become the subject of systematic research attention—phenomena such as participation in exciting activities and self-other confusions. And we hope that the model's metaphors will serve to continue to generate ways of thinking about relationships that do not entirely overlap with those embedded in other relationship models.

Chapter 7

Self-presentational Perspectives on Personal Relationships

Mark R. Leary

Wake Forest University, Winston-Salem, NC, USA

and

Rowland S. Miller

Sam Houston State University, Huntsville, TX, USA

Images matter. We may maintain that a person's image is superficial and bemoan the fact that people attach too much importance to how they are regarded by others. We may try to emphasize personal substance over public appearance in our own affairs, and we may even discourage our children from being concerned about what other people think of them. Yet, deep down, we know the truth: Images *do* matter. The perceptions that other people have of our personalities, abilities, and motives not only influence whether they begin to interact with us, but how they feel about us and whether they interact with us again. Whether we like it or not, their impressions of who we are and what we are like help to determine how they treat us and, thus, affect many of our outcomes in life. The nature and quality of our social lives are affected daily by the images that other people have of us.

The Social Psychology of Personal Relationships.
Edited by William Ickes and Steve Duck. © 2000 John Wiley & Sons Ltd.

The impressions that people have of their relational partners—whether those partners are family members, lovers, friends, co-workers, or other colleagues—are particularly important. Whether or not their impressions are accurate, people's images of one another fundamentally shape the nature of the relationship between them. As a result, whatever else they may be doing, people can rarely afford to disregard how others view them. Further, they will often have reason to behave in ways that will convey desired impressions of themselves to others and prevent others from forming undesired impressions. Of course, theorists and researchers have long been interested in relational partners' perceptions of one another and their relationship, and in the effects of those perceptions on the relationship itself (e.g., Murray, Holmes, & Griffin, 1996b; Sillars et al., 1994; Van Lange & Rusbult, 1995). Yet surprisingly little consideration has been given to the fact that people sometimes strive to shape relational partners' perceptions of them to their own ends.

This chapter will explore self-presentational processes that occur in personal relationships. After a brief conceptual introduction, we examine three factors that influence the degree to which people seek to manage others' impressions in a particular encounter or relationship. We then turn to situational and personal factors that influence the nature of the impressions that people try to create. The final section of the chapter explores people's occasional efforts to manage the images of their relational partners and of the relationship itself.

THE NATURE OF SELF-PRESENTATION

Self-presentation (also called impression management) refers to the various processes by which people try to control the impressions that other people form of them. Theory and research have explored the tactics that people use to manage their impressions, the features of the social context that influence people's self-presentations, personality characteristics that moderate self-presentational behaviors, and the effects of people's self-presentations on others' impressions of them (for reviews, see Baumeister, 1982a; Leary, 1995; Schlenker, 1980).

People try to control the impressions that others have of them in a variety of ways. Explicit verbal claims about one's characteristics are the most direct means, but people often employ more subtle tactics as well. They convey impressions through the topics they choose to talk about and the particular attitudes they express. They alter their appearance, choosing clothing, hairstyle, and make-up to convey desired impressions, and they try to enact selected nonverbal behaviors involving emotional expressions, body language, and gaze. People also use "props" to create desired impressions, displaying personal possessions that show them to be a particular kind of person. Almost any behavior can be used to convey desired impressions of oneself to other people. (See Leary, 1995, for a full discussion of self-presentational tactics.)

Obviously, not all behavior is self-presentational. An action should be regarded as self-presentational only if it is motivated, at least in part, by the individual's desire to make a specific impression on one or more other people. Consider, for example, the simple behavior of placing a particular magazine on the coffee table in one's living room. This action has no self-presentational basis in many instances; one may put the magazine on the table simply to keep it off the floor. However, the same action would be self-presentational if one hopes to convey a certain impression. For example, a man who has invited a woman to his house for dinner may display copies of *National Geographic* or *Atlantic Monthly* in the living room, but relegate his issues of *Guns and Ammo* and *Professional Wrestling Weekly* to a box in a closet.

Nor are people's self-presentations necessarily deceptive. Of course, people do occasionally lie, trying to make impressions that they know are inconsistent with how they see themselves (and, sometimes, with objective evidence). However, self-presentation more often merely involves a tactical choice of which aspects of oneself to show to other people. In interactions at work, a woman may seek to be seen as conscientious and hard-working whereas, with her boyfriend, she may try to be perceived as kind and fun-loving. If she is successful, the different audiences may have somewhat different impressions of her; nevertheless, in both instances, the fostered impressions may accurately reflect her personal characteristics. She may indeed be conscientious at work and playful at home, with those who know her in those different settings forming accurate, but incomplete judgments of her.

The strategic effort to influence what others think of us is especially consequential in close relationships. Not only is positive regard from a close partner exceptionally valuable (see Baumeister & Leary, 1995), but the impressions that intimates hold of us have important effects on what we think of ourselves (Wood, 1995b). Close partners are some of our most influential, compelling critics (see Baldwin, 1994), and when they find our self-presentations convincing, we are likely to internalize those images and incorporate them (if we haven't already) into our own self-concepts (e.g., Schlenker, Dlugolecki, & Doherty, 1994). A husband who, for whatever reasons, tries to appear dominant and controlling with his new wife—and who finds her accepting and respectful of his assertion and authority—may gradually come to think of himself as a really tough guy. Indeed, throughout our lives, there may be no more important images we construct than those that we believe are affirmed and denied by our partners in close relationships.

Self-presentation and Self-disclosure

Thus, it is a bit surprising that the scientific study of self-presentation has emerged along two relatively independent lines, neither of which has adequately examined self-presentation within the context of lasting relationships. On one hand, the vast majority of studies of self-presentation per se have examined encounters with strangers or acquaintances, and only recently have investigators begun to explore self-presentations among friends (e.g., Leary, Nezlek et al., 1994; Tice, Butler, Muraven, & Stillwell, 1995).

On the other hand, researchers who have studied **self-disclosure** have been very interested in personal relationships, but self-disclosure reflects only a narrow range of self-presentational processes. As usually defined, self-disclosure refers to information that people *directly* and *verbally* reveal about themselves to others (Derlega, Metts, Petronio, & Margulis, 1993)—what self-presentation researchers have called self-descriptions (Leary, 1995; Schlenker, 1980). Thus, self-disclosure studies have not dealt extensively either with indirect verbal means of conveying impressions of oneself (such as statements about other people or choices of conversation topics) or nonverbal tactics (such as the tactical use of facial expressions or physical props). Furthermore, self-disclosure has typically been viewed as an *accurate* characterization of oneself (or at least as information that the discloser believes is accurate); the term "disclosure" itself connotes revealing something that is true. Self-disclosure researchers have been far more interested in truthful disclosure than in the instances in which people distort the truth about themselves in small and large ways.

Oddly, despite their close conceptual connection, researchers interested in self-presentation and self-disclosure have paid scant attention to one another's work. As cases in point, Derlega and Berg's (1987) edited volume on self-disclosure contains only one mention of the term "self-presentation", and Leary's (1995) book on self-presentation contains only one mention of "self-disclosure". In part, the lack of connections between these literatures reflects their origins. Interest in self-presentation emerged along two fronts, one in sociology (Goffman, 1959) and the other in experimental social psychology (Jones, 1964). Investigators in both areas were more interested in self-presentation in isolated interpersonal encounters than in the context of ongoing relationships (see Duck, 1986). The study of self-disclosure, in contrast, emerged from humanistic psychology (Jourard, 1971; Rogers, 1970) and focused on the role of self-disclosure in fostering and maintaining genuine human relationships. Social psychological work on self-disclosure focused on relationships from its very beginnings (e.g., Altman & Taylor, 1973; Cozby, 1973).

In addition, studies of self-presentation and self-disclosure have emphasized different processes. Self-presentation researchers have tended to focus either on the role that self- presentational motives play in behavior and emotion (such as attitude change, embarrassment, nonverbal behavior, and group processes) or on the factors that determine the kinds of impressions people try to create (Leary, 1995; Schlenker, 1980). Self-disclosure researchers, on the other hand, have tended to emphasize the consequences of self-disclosure for others' reactions to the individual, the development of relationships, and the discloser's psychological well-being (Berg & Derlega, 1987; Pennebaker, 1997).

Our discussion of self-presentational processes in personal relationships will draw from both the self-presentation and self-disclosure literatures, but it will be cast within the broader self-presentational framework. The organization for the following two sections of the chapter is guided by the two-component model of impression management. Leary and Kowalski (1990) suggested that self-presentational behaviors are the product of two distinct sets of processes. One is the set of processes that motivate people to try to control others' impressions of them (*impression motivation*) and the other is the set of processes that are involved in their decisions about a particular image to convey (*impression construction*).

IMPRESSION MOTIVATION IN RELATIONSHIPS

Self-presentational motivation waxes and wanes as people go about their social lives. In some instances, people are very attuned to how they are being perceived by others and are highly motivated to control those perceptions. At other times, they are relatively unconcerned with how they are being regarded and are less motivated to regulate their public images. Thus, the first question to be addressed is: What determines the degree to which people desire to manage the impressions other people have of them? In this section, we will discuss three factors that influence impression motivation: (1) the extent to which a person's impressions influence the attainment of his or her goals; (2) the value of the goals that may be affected by the person's images; and (3) discrepancies between the impression the person desires to convey and the impression he or she is making.

Goal-relevance of Impressions

People are increasingly motivated to monitor and control how they are perceived by others as the impressions others form of them become more important to the attainment of their goals. In some situations, people believe that desirable outcomes are predicated on making certain impressions on other people whereas, in other situations, they believe that their goals do not depend on the impressions that they make. People will be more concerned with managing their impressions when those impressions are more rather than less relevant to their goals.

People's self-presentations may influence their success in attaining many different goals (see Baumeister, 1982a; Leary & Kowalski, 1990; Schlenker, 1980). Sometimes people manage their images in pursuit of desired outcomes that do not directly involve their relationships with others. In such instances, the ultimate goal involves a personal rather than a social outcome, and the person's relationship with the target of his or her self-presentation is only a means to an end. For example, an employee who feigns agreement with the boss's ideas or pretends to be working particularly hard in order to get a raise is using self-presentation to pursue a personal goal. The ultimate goal—

getting a raise—does not involve the relationship itself (although the relationship may be affected by his self-presentational tactics). Because they have focused primarily on people's self-presentations to strangers and acquaintances, many researchers have conceived of impression management primarily as a means of obtaining personal goals.

However, people may also try to shape others' impressions of them as they pursue certain relational goals, trying to influence (e.g., advance, maintain, or end) their relationships with those others. People's self-presentations to a relational partner often have the potential to transform the relationship, both for good and for bad. As a result, people sometimes seek to control the impressions that friends, lovers, family members, and co-workers have of them in order to influence how those targets relate to them.

For example, studies of self-disclosure typically reveal a reciprocal relationship between depth of self-disclosure and relational intimacy. Deep, revealing disclosures tend to enhance the closeness and intimacy of a relationship; in fact, two strangers who engage in structured, increasingly personal self-disclosure over a 45-minute period are likely to feel considerably closer to one another than they would have by simply sharing small talk (Aron, Melinat, Aron, Vallone, & Bator, 1997). Indeed, over time, intimate relationships are characterized by more self-revelation than ordinarily exists in less intimate partnerships (Canary, Stafford, Hause, & Wallace, 1993). Moreover, many adults view self-disclosure as an indispensable component of intimacy (Parks & Floyd, 1996). In light of this, people can regulate the intimacy of their relationships through tactical self-presentation involving intentional self-disclosure. For instance, when macho men are talking with women with whom they foresee the possibility of a closer relationship, they engage in more self-disclosure than when they converse with other men or with women they will not see again (Shaffer, Pegalis, & Bazzini, 1996).

In a similar manner, when people go to lengths to make a favorable impression on a first date, their goal is likely a relational one—to elicit the other person's interest and advance the relationship (either for just one night or for an extended time). Some of these efforts are undoubtedly more successful than others; for example, because we like those who like us (Huston & Levinger, 1978), people who try to attract a suitor by feigning disinterest and playing "hard-to-get" may often be disappointed (Wright & Contrada, 1986).

First Impressions

People are particularly concerned with others' impressions in initial encounters with them. First impressions exert an inordinate influence on others' reactions (Asch, 1946), so this concern about first impressions is not misplaced. Initial judgments about others tend to be rather lasting and, of course, may determine whether any subsequent interaction occurs at all (Jones & Goethals, 1972). From a self-presentational standpoint, then, people should be particularly motivated to manage their impressions in initial encounters; first impressions will often be more relevant to the accomplishment of their short- and long-term goals than are impressions that people form of them later. Indeed the high goal-relevance of first impressions is one reason why people are often particularly nervous about meeting people for the first time (Leary & Kowalski, 1995; Strahan, 1974).

Ordinarily, self-presentational motives will be even stronger in initial encounters when people expect to have contact with the target in the future. Impression motivation is often strong in one-shot interactions, but the prospect of future interactions ups the interpersonal ante; first impressions are typically more relevant to one's goals if they set the stage for future encounters. People do not necessarily present themselves more positively in first encounters when they expect subsequent interactions, however. The prospect of future contact sometimes leads people to adopt a more cautious self-presentational stance so that they do not make exaggerated claims about themselves that might be discredited later (Baumeister, 1982b). However, whether people are cautious or bold, their motivation to manage their impressions is generally higher when subsequent interactions are expected (Gergen & Wishnov, 1965; Schneider, 1969).

Dependency

People are also more motivated to manage their impressions carefully to the extent they are dependent upon another person for valued outcomes. In laboratory investigations, people engage in more tactical self-presentation to others who have the power to dispense and withhold desired rewards (Kowalski & Leary, 1990; Jones, Gergen, Gumpert, & Thibaut, 1965; Stires & Jones, 1969). In the workplace, for instance, people appear to be highly motivated to convey positive impressions of themselves to those who have control over their salaries, promotions, and job futures. As a result, employer–employee relationships are characterized by a great deal of self-presentation (Villanova & Bernardin, 1989).

One outcome for which everyone must depend on other people is social acceptance. Human beings appear to have a fundamental "need to belong" (Baumeister & Leary, 1995) and often convey impressions of themselves that will increase the chances that others will accept and include them (Leary, 1995). Thus, the more that people feel a need for acceptance, the stronger their motivation to impression-manage.

Relational Security, Familiarity, and Time: Waning Motivation

Self-presentational concerns are acute in initial encounters when we expect lasting contact with others, and dependency tends to keep people on a self-presentational edge. Remarkably, however, continued familiarity with a person typically causes concerns with self-presentation to decline. In general, people are ordinarily less concerned with the impressions they make on close friends than they are with the images they convey to those they hold less dear. For instance, in a diary study that encompassed hundreds of interactions, college students clearly engaged in less impression management with same-sex friends they saw often than with acquaintances or strangers with whom they were less intimate. With friends, they thought less about how they were coming across and tried less hard to appear likeable, competent, and ethical (Leary, Nezlek et al., 1994). Self-presentational motives in heterosexual inter-actions were always high in this particular study, but other investigations suggest that romantic partnerships are also characterized by waning impres-sion motivation over time. Guerrero (1997) found that people were actually less worried about what their lovers thought of them than they were about their friends' evaluations. Men and women spend less and less time preening and grooming themselves in the restroom during a dinner date the longer they have known their partners (Daly, Hogg, Sacks, Smith, & Zimring, 1983). Despite the higher interdependency and increased opportunity for things to go wrong, people even experience less frequent and less intense embarrass-ments among friends than they do before strangers (Tangney, Miller, Flicker, & Barlow, 1996).

This is a compelling irony, with key implications for the study of impression management in close relationships: We are often more actively concerned with impressing those who do not yet know us well than we are with managing acceptable images for those who are more important to us. For better or (often) for worse, people exert less attention and energy crafting their presen-tations of self to their intimate partners than they do for mere acquaintances. This is not to suggest that people are heedless of how they are judged by their lovers and friends; on occasion, especially when they have misbehaved, have bad news, or have done some harm, impression motivation in close relation-ships may be extremely high (see Cloven & Roloff, 1994; DePaulo & Bell, 1996; Hodgins, Liebeskind, & Schwartz, 1996). Nevertheless, intimate part-nerships routinely involve less active, intentional impression management than less meaningful associations do.

There may be several reasons why. For one thing, when a relationship becomes established and a partner is won, the pervasive human desire to establish close relationships with others (Baumeister & Leary, 1995) is re-duced, at least with regard to that particular partner. Relational security assuages affiliative need. If one's partner seems (at least temporarily) com-mitted to a relationship, there are fewer, weaker relational goals that remain unmet, and one's self-presentations take on less urgency. In short, "when we can rely on others' approbation and approval, we stop trying so hard to get them to like us" (Miller, 1997b, p. 19).

In addition, once a relationship is established and a partner is well known, any one self-presentational effort has progressively less of an effect on what the partner already thinks. Although there are often surprising things that it may take a long time to learn about a partner (Felmlee, 1995; Murstein, 1987), and people typically don't know their friends and lovers as well as they think they do (Murray & Holmes, 1997; Sillars et al., 1994), close partners ordinarily possess a great deal of data about each other (Planalp & Garvin-Doxas, 1994). As a result, most momentary impressions a partner conveys will either reiterate information that is already known or provide only small amounts of new insight. As their active attempts at impression management become less consequential, people's interest in going to such trouble may gradually fade. Self-disclosure, for instance, declines significantly even over the first year of marriage (Huston, McHale, & Crouter, 1986).

As we suggested above, people often busily prepare for novel interactions with others they are meeting for the first time. Such forethought and attention is effortful, however (see Osborne & Gilbert, 1992), and, as time goes by, such exertions may dwindle from simple laziness and fatigue. In particular, because polite and decorous behavior usually involves some form of active self-restraint, people are often much cruder with intimate partners than they are with others they know less well (Miller, 1997b). Thus, the same fellow who would desperately go to any lengths to avoid farting noticeably on a first date may become a husband who unapologetically passes gas at will around his wife because he lazily "couldn't help it". Various forms of attentive work may gradually decline in intimate interaction. Romantic partners interact with less fluency, longer pauses, fewer nods, and less attention and vocal interest than friends do (Guerrero, 1997), perhaps because they can lazily get away with it. Similarly, the longer two spouses have been married, the *less* accurately they read each other's thoughts and feelings, apparently because they work less hard at it (Thomas, Fletcher, & Lange, 1997).

Finally, and more subtly, impression motivation may decline in close relationships because the "self" that people present to intimate partners is gradually changed by closeness and interdependency. Often, intimates slowly drift from thinking of themselves as autonomous, independent actors to considering themselves one part of a couple, a larger collective that includes the other person too. They use different first-person pronouns, describing themselves as "we" rather than "I" (Agnew, Van Lange, Rusbult, & Langston, 1998), and stop blaming the other for mistakes they both make (Sedikides, Campbell, Reeder, & Elliot, 1998). An individual's self may "expand" as elements of the person's relationship with a close partner are incorporated into the person's self-concept (Aron & Aron, 1996). Thus, over time, some partners may not only become trusted confidantes, they may seem less like external audiences for whom an image need be constructed.

Altogether, then, several overlapping influences may combine to reduce the average motivation and interest with which people tend to the images they construct for intimate partners. Relational security allows one to relax, familiarity means that there is little new to learn, simple laziness reduces one's effort, and broader conceptualizations of the self emerge. Although the judgments of our intimates may be more important than those of anyone else, and although attentive, careful impression management with our intimates may remain advantageous (Miller, 1997b), people are usually less motivated to hone their images for lovers and friends than they are for acquaintances and strangers.

Value of Desired Goals

Still, people's efforts to manage the impressions they make on intimate partners never disappear completely, and this is another intriguing facet of self-
presentation in close relationships: after years of companionship and extraor-
dinarily diverse interpersonal exchanges, people will still strive to shape what
a close partner thinks of them. To the extent the partner controls resources or
rewards they value, they can hardly afford not to; indeed, a second broad
factor that influences the motivation with which people seek to manage their
impressions is the value of their desired goals. People attend to their images
more carefully when they believe those images have implications for important, valuable goals. The higher the interpersonal stakes, the more that self-
presentation comes into play.

For instance, partners who are committed to a romantic relationship tend
to display accommodative behavior: when they encounter rudeness or
thoughtlessness from their beloved, they actively suppress their authentic
displeasure at such mistreatment, biting their tongues and refraining from a
tit-for-tat counterattack (Rusbult, Yovetich, & Verette, 1996). This contrived
forbearance seems to minimize conflict and help to maintain valued relationships, but ironically, people in closer, more intimate relationships are often
less likely to intentionally withhold their irritations in an effort to maintain
false images of placid satisfaction than those in less intimate ones (Cloven &
Roloff, 1994). Still, even in old, close partnerships where lazy security might
prevail, lovers choose to maintain strategic silences about some of their dis-
contents (Cloven & Roloff, 1994). Taken to an extreme, such misrepresenta-
tion of one's heartfelt feelings is probably unhealthy; in fact, excessive
inhibition of authentic self-expression within a close relationship—or "self-
silencing"—has been linked to depression in both men and women (Page,
Stevens, & Galvin, 1996; Thompson, 1995). However, in the normal range,
accommodative behavior can be construed to be an adaptive tactic of self-
presentation born of the desire to protect valued outcomes.

One implication of this tendency is that people are more highly motivated
to control their images in the eyes of those whom they view positively—for
example, those who are likeable, competent, attractive, or of high status—
than by those they view less positively. Approval and acceptance from socially
desirable people are more highly valued than is positive regard from less
attractive folks (Schlenker, 1980), and people will work harder to get it. For
instance, men and women will go to the trouble of tailoring their self-
descriptions to fit the avowed preferences of an attractive, desirable person of
the other sex, but will not do so when the potential partner is believed to be
less desirable (Morier & Seroy, 1994; Zanna & Pack, 1975). Women also eat
lightly, fitting a feminine stereotype, when they want to make good impressions on desirable men, but do not refrain from snacking when they are
interacting with less attractive men (Mori, Chaiken, & Pliner, 1987).

A further implication of this phenomenon is that individuals who possess
socially valued characteristics are more likely than other people to be the

target of others' intentional, tactical self-presentations. They may inhabit social worlds populated by people who seem to be more thoughtful, accepting, and likeable than those typically encountered by people with less beauty or power. In general, flattery, feigned agreement, and other forms of ingratiatory behavior do succeed in making more positive impressions on the recipient than would otherwise exist (Gordon, 1996). Employers, in particular, may underestimate the degree to which their impressions of their employees are affected by their subordinates' efforts to ingratiate them (Baumeister, 1989). On the other hand, if others' ingratiation is clumsily transparent, negative impressions result (Gordon, 1996) and the recipients may come to believe that the world is full of exploitative fakers. This may be one reason why physically attractive women generally mistrust praise from men more than relatively unattractive women do (Major, Carrington, & Carnevale, 1984), and why women in general expect deception from men who are interested in them as sexual partners (Keenan, Gallup, Goulet, & Kulkarni, 1997).

Of course, a given goal may be more highly valued at some times than at others. For instance, people who currently feel accepted and loved by important people in their lives may not value positive evaluations from others as much as do people who have recently experienced disapproval or rejection (Leary & Downs, 1995; Walster, 1965). Similarly, aversive social events such as public failure or embarrassment momentarily increase people's self-presentational motivation, perhaps by increasing the temporary subjective value of interpersonal approval (Miller, 1996). Lasting individual differences can be influential here as well; people who are dispositionally high in need for approval have chronically greater impression motivation than do people with lower need for approval (Leary, 1995; Leary & Kowalski, 1995).

Another important pattern that may emerge from the effects of goal value is that heterosexuals are routinely more concerned about the impressions they make on the other sex than they are about the images they convey to those of their own sex (e.g., Leary, Nezlek et al., 1994). One interpretation of this disparity in impression motivation is that, at least for heterosexuals, members of the other sex control more valuable rewards than do those of one's own sex. Members of the other sex can provide all of the affordances of same-sex friends (e.g., companionship, support, acceptance) and more. They also offer opportunities for desired romantic and sexual outcomes that are lacking in same-sex encounters, and can provide valuable self-affirming feedback on important dimensions—such as physical attractiveness and sexual appeal—that same-sex individuals cannot. Furthermore, because most people have more same-sex than cross-sex relationships (Reis, Senchak, & Solomon, 1985), cross-sex relationships are scarcer and, thus, in an economic sense, more valuable. In light of this, it is not surprising that heterosexuals are usually more interested in making desired impressions on those of the other sex, feel more socially anxious in cross-sex than in same-sex interactions, and devote more effort to making themselves desirable to the other sex (Leary & Kowalski, 1995; Leary, Nezlek et al., 1994; Zimbardo, 1977).

Discrepancies between Desired and Current Images

A final influence on impression motivation involves people's perceived level of success at projecting the images they desire others to hold of them. People often have rather distinct ideas about the impressions they wish to convey to others and, as long as they believe that others' perceptions of them lie within some acceptable range, their motivation to manage their judgments may be quiescent. They may continue to monitor others' reactions to them at a preattentive level (Leary & Downs, 1995), but may not give much conscious thought to their public images or exert deliberate effort to modify them. However, if they realize that others' impressions of them fall outside of this latitude of acceptable images, they become motivated to actively manage the impressions they create in order to reestablish the desired image.

This process is especially striking when negative discrepancies between one's desired and current image occur. Such discrepancies typically cause negative affect (commonly embarrassment or shame) and elicit immediate remedial behaviors intended to repair whatever self-presentational damage has occurred (Goffman, 1955; Miller, 1996). In the throes of embarrassment, people are usually highly motivated to present themselves in a reparative, positive way. They may offer excuses for their behavior (Gonzales, Pederson, Manning, & Wetter, 1990), stress their other positive attributes (Baumeister & Jones, 1978; Leary, Landel, & Patton, 1996), try to redress any harm or fix any physical damage (Cupach & Metts, 1994), or otherwise invite goodwill, for example by volunteering their time for a charitable cause (Apsler, 1975). Eager to restore a more desirable image, people often respond to embarrassment with concerted efforts at impression management.

When the discrepancies involve impressions that are relevant to their close relationships, people's self-presentational concerns may be even more acute. Maintaining a viable relationship requires that the participants sustain minimally acceptable images of themselves in one another's eyes. For example, we generally want our friends and spouses to see us as people who are trustworthy, faithful, and concerned about their welfare. This is typically not hard to do because relational partners often hold idealized images of each other that actually improve on the real thing (Murray & Holmes, 1997; Murray et al., 1996a) and readily trivialize and explain away each other's small transgressions (Fincham & Bradbury, 1993). However, if a friend, relative, or spouse comes to see us as immoral, unfaithful, or selfish—images that strike at the heart of our suitability as relational partners—a discrepancy occurs between our desired and current images that can cause impression motivation to skyrocket. When an extramarital affair or other betrayal is discovered, for instance, people often try to assert either that their actions were innocuous and meaningless or that some benefit to the relationship may ultimately come from them; unfortunately, these views are almost never shared by their partners (Buunk, 1987; Jones & Burdette, 1994).

Self-presentational motivation also increases when the mere possibility of a discrepancy between desired and public images exists. For example, people may work hard to conceal information that, if it became known, would portray them in a negative light. In particular, people readily inconvenience themselves (Miller, 1996) or, on occasion, put themselves at real risk (Leary, Tchividjian, & Kraxberger, 1994) in order to avoid situations or actions that may embarrass them. Faced with the threat of an unwanted discrepancy, people may also engage in strategic impression management in advance so that, should the undesirable information come to light, they have already buttressed their image in other ways (Leary et al., 1996). Thus, a spouse who knows that his or her overspending will be apparent on the upcoming credit card statement may preempt the imminent predicament with excessive kindness and special favors for his or her partner before the bill arrives.

Summary

Although people are rarely heedless of the impressions they are making on others, they become more motivated to actively manage their impressions to the extent they believe that others' judgments of them are relevant to desired goals, those goals are valuable, and a discrepancy exists between the images they wish to convey and the impressions they are currently making. In close relationships, relational security, familiarity, fatigue, and expansion of the self may reduce one's motivation to monitor and manipulate the impressions one makes on a partner over time. However, because relational partners often control unique, invaluable rewards, self-presentation continues to pervade our partnerships and becomes especially acute when unwanted discrepancies exist.

IMPRESSION CONSTRUCTION IN RELATIONSHIPS

We have discussed several aspects of self-presentation at length without yet addressing the precise nature of the "self" that is presented when people impression-manage. The term, *self-presentation*, seems to imply that people simply display for others' observation a pre-existing self that otherwise lies hidden within them. Interestingly, in his seminal book on self-presentation, Goffman (1959) explicitly disavowed this interpretation. He suggested that, although a person's self-presentations may lead others "to impute a self to a performed character," the self that is imputed "is a *product* of a scene that comes off, and is not a *cause* of it" (p. 252). Thus, according to Goffman, the self is constructed, moment by moment, in the course of interaction.

Our own view lies between these views. Clearly, people possess views of themselves—real, desired, and imagined images of who they are and who they want to be—and these "selves" underlie and guide many of the impressions they try to create in others' minds. At the same time, however, identities, like all social realities, are negotiated and altered in the process of social interaction to fit the immediate circumstances. Thus, the self that is presented when people impression-manage reflects both the person's existing self-identity and the self-relevant images that are created, on the spot, during ongoing social interaction. In this section, we examine closely five primary sets of factors that influence the nature and content of the self-presentations that people attempt: (1) the audience's values; (2) salient roles and norms; (3) the person's current or potential social image; (4) the person's self-concept; and (5) the kind of individual the person does and does not desire to be (Leary & Kowalski, 1990).

Target's Values

The most obvious determinants of the images people select are the preferences and values of the person they are trying to impress. People routinely tailor their public images to the perceived prejudices and predilections of their self-presentational targets. No other finding in the history of impression management research is more well documented; people readily change the content of their self-presentations to conform to the presumed characteristics and values of their audiences (e.g., Carnevale, Pruitt, & Britton, 1979; Smith, Berry, & Whiteley, 1997; von Baeyer, Sherk, & Zanna, 1981).

People are not necessarily being deceptive when they adjust their images to different tastes. For one thing, they are not always aware they are doing so. People may shape their own self-presentations to those of a partner without realizing that they are making any changes at all (Vorauer & Miller, 1997); editorial fine-tuning of this sort clearly takes place with no intention of misrepresenting the truth.

Furthermore, as we noted earlier, people can easily show different, yet equally accurate, sides of themselves to different audiences without lying to any of them. In fact, the talents that allow a person to perceptively discern what images are appropriate and then to deftly adjust his or her behavior to fit those specifications are widely acknowledged to be normal components of good social skill (Riggio, 1986). Certainly, the ability to steer a conversation toward a partner's interests and to communicate enthusiasm and liking for the interaction have long been admired by the lay public (Carnegie, 1940), and people with those skills enjoy more intimate interactions earlier in their relationships than people without them (Snyder & Simpson, 1984). Being a deft, attentive conversationalist always involves impression management but only rarely has anything at all to do with intentional dishonesty and deceit.

Relational Interest

Over time, one of the most important impressions one can convey to a friend, spouse, or other close partner is that one is still interested and invested in the relationship. Thus, people who wish to maintain a relationship will ordinarily be motivated to communicate explicit affection and assurance to their partners (Dainton & Stafford, 1993). These communications often express genuine, heartfelt feelings, but they also can have a self-presentational function. Some (typically masculine) people deeply love their spouses without being openly affectionate, but such reticence is associated with noticeably lower satisfaction for the spouse than are partnerships that are imbued with effusive appreciation (Ickes, 1985). As a result, most insightful relationship veterans recognize the value of forthright expressions of affection that suggest that they are still interested, committed partners.

Of course, people do sometimes convey more interest in a relational partner than they actually feel. People may feign interest for many reasons—to avoid conflict, to avoid hurting the partner's feelings, to compliment the other person, or even to seduce him or her—but men may be somewhat more likely to do this than women. When they misrepresent themselves to potential partners, for instance, men are more likely than women to feign sincerity and commitment (and to exaggerate their status and wealth), whereas women are more likely to fake an attractive appearance (Tooke & Camire, 1991). Because men generally evidence less commitment to their relationships than women do (e.g., Miller, 1997a), feigned interest may be an especially useful tactic for them, assuming they can overcome women's typical suspicions about their sincerity (see Keenan et al., 1997).

At other times, people purposefully convey impressions of *low* relational interest that suggest that they do not fully value their relationship with another individual. These self-presentations are sometimes veridical, but they can involve dissimulation as well. People who "play hard to get", for example, may try to seem less interested in a potential relationship than they really are. (This is not very clever; it is ordinarily more profitable to appear to be a highly selective person who *is* interested in a special someone [Walster, Walster, Piliavin, & Schmidt, 1973; Wright & Contrada, 1986].) In established relationships, people may purposefully convey disinterest to evoke insecurity or jealousy in order to attract a partner's attention, test the partner's interest, or simply bolster their own self-esteem; this tactic appears to be more common among women than men (White, 1980). Exaggerated disinterest may also be used to punish a partner for perceived misbehavior (as when people give someone "the cold shoulder"; Williams, 1997) or to control the other person through coercive influence (as when a person conveys relational interest only when the partner behaves in specified ways).

Maladaptive Self-presentations

People usually want to make "good", socially desirable impressions—of being likeable, competent, ethical, or conscientious, for example—because other people are likely to value these desirable characteristics. However, they will present themselves in an unflattering, negative way if they are motivated to make an impression on a target who values negative attributes (Jellison & Gentry, 1978; Jones & Pittman, 1982). Perhaps the best example of this tactic involves people who "play dumb" by concealing their true knowledge from a target who might be threatened by such talent (Dean, Braito, Powers, & Britton, 1975; Gove, Hughes, & Geerken, 1980).

In other instances, the images that people think will "impress" a particular target involve unhealthy, reckless, or otherwise hazardous behaviors that pose a risk to the individual's well-being (Leary et al., 1994). In one sample of university students, for instance, over half of the respondents admitted having done very dangerous things (e.g., jumping from bridges, having "unsafe" sex, driving recklessly) in order to impress others as brave, fun-loving, or "cool" (Martin & Leary, 1998). In these cases, people's efforts to convey impressions that they believed were valued by other people posed serious risks to their physical safety, if not to their lives. Lest such self-presentational risks be viewed as peculiar to the young, we should note that the elderly sometimes risk injury by failing to use walkers in public because they do not want other people to view them as infirm or "old" (Martin, Leary, & Rejeski, in press).

Other maladaptive patterns of self-presentation may result in psychological distress or harm. In some cases, people feel nervously incapable of successfully managing the images they are supposed to maintain. The "imposter" phenomenon that leads some high-achieving people to feel secretly unsuited for their tasks may be one such example; such people are plagued with anxiety and low self-esteem (Chrisman, Pieper, Clance, Holland, & Gliekauf-Hughes, 1995). In other cases, people deny or disguise thoughts, emotions, or other personal information that they believe will threaten their relationships with others. Everyone does this now and then, but when such inauthenticity becomes chronic—a pattern variously labeled as "self-concealment" (Larson & Chastain, 1990) or "self-silencing" (Jack, 1991)—it may become debilitating. As we noted earlier, a continual pattern of self-silencing in romantic relationships is associated with depression (e.g., Page et al., 1996).

Chronic self-silencing is rare, but occasional lying is not. Across their many interactions with others, college students tell lies, on average, once or twice per day (DePaulo, Kashy, Kirkendol, Wyer, & Epstein, 1996). More impressively, people report lying in one out of every four interactions with their friends, and in one of every three interactions with their mothers and premarital lovers (DePaulo & Kashy, 1998)! These findings seem to paint a bleak portrait of close relationships but, of course, our partnerships are not quite as fraudulent and devious as the statistics may make them seem. For one thing, people do tell fewer lies to intimate partners than they tell to strangers and acquaintances. (Lies are told least frequently—in about 10% of all interactions—to spouses and children [DePaulo & Kashy, 1998].) For another thing, people tell more kind lies to their close partners than they tell to others. As partnerships become more intimate and meaningful, higher proportions of the lies people tell are motivated by altruistic concern for their partners' well-being and are designed either to protect the partner from hurt feelings and needless worry or to advance the partner's interests in some other way (DePaulo & Kashy, 1998; DePaulo et al., 1996).

People consider most of their lies to be inconsequential and do not worry much about being caught (DePaulo et al., 1996). Nevertheless, we have

chosen to discuss lying in the context of "maladaptive" self-presentation because it is not an innocuous tactic. The more lies people tell, the lower the
quality of their same-sex relationships (Kashy & DePaulo, 1996). Furthermore, interactions in which more lies occur are generally judged to be less
pleasant and intimate than ones in which few lies are told (DePaulo et al.,
1996). Lying is globally related, then, to lower satisfaction with one's interpersonal transactions. Moreover, people are more discomfited by lies in close
relationships than they are by lies told to strangers (DePaulo & Kashy, 1998).
Thus, lying—a tactic that is merely convenient and often trivial in superficial
transactions—is more momentous when it occurs among intimates (see Mc-
Cornack & Levine, 1990).

   In addition, lying can be particularly impactful when it involves the keeping
of secrets. Chronic deception takes work. To safeguard a secret, people must
take pains to monitor their behavior for unwanted leaks that could suggest the
secret to others (see Buller & Burgoon, 1994), and, ironically, this can mean
that the forbidden knowledge is never far from their thoughts (Lane &
Wegner, 1995). In particular, secret lovers are more likely to come to mind
and seem more attractive than are partners who have been openly acknowledged (Wegner, Lane, & Dimitri, 1994). Carefully keeping quiet about such
frequent streams of thought is demanding work, however (Wegner & Gold,
1995), and over time, relational secrets may become exhausting sources of
stress (Wegner & Lane, 1995). Thus, fraudulent self-presentations that must
be maintained over time (i.e., "living a lie") may have lasting, deleterious
implications for personal adjustment—as well as relational satisfaction—that
their instigators do not always foresee.

   Another—more subtle—maladaptive pattern of self-presentation may occur when people gradually change their motivation from winning a desirable
new partner to *trying not to lose* that same partner. Losses have a greater
emotional impact on people than comparable gains do (Kahneman &
Tversky, 1982), and the imposing threat of losing a lover one already has may
engender less effective behavior than the opportunity for gaining a new lover
does. Schreindorfer, Leary, and Keith (1998) demonstrated, for instance, that
people who were faced with being left out of a desirable group made poorer
impressions on observers than did people who were trying to get into the
same group. This phenomenon has not yet been studied in relationships over
time, but it suggests the possibility that people who are charming suitors as
they try to win another's interest may become less effective, less appealing
partners when they try to keep that partner from losing interest later. This
raises the provocative notion that we may be better at getting people to fall *in*
love with us than we are preventing them from falling *out* of love.

   A final adverse consequence of maladaptive self-presentations is that
people may gradually come to adopt chronic images of helplessness or dependency because those roles help induce others to maintain desired patterns of
interaction in a dysfunctional relationship or family. Family therapists
typically recognize that the client of record or "identified patient" (Gubrium,
1992)—the person who comes to them with a problem—may simply be a

representative of a group or family whose relationships are unhealthy. In order to gain acceptance or fit into a disordered group, people may portray themselves as eccentric or maladjusted (Satir, 1967).

Audience Segregation

People generally try to keep audiences to which they present different images separated from one another. Acute self-presentational problems arise when people find themselves in the presence of two or more individuals for whom they desire to make very disparate impressions. Thus, we should not be surprised that they do their best to keep these audiences segregated in order to avoid the stressful *multiple audience problem* (Fleming, Darley, Hilton, & Kojetin, 1990; Fleming & Rudman, 1993).

In many cases, such audiences are found in distinct locations and it is easy to keep them apart. For example, a man might convey very different images to (a) his teenage students in a Sunday school class, and (b) his Saturday-night drinking buddies, safe in the knowledge that these audiences are unlikely to cross paths. However, should his students happen upon his drunken revelry, he faces a serious self-presentational predicament. Other audiences are more difficult to segregate. For example, when a supervisor becomes close friends with a subordinate at work, tension and awkwardness may result when the supervisor cannot convey the same familiar impressions to the friend that naturally occur outside of the work setting because of how other subordinates would react (Zorn, 1995).

A slightly different multiple audience problem occurs when someone is in the company of two individuals to whom he or she wants to present the *same* impression, but doing so for either person would make an undesired impression on the other. A classic example is the woman who finds herself at a party attended by both her husband and her illicit lover; she might like to convey an impression of loving openness to each of them but cannot easily do so without arousing suspicion in her husband or making her lover jealous. Although this is an extreme example, situations analogous to this one may not be uncommon. Because people often maintain several close relationships of various types at once, overlapping and competing self-presentational demands of this sort may occasionally be inevitable (Baxter et al., 1997).

Audience segregation becomes an increasingly thorny problem as one's intimacy and interdependency with one or both of the audiences grows. The closer one's relationship with a self-presentational audience, the more difficult it is to keep that audience apart from other audiences. Spouses, for example, often accompany a person into various venues that would not be frequented by other partners with whom one was less interdependent.

Roles and Norms

The broader social context also exerts a strong influence on self-presentational behaviors. Specifically, both the roles that people occupy and the situational norms that are salient dictate and constrain the impressions people attempt to construct.

Role Constraints

Many interpersonal relationships occur between people who are filling explicit social roles. For example, the relationships between a professor and a student, an employer and employee, or a pastor and a member of the congregation are often circumscribed by the roles that the individuals play. Roles prescribe that individuals behave in certain ways (and refrain from behaving in other ways), and these prescriptions involve not only instrumental behaviors (the pastor is to lead the worship service) but expressive and self-presentational ones as well. Certain public images are often required by one's role; a pastor, for instance, should maintain an image of rectitude. Such self-presentational prescriptions strongly affect the behavior of people who are bound by them and often govern the course of his or her relationships with other people. Failures to maintain the appropriate image—as when the pastor is seen with the prostitute or the politician cries in public—have dire consequences for the individual's effectiveness in the role and, often, for his or her right to maintain the role at all.

The important point here is that the self-presentational requirements of certain roles can affect the person's relationships with others. To the extent that a person in a particular role must maintain certain public images, his or her behavioral options are constrained. As much as he might like to, a minister who once played guitar in a rock band may decline a parishioner's invitation to jam with a local heavy metal band because doing so simply wouldn't "look" right. Similarly, a business executive may refrain from confiding her personal problems to a friendly subordinate because doing so would appear inconsistent with her leadership role. Such self-presentational concerns can impede the development of relationships that might otherwise have flourished.

On the other hand, certain role-bound self-presentations may facilitate other kinds of relationships. One example involves psychotherapists, medical personnel, teachers, and others in helping roles that prescribe that the helpers appear to be concerned about those who consult them. Although such professionals are sometimes wholly uninterested in a particular client's, patient's, or student's problem, they typically convey an appearance of interest and concern. Although these expressions of concern may be entirely feigned, they have the benefit of fostering trust and rapport that may facilitate the development of a relationship between helper and helpee.

Gender roles are perhaps the most pervasive roles in social life, and they, too, influence self-presentation. The conversations of men and women are different enough that they can be distinguished by strangers who read anonymous transcripts of their interactions (Martin, 1997), and some of these differences are embodied in the impressions the sexes choose to project. In particular, women are expected to be more modest than men (Janoff-Bulman & Wade, 1996), so they may comport themselves with a public humility they do not privately accept (see Heatherington et al., 1993). This may be a regrettable, but necessary strategy; when women confidently announce their accomplishments and talents, they are often judged to be less attractive by both men and women than they would have been had they been more demure and self-effacing (Rudman, 1998). Men, on the other hand, are expected to be boastful and self-assured, and images of confidence are more valued for men than women in most cultures (Williams & Best, 1990). As a result, it's hard to get men to admit they *don't* know the answer to a question, even when they have no idea what the real answer is (Giuliano, Barnes, Fiala, & Davis, 1998)!

Normative Constraints

Social norms also influence people's self-presentations. When clear consensus exists about how one ought to behave in a particular situation, people typically try to ensure that their impressions are consistent with those norms. For example, norms dictate that people should be happy at parties and sad at funerals. As a result, dispirited party-goers will often try to look like they're having a good time, and nonchalant funeral-goers will maintain a countenance of solemnity despite their lack of emotion. Similarly, different styles of impression management may be appropriate at different times in the workplace. When they are interviewing for a job, people make better impressions when they engage in self-promotion than when they try to ingratiate themselves to the interviewer (Stevens & Kristof, 1995). Once they are hired, however, their salaries and promotions may be tied to their success at ingratiation and have less to do with their talent for self-promotion (Orpen, 1996).

The norms that delineate desirable images may vary from culture to culture (Bond, 1991), but some general norms are widely applied. One of these is the norm of reciprocation. In any given interaction, people's self-presentations are likely to be substantially shaped by the behavior of their interaction partners. Both among strangers and between spouses, for instance, people typically fit the depth or intimacy of their self-disclosures to that displayed by their partners (Dindia, Fitzpatrick, & Kenny, 1997). Indeed, failure to do so is often regarded negatively by other people (Derlega & Berg, 1987). Intimate partners don't always match a partner's level of disclosure during a particular interaction, but failure to abide by this norm over the long run may result in stress within the relationship (Rosenfeld & Bowen, 1991).

A norm of reciprocity also affects the positivity of people's self-presentations. Without being aware of it, people often adopt the style of impression management displayed by others in an interaction. Thus, when others are self-enhancing, people present themselves positively as well; in contrast, when others self-deprecate, people tend to be similarly modest (Baumeister, Hutton, & Tice, 1989). This reciprocal influence means that, over time in close relationships, people may fall into habitual patterns of self-presentation that emerge from their contact with those particular partners, routinely maintaining impressions that may be unlike the ones that they convey to anyone else. For instance, romantic partners may un-self-consciously address each other with babytalk that would embarrass them before any other audience (Bombar & Littig, 1996).

Current or Potential Social Image

A further key influence on impression management in relationships is that close partners know much more about us than most other people do. This means that people actually have less self-presentational freedom among their intimates than they do among acquaintances and strangers because people are reluctant to present themselves in any manner that is inconsistent with what others already know of them (Baumeister & Jones, 1978). People may understand, perhaps through hard-won experience, that others will like them better if their self-presentations do not contradict established fact (Schlenker & Leary, 1982). Thus, a man and woman on a first date have more leeway for exaggeration and embellishment of their images than they will ever have again; after they have dated for awhile, the familiar partner's discernment will limit the images each person can safely, acceptably present.

The creative emancipation people experience when they cannot be held accountable for their images is especially visible in computer "chat rooms" in which anonymous parties can, and do, present themselves in extravagant, fabricated ways (see Lea & Spears, 1995). Even in such a forum, however, people may be circumspect if they expect a relationship to develop: people's self-presentations are often constrained by what they believe someone might learn about them in the future (Schlenker, 1975). If others will ultimately be able to see them as they "really are", people will be unlikely to convey impressions that deviate too far from the truth. Thus, although people are more highly motivated to engage in impression management when they anticipate future interaction with someone, the prospect of future encounters also limits the kinds of impressions they try to present.

Altogether, then, people may routinely present themselves more boastfully to strangers than to friends (Tice et al., 1995). Not only (as we noted earlier) will people be less motivated to gain approval from others who already like them, but the friends' rich knowledge of their real strengths and weaknesses makes too proud an image perilous. More subtly, considerate friends and lovers will also be mindful of the effects of their self-presentations on the well-being of their relational partners. A person's successes can have negative effects on the self-esteem and mood of those who compare themselves to him or her (Wheeler & Miyake, 1992). By and large, people don't worry much about the implications of their successes on strangers and acquaintances, but they may be acutely aware that friends and lovers may have mixed feelings about their accomplishments, particularly if those accomplishments reflect negatively on or are highly self-relevant to the partner (Beach & Tesser, 1995). As a result, people may refrain from making positive self-presentations to close associates or loved ones that they would ordinarily make to almost anyone else.

Self-concept

The three determinants of people's self-presentations we have discussed thus far—the target's values, the prevailing norms and roles, and the interactants' current and potential social images—all involve aspects of the social context. However, people's self-presentations are also affected by their personal characteristics, including who they think are (their self-concepts) and who they would and would not like to be (their desired and undesired selves).

People typically want others to see them as they see themselves (Swann, Stein-Seroussi, & Giesler, 1992). This is especially true in relationships, where intimate partners become exceptionally influential judges of one's abilities and other attributes. In fact, the importance of a person's self-concept in regulating his or her interpersonal needs in a relationship may grow as the partnership develops and time goes by. Swann, De La Ronde, and Hixon (1994) demonstrated that dating partners generally sought acceptance and praise from each other, whereas married partners sought confirmation of their self-concepts; people had more intimate, interdependent marriages when their spouses thought of them as they thought of themselves. What makes this pattern remarkable is that people who had negative self-concepts—those who genuinely disliked themselves—felt closer to their spouses when their spouses affirmed their faults as well!

The specific implications of this pattern for self-presentation to one's intimate partners have not yet been studied, but there is no doubt that people try to construct social images that elicit the feedback they feel they deserve (see Schlenker & Weigold, 1992). Thus, we should expect different styles of self-presentation over time from partners with different self-concepts, as the desire to support and verify one's beliefs about oneself leads people to seek confirming reactions from others.

We should also note again that a person's self-concept is likely to change as he or she commits to a close relationship with another person. As the role of relational partner fills more of their lives, both they (Aron & Aron, 1996) and almost everyone else (Sedikides, Olsen, & Reis, 1993) are likely to think of them differently, gradually redefining the person as one-half of a couple and not just an autonomous individual. As these new self-definitions sink in, the images one constructs may change (when, for instance, a new father proudly trades in the two-seater sports car he owned as a bachelor for a family minivan).

Desired and Undesired Selves

A fifth and final determinant of people's self-presentations involves their desired and undesired selves—the kinds of people they do and do not wish to be. In general, people probably try to convey impressions that portray them more as the people they wish they were—for most of us, as likeable, competent, and moral—than as the people they really are, or don't want to be (Schlenker, 1985, 1986). Desired selves serve as general guides to the images one prefers, and they are usually, but not always, socially desirable; if people's desired selves involve undesirable attributes, they may actually convey images of themselves that are disagreeable. A person who wants to be "tough", for instance, may try to convey images that are ruthless and intimidating (Jones & Pittman, 1982).

What makes this phenomenon interesting in close relationships is that people may get a lot of help from their partners in pretending to be better than they are. Even with their considerable knowledge and experience, for instance, intimate partners tend to idealize their mates, rating those partners more positively than those partners rate themselves (Murray & Holmes, 1997; Murray et al., 1996a). These rosy perceptions appear to be beneficial in the short run, helping to foster relational satisfaction (Murray & Holmes, 1997). Even more importantly for our purposes, people may gradually come to share their partners' flattering views of them (Murray et al., 1996b). If one's efforts at (typically) positive self-presentation are uncritically accepted by intimate audiences, people can become convinced that they really are the wonderful folks they seem to be. Overly idealistic views of a partner may be risky, however, opening one to distressing disappointment as the motivation to manage impressions slowly wanes with increasing closeness (Miller, 1997b). Nevertheless, within limits, a partner's support may help people bring out their best as they gradually move closer to becoming the people they want to be.

Summary

The images of themselves that people try to construct in close relationships emerge out of a dynamic interplay of their partners' interests and values, their current roles, salient norms, and their real and desired selves. There is a dark side to this process; people may take risks and keep secrets in order to create presentable images. On the other hand, intimate partners are important collaborators who can help us to refine and improve the people we try to be.

RELATIONSHIP SELF-PRESENTATIONS

Thus far, we have examined various influences on the images that people try to present of themselves to relational partners. In this section, we take a somewhat broader view as we note that people are often motivated to manage impressions not only of themselves, but of their partners and their relationships, to others who are not in those relationships.

Managing Impressions of Relational Partners

In normal circumstances, people show concern for other people's public images and take steps to help others convey the kinds of impressions they want to convey. In fact, impression management is such an important theme in social life that people sometimes help manage the images of total strangers. For instance, witnesses will often help an embarrassed stranger to restore a desirable image by expressing sympathy for the person or suggesting an excuse for the predicament (Miller, 1996). Such actions may be purely generous, but they can also be self-serving; people may suffer empathic embarrassment when they watch another's predicament (Miller, 1987), and helping the other person to recover can soothe their own distress.

Concern for another's image is even higher when a person is meaningfully connected to the other individual in some way (Britt, 1995). Thus, people often take steps to manage the impressions of their relational partners (Rowatt & Cunningham, 1997). Typically, partners bolster each other's public images and refrain from criticizing one another in front of outsiders; they mention their partners' positive attributes but conceal or downplay unflattering characteristics. Among other examples, parents may announce their children's athletic ability but remain mum about their delinquency, and athletic team-mates may publicly praise other players' talent but say nothing about their missed practices. Norms prescribe that people should help relational partners sustain a desired social image and failure to do so may be viewed by the partner as a betrayal.

Two specific tactics people employ in this regard are "burnishing"—enhancing the positive features of people with whom one is linked—and "boosting"—minimizing their unfavorable features (Cialdini, 1989). Remarkably, even trivial connections between people can activate concerns for image and trigger the use of these tactics. In one study, people who were told that they shared their birthday with Rasputin, the "mad monk" of Russia, subsequently rated the despicable Rasputin more positively than did people who shared no connection with him at all (Finch & Cialdini, 1989). If people boost the image of a dead historical figure because of such a trifling association, one can only imagine the prevalence of burnishing and boosting that occurs for real relationship partners with whom we are connected.

Creating positive public images of our partners is often self-serving because our own public images are enhanced when we are associated with others who possess desirable characteristics (Cialdini & DeNicholas, 1989). Indeed, relational partners have interdependent images, and we can easily be embarrassed by the misbehavior of a partner even when we have personally done nothing wrong (Miller, 1996). However, some self-presentational efforts in another's behalf may be motivated by thoughtful concern for the other's well-being. Rowatt and Cunningham (1997) found that interpersonal warmth and dominance both predicted how interested people would be in controlling the social images of their relational partners.

Of course, people do not always promote their partners' positive images. Romantic couples sometimes belittle each other in public, parents complain about their children, and friends gossip about one another behind each other's back. We suspect that people who disparage a partner to others no longer feel (or are trying to change) a close connection between their own images and those of the partner.

Managing Impressions of the Relationship

People tend to perceive and think about relationships as entities that are separate and distinct from the individuals who comprise them (Acitelli, 1993). As a result, people are sometimes concerned with how their relationships are viewed by others and try to construct certain impressions of their relationships for external audiences. One familiar example involves denying that a relationship even exists; for instance, young lovers may tell their parents that they're not yet serious about anyone (Baxter & Widenmann, 1993). Another common instance involves spouses' efforts to "put a happy face" on their marriage no matter how distressed or strained the relationship really is; they may have argued fiercely all the way to a party—indeed, their marriage may be in its terminal stage—yet they treat one another pleasantly once they arrive. Similarly, co-workers may seem to be the greatest of friends when customers or clients are present, but return to sullen indifference or active hostility when the audience leaves. In Goffman's (1959) terms, these are "team performances" in which a group of people (whether romantic couples, families, work groups, or friendship cliques) collude to project particular impressions of the team to outsiders.[1]

In part, falsely positive relational self-presentations may be enacted out of simple courtesy to others. People may feign relationship harmony because they know that public discord is stressful for observers and is often impolite. Yet, some motivation may also lie in the fact that one's relational status reflects on—and constrains—one's personal images. To make a desired impression on an attractive stranger during a trip out-of-town, for instance, a relationships researcher may not only wish to avoid seeming too scholarly and erudite (Rudman, 1998) but may also not want to mention that she is engaged to be married. Obviously, people often have a personal self-presentational stake in ensuring that their relationships are perceived in particular ways.

Relational impression management can be consequential. For one thing, working together to craft a team image can create a bond of interdependence among the collaborators that fosters commitment to their relationship. For

---

[1] During the uproar following allegations of President Clinton's relationship with a White House intern in 1998, the President and Ms Clinton seemed to manage their relational impressions carefully. Not only did Ms Clinton angrily denounce the accusations, but the Clintons made a point to be photographed attending church, laughing together, and appearing to be untroubled by the controversy. Veteran observers of political image-making were not surprised by this response.

example, workers who cooperate to project a desired image of a company to customers or clients are bound to one another in theirs and others' eyes. This kind of self-presentational complicity can provide a source of cohesion across the organizational hierarchy (Goffman, 1959).

For another thing, concerns about a team image may occasionally constrain the kinds of interactions the members of a team share with one another. For example, members of a self-presentational team often conceal secrets and disagreements from outsiders, and, as a result, cannot always interact freely when other people are present. Likewise, when a team member jeopardizes the collective image with some public mistake, concerns for appearances may prevent other members from correcting or punishing the offender until the audience is no longer present.

Finally, when people do not think that a team member is willing or able to sustain the desired relational image, they may take steps to limit that individual's contact with certain key audiences. Children, in particular, may be kept ignorant of family secrets that they might unwittingly reveal, and may be excluded from social situations in which they may fail to sustain the desired family image. Indeed, when parents are concerned that children will not "behave themselves" in some situation, they are rarely worried about inconvenience to others; instead, they are more often worried that the kids will not maintain the desired relational image of a well-adjusted family with effective parents and well-bred children. Along the same lines, friends and family members who are carelessly indiscrete may not be invited to certain gatherings, and employees who do not uphold the company image may be tucked away out of sight of customers.

CONCLUSION

Throughout this chapter, we have offered several propositions about the nature of self-presentation in close relationships. As we have seen, the people with whom we enter into ongoing relationships are crucial audiences for impression management. They control highly valued resources on which we depend, and we ordinarily wish to present ourselves in ways that favorably impress them (although, ironically, our motivation to manage our images around them may wane as the relationship deepens).

Many of the phenomena and processes that we have examined in this chapter can be studied with little consideration of the nature of the relationship between the individual and the target of his or her self-presentations. Others, however, depend strongly on the nature of the relationship between them. Because self-presentational researchers have relied primarily upon samples of unacquainted college students, they have devoted little theoretical or empirical attention to self-presentational processes that occur in ongoing relationships. As a result, we know virtually nothing about how relationship variables—such as commitment, satisfaction, familiarity, trust, or status inequality—influence the motive to impression-manage, the nature of the images people try to convey, or the interpersonal consequences of partners' self-presentations. Nor have studies considered how self-presentations may differ in different types of relationships or how they may change over time through the course of relationship development. The possibilities for interesting, informative research on self-presentational processes in relationships are extensive, and we hope that this chapter provides an impetus for research in this area.

Chapter 8

Methods of Studying Close Relationships*

William Ickes

University of Texas, Arlington, TX, USA

Something unusual is happening here. For as long as you have known them, your best female friend Janice and your best male friend Don have simply not gotten along. As much as you like them as individuals, and as often as you have tried to bring them together, they have always seemed to get on each other's nerves. You can feel the tension between them whenever they are in the same room, and you have often wondered why it is that two people whom you like so much don't seem to like each other.

But what's really got you wondering lately is this: Why, three days after Janice broke off her engagement to her fiance, Bobby, did you see Don's car parked in front of her apartment as you drove by on your way to work? And why, after calling Janice last night and discovering that her line was busy, did it happen that when you tried to call Don, you discovered that *his* line was busy too? Could it be that Janice and Don are not as uncomfortable around each other as you thought? Could it be that the tension you have felt between them in the past was not the "push" of magnetic poles that repel each other but the "pull" of magnetic poles that attract?

Naturally, as nosy as you are, you won't be able to rest until you find out for sure, one way or the other . . .

---

* Reproduced by permission of Allyn & Bacon, Boston, USA.

The Social Psychology of Personal Relationships.
Edited by William Ickes and Steve Duck. © 2000 John Wiley & Sons Ltd.

HOW DO WE LEARN ABOUT CLOSE RELATIONSHIPS IN OUR EVERYDAY LIVES?

But where do you go from here? If you really want to know if (and when, and how, and why) the relationship between Janice and Don has changed, what options are available to you for obtaining this information? You quickly run through a mental list, which, if you took the time to organize it, might look something like this:

1. Ask Janice to tell me what is going on.
2. Ask Don to tell me what is going on.
3. Get them both together and confront them with my suspicions.
4. Get them both together, but play it cool and observe them closely.
5. Ask around and see if our mutual friends know anything.
6. Put a tap on Janice's telephone line. Ditto Don's.
7. Intercept Janice's mail. Ditto Don's.
8. Sneak a long look at Janice's diary. Don's too, if he has one.
9. Hire private detectives to follow them around and report back.
10. Bug their apartments with listening devices.
11. Bug their persons with locating devices.
12. Hide video cameras in their apartments to record their behavior.
13. Sit them down side-by-side, hooked up to a Libido Meter.
14. If all else fails, read their minds.

With the possible exception of items 13 and 14, which suggest that you were beginning to drift off into Fantasyland, the items in this list appear to provide a useful summary of the different methods you could use to investigate Janice and Don's relationship. Some of these methods are more exotic and complicated than others, but they all represent ways that people can and do use to investigate relationships in everyday life. Indeed, it may not surprise you to learn that social scientists have drawn from a highly similar list of methodological options in their more formal and systematic attempts to study close relationships. But which of these methodological options should you choose? And how should you decide?

   Like the social scientists who study relationships, you must choose one or more of these options based on a comparative analysis of the relative advantages and disadvantages (e.g., the pros and cons) associated with each. Moreover, this comparison of the different methods' advantages and disadvantages must be made within the context of your own goals as a researcher. In other words, like more formally trained students of close relationships, you will have to begin by dealing with what we will call *the trade-off problem*.

THE TRADE-OFF PROBLEM

Whenever you settle on a single method for studying any phenomenon, including a close relationship, you simultaneously gain some things and lose others. The choice you make represents a complex trade-off in which the combined strengths and weaknesses of the method that you decide to use are weighed against the combined strengths and weaknesses of any alternative method(s) that you decide not to use. Some of the trade-offs that are commonly encountered in the study of close relationships are described below.

Choosing One Perspective over Another

If you choose Option 1 from your list ("Ask Janice to tell me what's going on"), you may stand a good chance of getting Janice to give you her perspective on her relationship with Don. However, if Option 1 is the only option you choose, you will obtain Janice's perspective at the expense of the perspectives that you might have obtained if you had selected Option 2 ("Ask Don") or Option 5 ("Ask our mutual friends") instead. In deciding to seek one perspective at the expense of some other(s), you are implicitly making judgments about whose perspective is likely to be the most accurate, unbiased, uncensored, perceptive, fully informed, and so on. If you choose to seek the wrong perspective—one that is inaccurate, uninformed, biased, or misleading—you risk coming to the wrong conclusion about Janice and Don's relationship.

Choosing One Level of Analysis over Another

If you choose either Option 1 ("Ask Janice") or Option 2 ("Ask Don"), the information you obtain from each person as an individual may be different from the information you would obtain if you chose Option 4 and studied Janice and Don together, as a couple. For example, when interviewed separately, Janice and Don might deny that they have any romantic interest in each other; however, their verbal or nonverbal reactions when you observe them together might tell you just the opposite. If you choose to inquire about their relationship at the "wrong" level of analysis (e.g., at the individual, rather than the dyadic, level), you may again risk reaching a conclusion that is misleading or incorrect.

Choosing an Obtrusive Method over an Unobtrusive One

Some of the methods in your list (in particular, Options 1, 2, and 3) are obtrusive in that they blatantly convey to Janice and Don your interest in their relationship. All of the remaining methods are somewhat more unobtrusive in that they seek to obtain the same information without alerting Janice and Don to your interest. If you think that Janice and Don are motivated to lie to you or mislead you, an obtrusive method is likely to fail to tell you what you really want to know. On the other hand, the use of an unobtrusive method incurs certain risks as well. For example, what would happen if Janice and Don discover that you have been "spying" on them by listening in on their conversations (Options 6 and 10), reading their private thoughts and feelings (Options 7 and 8—and 14!) or covertly monitoring their behavior (Options 9, 11, and 12)? At best, they might become more suspicious and guarded around you in the future; at worst, they might sue you for invading their privacy!

Because unobtrusive methods involve some form of spying, there are potential ethical and practical costs associated with them. From an ethical standpoint, these methods can violate the subjects' rights to privacy and reveal things about them and their relationships that they would prefer to keep to themselves. From a practical standpoint, these methods can also be costly to implement. Installing a phone tap, purchasing video equipment, or retaining the services of a private detective can be expensive ways to find out what you want to know. These costs, like the others just mentioned, must also be considered when you choose among the various options on your list.

Choosing an Ethically Questionable Method over an Ethically Safe One

Let's face it—some of the methods in your list are either ethically questionable (Options 8 and 9, for example) or downright illegal (Options 6 and 7). Given the high potential costs associated with such ethically questionable methods (losing the trust of the people you are studying, being arrested, getting sued, and so on), when, and why, would you ever consider using them?

In general, you probably would *not* consider using them. Your society holds you accountable for your unethical behavior in the same way that various legal, professional, and social institutions hold social scientists accountable for their unethical behavior. In fact, social scientists typically have to submit descriptions of their proposed research projects for approval by Institutional Review Boards (IRBs) before they can even begin to collect their data. These review boards are charged with the task of ensuring that any research projects they approve are ethically defensible and involve only a minor and acceptable level of risk to any potential subject's well-being.

However, decisions of this type are not always easy to make. Ethical considerations such as invasion of the subjects' privacy must be balanced against the importance to society of the knowledge to be gained from the research. An assessment of the method's informativeness and freedom from self-presentation bias must also be weighed against its potential threat to the subjects' privacy and well-being. Finally, it should be recognized that a given research method may be more or less ethically defensible, depending on the circumstances in which it is applied. If, for example, subjects sign a consent form notifying them at the outset that certain behaviors may be observed and recorded unobtrusively, they have effectively granted their permission to allow some limited invasion of their privacy to occur. Even in cases such as this, however, the subjects' privacy is in a larger sense still protected by the researcher's pledge to keep their identities confidential and to use their data "for statistical purposes only".

Choosing a Method Reflecting One "Philosophy" versus Another

So far, this discussion of the trade-off problem has sounded like a cost–benefit analysis that takes no account of the researcher's own philosophy and theoretical commitments. It is time to correct that impression. The researcher's choice of a method is strongly (and, in some cases, perhaps entirely) determined by his or her theoretical and philosophical assumptions about the phenomenon being investigated. As Steve Duck (1992, personal communication) has noted:

> For instance, no one would do diary and interaction record studies who did not believe that subjects could recall or introspect about their personal relationships with a certain degree of acceptable accuracy. By contrast, someone who does observational studies is usually of the opinion that people can be biased and mistaken when they report on their behavior, and are influenced by psychological dynamics that do not corrupt an outside observer. In other words, the selection of methods is not necessarily an intellectually neutral enterprise, but instead involves the implicit adoption of a perspective from which to see things—and an implicit set of values as well.

SOLUTIONS TO THE TRADE-OFF PROBLEM

We will consider many more of these trade-off issues in this chapter and the following ones. Before we do, however, it may be useful to consider the most obvious and common-sense solution to the trade-off problem: using multiple methods that complement each others' strengths and compensate for each others' weaknesses.

For example, instead of seeking only Janice's perspective (Option 1), you might invest the extra time and effort required to seek Don's perspective (Option 2) and the perspective of your mutual friends (Option 5) as well. Although more costs are involved in obtaining these additional sources of data, some potential benefits may also result. In the ideal case, all three sources of data would agree, increasing your confidence that Janice and Don's relationship really has changed, consistent with your hypothesis. But even if all three sources of data do not converge on the same conclusion, the overall pattern of data may still provide you with greater insight into what is actually happening. Suppose that your mutual friends all agree that Don has fallen in love with Janice, but that neither Janice nor Don is willing to acknowledge that this is true. Considering (a) that Janice has just broken up with Robby, and may be feeling confused about whom she really loves—Robby or Don—and (b) that Don may be feeling guilty about being the cause of their break-up, you may be able to conclude that Janice and Don's relationship really has changed, although neither of them is yet willing to publicly acknowledge that it has.

Similarly, by complementing Janice and Don's individual accounts (Options 1 and 2) with information about how they relate to each other when they are observed together (Option 4), you may again be able to conclude that their relationship really has changed, but that neither of them is yet willing to acknowledge it publicly. Obtaining more unobtrusive measures of Janice and Don's behavior (Options 6 through 12) may further confirm your suspicions, despite their public denials. In other words, the convergence or triangulation of data obtained by different methods or from different sources is likely to provide a more complete and accurate view of the relationship than is any single type of data taken by itself (Duck, 1990).

HOW DO SOCIAL SCIENTISTS LEARN ABOUT CLOSE RELATIONSHIPS?

As the example of Janice and Don suggests, social scientists learn about close relationships in essentially the same ways that we do in our everyday lives. The methods that social scientists use are similar to ours, only more systematic, and in some cases, more sophisticated. In the sections to follow, we will briefly review these methods, which include *self-report*, *peer report*, *observational*, *life-event archival*, *experimental*, and *physiological* methods, along with *eclectic* approaches in which multiple methods are combined. Beginning in most cases with a representative research example, we will examine the purposes and procedures of each method and consider the kinds of questions that each is typically used to study. We will then turn to a discussion of the trade-off problem in close relationship research, and explore a range of possible solutions to this problem. As we will see, these solutions implicate both the methods that social scientists use and the theories that they apply in their study of close relationships.

Self-report Methods

Self-report methods have been used more frequently than any other type of method to study close relationships. These methods require one or more of the relationship members to serve as respondents, providing data in the form of verbal or written information about the relationship. This information is assumed to be subjective to the extent that it reflects the particular viewpoint of the respondent who provided it. Self-report methods in close relationship research include (a) questionnaire studies, (b) face-to-face or telephone interview studies, (c) diary and account studies, (d) interaction record studies, and (e) epistolary studies of written correspondence.

Questionnaire Studies

Leanne Lamke (1989) conducted a questionnaire study to determine how the gender-role orientations of married couples were related to their marital adjustment and satisfaction. In her study, nearly 300 couples living in rural Alabama were mailed paper-and-pencil survey questionnaires that about a third of these couples completed and returned. By having both husbands and wives complete the Personal Attributes Questionnaire (Spence, Helmreich, & Stapp, 1975), Lamke was able to measure the extent to which each partner reported having such "feminine" traits as nurturance, caring, gentleness, and kindness, and such "masculine" traits as assertiveness, dominance, and decisiveness. And, by having both husbands and wives complete the Spanier Dyadic Adjustment Scale (Spanier, 1976), Lamke was able to measure the extent to which each partner was satisfied with the marital relationship.

Lamke found that the wives' marital satisfaction was not predicted by their husbands' masculine traits such as dominance and decisiveness ($r = 0.05$), but was instead predicted by their husbands' more feminine traits such as being kind, affectionate, and caring ($r = 0.43$). Similarly, the husbands' marital satisfaction was not predicted by their wives' masculine traits ($r = 0.10$), but was strongly predicted by their wives' feminine traits ($r = 0.51$). For both husbands and wives, it appears that "happiness is having a feminine marriage partner" (Ickes, 1985, p. 200).

Lamke's questionnaire study is typical in that it attempted to relate one or more predictor variables (self-reported masculine and feminine traits) to one or more criterion variables (self-reported marital satisfaction). Most questionnaire studies of close relationships are of this type. They seek to relate external predictors such as demographic characteristics (e.g., age, ethnicity), personality traits (e.g., shyness, femininity), and situational factors (e.g., employment status, incidence of neighborhood crime) to the respondents' subjective perceptions about one or more aspects of their close relationship (e.g., satisfaction, conflict resolution). The typical goal of this research is to increase our understanding of how individuals' social identities, personalities, and life circumstances affect the way their close relationships are experienced and described (Harvey, Hendrick, & Tucker, 1988).

Not all questionnaire studies are conducted by mail, however. College-age respondents are often asked to respond to research questionnaires in classroom or laboratory settings (e.g., Simpson & Gangestad, 1991). They may enter their responses into a computer or mark them down on computer-scorable answer sheets instead of writing them directly on the questionnaire itself. While mail-out surveys can be a useful way to sample the responses of people in the community at large, such people can also be reached through survey questionnaires published in local or national newspapers and magazines (e.g., Shaver & Rubenstein, 1983).

As Susan and Clyde Hendrick (1992) have noted, "the development of relationship-oriented [questionnaire] measures has greatly increased in recent years, so that now there are measures for love (e.g., Hendrick & Hendrick,

1986), intimacy (e.g., Lund, 1985), romantic beliefs (e.g., Sprecher & Metts, 1989), self-disclosure (e.g., Miller, Berg, & Archer, 1983), and a host of other concepts" (p. 11).

Interview Studies

Self-report data can also be collected through either face-to-face or telephone interview studies. For example, John Antill and his students used face-to-face interviews to collect the same type of data that Lamke (1989) later collected by mailing out questionnaires (Antill, 1983). After recruiting potential subjects at various shopping centers in the metropolitan area of Sydney, Australia, Antill's research assistants conducted in-home interviews with 108 married couples. During these interviews, both spouses independently provided responses to the Bem Sex-Role Inventory (Bem, 1974) and the Spanier Dyadic Adjustment Scale (Spanier, 1976). Like Lamke (1989), Antill (1983) found that marital satisfaction for both husbands and wives was uniquely predicted by the degree to which their partners were seen as having the traditionally feminine traits of being kind, considerate, and emotionally supportive.

It is possible that the same data could also have been collected through telephone interviews. However, Antill's decision to conduct face-to-face interviews probably reflected his belief that subjects who were interviewed by telephone would have been less cooperative in providing a large number of responses about a highly personal matter (i.e., their marital satisfaction) to an anonymous caller.

Diary and Account Studies

Paul Rosenblatt, while doing research on romantic love, came across the diary of Mollie Dorsey Sanford (1959) and was so fascinated by it that he spent several years "tracking down unpublished nineteenth century diaries with material on close relationships". He soon realized that "grief was the most common aspect of the close relationships that was represented in the diaries. A few diaries dealt with marital disenchantment, a few with courtship, a few with problems in child-rearing; but many dealt with deaths and separation" (Rosenblatt, 1983, p. vii).

Rosenblatt's analysis of these diaries addressed a range of issues regarding the grief process, including the time course and patterning of grief, the events and occasions that re-invoke it, and the ways that individuals and family systems attempt to cope with it. Diary studies have not been frequently used in the study of close relationships, and they represent a rich and largely untapped source of data. It may be possible, for example, to compare the size and diversity of individuals' social networks through the data available in their diaries, with *The Diary of H. L. Mencken* providing a prototypical example.

Accounts of close relationships can be found in a variety of forms. "Naturalistically, they may appear in diary form or in recordings, letters and notes, and even videotapes" (Harvey et al., 1988, p. 108). In one recent study, subjects were asked to provide a running commentary on their conversation with a co-participant on a microcomputer network (Daly, Webster, Vangelisti, Maxwell, & Neel, 1989). The typical focus of most account studies is the differences that are found when separate accounts of the same relational event(s) are compared. For example, the accounts of marriage partners can reveal differences so striking that it appears "as if there are two different relationships cohabiting in one marriage" (Mansfield & Collard, 1988, p. 39). Even the accounts of the same individual can differ substantially as time passes and the benefits of hindsight accumulate (Burnett, 1987; Harvey et al., 1988).

Interaction Record Studies

The use of interaction record studies in relationship research is based on the assumption that people can monitor their social life while they are in the process of living it. To appreciate this assumption, imagine that as you interact with various people during the course of a typical day, you take mental notes on each of these interactions. You remember the time of day each interaction occurred, how long it lasted, the number of people you were with, the gender of these interaction partners, how pleasant or unpleasant the interaction was, and so on. Periodically, you retrieve these interaction records from your memory and convert them into written form. The data in these written records are subsequently analyzed to determine what your general pattern of social interaction looks like: whether you have many social contacts or only a few, whether your interactions are mostly with members of the same sex or with members of the opposite sex, how much you self-disclose and to whom, and so on.

Interest in this research method was stimulated by a series of studies conducted by Ladd Wheeler, John Nezlek, Harry Reis, and their colleagues at the University of Rochester (Reis & Wheeler, 1991). In these studies, college-age subjects used the Rochester Interaction Record (RIR)—a standardized form depicted in Figure 8.1—to make a record of each of their social interactions that lasted 10 minutes or longer. The subjects were asked to keep these records for an extended period of time (typically, 10–14 days) in order to adequately sample their general pattern of social activity. To date, the RIR has been used to study a range of topics that include loneliness (Wheeler, Reis, & Nezlek, 1983), adaptation to the college environment (Wheeler & Nezlek, 1977), the impact of physical attractiveness on one's social life (Reis, Nezlek, & Wheeler, 1980), and the tendency to withdraw from other relationships during the later stages of courtship (Milardo, Johnson, & Huston 1983).

More recently, Steve Duck and his colleagues at the University of Iowa have developed the Iowa Communication Record (ICR) to permit a more focused and intensive study of the conversations that take place between interaction partners (Duck, 1991). The ICR contains questions about the content of the conversation, the context in which it occurred, and its perceived quality, purpose, and impact on the participants' relationship. Steve Duck,

DATE OF INTERACTION ....
TIME .... AM/PM
LENGTH: ....HRS ....MIN
INITIALS IF MORE THAN 3 OTHERS:...
SEX   #OF FEMALES ....#OF MALES ....

INTIMACY: SUPERFICIAL   1 2 3 4 5 6 7   MEANINGFUL

I DISCLOSED: VERY LITTLE   1 2 3 4 5 6 7   A GREAT DEAL

OTHER DISCLOSED: VERY LITTLE   1 2 3 4 5 6 7   A GREAT DEAL

QUALITY: UNPLEASANT   1 2 3 4 5 6 7   PLEASANT

SATISFACTION: LESS THAN EXPECTED   1 2 3 4 5 6 7   MORE THAN EXPECTED

INITIATION: I INITIATED   1 2 3 4 5 6 7   OTHER INITIATED

INFLUENCE: I INFLUENCED MORE   1 2 3 4 5 6 7   OTHER INFLUENCED MORE

NATURE OF INTERACTION:

    WORK   TASK   PASTIME   CONVERSATION   DATE

Figure 8.1   The Rochester Interaction Record

Kris Pond, and Geoff Leatham (1991) have used the ICR in a recent study in which each pair of subjects was videotaped interacting for five minutes while a second pair of subjects observed their interaction. The results indicated that active participants (insiders) and passive observers (outsiders) have different views of the interaction, particularly with regard to its perceived quality and intimacy, even though they have presumably attended to the same behavioral cues. For research suggesting a similar conclusion, see Abbey (1982) and Floyd and Markman (1983).

Interaction record studies using the RIR and the ICR are event-contingent, requiring respondents to report their experience each time an appropriate event (e.g., an interaction at least 10 minutes long) has occurred. In contrast, other interaction record studies have been interval-contingent, requiring respondents to report at regular, predetermined intervals; or signal-contingent, requiring respondents to report whenever signaled by the researcher (Wheeler & Reis, 1991). For example, Dirk Revenstorf and his colleagues used an interval-contingent interaction record study when they asked couples involved in marital therapy to make daily ratings of six aspects of their relationship (Revenstorf, Hahlwegg, Schindler, & Kunert, 1984). These data were subsequently analyzed using time series statistics in order to assess the changes that occurred in the couples' relationships over time.

Signal-contingent studies require subjects to complete an interaction record whenever the experimenter signals them by means of a telephone call or the beeping of an electronic pager. In an elegant study using telephone calls to signal the subjects and to record their responses, Ted Huston and his colleagues phoned married couples nine times during a two- or three-week period. During these calls, each spouse was asked to report on activities in the past 24 hours that included household tasks, leisure activities, positive and negative interaction events, conflict, and conversations (Huston, Robins, Atkinson, & McHale, 1987). In a study which sampled the day-to-day experiences of 170 high school students, Maria Mei-Ha Wong and Mihaly Csikszentmihalyi (1991) used preprogrammed electronic pagers to signal their teenage subjects to complete a behavioral self-report measure at randomly determined intervals. One of their strongest findings was that the girls spent more time with friends and less time alone than the boys.

Epistolary Studies

An analysis of letters (e.g., epistles) and other forms of written correspondence (e.g., electronic mail) represents another way in which self-report data can be used to study relationships. As Catalin Mamali has noted in his epistolary study of the relationship between Theodore Dreiser and H. L. Mencken, the letters which two people exchange can provide coherent, chronological records of interpersonal cognitions, emotions, accounts, communications, and actions (Mamali, 1991). They can be very useful in documenting a consistent style of relating to others, as evidenced by the relentlessly irreverent letters of Groucho Marx (1987). Because written correspondence is also a mode of relating to others, epistolary studies may also have much to teach us about the dynamics of personal relationships as they are expressed in this as well as in other modes (Mamali, 1992).

Peer Report Methods

Peer report methods have rarely been used in the study of close relationships. These methods require one or more knowledgeable informants to serve as respondents, providing data in the form of verbal or written information about the relationship(s) of people with whom they are acquainted.

In contrast to research using self-report methods, which frequently seeks evidence of differences in the viewpoints of the individual relationship members, research using peer report methods frequently seeks evidence of agreement or consensus among the set of peer respondents in their perceptions of a given relationship. Whereas self-report research tends to focus on the different subjective reactions of the individual members of a relationship, peer report research tends to focus on the shared, intersubjective reactions of a set of peers who all view the relationship from the outside, as observers and knowledgeable informants. Theoretical interest in the agreement or consensus of peer reports is based on the assumption that such consensus is not coincidental, but points instead to genuine relational phenomena that are potentially worthy of study.

In theory, peer report methods in relationship research can take the same forms as self-report methods:

(a) questionnaire studies;
(b) face-to-face or telephone interview studies;
(c) diary and account studies;
(d) interaction record studies; and
(e) epistolary studies of written correspondence.

In practice, however, close relationship researchers have seldom attempted to collect peer report data—even though they are the kind of data that are routinely collected by biographers and social historians (see, for example, Jean Stein's (1982) biography of Andy Warhol's protégé Edith Sedgwick—a biography composed entirely of excerpts from the conversational accounts of people who knew Edie, or knew of her). Still, if researchers are willing to invest the time and effort required, they could probably learn much by asking knowledgeable observers of a given relationship to complete questionnaires, answer interview questions, provide written accounts, keep interaction records, or allow their own correspondence about the relationship to be examined.

Observational Methods

There is a simple way to distinguish peer report studies from observational studies in relationship research. Peer report studies, in the strictest sense of the term, involve verbal or written reports made by observer-acquaintances whose insights are based on their cumulative knowledge of the relationship members and the history of their relationship. In contrast, observational studies involve summary judgments or behavioral records made by trained raters who typically have no prior knowledge of the relationship members or the history of their relationship. An important consequence of this distinction is that peer report studies are extremely rare in close relationship research whereas observational studies are relatively common.

As Ickes and Tooke (1988, p. 80) have noted, the range of relationships that have been studied by observational methods is impressively large:

> To cite just a few representative examples, the observational method has been applied to the study of children's quarrels (Dawe, 1934) and children's friendships (Gottman and Parker, 1986). It has been used to explore the interactions of poker players (Hayano, 1980), police officers (Rubenstein, 1973), prison inmates (Jacobs, 1974) distressed and nondistressed married couples (Gottman, 1979), and the families of schizophrenics (Cheek and Anthony, 1970). In clinical and counseling psychology, its most common application has been to the study of therapist-client relationships (Jones, Reid, & Patterson, 1975; Scheflen, 1974).

The range of behaviors that can be observed and recorded is also impressively large, and may be limited only by the researcher's imagination.

According to Karl Weick (1968), researchers may study nonverbal behaviors such as facial expressions, directed gazes, body movements, and interpersonal distance; extralinguistic behaviors such as the pitch, amplitude, and rate of speech; and linguistic behaviors such as giving suggestions, expressing agreement, or asking for an opinion or evaluation. In some studies, researchers may examine only one behavior, such as the eyeblinks that people display when they are observed in natural settings (Ponder & Kennedy, 1927). In other studies, researchers may examine several behaviors, such as the talking, smiling, gazing and gesturing of opposite-sex strangers (Garcia, Stinson, Ickes, Bissonnette, & Briggs, 1991). Researchers may also explore more extensive patterns of behavior, such as the reciprocation of negative feelings during conflict by distressed versus nondistressed married couples (Gottman, 1979).

Although many observational studies are conducted in laboratory settings (e.g., Gottman, Markman, & Notarius, 1977; Ickes, 1984), many others are conducted in real-world settings as diverse as an auction (Clark & Halford, 1978), a party (Riesman & Watson, 1964), a high school (Barker & Gump, 1964), a hospital delivery room (Leventhal & Sharp, 1965), a police station (Holdaway, 1980), a subway train (Fried & DeFazio, 1974), and the United Nations building (Alger, 1966). Whatever setting is chosen, it is important that the observation itself be as unobtrusive as possible. Recording the subjects' interaction by means of a hidden video camera for later analysis (Ickes, 1983; Ickes et al., 1990a) provides one means of ensuring that the subjects' behavior will not be biased by the presence of trained raters on the scene. Having college roommates start an audio tape recorder in their dormitory room whenever they begin a conversation is also a relatively unobtrusive way to study their naturally occurring interactions (Ginsberg & Gottman, 1986). However, putting directional microphones in subjects' faces and requiring them to interact in front of a camera crew or in the presence of trained raters will virtually guarantee that their behavior will be altered or interfered with by the recording process itself.

Life-event Archival Methods

Some of the problems explored by relationship researchers can be studied by means of life-event data that are publicly available in archival sources. A good example is the archival study by Frank Trovato of the relationship between divorce and suicide in Canada (Trovato, 1986, 1987; Trovato & Lauris, 1989). Susan and Clyde Hendrick (1992, pp. 14–15) have described this study as follows:

> Trovato used census-type demographic data from all the Canadian provinces to assess the impact of divorce on suicide, taking into consideration the effects of other variables such as educational level, religious preferences, marriage rates, and geographical mobility between provinces. He determined that divorce has a substantial effect on suicide rate (1986), and he did this without administering a single questionnaire or making even one behavioral observation.

Trovato's findings were similar to those of Steven Stack, who used the same kinds of archival data to test the relationship between divorce and suicide in the United States (Stack, 1980, 1981) and in Norway (Stack, 1989). As this set of studies illustrates, data concerning major life events can be obtained from national agencies that compile statistics from official records such as divorce decrees and birth, marriage, and death certificates. Researchers such as Stack and Trovato can then use these archival data to test important hypotheses about personal relationships without having any direct contact with the subjects of their research. Of all of the methods available for conducting relationship research, the archival methods are the least obtrusive. For this reason, they are the least likely to be biased by the subjects' reactions to the researcher.

Experimental Methods

Experimental methods in relationship research are used to determine whether changes in the level of certain independent variables cause corresponding changes to be observed in the level of one or more dependent variables. In any application of the experimental method, the independent variables are the ones that are systematically manipulated by the experimenter, whereas the dependent variables are the ones that are subsequently measured by the experimenter. For a study to qualify as a true experiment, two criteria must be met. First, the experimenter must manipulate, or systematically vary, the level of the independent variable (the specific treatment that subjects receive) across the set of experimental conditions. Second, the experimenter must randomly assign the subjects (as individuals, dyads, groups, etc.) to each of the experimental conditions.

For example, William Ickes, Miles Patterson, D. W. Rajecki, and Sarah Tanford (1982) conducted a study in which one member of each pair of male strangers (the perceiver) was randomly assigned to receive one of three different kinds of pre-interaction information about the other member (the target). Specifically, some perceivers were led to expect that their target partners would act very friendly, others were led to expect that their partners would act very unfriendly, and a third (control) group was given no expectancy information. Of course, the information the perceivers received was in no case based on what their interactional partners were actually like; it was instead manipulated independently by the experimenters.

The results of the study converged to suggest that, relative to the no-expectancy perceivers, the friendly-expectancy perceivers adopted a reciprocal interaction strategy (one designed to reciprocate the friendly behaviors they expected their partner to display), whereas the unfriendly-expectancy perceivers adopted a compensatory interaction strategy (one designed to compensate for the unfriendly behaviors they expected their partner to display). Because the experimenters determined what kind of expectancy information the perceivers received, and the subjects (perceivers and targets) were randomly assigned to the three expectancy conditions, the differences in the perceivers' behavior in the three conditions could be attributed to the different expectancies that were created rather than to differences in the types of subjects assigned to the three conditions. In other words, the only plausible cause of the difference in the perceivers' behavior in the three conditions was the difference in the expectancies which the experimenters had established.

As this example suggests, researchers who use the experimental method in relationship research often seek to identify those independent variables whose manipulation establishes the varying conditions in which different types of relational phenomena (for example, reciprocity versus compensation) will be observed. Occasionally, however, experimenters may pursue the opposite goal of manipulating the presence or absence of certain relational phenomena in order to assess their effects on subjects' perceptions of the relationship (e.g., Clark, 1985; Clark & Mills, 1979).

Physiological Methods

Perhaps the most fanciful option in our list of ways to discover Janice and Don's true feelings about each other is Option 13: "Sit them down side-by-side, hooked up to a Libido Meter." This option may be more realistic than it sounds, however. A growing number of relationship researchers are using physiological methods to determine how their subjects respond to others at the visceral level, that is, the level at which various bodily reactions are measured. Men's sexual arousal, for example, is often assessed by means of a mercury-in-rubber strain gauge which measures changes in penile tumescence (i.e., degree of erection). If we could somehow persuade Don to wear the penile gauge while reading two sexual scenarios—one in which he made love to Janice and one in which he made love in the same way to his ex-girlfriend, Linda—we might expect his "Libido Meter" to reveal greater sexual arousal in response to Janice than to Linda.

It is important to realize, however, that the same method we might use to assess Don's passionate love for Janice could be used to assess socially undesirable forms of sexual arousal as well. As Neil Malamuth (1986) has noted, a measure called the penile tumescence rape index has proven useful in distinguishing rapists from nonrapists. Research with this index suggests that men whose maximum penile tumescence in response to a rape scenario is greater than their maximum tumescence to a consensual sex scenario may have a predisposition to rape (Quinsey, Chaplin, Maguire & Upfold, 1987).

Physiological methods have also been used to demonstrate that a high level of physiological arousal during marital conflict is strongly correlated with a long-term decline in marital satisfaction. Robert Levenson and John Gottman (1983, 1985) arranged to have 30 married couples argue about high-conflict issues in the laboratory while their physiological reactions (heart rate, skin conductance, etc.) were monitored. When they contacted the couples three years later, they found that the couples whose marital satisfaction had declined the most were the same couples who had displayed the greatest physiological arousal during the laboratory conflict. In fact, "the correlation between the husband's heart rate during the conflict discussion and decline in marital satisfaction was 0.92" (Gottman & Levenson, 1986, p. 41). Apparently, having a marital partner who makes your heart beat faster is not always a good thing!

Eclectic Approaches

In contemporary research on relationships, it is becoming increasingly common for researchers to use eclectic approaches which combine two or more of the types of methods described above. The researcher's goal in these cases is to combine the different methods in such a way that they build on each other's strengths and compensate for each other's weaknesses. A useful example of the eclectic approach is the unstructured dyadic interaction paradigm developed by William Ickes (who feels weird referring to himself in the third person) and his colleagues (who feel weird being referred to as "et al.") (Ickes, 1983; Ickes & Tooke, 1988; Ickes et al., 1990a).

The general procedure is as follows: the members of each dyad—who can be strangers, acquaintances, or intimates, depending on the purposes of the study—are led into a waiting room and left there together in the experimenter's absence. During this time in which the subjects are ostensibly waiting for the experiment to begin, their verbal and nonverbal behaviors are unobtrusively audio- and videotaped. When the experimenter returns at the end of the observation period, the subjects are partially debriefed and asked for their signed consent to release the videotape of their interaction for use as data. They are also asked to participate in a second part of the study that concerns the specific thoughts and feelings they had during the interaction.

If their signed consent is given, the subjects are then seated in separate but identical cubicles where they are each instructed to view a videotaped copy of the interaction. By stopping the videotape with a remote start/pause control at those points where they remember having had a specific thought or feeling, each subject makes a written, time-logged listing on a standardized form (see Figure 8.2(a)) of these *actual thought–feeling entries*. The subjects are then instructed to view the videotape a second time, during which the tape is stopped for them at each of those points at which their interaction partner reported a thought or feeling. The subject's task during this pass through the tape is to infer the content of their partner's thoughts and feelings and provide a written, time-logged listing on a second, standardized form (see Figure 8.2(b)) of these *inferred thought–feeling entries*. When both subjects have completed this task, they are asked to complete a posttest questionnaire assessing their perceptions of themselves and their partner during the interaction. They are then debriefed more completely, thanked, and released.

DATE_____

NUMBER _____

| | | M | F |

TIME	THOUGHT OR FEELING	+, 0, −	
	☐ I was thinking: ☐ I was feeling:	+ 0 −	
	☐ I was thinking: ☐ I was feeling:	+ 0 −	
	☐ I was thinking: ☐ I was feeling:	+ 0 −	
	☐ I was thinking: ☐ I was feeling:	+ 0 −	
	☐ I was thinking: ☐ I was feeling:	+ 0 −	
	☐ I was thinking: ☐ I was feeling:	+ 0 −	
	☐ I was thinking: ☐ I was feeling:	+ 0 −	
	☐ I was thinking: ☐ I was feeling:	+ 0 −	
	☐ I was thinking: ☐ I was feeling:	+ 0 −	
	☐ I was thinking: ☐ I was feeling:	+ 0 −	

Figure 8.2(a) Standardized thought/feeling reporting form

DATE_____

NUMBER_____

M   F

TIME	THOUGHT OR FEELING	+, 0, −	
	☐ He/she was thinking: ☐ He/she was feeling:	+ 0 −	
	☐ He/she was thinking: ☐ He/she was feeling:	+ 0 −	
	☐ He/she was thinking: ☐ He/she was feeling:	+ 0 −	
	☐ He/she was thinking: ☐ He/she was feeling:	+ 0 −	
	☐ He/she was thinking: ☐ He/she was feeling:	+ 0 −	
	☐ He/she was thinking: ☐ He/she was feeling:	+ 0 −	
	☐ He/she was thinking: ☐ He/she was feeling:	+ 0 −	
	☐ He/she was thinking: ☐ He/she was feeling:	+ 0 −	
	☐ He/she was thinking: ☐ He/she was feeling:	+ 0 −	
	☐ He/she was thinking: ☐ He/she was feeling:	+ 0 −	

Figure 8.2(b)   Standardized thought/feeling inference form

The unstructured dyadic interaction paradigm combines a number of the methods already described in this chapter. First, the observational method is used when the participants' interaction behavior is unobtrusively recorded on audio- and videotape for later analysis. Second, the subjects are cued by the events recorded on the videotape to make an event-contingent self-report interaction record of their own thoughts and feelings during the interaction. Third, they are then cued by the same videotape to make an event-contingent peer-report interaction record of the inferred thoughts and feelings of their interaction partners. Fourth, the subjects complete a posttest questionnaire in which they provide additional self-report and peer-report data. Fifth, in some cases the experimental method can be incorporated into this procedure, as illustrated by the previously described study in which one male dyad member was randomly designated to receive false feedback about the friendliness or unfriendliness of the other male dyad member before their interaction took place (Ickes et al., 1982, Experiment 1).

To further illustrate the eclecticism of this procedure, imagine that we are able to study Janice's and Don's relationship using the unstructured dyadic interaction paradigm. By means of the posttest questionnaire data, we can ask straightforward questions about Janice's view of the relationship (Option 1 of our original list) and about Don's view of the relationship (Option 2). By means of the unobtrusive audiotaping and videotaping procedure (Options 10 and 12), we can observe Janice and Don closely while they are left alone together (Option 4). By means of the thought–feeling records they are later asked to create, we can read their private thoughts and feelings as directly as if we were reading their personal diaries (Option 8)—and almost as directly as if we were reading their minds (Option 14!). And, by comparing the content of Janice's actual thoughts and feelings with the content of Don's inferences about her thoughts and feelings (and vice versa), we can even determine how good they are at reading each other's minds (Ickes et al., 1990a, 1990b; Stinson & Ickes, 1992)!

THE TRADE-OFF PROBLEM IN CLOSE RELATIONSHIP RESEARCH

Earlier in this chapter it was noted that any choice of method for studying relationships represents a complex trade-off—one in which the combined strengths and weaknesses of the method that the researcher decides to use are weighed against the combined strengths and weaknesses of any alternative method(s) that the researcher decides not to use. What are the strengths and weaknesses of the various methods we have reviewed above? What kinds of trade-offs do researchers typically make when choosing to use one method instead of another? In what ways can different methods be combined so as to complement each others' strengths and compensate for each others' weaknesses?

Strengths and Weaknesses of the Various Methods

Each type of method used by relationship researchers is characterized by its own distinctive strengths and weaknesses. Following are summaries of these strengths and weaknesses:

Self-report Methods

According to John Harvey and his colleagues (Harvey, Christenson, & Mc-Clintock, 1983; Harvey, Hendrick, & Tucker, 1988), there are at least three major advantages of using self-report methods to study relationships. First, self-reports are relatively easy, efficient, and inexpensive to obtain from the participants in the relationships. Second, they represent the only way researchers currently have to access purely subjective events, such as the participants' thoughts, feelings, perceptions, expectancies, and memories. Third, they enable researchers to obtain the participants' reports of certain overt behaviors that are typically private, and that might otherwise remain inaccessible to study (for example, conflict and sexual behavior).

Contrasted with these strengths are a variety of weaknesses (Duck & Sants, 1983; Harvey et al., 1983, 1988; Huston et al., 1987; Wheeler & Reis, 1991). First, participants may not understand the researchers' questions, or may interpret them differently from the way the researchers intended. Second, the participants' self-reports may be biased by:

(a) poor, selective, or distorted memory;
(b) reactions against what are perceived to be invasive and inappropriate questions by the researcher;
(c) egocentric reactions that fail to give appropriate weight to the relational perceptions of one's interaction partners;
(d) egodefensive reactions designed to promote a favorable view of oneself and one's actions; and
(e) "errors in the calculation of events, questionnaire response biases, and so on" (Harvey et al., 1988, p. 110).

Third, any single participant's view of the relationship is necessarily incomplete, and there is no guarantee that combining the individual views of all the participants will produce an image that is any more coherent than that of the blind men's views of the elephant. Fourth, the degree to which the researcher is perceived by the participants as an insider or outsider may not only affect their trust and willingness to self-disclose but can also alter the dynamics of the relationship itself (Levinger, 1977).

Of course, some types of self-report methods are less susceptible than others to the problems described above. For example, misunderstanding or misinterpreting the researchers' questions is not an issue that is relevant to diary and epistolary studies. And memory-based biases can be reduced, if not eliminated, in interaction record studies if relational events are recorded as soon as possible after they occur (Huston et al., 1987; Wheeler & Reis, 1991). Other forms of bias may be difficult to eliminate, however, and collectively may constitute the greatest potential threat to the validity of any methods that rely exclusively on the participants' self-reports.

Peer Report Methods

Peer report data can be used to obtain information about the subjective thoughts and feelings of relationship participants which they have confided to peer respondents. In addition, such data can provide some insight into private behaviors, such as sex and conflict, which the relationship members may have confided to their peers. However, peer report data are not as easily and as inexpensively obtained as self-report data, because they require the researcher to identify knowledgeable peer respondents and persuade them to provide information about the relationship of people who, if still living, may regard their cooperation in the research enterprise as both an invasion of privacy and a breach of trust. They are also susceptible to many of the same biases as self-report data, although some of the biases of individual respondents may be canceled out when their data are combined with those of other respondents.

Observational Methods

At their best, observational data can have the weight of objectively recorded facts. To the extent that they were obtained in an unobtrusive, nonreactive manner and are based on representative samples of the participants' behavior, observational data may be among the most valid types of data available. On the other hand, observational data are expensive and inconvenient to obtain. In most cases, they require sophisticated electronic equipment to record the succession of events that unfold over time in the relationships being studied. In nearly all cases, they require the presence of trained raters to code and often re-code various aspects of the participants' behavior from the resulting behavioral records. Moreover, the analyses of such data are typically complicated by the between-dyad and within-dyad interdependence of the participants' responses (Bissonnette, 1992; Kenny, 1988; Kenny & Kashy, 1991). Finally, observational methods may require that the participants' privacy be invaded, and may raise other ethical questions as well (Middlemist, Knowles, & Matter, 1976, 1977; Koocher, 1977).

Life-event Archival Methods

As noted earlier, life-event archival methods have a number of advantages. They do not require researchers to collect original data, allowing them to rely instead on statistical information about major life events (births, marriages, divorces, etc.) that have previously been compiled by various public agencies. Moreover, because archival methods do not require researchers to have any direct contact with the subjects of their research, they are among the most unobtrusive and nonreactive methods available. On the other hand, archival data can display some serious limitations as well. For example, "because of idiosyncrasies and/or shortcomings in methods of reporting", different institutions (different cities, counties, states, etc.) may provide data that differ substantially in their accuracy, their completeness, and the criteria used in compiling them (Cox, Paulus, & McCain, 1984, p. 1149). In addition, relationships based on summary statistics for large populations "may not accurately reflect the actual experience" of the individuals who comprise the summary statistics (Baum & Paulus, 1987, p. 541).

Experimental Methods

The major advantage of using experimental methods to study relationships is the ability of well-designed experiments to establish causal relationships between independent variables that are manipulated by the experimenter and dependent variables that are measured by the experimenter. There are three major disadvantages of using experimental methods, according to Charles Tardy and Lawrence Hosman (1991). First, many laboratory studies create interaction situations that may strike the participants as being somewhat artificial or unnatural—a criticism that is less often applied to field experiments conducted outside of the lab. Second, the typical experiment confronts the participants with a psychologically strong situation that encourages them to behave as passive reactors rather than as active agents (Ickes, 1982; Snyder & Ickes, 1985). Third, because the specific conditions established in the experiment may not match the real-world conditions of the participants' everyday lives, the results of experiments may lack ecological validity and may not always generalize well to other settings.

Physiological Methods

The most obvious and unique strength of using physiological measures to study relationships is their potential to measure people's visceral reactions to each other. Countering this strength, however, are certain barriers which John Cacioppo and Richard Petty have described as impeding the application of physiological procedures to the study of important social processes. Perhaps the most daunting of these barriers is the extensive "physiological background, technical sophistication, and elaborate instrumentation that are necessary for collecting, reducing, and analyzing interpretable psychophysiological data in already complex social-psychological paradigms" (Cacioppo & Petty, 1986, p. 649). Other obstacles include the high cost (in time, equipment, and trained personnel) of conducting this type of research, the participants' reactivity to certain kinds of physiological measures, and the fact that some physiological measures may be perceived as highly invasive (the strain gauge measure of penile tumescence, for example!).

TYPICAL TRADE-OFFS IN THE CHOICE OF A METHOD

What kinds of trade-offs do researchers typically make when choosing to use one method instead of another? In general, researchers who rely exclusively on self-report data benefit from the convenience of collecting such data and from the insights the data offer into the subjective experience and private behaviors of the relationship members. On the other hand, these researchers run the risk that their self-report data may be biased in any of a number of ways described previously. Moreover, unless they assess the subjective perceptions of all of the participants in the relationship, these researchers may run the risk of obtaining a very one-sided view that, in the worst case, represents the egocentric perceptions of only a single respondent. Finally, unless the researchers' self-report data take the form of interaction records, they may fail to learn much, if anything, about the specific behaviors on which their subjects' perceptions are presumably based.

Researchers who rely on peer report data will typically make the same kinds of trade-offs, but the problems will be magnified because their respondents are not the actual participants in the relationships being studied, but are instead peer informants. Because these peer informants may differ greatly in how much knowledge they actually have about the relationship, and how willing they are to report gossip and hearsay as fact, it is even more important than in the case of self-report data that the researchers seek evidence of convergence and consensus in their informants' responses.

Researchers who use observational, physiological, and life-event archival methods will typically benefit by obtaining information about the behavior of the relationship participants that is objective, reliable, and free from many of the sources of bias that can plague self-report research. On the other hand, researchers who rely exclusively on these methods may find it difficult to determine the meaning these behaviors have for the relationship members (Harvey et al. 1988). In order to establish this meaning, the objective recording of behavior must be supplemented by the participants' own self-reports.

Finally, researchers who rely exclusively on experimental methods will typically benefit from being able to identify specific causal relationships. As a trade-off, however, they will often incur the risk that these relationships may not generalize well beyond the specific conditions established within the experiment itself.

COMBINING METHODS AS A SOLUTION TO THE TRADE-OFF PROBLEM

Increasingly, relationship researchers have begun to use eclectic approaches as a solution to the trade-off problem. Their general strategy, as illustrated by the unstructured dyadic interaction paradigm described earlier in this chapter, is to combine different methods in such a way that they build on each other's strengths and compensate for each other's weaknesses. When this strategy is successfully applied, the integration of different methods within a single research project may enable researchers to demonstrate a convergence or triangulation of results across the various methods. It may also broaden the researchers' view of the relational phenomena they are studying in ways that can help them to account for any discrepancies in the patterns of results obtained by one method versus another. Obtaining these important advantages also involves a trade-off, however, in that eclectic approaches often require a greater investment of time, effort, and other resources than single-method approaches require.

CONCLUSIONS AND SUMMARY

What have you learned to this point? Well, you learned this morning from your friend Chris that Janice and Don eloped late last night, and are heading for Las Vegas where they plan to be married before continuing on to Lake Tahoe for a two-week honeymoon. Ironically, despite all of your interest, they didn't even bother to tell you; and, as it turns out, you are one of their last friends to know.

Fortunately, however, that is not all that you have learned. To remind you of what else you have learned in this this chapter, I offer the following summary statement: "This chapter has reviewed the different research methods by which social scientists have INQUIRED about PEOPLE'S relationships." If you can remember even two words of this summary statement (guess which two words), you should also be able to remember the different types of methods that relationship researchers have used. As you might have guessed, these two words are mnemonic devices or memory aids. More specifically, they are acrostic-anagrams that are formed by taking the first letters of the different types of methods and then reordering these letters to form the words INQUIRED and PEOPLE'S. The second word, PEOPLE'S, is an acrostic-anagram that gives you the first letters of the major types of methods used by relationship researchers. These, in their newly scrambled order, are Peer report, Experimental, Observational, Physiological, Life-event archival, Eclectic, and Self-report. The first word, INQUIRED, is an acrostic-anagram that gives you the first letters of the different subcategories of self-report methods that relationship researchers have used. These letters should help to remind you of INterview studies, QUestionnaire studies, Interaction Record studies, Epistolary studies of written correspondence, and Diary and account studies. In the interest of ensuring that our author–reader relationship will live on in your memory (for a while, at least), I leave these two words with you.

Chapter 9

On the Statistics of Interdependence: Treating Dyadic Data with Respect*

Richard Gonzalez

University of Michigan, Ann Arbor, MI, USA

and

Dale Griffin

University of British Columbia, Vancouver, Canada

> *"The time has come" the Walrus said,*
> *"to talk of many things:*
> *Of shoes and ships and sealing wax,*
> *of cabbages and kings...*
>   (LEWIS CARROLL, *Through the Looking Glass*)

Dyadic relationships form the core element of our social lives. They also form the core unit of study by relationship researchers. Then why (to paraphrase Woody Allen) do so many analyses in this area focus on only one consenting adult at a time? The reason, we suspect, has to do with the rather austere authority figures of our early professional development: statistics professors who conveyed the cherished assumption of independent sampling. However,

---

* This research was supported by a grant from the National Science Foundation (Gonzalez) and by a grant from the Social Sciences and Humanities Research Council of Canada (Griffin).

The Social Psychology of Personal Relationships.
Edited by William Ickes and Steve Duck. © 2000 John Wiley & Sons Ltd.

when we collect data in which the sample units do not arrive one at a time, as in the idealized world of independence, but instead arrive two at a time as in the real world of dyadic interdependence, we are faced with a frustrating dilemma. How do we capture the psychology of interdependence with the statistics of independence?

Unfortunately for the development of interpersonal relationships theory, the patterns laid down during the imprinting period of graduate statistics classes tend to dominate the rest of one's professional life. Interdependence in one's data is typically viewed as a nuisance and so dyadic researchers have developed strategies to sweep interdependence under the statistical rug. These strategies include (a) averaging interdependence away by creating a sample of "independent" dyad mean scores, (b) partialling interdependence out and thereby creating a sample of "independent" individual scores, and (c) dropping one dyad member's scores and thus creating a truncated sample of "independent" individual scores. This ritual mutilation of dyadic data comes at a high cost: important information about the similarity or dissimilarity between dyad members is lost.

In this chapter, we review some recent developments in dyadic data analysis that are aimed at making the statistics of interdependence as accessible as the statistics of independence (see Kenny, 1988, for a similar analysis from a slightly different perspective). These techniques give researchers the ability to study interdependence directly; they view interdependence as an opportunity to ask novel research questions, not as a problem to avoid. We focus on correlational and regression methods because these represent the areas of greatest confusion among researchers. The techniques we will describe should help prevent four particular errors of interpretation that haunt dyadic data analysis: the assumed independence error, the deletion error, the cross-level or ecological error, and the levels of analysis error. We first discuss these four common errors in the analysis of dyadic data and then present a general framework that can handle many data analysis issues that occur when subsets of subjects are interdependent.

FOUR COMMON ERRORS

We consider the problems and opportunities of dyadic data analysis in light of a specific example. Stinson and Ickes (1992) had pairs of male students interact in an unstructured "waiting room" situation. These interactions, some between friends and some between strangers, were videotaped and coded on a number of dimensions including the frequency of verbalizations and the frequency of gazes. How should researchers evaluate the strength of the linear relation between speaking and gazing in the context of individuals interacting in dyads? We point out four errors that researchers should avoid when evaluating the linear relation between two variables in the context of dyads.[1]

---

[1] These errors were not made by Stinson and Ickes, who used these data to answer different research questions than those being addressed here.

First, researchers must avoid the *assumed independence error*, which consists of correlating the $2N$ interdependent data points as if they were independent (where N represents the number of dyads). To do this would invalidate the statistical test of the correlation, which depends primarily on the appropriate sample size (see also Kenny, 1995b). One remedy is to adjust the significance test to take into account the degree and type of interdependence in the sample. This approach is described in more detail later in the chapter.

Second, researchers should not create independent data by throwing out half their sample, an error that we call the *deletion error*. Although in some situations this may not bias the actual correlation obtained, it is a waste of power to drop subjects. The deletion error also prevents the researcher from assessing the type and degree of interdependence in dyads. We view the assessment of interdependence as an opportunity to examine interesting theoretical questions, not as a statistical nuisance that needs to be eliminated.

Third, researchers must avoid the tendency to generalize from one level of aggregation to another, the *cross-level error*. In particular, researchers should not attempt to circumvent the independence problem by creating dyadic averages on each variable and then interpreting the correlation between averages as an index of the correlation for these individuals (Robinson, 1950, 1957). Depending on the degree of interdependence within dyads on each variable, the correlation between dyadic averages can be quite different from the correlation computed for individual scores. This will be discussed in more detail below.

Finally, researchers must avoid a common interpretational fallacy, the *levels of analysis error*. That is, they must avoid interpreting the correlation between dyad means as indicating "dyad-level processes" and similarly avoid interpreting the correlation between individual scores as indicating "individual-level processes". Instead, they must appreciate the fact that both of these correlations contain a *mix* of dyad-level and individual-level information. Separating the dyad-level and individual-level correlations requires an approach that explicitly identifies and models the degree of interdependence within and between variables at each level of analysis.

Identifying common errors is useful only to the extent that sensible alternatives are available. Having pointed out errors to avoid, we now turn to a technique that helps researchers avoid these errors. This technique, the *pairwise method*, is simple to use, produces Pearson-type correlations that are familiar to researchers, and permits relatively straightforward significance tests that adjust for the observed degree of interdependence within the dyads. The primary advantage of the pairwise method, however, is that it offers researchers a general framework in which to think about psychological processes in dyads. Within the pairwise approach, researchers can (a) ask questions at both the dyad level and the individual level simultaneously, (b) use data from both members of the dyad, and (c) test the significance of an observed correlation or regression slope in a manner that appropriately adjusts for the degree of interdependence in the dyad members' responses.

ASSESSING INTERDEPENDENCE ON A SINGLE VARIABLE

In this and the next few sections we deal with the problem of assessing interdependence in a dyad for a single dependent variable (i.e., univariate interdependence). In each case, we illustrate the concepts using data from Stinson and Ickes (1992). In the case of strangers, the dyadic partners were randomly assigned by the experimenter, so we can assume that individuals start off no more similar to their partners than they are to any other person in the sample. However, if interaction leads to interdependence—so that the dyads are no longer simply the "sum of their individual parts"—then interaction should generally lead to individuals becoming more similar to their partners than to the other people in the sample.[2]

There is a fundamental dimension on which both types of dyads in the Stinson and Ickes study (i.e., male friends and male strangers) differ from other kinds of dyads that researchers may study. In some dyads, such as heterosexual couples, the dyad members are *distinguishable* because sex can be used to differentiate the members within the dyads. That is, when computing a correlation, the researcher "knows whose score to put in column X and whose score to put in column Y" by virtue of the individual's sex. In this example, we are using sex as the variable to distinguish the dyad members, but the general point is that in the distinguishable case *some* meaningful variable can be used to distinguish the two dyad members. However, with same-sex platonic friends or homosexual couples, the dyad members are *exchangeable* because they are not readily distinguished on the basis of sex or any other non-arbitrary variable (i.e., the researcher does not know whose score to put in column X and whose score to put in column Y). When the dyad members are distinguishable it is possible for the scores of the members within each category to have different means, different variances, and different covariances. When the dyad members are exchangeable, however, their scores have the same mean, the same variance, and the same distribution because there is no meaningful way to divide them into distinct categories.

How do we assess the degree of interdependence in the distinguishable case? That is, on a single variable how similar are the two distinguishable dyad members? Most readers will realize that the standard interclass, or Pearson product moment correlation, can be used to assess interdependence when the two individuals in each dyad are distinguishable. The interclass correlation assesses "relative similarity"—for example, whether a woman who receives a high score on a variable *relative to other women* tends to be paired with a man

---

[2] Note that when dyadic sorting is nonrandom, as in the case of heterosexual romantic relationships or male friends as in the Stinson and Ickes (1992) study, this inference is not so straightforward. Similarity within dyads may indicate interdependence arising through interaction, but it may also be an artifact of sorting due to common interests, common abilities, or common status. In such cases, all the statistics presented here will still be appropriate, but their interpretation may be different depending on whether there was random or nonrandom sorting in how the dyads were created.

who receives a high score on that variable *relative to other men*. Because it assesses relative rather than absolute similarity, mean group differences do not affect the interclass correlation. This is an important point because the interclass correlation in this context cannot be interpreted as a measure of absolute similarity, or agreement, between the dyad members (Robinson, 1957).

How do we assess the degree of interdependence in the exchangeable case? In this situation the researcher cannot meaningfully distinguish the dyad members so the interclass correlation cannot be computed. However, it is possible to compute the intraclass correlation. The assumption of equal variance is guaranteed in this case because there is no meaningful way to separate the two members; they are both sampled from the same distribution. In the exchangeable case it is not possible to examine relative similarity but it is possible to examine absolute similarity.

It is also possible to measure absolute similarity in the distinguishable case when it can be assumed that the two groups come from populations with equal variances. The similarity measure is the intraclass correlation with mean differences partialled out. This index of interdependence generally yields a value that is very similar to the interclass correlation, but unlike the interclass correlation it can be used as the basis for the more complex measures that are introduced below.

We have argued that the intraclass correlation and the partial intraclass correlation can be useful in assessing intra-dyadic similarity. There have been several treatments in the literature on computing and testing the intraclass correlation (Haggard, 1958; Kenny, 1988; Kenny & Judd, 1996; Shrout & Fleiss, 1979); these treatments presented the intraclass correlation in the context of analysis of variance (ANOVA). The ANOVA framework does not always make concepts transparent to the researcher who (understandably) tends to be more interested in answering research questions than in learning statistical theory. We present a different framework, a correlational approach based on the pairwise coding of data, that, we hope, makes the relevant concepts more intuitive to the researcher. The advantage of the pairwise approach will become obvious when we generalize the univariate situation to the multivariate case. The complicated analysis problem of multivariate dyadic data will be seen as relatively simple when we apply the techniques developed in the next section. Another benefit of the approach used here is that significance tests are straightforward to derive (which is not necessarily the case in the ANOVA framework).

The Pairwise Intraclass Correlation as a Measure of Interdependence

Exchangeable Case

A useful measure of intra-dyadic similarity for a single variable is the *pairwise intraclass correlation* (Donner & Koval, 1980; Fisher, 1925). The pairwise intraclass correlation is so named because each possible within-group pair of scores is used to compute the correlation. For example, with individuals Adam and Amos in the first dyad, there are two possible pairings: Adam in column one and Amos in column two; or Amos in column one and Adam in column two. With three exchangeable dyads (Adam and Amos, Bob and Bill, and Colin and Chris) the pairwise set-up consists of the scores on X of Adam, Amos, Bob, Bill, Colin, and Chris in the first column (denoted X') and the scores on X of Amos, Adam, Bill, Bob, Chris, and Colin in the second column (denoted X'). Note that each pairing occurs twice, but in opposite orders (Adam in column one with Amos adjacent in column two, then Amos in column one and Adam adjacent in column two, etc.). Thus with $N = 3$ dyads, each column contains $2N = 6$ scores because each member is represented in both columns. This coding is represented symbolically in Table 9.1. The two columns (i.e., variables X and X') are then correlated using the usual product-moment correlation. This correlation is denoted $r_{xx'}$, is called the *pairwise intraclass correlation*, and is the maximum likelihood estimate of the intraclass correlation. The correlation $r_{xx'}$ indexes the absolute similarity between two exchangeable partners in a dyad. In other words, $r_{xx'}$ is the intraclass correlation of one person's score with his or her partner's score. It is important to point out that the intraclass correlation, unlike the usual Pearson correlation, carries a "variance accounted for" interpretation in the $r_{xx'}$ form, that is, there is no need to square the intraclass correlation (see, e.g., Haggard, 1958).

Table 9.1 Symbolic representation for the pairwise data setup in the exchangeable case. The first subscript represents the dyad and the second subscript represents the individual. Categorization of individuals as 1 or 2 is arbitrary.

Dyad	Variable		Dyad	Variable	
	X	X'		X	X'
No. 1	X_{11}	X_{12}	No. 3	X_{31}	X_{32}
	X_{12}	X_{11}		X_{32}	X_{31}
No. 2	X_{21}	X_{22}	No. 4	X_{41}	X_{42}
	X_{22}	X_{21}		X_{42}	X_{41}

The correlation $r_{xx'}$ is computed over all $2N$ pairs. However, because the correlation $r_{xx'}$ is based on $2N$ pairs rather than on N dyads, as in the usual case, the test of significance needs to be adjusted, i.e., a researcher cannot use the p-value printed by standard statistical packages. The sample value $r_{xx'}$ can be tested against the null hypothesis that $\rho_{xx'} = 0$ using the asymptotic test[3]

[3] To simplify matters, we have chosen to present large sample asymptotic significance tests throughout this chapter, unless a well-known and easily accessible "small sample" test was available. For most applications of these tests, "large sample" refers to approximately 30–40 (or more) dyads. We also present a null hypothesis testing approach rather than a confidence interval approach because the former is relatively simple in the pairwise domain. Readers interested in the relevant standard errors to compute confidence intervals can consult the more technical papers we cite.

$$Z = r_{xx'}\sqrt{N} \tag{9.1}$$

where N is the number of dyads and Z is normally distributed. The observed Z can be compared to critical values found in standard tables. Thus for applications where the researcher sets the Type I error rate at $\alpha = 0.05$ (two-tailed), the critical value for Z will be 1.96. An observed Z greater than or equal to 1.96 leads to a rejection of the null hypothesis that $\rho_{xx'} = 0$.

The pairwise intraclass correlation indexes the similarity of individuals within dyads, and so is closely related to other methods of estimating the intraclass correlation such as the ANOVA estimator (Fisher, 1925; Haggard, 1958). However, the pairwise method has several important advantages in the present situation. Most important, it is calculated in the same manner as the usual Pearson correlation: the two "reverse-coded" columns are correlated in the usual manner, thus offering ease of computation, flexibility in the use of existing computer packages, and an intuitive link to general correlational methods. As we will show, it also has certain statistical properties that make it ideal to serve as the basis for more complicated statistics of interdependence. Moreover, the same pairwise method used to compute the intraclass correlations within a single variable can be used to compute the "cross-intraclass correlation" across different variables—an important index that is discussed below.

Distinguishable Case

The calculation of the *partial pairwise intraclass correlation* in the distinguishable case follows the same general pattern. However, in the distinguishable case the pairwise correlation model requires one extra piece of information: a grouping code indexing the dyad member. This extra information is needed because each dyad member is distinguishable according to some theoretically meaningful variable, and that information needs to be incorporated into the value of $r_{xx'}$. Therefore, it is necessary to create an extra column of data to partial out mean class differences. This first column (labeled C) consists of binary codes representing the "class" variable, e.g., the sex of the subject. For example, if the researcher decided to code wives as "1" and husbands as "2", the first column would consist of "1" in the first row and "2" in the second row, and this pattern would be repeated for each of the N dyads in the sample, yielding $2N$ binary codes.

The second column (labeled X) consists of the scores on the variable of interest corresponding to the class code in column one. So, for example, adjacent to the first "1" in column one (representing the female member of the first dyad) the first woman's score would be placed. Below that, adjacent to the first "2" in column one (representing the male member of the first dyad) the first man's score would be placed. This pattern would then continue for the N dyads in the sample, again yielding a total of $2N$ scores. Column three is created by the pairwise reversal of column two. For example, adjacent to each person's score in column two is placed his or her partner's score in column three. Again, this pairwise "reversed" column of scores on X is referred to as X'. This coding is represented symbolically in Table 9.2.

The sample estimate of the partial pairwise intraclass correlation is simply the Pearson correlation between X and X' partialling out variable C. The partial pairwise intraclass correlation is denoted $r_{xx'.c}$. This correlation can be computed with standard statistical packages (e.g., the partial correlation routine in either *SAS* or *SPSS*). For completeness we present the formula for the partial correlation

$$r_{xx'.c} = \frac{r_{xx'} - r_{cx}r_{cx'}}{\sqrt{(1 - r_{cx}^2)(1 - r_{cx'}^2)}}$$

Table 9.2 Symbolic representation for the pairwise data setup in the distinguishable case. The first subscript represents the dyad and the second subscript represents the individual. Categorization of individuals as 1 or 2 is based on the class variable C.

		Variable				Variable	
Dyad	C	X	X'	Dyad	C	X	X'
No. 1	1	X_{11}	X_{12}	No. 3	1	X_{31}	X_{32}
	2	X_{12}	X_{11}		2	X_{32}	X_{31}
No. 2	1	X_{21}	X_{22}	No. 4	1	X_{41}	X_{42}
	2	X_{22}	X_{21}		2	X_{42}	X_{41}

The sample value $r_{xx'.c}$ can be tested against the null hypothesis that $\rho_{xx'.c} = 0$ using the large sample, asymptotic test

$$Z = r_{xx'.c}\sqrt{N}$$

where Z is normally distributed and can be compared to critical values found in standard tables. Note that the equality of variance assumption applies in the distinguishable case. For instance, the population variance for the men on variable X is assumed to be equivalent to the population variance for the women on variable X. Standard tests for the equality of two dependent variances can be used to determine if this assumption is valid (e.g., Kenny, 1979). See Gonzalez and Griffin (1998b) for advice about dealing with situations where the between-group variances are different.

Examples of the Pairwise Intraclass Correlation

In this section we present examples of the pairwise intraclass and partial pairwise intraclass correlations.

Exchangeable Case: Pairwise Intraclass Correlation

From the Stinson and Ickes data, we selected three variables on which to measure dyadic interdependence: gazes, verbalization, and gesture. Our example focuses on the 24 dyads of same-sex strangers. Each variable was coded in the pairwise fashion, creating a total of six columns of data for the three variables (e.g., the $2N$ gaze scores in column one, and the $2N$ gaze scores in reversed order in column two and so on). The resulting value of $r_{xx'}$ for the frequency of gazes was 0.57; for the frequency of verbalizations, 0.84; and for the frequency of gestures, 0.23 (i.e., 57%, 84%, and 23% of the variance in each variable, respectively, was shared between dyad members). These values of $r_{xx'}$ suggest that dyad members were quite similar on the frequency of their gazes and the frequency of their verbalizations, but it appears that the similarity between dyad members in the frequency of their gestures was low.

A direct application of Equation (9.1) yields significance tests for these three sample $r_{xx'}$ values against the null hypothesis that $\rho_{xx'} = 0$. In this example there were $N = 24$ dyads (thus 48 individuals). The corresponding values of Z were 4.12 for gaze, 2.79 for verbalization, and 1.11 for gestures. Thus, using a two-tailed $\alpha = 0.05$, the dyadic similarity was significantly different from zero for gaze and verbalization, but not for gestures.

Distinguishable Case: Partial Pairwise Intraclass Correlation

Consider the following example from a study of distinguishable dyads. Sandra Murray (1995) collected self-evaluations and partner-evaluations from both members of 163 heterosexual couples who were dating exclusively. A comparison of the men's and women's variances on these two variables revealed that, in each case, the between-group differences were very small (i.e., the men and women had approximately equal variance), justifying the use of pooled variances in the partial pairwise intraclass correlation. The partial pairwise correlation for self-evaluations was 0.218, which is statistically significant ($Z = 0.218\sqrt{163} = 2.78$) and the partial pairwise correlation for partner-evaluations was 0.365, also significant ($Z = 4.65$). Thus the partners resembled each other on each of the two variables. It is interesting to note that the interclass correlation between self-evaluation and partner-evaluation was 0.46, and the interclass correlation for the women was 0.55, which was not statistically significant ($Z = 1.08$).

Now that we have introduced the pairwise method of computing the intraclass correlation in the dyadic case, we will use this technique as a building block for more complicated correlational methods. In the remainder of the chapter we present methods for examining dyadic correlations between two variables, methods for separating individual and dyadic effects, and methods for testing actor–partner effects in dyadic research. We take each topic in turn.

OVERALL CORRELATION AND THE CROSS-INTRACLASS CORRELATION

Consider the situation where the researcher has two variables, X and Y, measured on each member of the dyad. For instance, suppose a trust scale and a satisfaction with relationship scale are given to each member of N dyads. There are two natural questions the researcher might ask: Is an individual's trust associated with his or her satisfaction? and is an individual's trust associated with his or her partner's satisfaction?

To answer these questions, the researcher might compute two Pearson correlations over all individuals: (a) a correlation between X and Y, which we call the *overall within-partner correlation* (e.g., individual's trust correlated with satisfaction), and (b) a correlation between an individual's X and his or her partner's Y, which we call the *cross-intraclass correlation* (e.g., individual's trust correlated with partner's satisfaction). The values of these two correlations serve as estimates of the underlying linear association. Unfortunately, the standard tests of significance for these two correlations will generally be incorrect. They commit the assumed independence error because the standard test assumes that there are $2N$ independent subjects, yet the data may not obey independence. This violation of independence can have a dramatic effect on the result of a significance test (e.g., Kenny & Judd, 1986).

Pairwise Approach for the Exchangeable Case

Fortunately, a straightforward solution for the test of significance for both the overall correlation and the cross-intraclass correlation can be found by using a generalization of the pairwise approach developed in the previous section. We first consider the case for exchangeable dyad members and then the case for distinguishable dyad members. The pairwise coding is done on each variable X and Y separately. That is, the $2N$ scores for X, the $2N$ scores for X that have been "reversed coded" (denoted X', as previously shown in Table 9.1), the $2N$ scores for Y, and the $2N$ scores for Y' are entered into four columns. This creates a total of four variables, X, X', Y, and Y', which are shown symbolically in Table 9.3. In this framework there are six possible correlations, which are depicted in Figure 9.1. Figure 9.1 shows that the pairwise intraclass correlations for X and Y are given by $r_{xx'}$ and $r_{yy'}$, respectively; the overall within-partner correlation is given by r_{xy}; and the cross-intraclass correlation is given by $r_{xy'}$. Note that in this framework $r_{xy'} = r_{x'y}$ and $r_{xy} = r_{x'y'}$.

Table 9.3 Symbolic representation for the pairwise data setup for two variables in the exchangeable case. The first subscript represents the dyad and the second subscript represents the individual. Categorization of individuals as 1 or 2 is arbitrary.

| Dyad | Variable | | | | Dyad | Variable | | | |
	X	X'	Y	Y'		X	X'	Y	Y'
No. 1	X_{11}	X_{12}	Y_{11}	Y_{12}	No. 3	X_{31}	X_{32}	Y_{31}	Y_{32}
	X_{12}	X_{11}	Y_{12}	Y_{11}		X_{32}	X_{31}	Y_{32}	Y_{31}
No. 2	X_{21}	X_{22}	Y_{21}	Y_{22}	No. 4	X_{41}	X_{42}	Y_{41}	Y_{42}
	X_{22}	X_{21}	Y_{22}	Y_{21}		X_{42}	X_{41}	Y_{42}	Y_{41}

With the four basic correlations found in Figure 9.1 it is possible to compute tests of significance for r_{xy} and $r_{xy'}$ that take into account the degree of interdependence. For details regarding the derivation of these tests and supporting simulations see Griffin and Gonzalez (1995). Under the null hypothesis that $\rho_{xy} = 0$, the approximate large-sample variance of r_{xy} is $1/N^*_1$, where

$$N^*_1 = \frac{2N}{1 + r_{xx'}r_{yy'} + r^2_{xy'}}$$

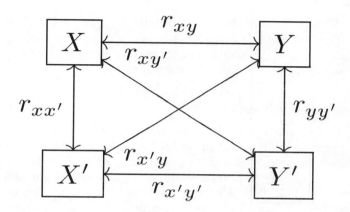

Figure 9.1   All possible pariwise correlations between variables X, Y, and their corresponding "reverse codes".

Thus the overall correlation r_{xy} can be tested using a Z test where

$$Z = r_{xy}\sqrt{N^*_1} \tag{9.2}$$

Intuitively, N^*_1 can be thought of as the "effective sample size" for r_{xy} adjusted for dependent observations (see Rosner, 1982, and Eliasziw & Donner, 1991, for the development of this intuition).

The formula for the effective sample size N^*_1 illustrates that a common practice used by some researchers may be flawed. Some researchers follow the practice of first testing the intraclass correlations, and if both intraclass correlations are close to zero, proceeding as though the data were independent. The problem with this practice is that there is another source of dependence relevant to the standard error of r_{xy}: the cross-intraclass correlation $r_{xy'}$. Only when all three sources of dependence are zero can the data be treated as independent. The Z test in Equation (9.2) is useful because it can be applied regardless of the values for the three sources of interdependence.

The correlation between an individual's score on variable X and his or her dyad partner's score on variable Y (i.e., the variable Y') is the cross-intraclass correlation. The cross-intraclass correlation $r_{xy'}$ assesses the strength of the relationship between two variables measured on different dyadic partners. Under the null hypothesis that $\rho_{xy'} = 0$, the asymptotic variance of $r_{xy'}$ is $1/N*_2$, where

$$N*_2 = \frac{2N}{1 + r_{xx'}r_{yy'} + r^2_{xy}}.$$

The cross-intraclass correlation $r_{xy'}$ can be tested using a Z test, where

$$Z = r_{xy'}\sqrt{N*_2}$$

Like $N*_1$, $N*_2$ can be thought of as the "effective sample size" for $r_{xy'}$ adjusted for dependent observations. Again, we see that the test of significance is influenced by sources of interdependence as measured by the two intraclass correlations and the overall within-partner correlation.

An Example of the Exchangeable Case

Consider the 24 same-sex, stranger dyads studied by Stinson and Ickes. Researchers might be interested in the following questions. Over all individuals, were the three variables (frequency of gazes, frequency of verbalizations, and frequency of gestures) significantly related to each other? Examination of the boxed values in Table 9.4 reveals that all three overall correlations are positive and moderately large: the overall correlation between verbalization frequency and gaze frequency was 0.386, the overall correlation between verbalization frequency and gesture frequency was 0.449, and the overall correlation between gaze frequency and gesture frequency was 0.474. Recall that the significance test of the overall correlation r_{xy} depends on the effective sample size $N*_1$. Between verbalizations and gazes,

$$N*_1 = \frac{48}{1 + (0.841)(0.570) + 0.471^2} = 28.22;$$

between verbalizations and gestures $N*_1 = 33.81$; and between gazes and gestures $N*_1 = 38.88$. The resulting significance tests were $Z = 0.386\sqrt{28.22} = 2.05, p < 0.05$; $Z = 2.61, p < 0.05$; and $Z = 2.96, p < 0.05$, respectively. All three overall correlations were significantly positive.

We now turn to the assessment of the cross-intraclass correlation $r_{xy'}$. Is an individual's score on one variable related to his partner's score on a second variable? The cross-intraclass correlation $r_{xy'}$ between verbalizations and gazes was 0.471. The effective sample size was

$$N*_2 = \frac{48}{1 + (0.841)(0.570) + 0.386^2} = 29.48;$$

and the resulting Z was $0.471\sqrt{29.48} = 2.56$, $p < 0.05$. The correlation $r_{xy'}$ between verbalization frequency and gesture frequency was 0.479. Testing $r_{xy'}$ against its standard error (with $N*_2 = 34.49$) yielded an observed $Z = 2.82, p <$

Table 9.4 Pairwise correlation matrix for randomly sampled, same-sex strangers (Stinson & Ickes, 1992).

	Verb	Verb'	Gaze	Gaze'	Gest	Gest'
Verb	1.000					
Verb'	**0.841**	1.000				
Gaze	0.386	0.471	1.000			
Gaze'	0.471	0.386	**0.570**	1.000		
Gest	0.449	0.479	0.476	0.325	1.000	
Gest'	0.479	0.449	0.325	0.474	**0.226**	1.000

Pairwise intraclass correlations are typed in bold. Verb = Frequency of verbalizations. Gaze = Frequency of gazes. Gest = Frequency of gestures.
Notes: Boxed values are the overall r_{xy} correlations.

0.01. Similarly, the cross-intraclass correlation $r_{xy'}$ between gaze frequency and gesture frequency was 0.325. Testing $r_{xy'}$ against its standard error (with $N*_2 = 35.46$) yielded an observed $Z = 1.94$, $p = 0.053$. The significant, positive values for $r_{xy'}$ indicate that individuals who speak frequently are associated with partners (in this case strangers) who gaze and gesture frequently; individuals who gaze frequently are moderately associated with partners who gesture frequently.

Pairwise Approach for the Distinguishable Case

The computational setup for the overall within-partner and the cross-intraclass correlations in the distinguishable case parallels the setup in the exchangeable case. As with the pairwise intraclass correlation, the distinguishable case is treated differently than the exchangeable case only in terms of the coding variable that is partialled out. The basic data arrangement is shown in Table 9.5, which is similar to Table 9.3 for the exchangeable case except for the extra column representing the categorization of individuals within the dyad. The coding variable C is partialled from all correlations. Figure 9.2 shows the possible correlations between the four variables, using a ".c" in the subscript to denote that variable C has been partialled out. Again, the standard formula for the partial correlation is used. The partial overall correlation $r_{xy.c}$ is computed according to the formula

$$r_{xy.c} = \frac{r_{xy} - r_{cx}r_{cy}}{\sqrt{(1 - r_{cx}^2)(1 - r_{cy}^2)}} \qquad (9.3)$$

and the partial cross intraclass correlation $r_{xy'c}$ is computed as

$$r_{xy'.c} = \frac{r_{xy'} - r_{cx}r_{cy'}}{\sqrt{(1 - r_{cx}^2)(1 - r_{cx'}^2)}} \qquad (9.4)$$

Table 9.5 Symbolic representation for the pairwise data setup for two variables in the distinguishable case. The first subscript represents the dyad and the second subscript represents the individual. Categorization of individuals as 1 or 2 is based on the class variable C. The primes denote the reverse coding described in the text.

Dyad	C	Variable X	X'	Y	Y'	Dyad	C	Variable X	X'	Y	Y'
No. 1	1	X_{11}	X_{12}	Y_{11}	Y_{12}	No. 3	1	X_{31}	X_{32}	Y_{31}	Y_{32}
	2	X_{12}	X_{11}	Y_{12}	Y_{11}		2	X_{32}	X_{31}	Y_{32}	Y_{31}
No. 2	1	X_{21}	X_{22}	Y_{21}	Y_{22}	No. 4	1	X_{41}	X_{42}	Y_{41}	Y_{42}
	2	X_{22}	X_{21}	Y_{22}	Y_{21}		2	X_{42}	X_{41}	Y_{42}	Y_{41}

Once data have been arranged as in Table 9.5, these partial correlations can be computed in standard statistical packages such as *SAS* or *SPSS*. The partial pairwise intraclass correlations for X and Y are denoted by $r_{xx'.c}$ and $r_{yy'.c}$, respectively; the partial overall correlation is denoted by $r_{xy.c}$; and the partial cross-intraclass correlation is denoted by $r_{xy'.c}$

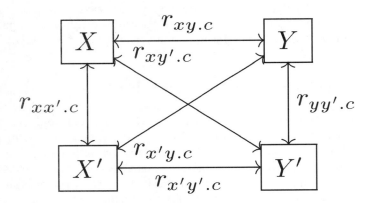

Figure 9.2 All possible pairwise correlations between X, Y, and their corresponding "reverse codes" in the distinguishable case. Variable C has been partialled out from all correlations.

Unlike the exchangeable case, there are three assumptions that need to be checked before proceeding: (a) equality of variance between the two classes on each variable (e.g., the variance for men on X needs to equal the variance for women on X; the variance for men on Y needs to equal the variance for women on Y), (b) equality of covariances between the two variables across classes (e.g., the covariance between X and Y for men needs to equal the covariance between X and Y for women), and (c) equality of cross covariances between the two variables (e.g., the covariance between the women's X and the men's Y needs to equal the covariance between the men's X and the women's Y). The reason these assumptions were not made in the exchangeable case was because the individuals could not be meaningfully separated into two classes (e.g., men vs women). However, in the distinguishable case the individuals can be separated into two classes; consequently, the equivalence of the variance and covariances must be checked before the data from the two groups are pooled for the partial overall and partial cross-intraclass correlations. Recall that the equality-of-variance assumption was also made for the partial pairwise intraclass case. Gonzalez and Griffin (in press) discuss the details for testing these assumptions. In general, when these assumptions are met the computation of the relevant correlations will be more efficient and the corresponding tests more powerful compared to the usual strategy of analyzing data of each class separately. There are also substantive reasons for making these assumptions (see Griffin & Gonzalez, in press).

Given the four basic correlations found in Figure 9.2 it is possible to compute tests of significance for $r_{xy.c}$ and $r_{xy'.c}$ that take into account the degree of interdependence. For details regarding the derivation of these tests, supporting simulations, and a discussion of how to perform the tests using standard structural equations modeling programs, see Gonzalez and Griffin (in press). Under the null hypothesis that $\rho_{xy.c} = 0$, the approximate large-sample variance of $r_{xy.c}$ is $1/N^*_1$, where

$$N^*_1 = \frac{2N}{1 + r_{xx'.c}r_{yy'.c} + r^2_{xy'c}} \tag{9.5}$$

Thus the partial overall correlation $r_{xy.c}$ can be tested using a Z test where

$$Z = r_{xy'c}\sqrt{N^*_1}$$

The partial cross-intraclass correlation assesses the strength of the relationship between two variables measured on different dyadic partners partialling out mean differences between the two partners. Under the null hypothesis that $\rho_{xy'.c} = 0$, the asymptotic variance of $r_{xy'.c}$ is $1/N^*_2$, where

$$N^*_2 = \frac{2N}{1 + r_{xx'.c}r_{yy'.c} + r^2_{xy.c}} \tag{9.6}$$

The partial cross-intraclass correlation $r_{xy'.c}$ can be tested using a Z test, where

$$Z = r_{xy'.c}\sqrt{N^*_2}$$

An Example of the Distinguishable Case

Recall that Murray (1995) found that for the 163 couples the correlation between self- and partner-evaluations for the men was 0.46, and the correlation between the same two variables was 0.55 for the women, which was not statistically significantly. The correlation between the women's self-evaluation and the men's partner-evaluation was 0.37, and the correlation between the men's self-evaluation and the women's partner-evaluation was 0.41. Further, the variances for the men were similar to the variances for the women (on each variable). Thus, the necessary conditions for computing the overall partial and cross-intraclass correlation are met for these data.

The partial overall correlation (with sex partialled out) between self-evaluations and partner-evaluations was 0.501. That is, controlling for sex differences, it appears that each individual's self-evaluations was strongly related to his or her evaluation of the partner. This result, along with the previously-reported partial intraclass correlations of 0.218 for self-evaluations and 0.364 for partner-evaluations, gives

$$N^*_1 = \frac{163 * 2}{1 + 0.218 * 0.364 + 0.392^2} = 264.39,$$

a straightforward application of Equation (9.5). The Z-value for this overall correlation was $0.501\sqrt{264.39} = 8.15$, $p < 0.001$.

The partial cross-intraclass correlation between one person's self-evaluations and the other's partner was 0.392. That is, controlling for sex differences, it appears that an individual's self-evaluation was moderately correlated to his or her partner's evaluation of the individual. The partial cross-intraclass correlation can be tested using the effective sample size given by substituting sample size N, the two partial pairwise intraclass correlations, and the partial overall correlation into Equation(9.6), which for this sample was 244.30. The Z-value for this sample $r_{xy'.c}$ was $0.392\sqrt{244.30} = 6.13$, $p < 0.001$.

A LATENT VARIABLE MODEL FOR SEPARATING INDIVIDUAL AND DYADIC EFFECTS

We now apply the pairwise framework to address the levels of analysis problem present in dyad research. A researcher studying dyads can ask questions at either the level of the individual, the level of the dyad, or both (Kenny & La Voie, (1985). To make this issue concrete we refer to the Stinson and Ickes (1992) study. A researcher can ask the question: Do *individuals* who gesture more also verbalize more? A researcher can also ask the question: Are *dyads* where both individuals gesture more also the dyads where both individuals verbalize more? The two questions differ in their level of analysis: individuals or dyads.

Both levels of analysis can be informative, and focusing on only one level is wasteful of information that might theoretically be interesting. Further, it is possible to find situations in which the direction of the relationship between two variables differs in sign across the two levels. For instance, imagine that trust and satisfaction scales are taken from married couples. Each partner answers both scales so there are a total of four observations per couple: two trust scores and two satisfaction scores. It is plausible that the relationship between trust and satisfaction at the dyad-level is positive (more trusting dyads are more satisfied with the relationship) whereas at the individual-level the relationship could be negative (the individual within a dyad who is relatively more trusting could be relatively less satisfied because his or her trust is not reciprocated). Thus, it is possible to find correlations in different directions (positive or negative) at different levels of analysis. Such patterns are interesting both in terms of theory development and theory testing because a complete understanding of dyadic interaction must address both levels of analysis.

The problem of separating the individual-level analysis from the dyad-level analysis has bothered methodologists for a long time. Robinson (1950) pointed out that the correlation between two aggregated variables (e.g., mean educational attainment and mean income correlated *across* states) is not equivalent to the correlation between the same two variables measured on individuals (e.g., educational attainment and average income *within* a state). In sociology, the cross-level error, or the erroneous generalization from one level to another, is termed the "ecological correlation fallacy" (Hauser, 1974; Robinson, 1950). The need for statistical techniques that permit analysis at different levels ("multi-level analysis") has led to a cottage industry of different viewpoints and statistical programs (see Bock, 1989; Bryk & Raudenbush, 1992; Goldstein, 1987; Goldstein & McDonald, 1988; Kreft, de Leeuw, & van der Leeden, 1994).

In this section we show how different levels of analysis can be incorporated into the pairwise approach. Our own work has been greatly influenced by Kenny and La Voie (1985), who proposed a group correlation model to decompose individual-level and group-level effects. Kenny and La Voie derived their group correlation model in the context of ANOVA. We present the pairwise version of Kenny and La Voie's group correlation model. We call it the *pairwise latent variable model*. The ingredients for this model again depend on whether the dyad members are exchangeable or distinguishable.

Pairwise Latent Variable Model for the Exchangeable Case

Figure 9.3 shows a simple latent variable model for the exchangeable dyadic design. In this model, each measured variable is coded in a pairwise fashion so that the variables X and X' (and, by the same logic, Y and Y') are identical except for order. The variance of a given observed variable is assumed to result from two different latent (not measured) sources: a dyadic component representing the portion of that variable that is shared between dyadic partners and an individual component representing the portion of that variable that is unshared or unique.

As Figure 9.3 illustrates, there are two levels at which the variables can be related. The shared dyadic variance of X and Y can be related through the dyadic correlation r_d. The unique individual variance of X and Y can be related through the individual-level correlation r_i. The model depicted in Figure 9.3 permits simultaneous estimation and testing of r_d and r_i.

The individual-level correlation, r_i, and the latent dyad-level correlation, r_d, can be computed as follows:

$$r_i = \frac{r_{xy} - r_{xy'}}{\sqrt{1 - r_{xx'}}\sqrt{1 - r_{yy'}}} \tag{9.7}$$

and

$$r_d = \frac{r_{xy'}}{\sqrt{r_{xx'}}\sqrt{r_{yy'}}}. \tag{9.8}$$

Note that both r_i and r_d are computed from the four basic correlations shown in Figure 9.1. The numerator of the individual-level correlation r_i is the difference between the observed correlation r_{xy}, which combines dyad-level and individual-level effects, and the cross-intraclass correlation $r_{xy'}$, which contains only dyad-level effects. Thus r_i is a measure of the individual-level relation uncontaminated by dyad-level effects. The numerator of the dyad-level correlation r_d is simply the pairwise cross-intraclass correlation $r_{xy'}$, and in this model corresponds to the direct measure of the dyad-level relations. The denominators, too, are conceptually straightforward: they correct the scale of the correlations for the fact that only "part" of each observed variable is being correlated. When the individual components of variables X and Y are correlated, the denominator adjusts for the proportions of variance in the observed X and Y that correspond to the *non-shared* effects ($\sqrt{1 - r_{xx'}}$, and $\sqrt{1 - r_{yy'}}$, respectively). Similarly, when the *dyadic* components of the variables X and Y are correlated, the denominator adjusts for the proportions of variance in the observed X and Y that correspond to the shared dyadic effects ($\sqrt{r_{xx'}}$ and $\sqrt{r_{yy'}}$, respectively). Note that r_d can be interpreted as $r_{xy'}$ that has been disattenuated (i.e., divided by the intraclass correlations representing the proportion of dyadic variance). The pairwise latent variable model is equivalent to the maximum likelihood group-level correlation suggested by Gollob (1991).

Testing the Underlying Correlations r_i and r_d in the Exchangeable Case

For the special case of dyads, r_i can be computed by Equation (9.7) or equivalently by correlating the deviation scores on X and on Y. That is, the dyad mean on X is subtracted from each X score and the dyad mean on Y is subtracted from each Y score, then the $2N$ deviations on X are correlated with the $2N$ deviations on Y. For dyads, Equation (9.7) and the deviation method yield identical values for r_i, which can be tested using the usual Pearson correlation table (or the associated t-test formula) with $N - 1$ degrees of freedom (Kenny & La Voie, 1985).

Note that when either of the intraclass correlations $r_{xx'}$ or $r_{yy'}$ (or both) are small, r_d will tend be large and may even exceed 1.0. Because the dyadic model is based on the assumption of dyadic similarity, the model should only be tested when *both* intraclass correlations are significantly positive. In general, the practice of restricting the application of this model to cases when both intraclass correlations are significantly positive should reduce the occurrence of out-of-bounds values for r_d. A significance test for r_d is reported in Griffin and Gonzalez (1995). Interestingly, the *p*-value associated with r_d is identical to the *p*-value associated with $r_{xy'}$. Therefore, when both intraclass correlations are significant, implying significant dyad-level variance in both X and Y, we recommend interpreting $r_{xy'}$ as the raw-score version of r_d (i.e., r_d is the disattenuated version of $r_{xy'}$).

The Mean-Level Correlation

It may appear that the correlation between the means of each dyad on the two variables should yield an estimate of the dyad-level correlation. Contrary to this intuition, the "mean-level" correlation (which we denote r_m) reflects both individual and dyad-level effects and can best be thought of as a "total" correlation. The mean-level correlation r_m should not be used as an index of dyad-level relations because it can be significantly positive or negative even when $r_d = 0$. According to the model in Figure 9.3, a positive dyad-level correlation exists only when the tendency of *both* dyad members to be high on X is matched by the tendency of *both* dyad members to be high on Y. However, this is only one of several circumstances that can lead to a positive value of r_m, indicating that a high *average* value on X is matched with a high *average* value on Y. For example, a positive mean-level correlation will result when the tendency of one member to be extremely high on X is matched with the tendency of that member to be extremely high on Y—regardless of the score of his or her dyadic partner on either variable. See Griffin and Gonzalez (1995) for a more systematic treatment of r_m.

An Example of the Exchangeable Case

We continue using the Stinson and Ickes (1992) data to illustrate the exchangeable case. Having determined that there was dyad-level variance—as indexed by the pairwise intraclass correlation—in at least two of the three variables of interest, we calculate and test r_d and r_i. In the case of verbalizations and gazes,

$$r_d = \frac{0.471}{\sqrt{(0.841)(0.570)}} = 0.680.$$

The observed Z- and *p*-value for r_d was identical to that found for $r_{xy'}$ (i.e., $Z = 2.56$, $p < 0.01$). The latent dyad-level correlation (r_d) between gaze frequency and gesture frequency was 0.906, $Z = 1.94$, $p = 0.052$, just shy of statistical significance. The dyad-level correlation (r_d) between verbalization frequency and gesture frequency was 1.10, which is "out of bounds". Such

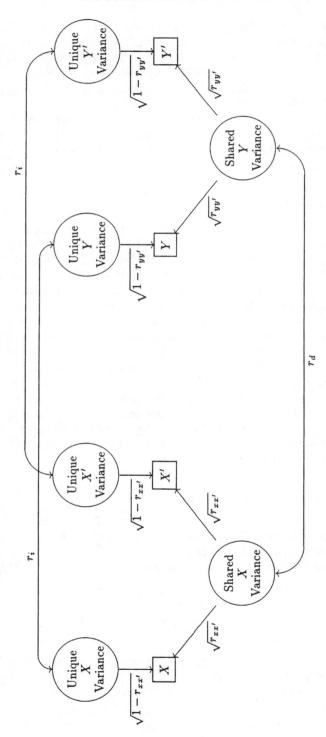

Figure 9.3 A latent variable model separating individual-level (unique) and dyad-level (shared) effects.

out-of-bounds values are most likely to occur when the intraclass correlation for one or both of the variables is marginal or non-significant (as in the case of gestures). In sum, the significant, positive values of r_d (and $r_{xy'}$) indicate that dyads in which both members gaze frequently are also dyads in which both members speak to each other frequently and gesture to each other frequently.

Were the three variables related at the level of *individuals* within dyads? The computation of the individual-level correlation, r_i, between verbalizations and gazes is straightforward:

$$\frac{r_{xy} - r_{xy'}}{\sqrt{1 - r_{xx'}}\sqrt{1 - r_{yy'}}} = \frac{0.386 - 0.471}{\sqrt{(1 - 0.841)(1 - 0.570)}} = -0.325.$$

In contrast to the positive dyad-level correlation between verbalization and gaze (0.680), the individual-level correlation is negative. That is, the dyad member who speaks *more* often tends to be the dyad member who looks at the other *less* often. This negative individual-level correlation emerges despite the fact that dyads in which there is frequent speaking also tend to be dyads in which there is frequent gazing. However, the individual-level correlation is also only marginally significant ($p < 0.010$),

$$
\begin{aligned}
t_{N-1} &= \frac{r_i \sqrt{N-1}}{\sqrt{1 - r_i^2}} \\
&= \frac{-0.325\sqrt{23}}{\sqrt{1 - 0.325^2}} \\
&= 1.65.
\end{aligned}
$$

Note that this significance test relies on the usual formula for testing a correlation, except that in this case the degrees of freedom are $N - 1$ (rather than $N - 2$). The individual-level correlations for the other pairs of variables were relatively small and nonsignificant. For verbalizations and gestures $r_i = -0.086$, and for gestures and gazes $r_i = 0.258$. All three values of r_i were markedly discrepant from the corresponding values of r_d and $r_{xy'}$, underlining the importance of separating the dyad-level and individual-level relations.

Recall that all three overall correlations were moderate and positive. However, the overall correlation represents a combination of underlying dyadic and individual-level correlations. A more detailed picture of the social interactions that occurred in this study emerges when the two levels are decomposed. Verbalizations and gazes were negatively correlated at the individual level, but positively correlated at the dyad level. Verbalizations and gestures were unrelated at the individual level, but positively correlated at the dyad level. Finally, gazes and gestures were positively correlated at both the individual and dyadic levels.

Pairwise Latent Variable Model for the Distinguishable Case

The pairwise latent variable model for the distinguishable case is similar to the model for the exchangeable case except that the "class" or grouping variable C needs to be partialled out of the four variables X, X', Y, and Y. Thus the corresponding model is identical to the model depicted in Figure 9.3 for the exchangeable case except that all observed correlations are partial correlations (with the grouping variable C being the control variable). In this section we simply sketch the pairwise latent variable model for the distinguishable case and refer interested readers to Gonzalez and Griffin (in press) for more detail.

The formula for the partial individual-level correlation r_i can be expressed in terms of the observed partial correlations given in Figure 9.2

$$r_i = \frac{r_{xy.c} - r_{xy'.c}}{\sqrt{1 - r_{xx'.c}}\sqrt{1 - r_{yy'.c}}}$$

Note that because the individual-level correlation r_i uses the correlations $r_{xy.c}$ and $r_{xy'.c}$ in its computation, the assumptions needed for computing the partial overall and partial cross-intraclass correlations apply to r_i as well. The implication of these assumptions is that the individual-level relationship is required to be the same for each level of the category variable (e.g., r_i for husbands equals r_i for wives).

The sample r_i can be tested against the null value of 0 using the standard t-test for a correlation. In the distinguishable case, the test has $N - 2$ degrees of freedom (one degree of freedom less than the r_i for the exchangeable case because the binary class variable C is used in the distinguishable case). For the Murray data sample, r_i between the self-evaluation and the partner's evaluation was 0.155, yielding an observed $t = 2.00$, $p < 0.05$.

The partial dyad-level correlation r_d can be expressed in terms of the observed correlations given in Figure 9.2

$$r_d = \frac{r_{xy'.c}}{\sqrt{r_{xx'.c}}\sqrt{r_{yy'.c}}}. \tag{9.9}$$

Again, the estimation of r_d for the pairwise model requires an assumption that the partial cross-intraclass correlations are equal to each level of the class variable. For instance, the population correlation between the husband's self-evaluation and the wife's partner-evaluation is assumed to equal the population correlation between the wife's self-evaluation and the husband's partner-evaluation. If this assumption is plausible given the sample data, then the partial cross-intraclass correlation can be used as the raw-score version of the dyad-level correlations (i.e., not disattenuated by the partial intraclass correlations). If this assumption appears to be violated, then a more general model can be estimated using a structural equations approach (see Gonzalez & Griffin, in press).

For the Murray data, the equality of cross-partner correlations appears to hold ($r_{xy'.c} = 0.41$ for the men and $r_{xy'.c} = 0.37$ for the women; the difference was not statistically significant). Also, recall that the partial intraclass correlations for self-evaluation was 0.22 and for partner-evaluation was 0.364. Even though both of these values are statistically different from zero, they are still relatively small and we anticipate that this could produce an out-of-bounds value for r_d. The dyad-level correlation r_d for the Murray data turned out to be out-of-bounds, $r_d = 1.39$, making it difficult to interpret as a correlation. Fortunately, because the partial intraclass correlations were significant we can interpret $r_{xy'.c}$ as the raw-score estimate of r_d (i.e., the dyad-level correlation that has not been disattenuated by the partial intraclass correlations), which was 0.392. The Z test for this sample $r_{xy'.c}$ was 6.13, as we saw before. Thus, the Murray et al data suggest that self-evaluation and partner-evaluation are positively correlated at both the individual-level and the couple-level.

STRUCTURAL MODELS IN DYADIC RESEARCH

Researchers often wish to go beyond calculating the strength of linear relation between variables. Most commonly, they wish to go beyond the correlational index and estimate parameters in a structural model in which one or more independent variables determine the value of a dependent variable. There are a number of ways that this can be accomplished with dyadic data. We will briefly outline a few of these models, focusing on examples of their use rather than on detailed computational descriptions.

Regression Models for Dyadic-Level and Individual-Level Effects

The correlational methods for separating dyadic- and individual-level effects presented above can be extended to cases with multiple predictor variables. Although such analyses are straightforward for the individual level of analysis, the extensions to the dyadic level is more complex. The individual-level analysis is relatively simple because the interdependence between dyadic partners has been "partialled out" of the individual-level correlations, and so the individual-level correlations can be entered as input to standard multiple regression routines or structural equation modeling programs, allowing complete estimation and significance testing through the standard programs. The dyad-level correlations, in contrast, measure only interdependent information and therefore violate the independence assumption that is essential to standard regression routines. Thus, even though the dyad-level correlations can also be entered as input to multiple regression routines, the resulting significance tests are not appropriate.

Consider again the results of Stinson and Ickes' (1992) study. In our earlier analysis of the dyad-level and individual-level correlations, we assessed whether the three relevant variables were interrelated at the dyadic level of analysis, at the individual level of analysis, or at both levels of analysis. As an extension of these correlational analyses, we have formulated a psychological model illustrated in Figure 9.4. This path diagram implies that gesture frequency and gaze frequency are both predictors of verbalization frequency. For a possible psychological theory that relates those three variables, see

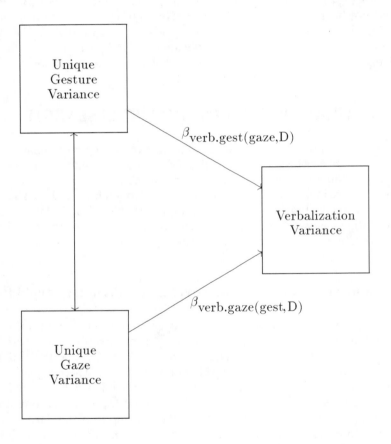

Figure 9.4 Representation for the regression between individual-level effects. All input correlations are the individual-level r_i's. The variable D represents a set of N-dummy codes. We follow the standard notation in the regression literature: the variable to the left of the dot is the dependent variable, the variable(s) to the right of the dot are the predictors, and the variable(s) in the parentheses are variables that have been controlled for, i.e., entered in a previous step.

Duncan and Fiske (1977). Because the goal in this chapter is to illustrate the application of several statistical models, we do not provide psychological motivation for the particular examples we selected.

This multiple regression model must be estimated separately for the two levels of analysis. Turning first to the individual level, we know that the individual-level correlation between the two predictors (gestures and gazes) is 0.258. This remains unchanged in the regression model and, because it is rather small, we will expect little change between the zero-order correlations and the standardized partial regression coefficient. When the three individual-level correlations (and the appropriate N, see below) are entered into a multiple regression program that accepts correlations as input (such as the REGRESSION command in *SPSS*; see Table 9.6 for example code), we find that the standardized coefficient for predicting verbalizations from gazes is -0.324 (virtually identical to the individual-level correlation). The coefficient for predicting verbalizations from gestures is -0.002, again virtually the same as the comparable individual-level correlation. These two standardized regression coefficients are denoted $\beta_{verb.gaze(gest)}$ and $\beta_{verb.gest(gaze)}$, respectively.

For this individual-level analysis, the appropriate significance test depends on the number of subjects. However, because the individual-level correlations are actually derived from one score for each dyad, the appropriate N to enter into the multiple regression routine is the number of dyads, *not* the number of subjects. In this case, the correct "sample size" to enter in the multiple regression routine is 24. At this sample size, neither coefficient is significant, although the regression coefficient for gazes is marginal ($t = 1.52$, $p < 0.15$). A method equivalent to that described here is to create $N - 1$ dummy codes that represent the dyads, and run the regression of verbalization on the dummy codes, the gesture variable, and the gaze variable. The dummy codes will account for the sum of squares due dyads.

The analysis is more complicated for the dyad-level portion of the analysis because of the sample size problem caused by interdependence. That is, each dyadic correlation is based on a different "effective sample size" depending on the degree of dyadic interdependence in the two relevant variables. Two possible, but inexact, solutions to this problem come to mind. First, because each dyadic correlation will be associated with an effective sample size of at least N, the number of dyads, this could be entered into the program as a conservative estimate of sample size. Second, one could use the smallest effective sample size associated with any of the dyad-level correlations in the model. In our example, we will use the second strategy, entering the smallest effective sample size, 29.5 (rounded down to 29), and the three cross-intraclass correlations into the *SPSS* multiple regression routine. All possible cross-intraclass correlations between the relevant variables (i.e., the raw-score index of the dyad-level correlations) are submitted as input to the regression procedure. In this case, the cross-intraclass correlation between the predictors is again moderate, 0.325, indicating that the standardized coefficients will not be much different than the corresponding zero-order correlations. In fact,

Table 9.6 Example SPSS code for executing the regression model described in the text. The input correlations are the individual-level correlations r_i between all possible pairs of gestures, gaze, and verbilization frequency.

```
matrix data variable=gest gaze verb
  /contents=corr
  /n=24.
begin data
  1
    .258  1
   -.086  -.325  1
end data.
regression matrix in (*)
  /noorigin
  /dependent=verb
  /method=enter gest gaze.
```

both standardized regression coefficients remain significant when the two predictors are entered together. The coefficient for gestures is somewhat reduced (0.364, $p < 0.05$, compared to the cross-intraclass correlation of 0.479), as is the coefficient for gazes (0.352, $p < 0.05$, compared to 0.471).

This approach can be used for either exchangeable or distinguishable dyads. In addition, for distinguishable dyads one may use structural equation modeling, which will yield significance tests in the distinguishable case for a more direct approach. In such a case, the covariance matrix is entered directly into a structural equation modeling program such as *LISREL* or *EQS*, following the general procedures outlined in Gonzalez and Griffin (in press). Note again that it is not appropriate to enter the pre-computed dyadic correlations into a structural equation modeling program.

A Regression Model for Separating Actor and Partner Effects

Earlier we noted that the overall correlation in a dyadic design can be decomposed into underlying correlations representing the dyadic-level and individual-level relations. It is these correlations that were entered into the multiple regression models discussed in the preceding section. However, this

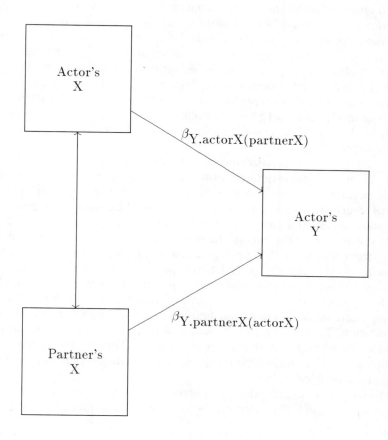

Figure 9.5   Representation of the actor–partner regression model.

particular decomposition is only one of a number of possible models that can be applied in this situation. Another useful way to model the social interaction within a dyad is as a combination of two paths linking X and Y: an actor effect, which represents the extent to which a dyad member's (the "actor") standing on variable X determines that actor's standing on variable Y, and a partner effect, which represents the extent to which the partner's standing on X determines the actor's standing on Y. We now turn to an example of an actor–partner model.

In the Stinson and Ickes example, we might ask: "What predicts an individual's verbalization frequency?" An individual actor's speech frequency might be caused by the joint effect of the individual's own gazes and his or her partner's gazes. Following the structural model illustrated in Figure 9.5 leads to the interpretation of the (semi-partial) pairwise r_{xy} as the "actor correlation" and the (semi-partial) pairwise $r_{xy'}$ as the "partner correlation". To obtain the actor and partner effects in the exchangeable case, it is necessary to partial out the shared component of the actor and partner variance—which means partialling out $r_{xx'}$, the pairwise intraclass correlation on X. The comparison of this model (depicted in Figure 9.5) with the decomposition presented earlier in this chapter (Figure 9.3) illustrates the importance of a theoretical model in guiding and formulating how an analysis should be conducted. Under different models the same correlations r_{xy} and $r_{xy'}$ carry different interpretations.

The actor–partner regression model (introduced in its most general form by Kenny, 1995a) can be estimated with the pairwise method. The dependent variable of interest (Y) is simply regressed on the X and X' columns, using a standard regression program on the pairwise data setup we have used throughout this chapter (where each column contains $2N$ data points). Either the raw regression coefficients or the standardized regression coefficients can be read from the program output and tested for significance (see Griffin & Gonzalez, 1998). Like the tests for the pairwise model given earlier, the significance tests for the actor and partner regression coefficients are made up of the four pairwise correlations: $r_{xx'}$, $r_{yy'}$, r_{xy}, and $r_{xy'}$. We will not go through the computational details here, but simply present examples and discuss their interpretation. Technical details as well as a generalized model that includes an interaction term that permits estimation of the Thibaut and Kelley (1959) concepts of reflexive control, fate control, and behavioral contrast are given in Griffin and Gonzalez (1998).

It is instructive to express these raw-score regression coefficients in terms of pairwise correlations. The actor regression coefficient is given by

$$\frac{s_y \left(r_{xy} - r_{xy'} r_{xx'}\right)}{s_x \left(1 - r^2_{xx'}\right)} \tag{9.10}$$

where s_y and s_x are the standard deviations of the criterion variable and the predictor variable, respectively. This formula produces a value that is identical to the coefficient produced by standard regression programs. The regression coefficient for the partner effect has the same form with the role of r_{xy} and $r_{xy'}$ interchanged. Under the null hypothesis that the population $\beta = 0$, the variance for the actor regression slope is

$$V\left(\beta_{\text{actor}}\right) = \frac{s^2_y \left(r^2_{xy'} r^2_{xx'} - r_{xx'} r_{yy'} + 1 - r^2_{xy'}\right)}{2N s^2_x \left(1 - r^2_{xx'}\right)} \tag{9.11}$$

The test of significance for the actor effect is computed with a Z test using $\beta / \sqrt{V_{(\beta)}}$. The test for the partner effect is analogous, except that r_{xy} appears in Equation (9.11) in place of $r_{xy'}$.

For the Stinson and Ickes' data that we have been using throughout this chapter, the actor correlation r_{xy} between gaze and verbalization was 0.386. In the context of the model shown in Figure 9.5, the standardized regression coefficient was 0.173 ($Z = 0.97$). This standardized regression coefficient is interpreted as the influence on an actor's frequency of verbalization given one standard deviation change on the actor's frequency of gaze, holding constant the partner's frequency of gaze. In this case, the actor effect was not statistically significant. Similarly, the partner correlation $r_{xy'}$ between gaze and verbalization was 0.471. The standardized regression coefficient was 0.372 ($Z = 2.09$). In other words, the influence on the actor's frequency of verbalization given one standard deviation change on the partner's frequency of gaze, holding constant the actor's frequency of gaze, was statistically significant. The partner's gaze frequency was a more powerful predictor of the actor's verbalization frequency than the actor's own gaze frequency. For one possible theoretical analysis of these results see Duncan and Fiske (1977).

A more complicated form of the actor–partner regression model is used for analyzing data from distinguishable dyads because when there are two different types of dyad members it is usually of interest to examine whether the actor effects and the partner effects vary across the two types of individuals. For example, consider the model presented in Figure 9.6, adapted from the study by Murray, Holmes, and Griffin (1996a) of married couples. In this model, a woman's image of her partner is determined by two causes: her own self-image (the "projection" path labeled "a", which is an actor effect) and her partner's self-reported self-image (the "matching" path labeled "b", which is a partner effect). A man's image of his partner is similarly determined by an actor effect "d" and a partner effect "c".

In such a model it is of central interest to test whether the actor (projection) paths are equal across sexes, or whether the partner (matching) paths are equal across sexes. This can be most easily done using structural equation modeling, as in the Murray et al. study, where the fit of the model under equality constraints is compared to the model where the constraints are not imposed. If both the actor and the partner effects are equal across the two classes, then "a" and "d" can be pooled and "b" and "c" can be pooled. In a simple model such as this, the pooled structural equation model is essentially equivalent to carrying out the pairwise regression model adjusted for distinguishable dyads because there the parameters are also averaged across the two types of people. The structural modeling approach can be extended to estimate much more complex models, as illustrated in the Murray et al. study.

In the Murray et al. example, the tests revealed that both the actor and partner effects were equal across husbands and wives. Furthermore, both the actor and partner effects were highly significant and almost equal in magnitude (standardized regression coefficients = 0.315 and 0.304, respectively).

The actor–partner regressions are interpreted quite differently than the regressions based on the dyadic- or individual-level correlations. The actor–partner models are simple regressions, and are used to answer whether an actor's score on an outcome variable is determined by that actor's score

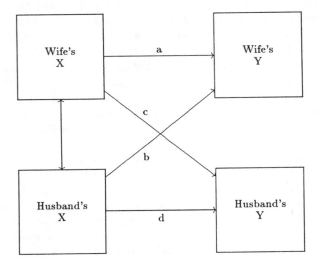

Figure 9.6 Representation of the actor–partner regression model for testing differences in regression coefficients between two classes.

on a predictor variable or by his or her partner's score on the predictor variable. These models provide estimates and significance tests that are corrected for interdependence, but they do not specifically model the interdependence itself. The dyadic-level regressions, in contrast, can be bivariate or multiple regressions, but they explicitly model the interdependence within dyads and answer questions at a different level of analysis. Finally, the individual-level regressions may be bivariate or multiple regressions, and they answer whether the unique or unshared qualities of an individual on the outcome variable are determined by some combination of his or her unique qualities on the predictor variables.

EXCHANGEABLE AND DISTINGUISHABLE DYADS IN THE SAME DESIGN: A SPECIAL ACTOR–PARTNER EFFECT

A special case of the actor–partner model is the Kraemer–Jacklin method (Kraemer & Jacklin, 1979). As Kenny (1995) has pointed out, this is a model for analyzing "mixed" dyads. This is applicable when some dyads are made up of distinguishable members and others are made up of exchangeable members. The classic use of the Kraemer–Jacklin method is to examine whether sex differences in mixed-sex dyads arise from direct (actor) effects or indirect (partner) effects. For example, are men in heterosexual couples more aggressive than their partners because they are men (the actor effect) or because they are paired with women (the partner effect)? In the terminology used by Kenny (1995), is the effect of sex on aggression due to an actor effect or a partner effect? This question cannot be answered in a design where all the dyads contain both men and women—instead it requires a mixed design where some dyads contain a man and a woman, some contain two men, and some contain two women. This design allows the researcher to separate the effect of being a man from the effect of being paired with a woman. Mendoza and Graziano (1982) presented an extension of the Kraemer–Jacklin model to multivariate data. This method uses contrasts to test the hypotheses of the model.

The basic Kraemer–Jacklin design can also be handled by the pairwise regression model. In the classic balanced design (using sex differences as an example), k dyads are male–male, k dyads are female–female, and $2k$ dyads are mixed sex, where $k = \frac{1}{4}N$ (other divisions are possible, but this offers the greatest power because it yields an orthogonal test of the actor and partner hypotheses, see Kenny, 1995). One column codes the sex of the subject and a second column codes the sex of the partner. Two more columns of data are used to code the dependent variable, one coding the outcome variable for the subject and the other coding the outcome variable for the partner.

In the original Kraemer and Jacklin example, there were 12 male–male, 12 female–female, and 21 mixed dyads. The outcome variable was the frequency of offering one's partner a toy. In the columns representing subject sex and partner sex, it is convenient to code boys -1 and girls +1 (although the codes could be reversed without loss of generality). When the outcome variable is regressed upon these two pairwise variables, the actor effect is simply the partial regression coefficient for the subject sex column and the partner effect is the partial regression coefficient for the partner sex column. Again, these coefficients are tested by a formula based on the four pairwise correlations $r_{xx'}$, $r_{yy'}$, r_{xy}, and $r_{xy'}$ Griffin & Gonzalez, 1998). In a perfectly balanced design, such as the one described in the preceding paragraph, the actor and partner effects are orthogonal, so that $r_{xx'} = 0$. This restriction simplifies the hypothesis testing phase. However, in the original Kraemer and Jacklin study, the design was not orthogonal because there are 21 rather than 24 mixed dyads.

In this example, the unstandardized coefficient for the actor effect is one-half the mean difference between toy offers made by girls versus boys. The partner effect represents one-half the mean difference between toy offers made to girls versus boys. (Actually, the means are slightly adjusted for the fact that this was an unbalanced design but the principle is the same). The raw-score coefficients in this case are 0.29 for the actor effect, indicating that girls were more likely to offer toys, and 0.48 for the actor effect, indicating that girls were more likely to be offered toys. Both of these values are identical to the estimates from the original method proposed by Kraemer and Jacklin, which involves a much more tedious method of estimation. The Z tests for the two effects were 1.1 (nonsignificant) and 1.80 (marginally significant), both very similar to the values obtained by the original method. For more details about the pairwise formulation of the Kraemer and Jacklin method, along with derivations and supporting simulations, see Griffin and Gonzalez (1998).

CONCLUSION

> *"But wait a bit", the Oysters cried,*
> *"before we have our chat.*
> *For some of us are out of breath*
> *and all of us are fat."*
> (LEWIS CARROLL, *Through the Looking Glass*)

We have given several examples of research questions that can be answered using the pairwise approach. Our approach differs from those that have been suggested by others. The usual approach to dealing with interdependence has been to define new statistics for a variety of special cases. Some of these statistics have not been readily accessible and have been difficult to implement. In contrast, our approach is to alter the way the data are arranged in the data matrix and then use well-known estimators (such as the Pearson correlation, the partial correlation, correction for disattenuation, regression slopes). The pairwise approach is relatively easy to implement and, as demonstrated here, fairly general in the range of possible research questions that it permits.

However, statistics should not be used in a vacuum. The use of statistics in research should be guided by the substantive theory relevant to the particular domain, the measurement concerns, and the design issues (Gonzalez, 1995). The pairwise technique provides one piece of the puzzle. The other pieces, equally as important, are also necessary for full advancement of a research area. For instance, researchers should develop paradigms that permit interdependence to emerge (see, for example, the paradigm described by Ickes, Robertson, Tooke, & Teng, 1986; Ickes, 1990). Then, armed with statistics for interdependence, relationship researchers can ask new research questions, develop new theory, grapple with measurement issues, and construct new paradigms and research designs. Our own interest in studying the statistics of interdependence grew out of an eagerness to return to research questions that were important during the early stages of our field, which in our opinion have not been adequately resolved.

One of the central phenomena of interest in the history of social psychology was the nature and character of the "group mind". At the turn of the century, French sociologists such as Tarde and Le Bon were fascinated by the difference between the irrational crowd and the rational individual. To them, the crowd was an entity in itself, something more than the sum of its individual parts. However, the phenomenology of the crowd was not amenable to controlled, experimental research and soon dropped out of favor as a topic for research. Later in the 1930s and 1940s, the group again became the focus of an influential school of researchers in social psychology: the Group Dynamics researchers. Once again, however, this group-based approach to social psychology was soon left behind, in part because of statistical design considerations. In particular, the realization that statistical dependency among group members' scores made the analysis of group data more complicated than individual data led to the virtual abandonment of experimental group research in favor of the use of confederates, paper-and-pencil descriptions, audiotapes, and similar individual-focused methods (Steiner, 1974, 1986).

It is our contention that with the introduction of conceptually and computationally straightforward techniques for assessing and separating group- and individual-level effects, we can return to the classic questions that fascinated earlier generations. Some of these questions have been addressed in recent years because of the availability of models developed by David Kenny and his colleagues (Kenny, 1995a, 1996; Kenny & La Voie, 1984, 1985; see Kenny & Albright, 1987, for an applied example). Our own work on the pairwise framework has been greatly influenced by the models of Kenny and his colleagues. We can imagine few questions more central to social psychology than those pertaining to when—or whether—groups act as more than the sum of their parts. A good place to start addressing these questions is with the simplest possible group structure: the dyad. (We are currently generalizing the pairwise method presented here to groups of arbitrary size; Gonzalez & Griffin, 1998a) We hope that the techniques presented in this chapter for dyadic data will provide tools that will be useful in asking and answering theoretical questions about dyads and the individuals that comprise them.

Acknowledgments

We thank Bill Ickes for supplying data and for his general support of our efforts. We also thank Sandra Murray for supplying data, as well as Marvin Hecht and Laura Reynolds for her help with editing. Work presented in this chapter was funded by an NSF grant.

Correspondence concerning this article can be addressed to either author: Richard Gonzalez, Department of Psychology, University of Michigan, Ann Arbor, MI 48109, or Dale Griffin, Faculty of Commerce and Business Administration, University of British Columbia, Vancouver, BC, Canada, V6T 1Z2. Electronic mail may be sent to either gonzo@u.washington.edu (Gonzalez) or dale.griffin@commerce.ubc.ca (Griffin).

Chapter 10

Embracing the *Social* in Personal Relationships and Research

Linda K. Acitelli

University of Houston, Houston, TX, USA

Steve Duck

and

Lee West

University of Iowa, Iowa City, IA, USA

The question "What is a personal relationship?" was offered over ten years ago as a central issue facing researchers of personal relationships (Kelley, 1979; Duck, 1990), but the importance of the question is not limited to local issues within the field of personal relationships (or interpersonal attraction and close relationships). Relational studies, and the issues surrounding them, are significant for the larger field of social psychology as it heeds the call to embrace the *social* more warmly (Ickes & Gonzalez, 1996). Some form of interpersonal relationship must be presupposed in any explanation of social behavior. As Berscheid and Reis (1998) observe, "knowledge about interpersonal relationships is essential to the further development of social psychology" (p. 196).

The Social Psychology of Personal Relationships.
Edited by William Ickes and Steve Duck. © 2000 John Wiley & Sons Ltd.

Three aspects of the *social* are quintessentially relational:

1. *Psychological congruence and empathic understanding between two people.*
   For example, Ickes and colleagues (Ickes & Dugosh, in press; Ickes &
   Gonzalez, 1996) note the incompleteness of accounts of social behavior
   based solely on individuals' reactions to experimentally manipulated "social" stimuli. They have observed that congruence between the perceptions
   of two social actors is not only the essential subject matter of relational
   studies but also a prerequisite for social interaction (see also Kenny, 1994).
   Thus, a strong psychological account of any genuinely *social* behavior will
   involve consideration of the intersubjectivity between at least two conscious minds (Ickes & Gonzalez, 1996) as well as the coordination of social
   behavior (Kenny, 1994).
2. *Interdependence of behavior.* Many examples of interdependence abound in
   relational theories that permeate social psychological theory more generally,
   such as Kelley (1979), Kelley et al. (1983), and Rusbult and Arriaga (1997).
3. *Larger social contexts.* Contexts impinge strongly on the form that relationships take and how they are enacted. As a range of social psychologists
   have argued, place and situation affect the ways in which roles and other
   social behaviors are carried out (Altman, Vinsel, & Brown, 1981; Argyle,
   Furnham, & Graham, 1981).

Moreover, relational processes underlie many other social psychological processes as well (Reis, 1998). For example, Taylor (1998) notes that social
cognition's vision of the self "insufficiently incorporates the centrality of interpersonal relationships" (p. 77) and that the ties between social cognition
and the literature on interpersonal relationships are not as developed as they
should be. Duck (1998) notes other examples of the dynamic interplay between personal relationships and social psychological processes. For example,
attitude change and persuasion function differently when one is persuading an
anonymous target as distinct from a friend, who is likely to respond differently
to a person with whom future close interactions are expected. Thus one might
do favors for friends that one could not be persuaded to do for strangers.
Furthermore, of all the studies that have looked at group dynamics and jury
decision-making, remarkably few have tied personal relationship work to such
dynamics and decisions. Yet it seems plausible to assume that 12 unacquainted strangers called upon to make life-or-death decisions spend at least
some time getting to know each other and that the results of such a process
might tinge their final decisions. Although it is taken as canon that socioemotional factors are at play in groups, personal relationship theories have
rarely been taken into that area directly. Moreover, the social psychology of
health, social support, group identification, stereotyping, prejudice, altruism,
social comparison, language, attributions, and a large set of other social psychological phenomena are also intricately connected with interpersonal factors (Gaines & Ickes, 1997; Rusbult & Arriaga, 1997), such as impression
formation and self-presentation (Leary & Miller, this volume).

Our commentary on the social psychology of personal relationships is therefore on two levels of specificity. We point towards some important directions specifically for personal relationship researchers and for social scientists more generally. At one level, our analysis is based on the fact that as attraction research has become relational research, social psychologists have increasingly recognized the inherently social nature of these interpersonal research domains. They have begun to apply methodologies that are explicitly designed to focus on and capture the processes that are genuinely social within these domains. The second level of commentary is aimed at locating places where social psychological processes are either based on, or moderated by, relational conditions.

In keeping with a developing trend in social psychology (Berscheid & Reis, 1998), we focus on personal relationships not as abstract constructs or attitudinal products of various precipitating factors, but as lived experiences of social life. Such everyday social and personal experiences pose special dilemmas for individuals that are not fully captured when one taps only into social cognitive processes—particularly if one focuses on the cognitions of just one relational participant (Ickes & Dugosh, in press; Ickes & Duck, this volume). The truly social aspects of social psychology and of social experience are only partially reflected in one person's thoughts about social objects. Increasingly, researchers are recognizing that social interactions may be perceived differently by the partners, and appreciate the importance of assessing the degree and type of congruence or incongruence between the perceptions of dyad or group members (Acitelli, Veroff, & Douvan, 1993; Kenny, 1994; Ickes & Gonzalez, 1996). A *social* point is that in the real-life conduct of relationships, such differences of perspective are understood, or tacitly accepted in varying degrees, by the partners. These cognitive differences can have significant behavioral consequences that can manifest themselves in several interactions.

Moreover, social experiences are deeply rooted in selective perception. When researchers select particular aspects for attention according to their own preferences, they may therefore do incomplete justice to the subjective experience of partners. Accordingly, Berscheid and Reis (1998) note that relationship scholars themselves still do not agree about which aspects (frequency, type, nature, etc., or combination thereof) of interaction actually define a relationship. In essence, then, researchers must attend to all behavioral enactments and contingent interdependencies that we recognize as "relationships", even if those interactions are, at some level, routine and trivial.

In lived experience, choices regarding interactions are made concerning the distribution of available time and social energies, the behavioral pressures and constraints created during interaction, the responses to the moral control exerted by others, and the expressions of individual identity within the context provided by other people (Shotter, 1992). However much one (cognitively) covets one's neighbor's ox, the realities of social convention restrain the playing out of the desire. Furthermore, social actors routinely face choices between the company of two friends liked equally, and are confronted with time constraints and divided loyalties that present real dilemmas about enacting relationships. Often people must choose to give time to one equally deserving and important relationship over another or to devote time to work instead of family (Crouter & Helms-Erickson, 1997).

Relationship researchers have documented the pitfalls of attempting to study social processes without full acknowledgment of such interpersonal contexts of everyday lived experience (Parks & Eggert, 1991; Duck, 1993, 1994a), but such contexts are complex in their influence. A weak view of context is the momentary backdrop against which actions are carried out (such as place, environment, or situation; Argyle, Furnham, & Graham, 1981). This view is rather like a scenic backdrop in a stage play and can give the play its texture. It is similar to a black back-cloth giving a portrait photograph a different feel from a white one, or the presence of one type of social audience shaping behavior one way rather than another. A stronger view of context is that place, time, ritual, ceremony, celebration, and other temporal contexts render different the experiences of relaters on those occasions or in those places (Werner, Altman, Brown, & Ginat, 1993). The strongest view is that context is like the water in which fishes swim; it is the essential medium for the conduct of human relationships and social interaction. Personal relationships are steeped in cultural, attitudinal, societal, normative, conversational, cognitive, economic, and dialectical contexts that subtly modify individual tendencies to process information in particular ways as those individuals accommodate to the inputs of other minds (Allan, 1993; Ickes & Dugosh, in press). As Berger and Kellner's (1964) far-sighted work on marriage indicated, the marital relationship becomes more structured through the processes and behaviors by which people coordinate their daily activities. The authors do not assume that the awareness of this process means that the spouses' lives *are* orderly. In fact, Berger and Kellner (1964) assume that the spouses do not apprehend this process and that they are unable to articulate the process of creating their shared reality.

In essence, then, we argue that a truly *social* psychology attends to the fact that relationships are outside the scope of single minds and that the gathering of information from single minds alone distorts our understanding of relationships. To comprehend them fully we must explore not only the congruence between individuals but also the behaviors, practices and processes that make a social experience truly social. This argument requires that we consider briefly the ways in which cutting-edge research is making new choices about phenomena that require attention, as well as reinterpreting phenomena that are considered traditional or mainstream within social psychology.

REPRESENTING THE SOCIAL THROUGH THE CHOICE OF WHAT TO STUDY

. . . in describing a given system, the scientist makes many choices. He chooses his words, and he decides which parts of the system he will describe first; he even decides into what parts he will divide the system to describe it. These decisions will affect the description as a whole in the sense that they will affect the map upon which the typological relationships between the elementary messages of description are represented. (Bateson, 1991, p. 62)

Research scholars must necessarily select from any phenomenal pool in order to collect data or describe behavior. Not all things in a situation count as data. Neither do all behaviors in an interaction merit inclusion in a description of the occurrences. Decisions about inclusion or exclusion are taken according to the observers' judgments and determinations of relevance. We observe that those things less represented in many research studies are the routine, tedious and repetitious, the varieties and fluctuations of experience, and the negative side of relating. Exceptions are daily hassles (Bolger & Kelleher, 1993), the dark side of relating (Cupach & Spitzberg, 1994; Duck, 1994b), and turning points of relating (Surra, 1987). Significant, dramatic and, as it happens, rare behaviors are well-researched. Relatively large amounts of research, for example, have focused on the role of self-disclosure in intimacy growth (Metts, 1997; Prager, 1995), yet recent field studies show that it actually occurs less than 2% of the time in natural interactions (Dindia, 1997). However, researchers do acknowledge that self-disclosure is not a monolithic concept and that there are distinct types or levels of self-disclosure that have different effects on the development of an intimate relationship (e.g., Derlega, Metts, Petronio, & Margulis, 1993; Reis & Shaver, 1988). Further, researchers are discovering that there is more to developing a close relationship than self-disclosure (Acitelli & Duck, 1987; Berscheid & Reis, 1998; Prager, 1995). Some of what constitutes relationships appears to be routine repetition and cementing of relationships through the ordinary practices and arrangements of leisure and routine life (Huston, Surra, Fitzgerald, & Cate, 1981).

Such practices and routines are sometimes irrational, disorganized, and mindless. Relationship research generally has developed a good understanding of the rational side of relationships (Andersen, 1993; Berger, 1988, 1993; Berscheid, 1994; Fehr, 1993; Fincham & Bradbury, 1987; Fletcher & Fitness, 1993; Honeycutt, 1993; Kelley et al., 1983), but has increasingly included efforts devoted to the apparently irrational or emotional experiences that occur in life (Fitness & Strongman, 1991). Important in the real-life management of relationships are aspects such as embarrassment (Miller, 1996), shame and anger (Retzinger, 1995), daily hassles (Bolger & Kelleher, 1993), the dark side of relationships (Cupach & Spitzberg, 1994; Duck, 1994b) or aversive relationships and social behaviors (Kowalski, 1997, and in press). Expanding the work on the negative side of such specific social behaviors as caring (Stein, 1993; Wood, Dendy, Dordek, Germany, & Varallo, 1994) or social support (La Gaipa, 1990; Rook, 1984), researchers are now attending to the fact that all relationships have simultaneously both bonds and binds (Wiseman, 1986), all have darkness and light, and all have hassles and irritations that have to be not only experienced but managed in daily life (Bolger & Kelleher, 1993; Duck & Wood, 1995).

These moves toward balance and complexity are particularly important when one acknowledges the methodological significance of the fact that relationships have often been depicted at the moment of measurement rather than in the context of a longer and more variegated flow of experience from the relaters' point of view. Recent research has recognized the risks of depicting relationship processes themselves in a form generalized from that moment as if it implies that close relationships are entities characterized totally by that measurement (Berscheid & Reis, 1998; Duck, 1994a). Relationships are not states or plateaus, and researchers now recognize the simultaneous presence of a number of features and observe the pressures of real alternatives to the path actually taken (Kelly, 1955). For example, "turning points" (Surra, 1987) are choices between actual alternative options: to understand the choice one has to understand the psychological and social context of alternatives in which it was made (Duck, 1994a; Dixson & Duck, 1993; Kelly, 1955).

Equally, the everyday conduct of relationships can involve choices between different relationships, between different distributions of time with different partners, and even strains on loyalties to different persons who may make simultaneous, competing demands on one's relational resources or provisions (Nicholson, 1998). A person may be faced with conflicts between or among different relationships—having to decide whether to spend time with spouse or with children, with friends or with co-workers, with partner or with family, staying longer at a work event or going home to play with the kids, in fulfilling obligations to parents or to neighbors (Baxter, et al, 1997). In real-life everyday relationships, a person's commitments to a particular relationship can be assessed as much by the relative distribution of time *between* relationships as by the balance between internal reward and cost systems *within* relationships (Stein, Bush, Ross, & Ward, 1992; Timmer, Veroff, & Hatchett, 1996).

Over and above such choices, recent research trends recognize that persons occasionally report selectively on the nature of their relationships, see partners as simultaneously "good" and "bad", change their affective appraisal of particular cues from negative to positive (Murray, Holmes, & Griffin, 1996b), or reflect negatively on each other without actually leaving the relationship (Felmlee, 1995). Indeed, positive affect and negative affect have been consistently shown to be two independent dimensions (e.g., Cacioppo & Bernston, 1994). Partners can feel good about a relationship at some times and not at other times, can quarrel and make up (i.e., cycle through different feelings and characterizations of the same relationship) or can have good days and bad days in the same relationship (Barbee, 1990)—an important development toward a complete story that recognizes a relationship's variabilities and vicissitudes. Because relationships are truly dynamic and complex, capturing the experiential and often uneven process of relating becomes a primary research goal. Implicit in this goal is the recognition that relationships are not well represented by unitary labels that obscure their seething processes or imply a calm uniformity (Berscheid & Reis, 1998; Duck & Wood, 1995).

In sum, recent research increasingly recognizes that social life is not exclusively an individual experience; it is not controlled by individuals personally; it is not all important, not all predictable, not all exciting or dramatic, not all consistent, and not all positive. It's life.

PARADIGMS OF RELATING AND SOCIAL EXPERIENCE

Cultural norms about relational conduct are locked into the interpretations of interaction that occur in everyday relationships. It is important to include such norms in efforts to understand the truly social aspects of relating. The proper and appropriate relationships permissible between persons, for example, depend on cultural values, such as whether equality, hierarchy, independence, individualism, or collectivism is the preferred mode (Gudykunst, 1992). Daily and routine direct interactions with neighbors and third parties in real life sharply increase a person's contact with an abstraction like "culture". Such regular, routine contacts provide interpretive cultural contexts for daily conduct since such third parties often comment on, and even constrain, behavior within a personal relationship (Klein & Johnson, 1997) or else actively intervene in conflicts within the couple (Klein & Milardo, 1993). In addition, social networks often respond/interact/relate to a couple, instead of to relational partners as separate individuals (Bendtschneider & Duck, 1993; Stein et al., 1992). In short, the relationship is not a functionally autonomous social unit but is circumscribed by other persons who are separate from the relationship itself and yet influence its own internal conduct (see Wellman, 1985 or Milardo & Wellman, 1992, for a critique). Increasing attention is now paid, especially by sociologists, to the fact that each partner in the dyadic relationship is simultaneously constituting a relationship with each individual in the network, often several relationships simultaneously (Berscheid, 1995; Klein & Johnson, 1997; Klein & Milardo, 1993; Sarason, Sarason, & Gurung, 1997).

External Influences on Individual Minds

A *social* psychology must continue to explore the ways in which such exterior influences impinge upon individual minds and, as a result, dyads. For instance, research on same-sex friendship assumes that the relationship is normatively supported by culture, family and other friends tacitly, unannounced, and without fuss. By contrast, Werking (1997) indicates that cross-sex non-romantic friendships are often seriously questioned or challenged by other people and hence require extra effort, additional layers of accounting, and auxiliary social psychological *work*. Huston and Schwartz (1995) show that gay and lesbian partners experience extra social burdens in carrying out their relationships in a context where other people's reactions are extremely influential. Further, Weston (1991) argues that "blood-family" is often replaced for homosexuals by "families of choice." Because homosexuals often are not "out" to blood-family, or may be estranged from their blood-families specifically because of their homosexuality, the blood-family can function very differently for gays and lesbians. Not only are gays and lesbians less likely to tell their parents and siblings of developing relationships, they are less likely to talk of developed intimate relationships (Huston & Schwartz, 1995). In examining the relation-ship between lesbian couples and their families of origin, Murphy (1989) reports that even when the parents of lesbians are aware of their daughter's significant romantic relationship, they often deny the bond or connection (e.g. by inviting only the daughter home for holidays). In short, then, key difficulties—and consequent social psychological processes—in the everyday social or relational experience of typical people may be overlooked in our examination of college sophomores.

A truly *social* psychology notes further that each "purely cognitive" or attitudinal concept in social psychology has real-life, structural counterparts. Duck (1994a) lamented that similarity has been interpreted as a primarily cognitive, rather than social, construct and as a state, not as an open-ended process of continually perceived and/or reconstructed congruence. Indeed, similarity is both a cognitive and a social construct. Early attraction re-searchers often noted the importance of similarity as a cognitive-affective mechanism for relational development (Byrne, 1971), whereas more recent work attends also to the social facts that constrain and circumscribe the influ-ences of cognitive similarity in the real social world (Byrne, 1997). Functional proximity preceded similarity as an important theoretical explanation for relational initiation (Festinger, Schachter, & Back, 1950), yet proximity is not merely physical nearness in a particular context (Kerckhoff, 1974; Murstein, 1971). Similarity and proximity both structure social experience (Allan, 1993). We are closer to those of social standing similar to our own.

Socio-economic positioning plays an enormous role in the range of people who are considered available for relationships (Kerckhoff, 1974; Whitbeck & Hoyt, 1994). It could be argued, therefore, that socio-economic standing or social group membership is largely presumed under the rubric "attitudinal similarity". In like manner, Kenny and Acitelli (1994) have shown that there is a distinction between the unique similarity of two people and a general similarity between one person and all others (within the particular population of study). Their work demonstrated that the general or "stereotypic" similarity inflates our assessments of partner similarity, but it has more power to affect relationship outcomes than is commonly assumed. Presuming that this ster-eotypic similarity has a cultural or normative base, their findings lend credence to the idea that social structures can create a psychological similarity.

Furthermore, social structure itself determines the factors that are deemed to be bases for judgments of similarity in the first place (e.g., in the USA, race or ethnicity is emphasized as an issue, but in some cultures, caste or class or religion is an issue that precludes or disparages certain sorts of relationship candidates and approves or prescribes certain others). The psychological similarity between individuals is best understood as partly created and played out by social contexts and not as a purely psychological (cognitive) relationship existing between individuals. Social stratification pre-sorts people in ways that affect the probability that they will have certain kinds of similarity (such as socio-economic, ethnic, religious, or political values), and the importance of the similarity to a particular relationship is determined or constrained by the social context.

Relationships are conducted in a context that takes a view about the ways in which individuals are supposed to progress in building a relationship (Allan, 1993). The path attributed to a relationship is partly an explanatory narrative referring to events and occurrences perceived within a particular social context as a reasonable path (Beall & Sternberg, 1995). For instance, "We met and fell in love and got married" is more acceptable in North America than "I ate some ground almond paste and the relationship just developed from there" or "Our parents picked our partners from a catalogue and naturally we got married the next day". Cultural contexts provide individuals not only with views of how relationships are supposed to develop, but also with vocabularies for representing relationship growth. "We fell in love" is a common style of explanation in most Western cultures; "It is a good match for both families" is more acceptable in many other parts of the world.

Because culture provides individuals with their vocabulary for relationships, expressions or explanations of feelings towards other people are likely to be modified by context, and so are researchers' views of them. Hendrick and Hendrick (1993) observed that researchers would more likely focus on the different types of love as absolute and relatively constant entities than on the variety of ways in which love could be expressed in different contexts or to different audiences (e.g., to a researcher, to parents, to a priest, or to a sexual partner). Research, therefore, could also explore the various ways in which the same person can express different sorts of love to the same partner as a function of place, context, or perceived appropriateness to situation—e.g., the expressions of love made in proposing marriage, on honeymoon, during a request for support, or after the discovery of unfaithfulness (Duck, 1994a).

If social psychologists view relationships as a matter of personal choice to the exclusion of such molding influences, they are less likely to attend to social contexts (Bradbury, Cohen, & Karney, 1998) because involuntary relationships are presumed to be formed by something external to the people in it (Berscheid & Reis, 1998; Hepburn & Crepin, 1984). Yet the arbiter for any relationship identity and relational form will ultimately also be some reference group outside of the relationship or individual that gets inside the person's head by repeated contact with other minds (Simmel, 1950). The identity of a person in a relationship, and of relationships themselves, will thus ultimately be influenced by reference to social communities rather than only to the two constituent individuals.

External Influences as Modifiers of Relationship Experiences

Common usage often applies the term *the relationship* as if there is only one appropriate way to represent it, and hence that "a relationship is a relationship is a relationship" to all people equivalently, or to both partners identically, or to each person consistently at all times. Social psychologists observed early on that there are "insider" and "outsider" ways to look at relationships (Olson, 1977; Duck & Sants, 1983; Surra & Ridley, 1991). More recently it has also been observed (Acitelli, 1993; Wood & Cox, 1993) that the outsider position is not simply outside the experience of the insiders, but that "being outside" has consequences for the depiction of inside phenomena. We tend to forget that outsiders' purposes in observing relationships usually involve a limited depiction or understanding of an insider's perspective. For one thing, the outsider position often represents only one cross-section in time, whereas the insider position is enriched by many cross sections in time because partners rely on memory as well as any particular observation. Also the outsider position necessarily "stabilizes" the interior dynamics of the participants by recording their momentary position rather than their fluctuations (Dixson & Duck, 1993). Finally, men and women view the "insides" of their relationships differently. The reported differences are specifically tied to sex: thus the experience of many aspects of relationships is a gendered social phenomenon, such that full investigation of relationships involves not merely identifying relationship behaviors but locating relationship behaviors in their gendered contexts and histories (Acitelli & Young, 1996; Maccoby, 1990; Peplau & Gordon, 1985; Wood, 1995a).

Relational scholars are now less likely to neglect the economic influences on relationship behavior provided by various social conditions and expectations (Allan, 1993). In fact, friendships are never "just behaviors" produced by individual minds, but are acts conducted in a place at a time (Werner et al., 1993) and "place" has ramifications that affect the style and range of behaviors of friendship that will be enacted (Allan, 1995). For instance people who do not have the money to entertain at home or who have small inconvenient homes—or no homes at all—are more likely to conduct their relationships in a place that reflects those economic conditions. Such places also happen to limit the financial resources required of the respective partners—for example, the British pub, where reciprocity extends to the cost of a round of drinks rather than an exchange of meals within the home (Allan, 1995). But such places also restrict privacy and so they generally affect the nature and conduct of self-disclosure and information flow, making it less likely for people to trade private information and more likely that they will express what is "public knowledge".

The construction of form for a relationship is thus a matter not only of cognition but also of coordination of one's own behavior with that of the partner, with the network, and with the wider social group (Milardo, 1984; Parks & Eggert, 1991; Milardo & Wellman, 1992). Such behavior is responsive to places, times, and social rules (Ginsburg, 1988). All these constructions are essentially manipulations of meaning systems that involve the sharing and coordination of meaning—or rather more particularly, the coordination of meanings embodies expectations for one's own and others' behavior—which takes us back to issues of congruence.

Relationships as Modifiers of Other Social Psychological Processes

Our argument has so far focused on the fact that relational processes parallel broader social processes, and social psychologists have given less direct attention than they should to the claim that relational processes underpin other social behaviors. When Watzlawick, Beavin, and Jackson (1967) noted that all messages contain both content and relational themes, they were, we believe, pointing to something widely relevant to social behavior.

Most social processes studied by social psychologists contain tacit assumptions regarding the underlying nature of the relationship between the participants, and yet the effects of different relational forms upon these processes are rarely explored. If they were to be explored, then we social psychologists would likely find that there is a large number of topics where the nature of the relationship between one person and the next would affect social psychological processes. For example, we have already noted that relationship processes could be defined as independent variables in studies of persuasion, stereotyping, altruism, self-presentation, and group dynamics. We would now simply observe that many other social psychological processes are also modified by the relationship between one person and another, whether they be accounts, attributions, nonverbal behaviors, judgments of testimony in court, physician–patient interaction, dissonance, conflict, emotional expression, anxiety, or use of language in social behavior.

Relational processes at the very least intersect with other social psychological processes that are usually demarcated from relational analysis. For example, in the case of embarrassment and social predicaments (Miller, 1996; Metts, 1997), at least a part of the concern of the key players is connected with consideration of the way in which they will appear to esteemed others in their relational circle, whereas the impacts of embarrassing behaviors can also be reduced in an intimate setting. The processes of social comparison that are accomplished in gossip (Suls, 1977) are connected to comparison with others to whom one has a close relationship, whereas gossip and the spreading of news and rumor also instantiate the structure of social groups. Bergmann (1993) notes that news (for example, about births, engagements, marriages, and deaths) is spread in a way that reflects the inherent relational structure of the group, with certain members having the right to take personal offense if they hear about it after some other person has heard about it, instead of before. Group and organizational social behavior likewise reflect relational structure whether the issue is power (Kelvin, 1977), annoyance at work (Cunningham, Barbee, & Druen, 1997), or social ostracism (Williams, 1997). Finally, some social psychological analyses of personality traits like egotism (Leary, Bednarski, Hammon, & Duncan, 1997), or need for control (Williams, 1997) and of psychological illnesses such as depression and schizophrenia (Segrin, in press) have begun to point to the relational processes that underlie them.

Social psychology in the past has viewed the connection between relationships and other social processes as primarily one of the dependency of relationships on other social processes, preferring to see the variations in intimacy as a consequence of processes such as embarrassment, self-disclosure, or normative behaviors. We now challenge social psychology to look at things the other way around and to see the moderation of embarrassment, self-presentation, self-disclosure, norms and so forth as dependent on the nature of the relationship between the two persons involved. For example, there is mounting evidence that social psychological influences on health are, at least in part, products of relational status and functioning (Sarason, Sarason, & Gurung, 1997; Heller & Rook, 1997).

CONCLUSION

As noted by Ickes and Dugosh (in press), any social psychology that emphasizes the individual is naturally tested and stretched by the study of dyads or personal relationships. We, as social psychologists, need to look both within and outside the relationship to create a broader picture of relationships in context. Thus researchers should look within individual relationships on several occasions in order to depict patterns, rather than presume the fixed pattern of experience that may be falsely deduced from a reliance on single-participant, one-shot measurements taken out of context. Where Hinde (1981) called for more description of relationships (using an ethological analogy), we call for more work on the variabilities perceived by relationship partners such as the contradictions and uncertainties with which partners must cope (Duck, 1994b; Duck & Wood, 1995), variations in expectations about the relationship (Miell, 1987), and the changing patterns of talk in and about relationships (Acitelli, 1988, 1993; Duck, Rutt, Hurst, & Strejc, 1991).

We also place emphasis on external, behaviorally based descriptions of the social structures and contexts wherein relationship are enacted. Though the number on the thermometer can say a great deal about the state of the water, the real point about boiling water is not the particular mark on the thermometer, but the interior ebullience and structural change that takes place in the boiling process. Nor is "good sex" merely a check mark in a diary but rather something energetic, dynamic, and composed of complex and congruent actions, based on shared understandings, purposes, and feelings. In keeping with our arguments about representations that have integrity, we suggest that external observations be more consistently combined with internal observations gathered over a long enough time period to display internal variabilities. Researchers are also replacing the simple emphasis on reliability (which deliberately seeks to strip out variability) and instead recalling what it is that reliability leaves out of our understanding of relationships.

As relationship researchers, we should ask ourselves what our research designs would look like if we were to investigate relating rather than relationships. A shift from focusing on the noun to the verb could be profitable in our quest to see how behaviors construct (over and over again) the loose definition of partners, friends and family. The answers to such questions are to be found partly in this volume and partly in the future of the field of research on personal relationships and their conduct.

Acknowledgment

We are grateful to Bill Ickes for his helpful comments on previous drafts of this chapter.

REFERENCES

Abbey, A. (1982). Sex differences in attributions for friendly behavior: Do males misperceive females' friendliness? *Journal of Personality and Social Psychology*, **42**, 830–838.

Acitelli, L. K. (1988). When spouses talk to each other about their relationship. *Journal of Social and Personal Relationships*, **5**, 185–199.

Acitelli, L. K. (1993). You, me, and us: Perspectives on relationship awareness. *Understanding relationship processes 1: Individuals in relationships* (pp. 144–174). Newbury Park: Sage.

Acitelli, L. K. (1995). Disciplines at parallel play. *Journal of Social and Personal Relationships*, **12**, 589–596.

Acitelli, L. K., & Duck, S. W. (1987). Intimacy as the proverbial elephant. In D. Perlman & S. W. Duck (Eds) *Intimate relationships: Development, dynamics, and deterioration* (pp. 297– 308). London: Sage.

Acitelli, L. K., & Young, A. M. (1996). Gender and thought in relationships. In G. Fletcher & J. Fitness, *Knowledge structures and interactions in close relationships: A social psychological approach*. Hillsdale, NJ: Lawrence Erlbaum Associates.

Acitelli, L. K., Douvan, E., & Veroff, J. (1993). Perceptions of conflict in the first year of marriage: How important are similarity and understanding? *Journal of Social and Personal Relationships*, **10**, 5–19.

Adams, J. S. (1965). Inequity in social exchange. In L. Berkowitz (Ed.), *Advances in experimental social psychology* (Vol. 2, pp. 267–299). New York: Academic Press.

Agnew, C. R., Van Lange, P. A. M., Rusbult, C. E., & Langston, C. A. (1998). Cognitive interdependence: Commitment and the mental representation of close relationships. *Journal of Personality and Social Psychology*, **74**, 939–954.

Ahuvia, A. (1993). *I love it! Towards a unifying theory of love across diverse love objects*. Unpublished Ph.D. Dissertation, Northwestern University.

Ainsworth, M. D. S., Blehar, M. C., Waters, E., & Wall, S. (1978). *Patterns of attachment: Assessed in the strange situation and at home*. Hillsdale, NJ: Erlbaum.

Alcock, J. (1993). *Animal behavior*, 5th edn. Sunderland, MA: Sinauer.

Aldridge, D. P. (1978). Interracial marriages: Empirical and theoretical considerations. *Journal of Black Studies*, **8**, 355–368.

Aldridge, D. P. (1991). *Focusing: Black male–female relationships*. Chicago: Third World Press.

Alger, C. E . (1966). Interaction in a committee of the United Nations General Assembly. *Midwest Journal of Political Science*, **10**, 411–447.

Allan, G. A. (1993). Social structure and relationships. *Social contexts of relationships [Understanding relationship processes 3]* (pp. 1–25). Newbury Park: Sage.

Allan, G. A. (1995, June). *Friendship, class, status and identity*. Paper presented at the *International Network on Personal Relationships*, Williamsburg, VA.

Allan, G. A., & Milardo, R. M. (1997). Social Networks and Marital Relationships, *Handbook of personal relationships*, 2nd edn (pp. 505–522). Chichester, UK: Wiley.

Allen, J. B., Kenrick, D. T., Linder, D. E., & McCall, M. A. (1989). Arousal and attraction: A response-facilitation alternative to misattribution and negative-reinforcement models. *Journal of Personality and Social Psychology*, **57**, 261–270.

Allport, G. W. (1954/1979). *The nature of prejudice*. Chicago: Addison-Wesley.

Altman, I., & Taylor, D. (1973). *Social penetration: The development of interpersonal relationships*. New York: Holt, Rinehart & Winston.

Altman, I., Vinsel, A., & Brown, B. B. (1981). Dialectic conceptions in social psychology: An application to social penetration and privacy regulation. In L. Berkowitz (Ed.) *Advances in experimental social psychology*, Vol. 14, pp. 107–160. New York: Academic Press.

Andersen, P. A. (1993). Cognitive schemata in personal relationships. In S. W. Duck (Ed.) *Understanding relationship processes 1: Individuals in relationships* (pp. 1–29). Newbury Park: Sage.

Antill, J. K. (1983). Sex role complementarity versus similarity in married couples. *Journal of Personality and Social Psychology*, **45**, 145–155.

Apsler, R. (1975). Effects of embarrassment on behavior toward others. *Journal of Personality and Social Psychology*, **32**, 145–153.

Argyle, M., Furnham, A., & Graham, J. (1981). *Social situations*. Cambridge: Cambridge University Press.

Aron, A. (1970). *Relationship variables in human heterosexual attraction*. Unpublished doctoral dissertation, University of Toronto.

Aron, A., & Aron, E. N. (1986). *Love and the expansion of self: Understanding attraction and satisfaction* (pp. 19–67). Washington: Hemisphere.

Aron, A., & Aron, E. N. (1997). Self-expansion motivation and including other in the self. In S. W. Duck (Ed.) *Handbook of personal relationships: Theory, research, and interventions*, 2nd edn (pp. 251–270). Chichester: Wiley.

Aron, A., & Rodriguez, G. (1992, July). Scenarios of falling in love among Mexican, Chinese, and Anglo-Americans. In A. Aron (chair), *Ethnic and cultural differences in love*. Symposium conducted at the Sixth International Conference on Personal Relationships, Orono, ME.

Aron, A., Aron, E. N., & Allen, J. (1998). Motivations for unrequited love. *Personality and Social Psychology Bulletin*, **24**, 787–796.

Aron, A., Aron, E. N., & Smollan, D. (1992). Inclusion of Other in the Self Scale and the structure of interpersonal closeness. *Journal of Personality and Social Psychology*, **63**, 596–612.

Aron, A., Aron, E. N., Tudor, M., & Nelson, G. (1991). Close relationships as including other in the self. *Journal of Personality and Social Psychology*, **60**, 241–253.

Aron, A., Dutton, D. G., Aron, E. N., & Iverson, A. (1989). Experiences of falling in love. *Journal of Social and Personal Relationships*, **6**, 243–257.

Aron, A., Melinat, E., Aron, E. N., Vallone, R. D., & Bator, R. J. (1997). The experimental generation of interpersonal closeness: A procedure and some preliminary findings. *Personality and Social Psychology Bulletin*, **23**, 363–377.

Aron, A., Paris, M., & Aron, E. N. (1995). Falling in love: Prospective studies of self-concept change. *Journal of Personality and Social Psychology*, **69**, 1102–1112.

Aron, E. N., & Aron, A. (1996). Love and expansion of the self: The state of the model. *Personal Relationships*, **3**, 45–58.

Aronson, E., & Linder, D. (1965). Gain and loss of esteem as determinants of interpersonal attraction. *Journal of Experimental Social Psychology*, **1**, 156–171.

Arriaga, X. B., & Rusbult, C. E. (1998). Standing in my partner's shoes: Partner perspective-taking and reactions to accommodative dilemmas. *Personality and Social Psychology Bulletin*, **9**, 927–948.

Asante, M. (1987). *The Afrocentric idea*. Philadelphia: Temple University Press.

Asch, S. (1946). Forming impressions of personality. *Journal of Abnormal and Social Psychology*, **41**, 258–290.

Axelrod, R. (1984). *The evolution of cooperation*. New York: Basic Books.

Axelrod, R., & Hamilton, W. D. (1981). The evolution of cooperation. *Science*, **211**, 1390–1396.

Backman, C. W. (1959). The effect of perceived liking on interpersonal attraction. *Human Relations*, **12**, 379–384.

Bailey, J. M., & Pillard, R. C. (1991). A genetic study of male sexual orientation. *Archives of General Psychiatry*, **48**, 1089–1096.

Bailey, J. M., Gaulin, S., Agyei, Y., & Gladue, B. A. (1994). Effects of gender and sexual orientation on evolutionarily relevant aspects of human mating psychology. *Journal of Personality and Social Psychology*, **66**, 1074–1080.

Bakan, D. (1966). *The duality of human existence: Isolation and commitment in Western man*. Boston: Beacon Press.

Baldwin, M. W. (1992). Relational schemas and the processing of social information. *Psychological Bulletin*, **112**, 461–484.

Baldwin, M. W. (1994). Primed relational schemas as a source of self-evaluative reactions. *Journal of Social and Clinical Psychology*, **13**, 380–403.

Bandura, A. (1977). Self-efficacy: Toward a unifying theory of behavioral change. *Psychological Review*, **84**, 191–215.

Barbee, A. P. (1990). Interactive coping: The cheering up process in close relationships, *Personal Relationships and Social Support* . London: Sage.

Barker, R. G., & Gump, R V. (1964). *Big school, small school: High school size and student behavior.* Stanford, CA: Stanford University Press.

Barkow, J. H., Cosmides, L., & Tooby, J. (1992). *The adapted mind: Evolutionary psychology and the generation of culture.* New York: Oxford University Press.

Bartholomew, K., & Horowitz, L. M. (1991). Attachment styles among young adults: A test of a four category model. *Journal of Personality and Social Psychology*, **61**, 226–244.

Bateson, G. (1991). Naven: Epilogue 1958. In R. E. Donaldson (Ed.) *A sacred unity: Further steps to an ecology of mind* (pp. 49–69). New York: Harper Collins.

Batson, C. D. (1987). Prosocial motivation: Is it ever truly altruistic? In L. Berkowitz (Ed.) *Advances in experimental social psychology* (Vol. 20, pp. 65–122). New York: Academic Press.

Baum, A., & Paulus, P. B. (1987). Crowding. D. Stokols & I. Altman (Eds) In *Handbook of environmental psychology*, (pp. 533–70. New York: John Wiley & Sons.

Baumeister, R. F. (1982a). A self-presentational view of social phenomena. *Psychological Bulletin*, **91**, 3–26.

Baumeister, R. F. (1982b). Self-esteem, self-presentation, and future interaction: A dilemma of reputation. *Journal of Personality*, **50**, 29–45.

Baumeister, R. F. (1989). Motives and costs of self-presentation in organizations. In R. A. Giacalone & P. Rosenfeld (Eds) *Impression management in the organization* (pp. 57–71). Hillsdale, NJ: Lawrence Erlbaum Associates.

Baumeister, R. F., & Jones, E. E. (1978). When self-presentation is constrained by the target's knowledge: Consistency and compensation. *Journal of Personality and Social Psychology*, **36**, 608–618.

Baumeister, R. F., & Leary, M. R. (1995). The need to belong: Desire for interpersonal attachment as a fundamental human motivation. *Psychological Bulletin*, **117**, 497–529.

Baumeister, R. F., Hutton, D. G., & Tice, D. M. (1989). Cognitive processes during deliberate self-presentation: How self-presenters alter and misinterpret the behavior of their interaction partners. *Journal of Experimental Social Psychology*, **25**, 59–78.

Baxter, L. A., & Dindia, K. (1990). Marital partners' perceptions of marital maintenance strategies. *Journal of Social and Personal Relationship*, **7**, 187–208.

Baxter, L. A., & Widenmann, S. (1993). Revealing and not revealing the status of romantic relationships to social networks. *Journal of Social and Personal Relationships*, **10**, 321–337.

Baxter, L. A., Mazanec, M., Nicholson, J., Pittman, G., Smith, K., & West, L. (1997). Everyday loyalties and betrayals in personal relationships. *Journal of Social and Personal Relationships*, **14**, 655–678.

Beach, F. A. (1976). Sexual attractivity, proceptivity and receptivity in female mammals. *Hormones and Behavior*, **7**, 105–138.

Beach, S. R. H., & Tesser, A. (1995). Self-esteem and the extended self-evaluation maintenance model: The self in social context. In M. H. Kernis (Ed.), *Efficacy, agency, and self-esteem* (pp. 145–170). New York: Plenum.

Beall, A., & Sternberg, R. (1995). The social construction of love. *Journal of Social and Personal Relationships*, **12**, 417–438.

Becker, H. S. (1960). Notes on the concept of commitment. *American Journal of Sociology*, **66**, 32–40.

Belk, R. W. (1988). Possessions and the extended self. *Journal of Consumer Research*, **15**, 139–168.

Belsky, J., Steinberg, L., & Draper, P. (1991). Childhood experience, interpersonal development, and reproductive strategy: An evolutionary theory of socialization. *Child Development*, **62**, 647–670.

Bendtschneider, L., & Duck, S. W. (1993). What's yours is mine and what's mine is yours: Couple friends. In P. Kalbfleisch (Ed.) *Developments in interpersonal communication* (pp. 169–186). Hillsdale, NJ: Erlbaum.

Berg, J. H. (1984). Development of friendship between roomates. *Journal of Personality and Social Psychology*, **46**, 346–356.

Berg, J. H., & Derlega, V. J. (1987). Themes in the study of self-disclosure. In V. J. Derlega & J. H. Berg (Eds) *Self-disclosure: Theory, research, and therapy* (pp. 1–8). New York: Plenum.

Berger, C. R. (1988). Uncertainty and information exchange in developing relationships. In S. W. Duck, D. F. Hay, S. E. Hobfoll, W. Ickes & B. Montgomery (Eds) *Handbook of personal relationships* (pp. 239–256). Wiley: Chichester.

Berger, C. R. (1993). Goals, plans and mutual understanding in personal relationships, *Understanding relationship processes 1: Individuals in relationships* (pp. 30–59). Newbury Park: Sage.

Berger, P., & Kellner, H. (1964). Marriage and the construction of reality: An exercise in the microsociology of knowledge. *Diogenes*, **46**, 1–24.

Bergler, E. (1946). *Unhappy marriage and divorce: A study of neurotic choice of marriage partners.* New York: International Universities Press.

Bergmann, J. R. (1993). *Discreet indiscretions: The social organization of gossip.* New York: Aldine de Gruyter.

Berkowitz, L., & Daniels, L. R. (1963). Responsibility and dependency. *Journal of Abnormal Social Psychology*, **66**, 429–436.

Berlyne, D. E. (1960). *Conflict, arousal, and curiosity.* New York: McGraw-Hill.

Bern, S. L. (1974). The measurement of psychological androgyny. *Journal of Consulting and Clinical Psychology*, **42**, 155–162.

Bernstein, I. S. (1964). The integration of rhesus monkeys introduced to a group. *Folia Primatologica*, **2**, 50–63.

Bernstein, I. S. (1969). Introductory techniques in the formation of pigtail monkey troops. *Folia Primatologica*, **10**, 1–19.

Bernstein, I. S. (1971). The influence of introductory techniques on the formation of captive mangabey groups. *Primates*, **12**, 33–44.

Berscheid, E. (1983). Emotion. In H. H. Kelley, E. Berscheid, A. Christensen, J. H. Harvey, T. L. Huston, G. Levinger, E. McClintock, L. A. Peplau & D. R. Peterson (Eds) *Close relationships* (pp. 110–168). New York: Freeman.

Berscheid, E. (1985). Interpersonal attraction. In G. Lindzey & E. Aronson (Eds) *Handbook of social psychology*, 3rd edn (pp. 413–484). Reading, MA: Addison-Wesley.

Berscheid, E. (1994). Interpersonal relationships. *Annual Review of Psychology*, **45**, 79–129.

Berscheid, E. (1995). Help wanted: A grand theorist of interpersonal relationships, sociologist or anthropologist preferred. *Journal of Social and Personal Relationships*, **12**, 529–533.

Berscheid, E., & Graziano, W. (1979). The initiation of social relationships and social attraction. In R. L. Burgess & T. L. Huston (Eds) *Social exchange in developing relationships*. New York: Academic.

Berscheid, E., & Reis, H. T. (1998). Attraction and close relationships. In D. T. Gilbert, S. F. Fiske & G. Lindzey (Eds) *The handbook of social psychology*, 4th edn (Vol. 2, pp. 193–281), Boston: McGraw-Hill.

Betzig, L. (1989). Causes of conjugal dissolution: A cross-cultural study. *Current Anthropology*, **30**, 654–676.

Betzig, L. (1992). Roman polygyny. *Ethology and Sociobiology*, **13**, 309–349.

Bissonnette, V L. (1992). *Interdependence in dyadic gazing*. Unpublished doctoral dissertation, University of Texas at Arlington.

Blau, P. M. (1964). *Exchange and power in social life*. New York: Wiley.

Blieszner, R., & Adams, R. G. (1992). *Adult friendship*. Newbury Park, CA: Sage.

Blood, R. O., & Wolfe, D. W. (1960). *Husbands and wives*. Glencoe, IL: The Free Press.

Bloom, B. L., Asher, S, J., & White, S. W. (1978). Marital disruption as a stressor: A review and analysis. *Psychological Bulletin*, **85**, 867–894.

Blumstein, P., & Schwartz, P. (1983). *American couples: Money, work, sex*. New York: William Morrow.

Bock, R. D. (1989). *Multilevel analysis of educational data*. San Diego: Academic Press.

Bolger, N., & Kelleher, S. (1993). Daily Life in Relationships. *Social contexts of relationships [Understanding relationship processes 3]* (pp. 100–109). Newbury Park: Sage.

Bolig, R., Stein, P. J., & McKenry, P. C. (1984). The self-advertisement approach to dating: Male–female differences. *Family Relations*, **33**, 587–592.

Bombar, M. L., & Littig, L. W., Jr. (1996). Babytalk as a communication of intimate attachment: An initial study in adult romances and friendships. *Personal Relationships*, **3**, 137–158.

Bond, M. H. (1991). Cultural influences on modes of impression management. In R. A. Giacalone & P. Rosenfeld (Eds) *Applied impression management: How image-making affects managerial decisions* (pp. 195–215). Newbury Park, CA: Sage.

Bowen, S. P., & Michal-Johnson, P. (1995). HIV/AIDS: A crucible for understanding the dark side of sexual interactions. In S. W. Duck & J. T. Wood (Eds) *Confronting relationship challenges [Understanding relationship processes 5]* (pp. 150–179). Thousand Oaks, CA: Sage.

Bower, G. H., & Gilligan, S. G. (1979). Remembering information related to one's self. *Journal of Research in Personality*, **13**, 420–432.

Bowlby, J. (1944). Forty-four juvenile thieves: Their characters and home life. *International Journal of Psychoanalysis*, **25**, 19–52.

Bowlby, J. (1969/1982). *Attachment and loss, Vol. I. Attachment*, 2nd edn. New York: Basic Books.

Bowlby, J. (1973). *Attachment and loss, Vol. II. Separation: Anxiety and anger*. New York: Basic Books.

Bowlby, J. (1979). *The making and breaking of affectional bonds*. London: Tavistock Publications.

Bowlby, J. (1980). *Attachment and loss, Vol. III. Loss: Sadness and depression*. New York: Basic Books.

Bowlby, J. (1988). *A secure base: Parent–child attachment and healthy human development*. New York: Basic Books.

Bradbury, T. N., & Fincham, F. D. (1990). Attributions in marriage: Review and critique. *Psychological Bulletin*, **107**, 3–33.

Bradbury, T. N., Cohen, C. L., & Karney, B. R. (1998). Optimizing longitudinal research for understanding and preventing marital dysfunction. In T. N. Bradbury (Ed.) *The developmental course of marital dysfunction*. New York: Cambridge University Press.

Brake, S., Shair, H., & Hofer, M. A. (1988). Exploiting the nursing niche: The infant's sucking and feeding in the context of the mother–infant interaction. In E. M. Blass (Ed.) *Handbook of behavioral neurobiology* (Vol. 9, pp. 347–388). New York: Plenum.

Brehm, S. S. (1985). *Intimate relationships*. New York: Random House.

Brehm, S. S. (1988). Passionate love. In R. J. Sternberg & M. L. Barnes (Eds) *The psychology of love* (pp. 232–263). New Haven, CT: Yale University Press.

Brehm, S. S. (1992). *Intimate relationships*, 2nd edn. New York: McGraw-Hill.

Brennan, K. A., Shaver, P. R., & Tobey, A. E. (1991). Attachment styles, gender, and parental problem drinking. *Journal of Social and Personal Relationships*, **8**, 451–466.

Brewer, M. (1991). The social self: On being the same and different at the same time. *Personality and Social Psychology Bulletin*, **17**, 475–482.

Brewer, M. B., & Miller, N. (1988). Contact and cooperation: when do they work? In P. A. Katz and D. A. Taylor (Eds) *Eliminating racism: Profiles in controversy*. pp. 315–326. New York: Plenum.

Brickman, P., Dunkel-Schetter, C., & Abbey, A. (1987). The development of commitment. In P. Brickman (Ed.) *Commitment, conflict, and caring* (pp. 145–221). Englewood Cliffs, NJ: Prentice Hall.

Britt, T. W. (1995, August). *The identity regulation of romantic partners*. Paper presented at the meeting of the American Psychological Association, New York.

Brockner, J., & Rubin, J. Z. (1985). *Entrapment in escalating conflicts: A social psychological analysis*. New York: Springer-Verlag.

Broude, G. J. (1992). The May-September algorithm meets the 20th century actuarial table. *Behavioral and Brain Sciences*, **15**, 94–95.

Brown, D. E. (1991). *Human universals*. New York: McGraw-Hill.

Brown, R. (1986). *Social psychology*, 2nd edn. New York: Free Press.

Bryk, A. S., & Raudenbush, S. W. (1992). *Hierarchical linear models: Applications and data analysis methods*. Newbury Park: Sage.

Buber, M. (1937). *I and thou*. New York: Scribners.

Buller, D. B., & Burgoon, J. K. (1994). Deception: Strategic and nonstrategic communication. In J. A. Daly & J. M. Wiemann (Eds) *Strategic interpersonal communication* (pp. 191–223). Hillsdale, NJ: Erlbaum.

Burnett, R. (1987). Reflection in personal relationships. In R. Burnett, P. McGhee & D. D. Clarke (Eds) *Accounting for relationships: Explanation, representation, and knowledge*. London: Methuen.

Burnstein, E., Crandall, C., & Kitayama, S. (1994). Some neo-Darwinian rules for altruism: Weighing cues for inclusive fitness as a function of the biological importance of the decision. *Journal of Personality and Social Psychology*, **67**, 773–789.

Buss, D. M. (1988a). The evolution of human intrasexual competition: Tactics of mate attraction. *Journal of Personality and Social Psychology*, **54**, 616–628.

Buss, D. M. (1988b). From vigilence to violence: Tactics of mate retention in American undergraduates. *Ethology and Sociobiology*, **9**, 291–317.

Buss, D. M. (1989a). Sex differences in human mate preferences: Evolutionary hypotheses tested in 37 cultures. *Behavioral and Brain Sciences*, **12**, 1–49.

Buss, D. M. (1994). *The evolution of desire*. New York: Basic Books.

Buss, D. M. (1995). Evolutionary psychology: A new paradigm for psychological science. *Psychological Inquiry*, **6**, 1–30.

Buss, D. M., & Barnes, M. F. (1986). Preferences in human mate selection. *Journal of Personality and Social Psychology*, **50**, 559–570.

Buss, D. M., & Kenrick, D. T. (1998). Evolutionary social psychology. In D. Gilbert, S. Fiske & G. Lindzey (Eds) *Handbook of social psychology*, 4th edn. (Vol. 2, pp. 982–1026). New York: McGraw-Hill.

Buss, D. M., & Schmitt, D. P. (1993). Sexual strategies theory: An evolutionary perspective on human mating. *Psychological Review*, **100**, 204–232.

Buss, D. M., Larsen, R., Westen, D., & Semmelroth, J. (1992). Sex differences in jealousy: Evolution, physiology, and psychology. *Psychological Science*, **3**, 251–255.

Buunk, A. P. (1987). Conditions that promote breakups as a consequence of extradyadic involvements. *Journal of Social and Clinical Psychology*, **5**, 271–284.

Buunk, A. P. (1991). Jealousy in close relationships: An exchange-theoretical perspective. In P. Salovey (Ed.) *The psychology of jealousy and envy* (pp. 148–177). New York: Guilford.

Buunk, A. P., & Hupka, R. B. (1987). Cross-cultural differences in the elicitation of sexual jealousy. *Journal of Sex Research*, **23**, 12–22.

Buunk, A. P., & Van Yperen, N. W. (1991). Referential comparisons, relational comparisons, and exchange orientation: Their relation to marital satisfaction. *Personality and Social Psychology Bulletin*, **17**, 709–717.

Buunk, A. P., Angleitner, A., Oubaid, V., & Buss, D. M. (1996). Sex differences in jealousy in evolutionary and cultural perspective: Tests from the Netherlands, Germany, and the United States. *Psychological Science*, **7**, 359–363.

Buunk, B. (1987). Conditions that promote breakups as a consequence of extradyadic involvements. *Journal of Social and Clinical Psychology*, **5**, 271–284.

Byers, J. A., & Byers, K. Z. (1983). Do pronghorn mothers reveal the locations of their hidden fawns? *Behavioral Ecology and Sociobiology*, **13**, 147–156.

Byrne, D. (1971). *The attraction paradigm*. New York: Academic Press.

Byrne, D. (1997). An overview (and underview) of research and theory within the attraction paradigm. *Journal of Social and Personal Relationships*, **14**, 417–431.

Cacioppo, J. T., & Bernston, G. C. (1994). Relationship between attitudes and evaluative space: A critical review, with emphasis on the separability of positive and negative substrates. *Psychological Bulletin*, **115**, 401–423.

Cacioppo, J. T., & Petty, R. E. (1986). Social processes. In M. G. H. Coles, E. Donchin, & S. W. Porges (Eds) *Psychophysiology: Systems, processes, and applications*, (pp. 646–79). New York: Guilford Press.

Cameron, C., Oskamp, S., & Sparks, W. (1977). Courtship American style—newspaper ads. *Family Coordinator*, **26**, 27–30.

Campbell, A., Converse, P. E., & Rodgers, W. L. (1976). *The quality of American life*. New York: Russell Sage.

Campbell, D. T. (1975). On the conflicts between biological and social evolution and between psychology and moral tradition. *American Psychologist*, **30**, 1103–1126.

Campos, J., Barrett, K., Lamb, M., Goldsmith, H., & Stenberg, C. (1983). Socioemotional development. In P. Mussen (Ed.) *Handbook of child psychology*, Vol. 2, pp. 783–917.

Canary, D. J., Stafford, L., Hause, K. S., & Wallace, L. A. (1993). An inductive analysis of relational maintenance strategies: Comparisons among lovers, relatives, friends, and others. *Communication Research Reports*, **10**, 5–14.

Carnegie, D. (1940). *How to win friends and influence people*. New York: Pocket Books.

Carnevale, P. J. D., Pruitt, D. G., & Britton, S. D. (1979). Looking tough: The negotiator under constituent surveillance. *Personality and Social Psychology Bulletin*, **5**, 118–121.

Carter, C. S. (1992). Oxytocin and sexual behavior. *Neuroscience and Biobehavioral Reviews*, **16**, 131–144.

Chapman, L. J., & Chapman, J. P. (1969). Genesis of popular but erroneous psychodiagnostic observations. *Journal of Abnormal Psychology*, **74**, 272–280.

Cheek, F E., & R. Anthony, R. (1970). Personal pronoun usage in families of schizophrenics and social space utilization. *Family Process*, **9**, 431–448.

Cherlin, A. (1989). Remarriage as an incomplete institution. In J. M. Henslin (Ed.) *Marriage and family in a changing society* (pp. 442–501). New York: Free Press.

Chrisman, S. M., Pieper, W. A., Clance, P. R., Holland, C. L., & Gliekauf-Hughes, C. (1995). Validation of the Clance Imposter Phenomenon Scale. *Journal of Personality Assessment*, **65**, 456–467.

Cialdini, R. B. (1989). Indirect tactics of image management: Beyond basking. In R. A. Giacalone & P. Rosenfeld (Eds) *Impression management in the organization* (pp. 45–56). Hillsdale, NJ: Lawrence Erlbaum Associates.

Cialdini, R. B., & DeNicholas, M. E. (1989). Self-presentation by association. *Journal of Personality and Social Psychology*, **57**, 626–631.

Clark, M. S. (1985). Implications of relationship type for understanding compatibility In W. Ickes (Ed.) *Compatible and incompatible relationships* (pp. 119–40). New York: Springer-Verlag.

Clark, M. S., & Mills, J. (1979). Interpersonal attraction in exchange and communal relationships. *Journal of Personality and Social Psychology*, **37**, 12–24.

Clark, M. S., Mills, J., & Powell, M. C. (1986). Keeping track of needs in communal and exchange relationships. *Journal of Personality and Social Psychology*, **51**, 333–338.

Clark, R. D., & Hatfield, E. (1989). Gender differences in receptivity to sexual offers. *Journal of Psychology and Human Sexuality*, **2**, 39–55.

Clark, R. E., & Halford, L. J. (1978). Going going gone: Some preliminary observations on "deals" at auctions. *Urban Life*, **7**, 285–307.

Cloven, D. H., & Roloff, M. E. (1994). A developmental model of decisions to withhold relational irritations in romantic relationships. *Personal Relationships*, **1**, 143–164.

Clulow, C. (1993). Marriage across frontiers: National, ethnic and religious differences in partnership. *Sexual and Marital Therapy*, **81**, 81–87.

Collins, N. L., & Read, S. J. (1990). Adult attachment, working models, and relationship quality in dating couples. *Journal of Personality and Social Psychology*, **58**, 644–663.

Cook, W. L. (1993). Interdependence and the interpersonal sense of control: An analysis of family relationships. *Journal of Personality and Social Psychology*, **64**, 587–601.

Cosmides, L., & Tooby, J. (1989). Evolutionary psychology and the generation of culture. Part II: A computational theory of social exchange. *Ethology and Sociobiology*, **10**, 51–97.

Cox, V C., Paulus, R B., & McCain, G. (1984). Prison crowding research: The relevance for prison housing standards and a general approach regarding crowding phenomena. *American Psychologist*, **39**,1148–1160.

Cozby, P. C. (1973). Self-disclosure: A literature review. *Psychological Bulletin*, **79**, 73–91.

Crawford, C. B., & Anderson, J. L. (1989). Sociobiology: An environmentalist discipline. *American Psychologist*, **44**, 1449–1459.

Crittenden, P. M. (1988), Relationships at risk. In J. Belsky & T. Nezworski (Eds) *Clinical implications of attachment* (pp. 136–174). Hillsdale, NJ: Lawrence Erlbaum Associates.

Crosby, F. (1976). A model of egoistical relative deprivation. *Psychological Review*, **83**, 85–113.

Crouter, A. C., & Helms-Erickson, H. (1997). Work and family from a dyadic perspective: Variations in inequality. *Handbook of personal relationships*, 2nd edn (pp. 487–504). Chichester, UK: Wiley.

Cunningham, M. R., Barbee, A. P., & Druen, P. B. (1997). Social allergens and the reactions that they produce: Escalation of annoyance and disgust in love and work. In R. Kowalski (Ed.) *Aversive interpersonal behaviors* (pp. 190–215). New York: Plenum.

Cunningham, M. R., Roberts, A. R., Barbee, A. P., Druen, P. B., & Wu, C. (1995). "Their ideas of beauty are, on the whole, the same as ours": Consistency and variability in the cross-cultural perception of female physical attractiveness. *Journal of Personality and Social Psychology*, **68**, 261–279.

Cupach, W. R., & Metts, S. (1994). *Facework*. Thousand Oaks, CA: Sage.

Cupach, W. R., & Spitzberg, B. H. (Eds). (1994). *The dark side of interpersonal communication*. Hillsdale NJ: LEA.

Curtis, R. C., & Miller, K. (1986). Believing another likes or dislikes you: Behaviors making the beliefs come true. *Journal of Personality and Social Psychology*, **51**, 284–290.

Cutler, W. B., Garcia, C. R., Huggins, G. R., & Preti, G. (1986). Sexual behavior and steroid levels among gynecologically mature premenopausal women. *Fertility and Sterility*, **45**, 496–502.

Cutler, W. B., Preti, G., Huggins, G. R., Erickson, B., & Garcia, C. R. (1985). Sexual behavior frequency and biphasic ovulatory type menstrual cycles. *Physiology and Behavior*, **34**, 805–810.

Dainton, M., & Stafford, L. (1993). Routine maintenance behaviors: A comparison of relationship type, partner similarity and sex differences. *Journal of Social and Personal Relationships*, **10**, 255–271.

Daly, J. A., Hogg, E., Sacks, D., Smith, M., & Zimring, L. (1983). Sex and relationship affect social self-grooming. *Journal of Nonverbal Behavior*, **7**, 183–189.

Daly, J. A., Weber, D. J., Vangelisti, A. L., Maxwell, M., & Neel, H. (1989). Concurrent cognitions during conversations: Protocol analysis as a means of exploring conversations. *Discourse Processes*, **12**, 227–244.

Daly, M., & Wilson, M. I. (1983). *Sex, evolution, and behavior*, 2nd edn. Belmont, CA: Wadsworth.

Daly, M., & Wilson, M. I. (1988a). *Homicide*. New York: Aldine de Gruyter.

Daly, M., & Wilson, M. I. (1988b). Evolutionary social psychology and family homicide. *Science*, **242** (October), 519–524.

Daly, M., & Wilson, M. I. (1989). Homicide and cultural evolution. *Ethology and Sociobiology*, **10**, 99–110.

Daly, M., & Wilson, M. I. (1994). Some differential attributes of lethal assaults on small children by stepfathers versus genetic fathers. *Ethology and Sociobiology*, **15**, 207–217.

Daly, M., Wilson, M. I., & Weghorst, S. J. (1982). Male sexual jealousy. *Ethology and Sociobiology*, **3**, 11–27.

Darwin, C. (1859). *The origin of species*. London: Murray.

Darwin, C. (1872). *The expression of emotions in man and animals*. London: Murray.

Davidson, J. R. (1992). Interracial marriages: A clinical perspective. *Journal of Multicultural Counseling and Development*, **20**, 150–157.

Davies, J. C. (1962). Toward a theory of revolution. *American Sociological Review*, **27**, 5–13.

Davis, M. H., & Oathout, H. A. (1987). Maintenance of satisfaction in romantic relationships: Empathy and relational competence. *Journal of Personality and Social Psychology*, **53**, 397–410.

Dawe, H. C. (1934). An analysis of two hundred quarrels of pre-school children. *Child Development*, **5**, 139–57.

Dawkins, R. (1976). *The selfish gene*. Oxford: Oxford University Press.

Deag, J. M. (1977). Aggression and submission in monkey societies. *Animal Behaviour*, **25**, 465–474.

Dean, D. G., Braito, R., Powers, E. A., & Britton, B. (1975). Cultural contradictions and sex roles revisted: A replication and a reassessment. *Sociological Quarterly*, **16**, 201–215.

Deci, E. L. (1975). *Intrinsic motivation*. New York: Plenum Press.

Dehue, F. M. J., McClintock, C. G., & Liebrand, W. B. G. (1993). Social value related response latencies: Unobtrusive evidence for individual differences in information processes. *European Journal of Social Psychology*, **23**, 273–294.

Denzin, N. K. (1970). Rules of conduct and the study of deviant behavior: Some notes on social relationships. In G. J. McCall, M. McCall, N. Denzin & S. Kurth (Eds) *Social relationships* (pp. 62–94). Chicago: Aldine.

DePaulo, B. M. (1992). Nonverbal behavior and self-presentation. *Psychological Bulletin*, **111**, 203–243.

DePaulo, B. M., & Bell, K. L. (1996). Truth and investment: Lies are told to those who care. *Journal of Personality and Social Psychology*, **71**, 703–716.

DePaulo, B. M., & Kashy, D. A. (1998). Everyday lies in close and casual relationships. *Journal of Personality and Social Psychology*, **74**, 63–79.

DePaulo, B. M., Kashy, D. A., Kirkendol, S. E., Wyer, M. M., & Epstein, J. A. (1996). Lying in everyday life. *Journal of Personality and Social Psychology*, **70**, 979–995.

Derlega, V. J., & Berg, J. H. (1987). *Self-disclosure: Theory, research, and therapy*. New York: Plenum.

Derlega, V. J., Metts, S., Petronio, S., & Margulis, S. T. (1993). *Self-disclosure*. Newbury Park, CA: Sage.

Deutsch, F. M., Zalenski, C. M., & Clark, M. E. (1986). Is there a double standard of aging? *Journal of Applied Social Psychology*, **16**, 771–775.

Deutsch, M. (1975). Equity, equality, and need: What determines which value will be used as the basis of distributive justice? *Journal of Social Issues*, **31**, 137–149.

deWaal, F. (1989). *Chimpanzee politics*. Baltimore: Johns Hopkins University Press.

Dindia, K. (1997). Self-disclosure, self-identity, and relationship development: A transactional/dialectical perspective. *Handbook of personal relationships*, 2nd edn (pp. 411–425). Chichester, UK: Wiley.

Dindia, K., & Baxter, L. A. (1987). Strategies for maintaining and repairing marital relationships. *Journal of Social and Personal Relationships*, **4**, 143–158.

Dindia, K., Fitzpatrick, M. A., & Kenny, D. A. (1997). Self-disclosure in spouse and stranger interaction: A social relations analysis. *Human Communication Research*, **23**, 388–412.

Dixson, M. D., & Duck, S. W. (1993). Understanding relationship processes: Uncovering the human search for meaning. *Understanding relationship processes 1: Individuals in relationships* (pp. 175–206). Newbury Park: Sage.

Doherty, R. W., Hatfield, E., Thompson, K., & Chao, P. (1994). Cultural and ethnic influences on love and attachment. *Personal Relationships*, **1**, 391–398.

Dollard, J., & Miller, N. E. (1950). *Personality and psychotherapy*. New York: McGraw-Hill.

Donner, A., & Koval, J. J. (1980). The estimation of intraclass correlation in the analysis of family data. *Biometrics*, **36**, 19–25.

Drigotas, S. M., & Rusbult, C. E. (1992). Should I stay or should I go? A dependence model of breakups. *Journal of Personality and Social Psychology*, **62**, 62–87.

Drigotas, S. M., Rusbult, C. E., & Verette, J. (in press). Level of commitment, mutuality of commitment, and couple well-being. *Personal Relationships*.

Drigotas, S. M., Rusbult, C. E., Wieselquist, J., & Whitton, S. (in press). Close partner as sculptor of the ideal self: Behavioral affirmation and the Michelangelo phenomenon. *Journal of Personality and Social Psychology*.

Du Bois, W. E. B. (1903/1969). *The souls of Black folk*. New York: Signet.

Du Bois, W. E. B. (1947/1965). *The world and Africa*. New York: International Publishers.

Du Bois, W. E. B. (1986). *Writings*. New York: Library of America.

Duck, S. W. (1986). *Human relationships*. Newbury Park, CA: Sage.

Duck, S. W. (1990). Relationships as unfinished business: Out of the frying pan and into the 1990s. *Journal of Social and Personal Relationships*, **7**, 5–29.

Duck, S. W. (1991). Diaries and logs. In B. M. Montgomery & S. W. Duck (Eds) *Studying interpersonal relationships*, (pp. 141–61). New York: Guilford Press.

Duck, S. W. (1993). *Understanding relationship processes 3: Social contexts of relationships*. Newbury Park: Sage.

Duck, S. W. (1994a). *Meaningful relationships: Talking, sense, and relating*. Thousand Oaks, CA: Sage.

Duck, S. W. (1994b). Stratagems, spoils and a serpent's tooth: On the delights and dilemmas of personal relationships. *The dark side of interpersonal communication*, (pp. 3–24). Mahwah, NJ: Erlbaum.

Duck, S. W. (1998). *Human relationships*, 3rd edn. London: Sage.

Duck, S. W., & Miell, D. E. (1986). Charting the development of personal relationships. In R. Gilmour & S. W. Duck (Eds) *The emerging field of personal relationships* (pp. 133–144). Hillsdale, NJ: Erlbaum.

Duck, S. W., & Sants, H. K. A. (1983). On the origin of the specious: Are personal relationships really interpersonal states? *Journal of Social and Clinical Psychology*, **1**, 27–41.

Duck, S. W., & Wood, J. T. (1995). *Confronting relationship challenges [Understanding relationship processes 5]*. Newbury Park: SAGE.

Duck, S. W., Pond, K., & Leatham, G. (1991). *Remembering as a context for being in relationships: Different perspectives on the same interaction*. Paper presented at the Third Conference of the International Network on Personal Relationships, Normal/Bloomington, Illinois.

Duck, S. W., Rutt, D. J., Hurst, M., & Strejc, H. (1991). Some evident truths about communication in everyday relationships: All communication is not created equal. *Human Communication Research*, **18**, 228–267.

Duck, S. W., West, L., & Acitelli, L. K. (1997). Sewing the field: The tapestry of relationships in life and research. In S. W. Duck, K. Dindia, W. Ickes, R. M. Milardo, R. S. L. Mills & B. Sarason (Eds) *Handbook of Personal Relationships*, 2nd edn (pp. 1–24). Chichester, UK: Wiley.

Duckitt, J. (1994). *The social psychology of prejudice*. Westport, CT: Praeger.

Duncan, S., & Fiske, D. W. (1977). *Face-to-face interaction: Research, methods, and theory*. New Jersey: Lawrence Erlbaum Associates.

Durodoye, B. (1994). Intermarriage and marital satisfaction. *TCA Journal*, **22**, 3–9.

Dutton, D. G., & Aron, A. (1974). Some evidence for heightened sexual attraction under conditions of high anxiety. *Journal of Personality and Social Psychology*, **30**, 510–517.

Dutton, D. G., & Aron, A. (1989). Romantic attraction and generalized liking for others who are sources of conflict-based arousal. *Canadian Journal of Behavioural Science*, **21**, 246–257.

Early, G. (1993). Introduction. In G. Early (Ed.) *Lure and loathing: Essays on race, identity, and the ambivalence of assimilation* (pp. xi–xxiv). New York: Penguin.

Eibl-Eibesfeldt, I. (1975). *Ethology: The biology of behavior*, 2nd edn. New York: Holt, Rinehart & Winston.

Eibl-Eibesfeldt, I. (1989). *Human ethology*. New York: Gruyter.

Ekman, P. (1992). An argument for basic emotions. *Cognition and Emotion*, **6**, 169–200.

Ekman, P., & Friesen, W. V. (1971). Constants across cultures in the face and emotion. *Journal of Personality and Social Psychology*, **17**, 124–129.

Ekman, P., Friesen, W. V., O'Sullivan, M., Chan, A., Diacoyanni-Tarlatzis, I., Heider, K., Krause, R. LeCompte, W. A., Pitcairn, T., Ricci-Bitti, P. E., Scherer, K., Tomita, M., & Tzavaras, A. (1987). Universals and cultural differences in the judgments of facial expressions of emotion. *Journal of Personality and Social Psychology*, **53**, 712–717.

Eliasziw, M., & Donner, A. (1991). A generalized non-iterative approach to the analysis of family data. *Annals of Human Genetics*, **55**, 77–90.

Ellis, B. J., & Symons, D. (1990). Sex differences in sexual fantasy: An evolutionary psychological approach. *Journal of Sex Research*, **27**, 527–556.

Ellis, L., & Ames, M. A. (1987). Neurohormonal functioning and sexual orientation: A theory of homosexuality-heterosexuality. *Psychological Bulletin*, **101**, 233–258.

Erikson, E. H. (1950). *Childhood and society*. New York: Norton.

Essed, P. (1991). *Understanding everyday racism: An interdisciplinary theory*. Newbury Park, CA; Sage.

Fairchild, H. H. (1991). Scientific racism: The cloak of objectivity. *Journal of Social Issues*, **47**, 101–115.

Feeney, J., & Noller, P. (1990). Attachment style as a predictor of adult romantic relationships. *Journal of Personality and Social Psychology*, **58**, 281–291.

Fehr, B. (1993). How do I love thee? . . . Let me consult my prototype. *Understanding relationship processes 1: Individuals in relationships* (pp. 87–120). Newbury Park: Sage.

Felmlee, D. H. (1995). Fatal attractions: Affection and disaffection in intimate relationships. *Journal of Social and Personal Relationships*, **12**, 295–311.

Felmlee, D., Sprecher, S., & Bassin, E. (1990). The dissolution of intimate relationships: A hazard model. *Social Psychology Quarterly*, **53**, 13–30.

Festinger, L. (1954). A theory of social comparison processes. *Human Relations*, **7**, 117–140.

Festinger, L., Schachter, S., & Back, K. W. (1950). *Social pressure in informal groups: A study of human factors in housing*. New York: Harper.

Finch, J. F., & Cialdini, R. B. (1989). Another indirect tactic of (self-) image management: Boosting. *Personality and Social Psychology Bulletin*, **15**, 222–232.

Fincham, F. D., & Bradbury, T. N. (1987). The impact of attributions in marriage: A longitudinal analysis. *Journal of Personality and Social Psychology*, **53**, 510–517.

Fincham, F. D., & Bradbury, T. N. (1993). Marital satisfaction, depression, and attributions: A longitudinal analysis. *Journal of Personality and Social Psychology*, **64**, 442–452.

Fine, M. A., McKenry, P. C., Donnelly, B. W., & Voydanoff, P. (1992). Perceived adjustment of parents and children: Variations by family structure, race, and gender. *Journal of Marriage and the Family*, **54**, 118–127.

Fine, M., Schwebel, A. I., & James-Myers, L. (1987). Family stability in Black families: Values underlying three different perspectives. *Journal of Contemporary Family Study*, **18**, 1–23.

Fisher, H. E. (1992). *Anatomy of love*. New York: Norton.

Fisher, R. A. (1925). *Statistical Methods for Research Workers*. Edinburgh: Oliver & Boyd.

Fiske, S. T. (1992). Thinking is for doing: Portraits of social cognition from daguerreotype to laserphoto. *Journal of Personality and Social Psychology*, **63**, 877–889.

Fiske, S. T. (1993). Controlling other people: The impact of power on stereotyping. *American Psychologist*, **48**, 621–628.

Fiske, S. T., & Taylor, S. E. (1984). *Social cognition*. Reading, MA: Addison-Wesley.

Fitness, J., & Strongman, K,. (1991). Affect in close relationships. *Cognition in close relationships*, 175–202.

Fleming, J. H., & Rudman, L. A. (1993). Between a rock and a hard place: Self-concept regulating and communicative properties of distancing behaviors. *Journal of Personality and Social Psychology*, **64**, 44–59.

Fleming, J. H., Darley, J. M., Hilton, J. L., & Kojetin, B. A. (1990). Multiple audience problem: A strategic communication perspective on social perception. *Journal of Personality and Social Psychology*, **58**, 593–609.

Fletcher, G. J. O., & Fincham, F. D. (1991a). Attribution processes in close relationships. In G. J. O. Fletcher & F. D. Fincham (Eds) *Cognition in close relationships* (pp. 7–35). Hillsdale, NJ: Erlbaum.

Fletcher, G. J. O., & Fincham, F. D. (1991b). *Cognition in close relationships*. Hillsdale, NJ: Lawrence Erlbaum.

Fletcher, G. J. O., & Fitness, J. (1993). Knowledge structures and explanations in intimate relationships, *Understanding relationship processes 1: Individuals in relationships* (pp. 121–143). Newbury Park: Sage.

Floyd, F., & Markman, H. (1983). Observational biases in spouse interaction: Toward a cognitive/behavioral model of marriage. *Journal of Consulting and Clinical Psychology*, **51**, 450–457.

Form, W. H., & Nosow, S. (1958). *Community in disaster*. New York: Harper.

Frable, D. E. S., Blackstone, T., & Scherbaum, C. (1990). Marginal and mindful: Deviants in social interactions. *Journal of Personality and Social Psychology*, **59**, 140–149.

Freeman, D. (1983). *Margaret Mead and Samoa*. Cambridge, MA: Harvard University Press.

French, M. (1985). *Beyond power: On women, men, and morals*. New York: Ballantine.

Fried, M. L., & DeFazio, V. J. (1974). Territoriality and boundary conflicts in the subway *Psychiatry*, **37**, 47–59.

Frijda, N. H. (1988). The laws of emotion. *American Psychologist*, **43**, 349–358.

Funderberg, L. (1994). *Black, White, Other: Biracial Americans talk about race and identity*. New York: Morrow.

Furman, W. (1985). Compatibility and incompatibility in children's peer and sibling relationships. In W. Ickes (Ed.) *Compatible and incompatible relationships* (pp. 61–87) New York: Springer-Verlag.

Gaines, S. O., Jr. (1996). Impact of interpersonal traits and gender-role compliance on interpersonal resource exchange among dating and engaged/married couples. *Journal of Social and Personal Relationships*, **13**, 241–261.

Gaines, S. O., Jr., & Reed, E. S. (1994). Two social psychologies of prejudice: Gordon W. Allport, W. E. B. Du Bois, and the legacy of Booker T. Washington. *Journal of Black Psychology*, **20**, 8–28.

Gaines, S. O., Jr., & Reed, E. S. (1995). Prejudice: From Allport to Du Bois. *American Psychologist*, **50**, 96–103.

Gaines, S. O., Jr., Marelich, W. D., Bledsoe, K. L., Steers, W. N., Henderson, M. C., Granrose, C. S., Barájas, L., Hicks, D., Lyde, M., Takahashi, Y., Yum, N., Ríos, D. I., García, B. F., Farris, K. R., & Page, M. S. (1997). Links between race/ethnicity and cultural values as mediated by racial/ethnic identity and moderated by gender. *Journal of Personality and Social Psychology*, **72**, 1460–1476.

Gaines, S. O., Jr., Ríos, D. I., Granrose, C. S., Bledsoe, K. L., Farris, K. R., Page, M. S., & García, B. F. (1999). Romanticism and interpersonal resource exchange among African American–Anglo and other interracial couples. *Journal of Black Psychology*, **25**, 461–489.

Gaines, S. O., & Ickes, W. (1997). Perspectives on interracial relationships. In S. W. Duck (Ed.) *Handbook of personal relationships*, 2nd edn (pp. 197–220). Chichester, UK: Wiley.

Gangestad, S. W., & Simpson, J. A. (1990). Toward an evolutionary history of female sociosexual variation. *Journal of Personality*, **58**, 69–96.

Garcia, S., Stinson, L., Ickes, W., Bissonnette, V., & Briggs, S. (1991). Shyness and physical attractiveness in mixed-sex dyads. *Journal of Personality and Social Psychology*, **61**, 35–49.

Geary, D. C. (1998). *Male, female: The evolution of human and sex differences*. Washington, DC: American Psychological Association.

Gecas, V. (1989). Social psychology of self-efficacy. *American Sociological Review*, **15**, 291–316.

Gelles, R. J. (1979). *Family violence*. Beverly Hills, CA: Sage.

Gelles, R. J., & Straus, M. A. (1985). Violence in the American family. In A. J. Lincoln & M. A. Straus (Eds) *Crime and the family* (pp. 88–110). Springfield, Ill.: Thomas.

Gergen, K. J., & Wishnov, V. B. (1965). Others' self-evaluation and interaction anticipation as determinants of self-presentation. *Journal of Personality and Social Psychology*, **2**, 348–358.

Gilbert, D. T., Pelham, B. W., & Krull, D. S. (1988). On cognitive busyness: When person perceivers meet persons perceived. *Journal of Personality and Social Psychology*, **54**, 733–740.

Ginsberg, D., & Gottman, J. M. (1986). Conversations of college roommates: Similarities and differences in male and female friendship. In J. M. Gottman & J. G. Parker (Eds) *Conversations of friends* (pp. 241–91). New York: Cambridge University Press.

Ginsburg, G. P. (1988). Rules, scripts and prototypes in personal relationships. In S. W. Duck (Ed.) *Handbook of personal relationships* (pp. 23–39). Chichester: Wiley.

Giuliano, T. A., Barnes, L. C., Fiala, S. E., & Davis, D. M. (1998, April). *An empirical investigation of male answer syndrome*. Paper presented at the meeting of the Southwestern Psychological Association, New Orleans.

Givens, D. B. (1978). The nonverbal basis of attraction: Flirtation, courtship, and seduction. *Psychiatry*, **41**, 346–359.

Glenn, N. D. (1990). Quantitative research on marital quality in the 1980s: A critical review. *Journal of Marriage and the Family*, **52**, 818–831.

Goffman, E. (1955). On facework. *Psychiatry*, **18**, 213–231.

Goffman, E. (1959). *The presentation of self in everyday life*. Garden City, NJ: Doubleday Anchor.

Goffman, E. (1963). *Stigma: Notes on the management of spoiled identity*. Englewood Cliffs, NJ: Prentice Hall.

Goldberg, L. R. (1981). Unconfounding situational attributions from uncertain, neutral, and ambiguous ones: A psychometric analysis of descriptions of oneself and various types of others. *Journal of Personality and Social Psychology*, **41**, 517–552.

Goldstein, H. (1987). *Multilevel models in educational and social research*. New York: Oxford.

Goldstein, H., & McDonald, R. P. (1988). A general model for the analysis of multilevel data. *Psychometrika*, **53**, 455–467.

Gollob, H. F. (1991). Methods for estimating individual- and group-level correlations. *Journal of Personality and Social Psychology*, **60**, 376–381.

Gonzales, M. H., Pederson, J. H., Manning, D. J., & Wetter, D. W. (1990). Pardon my gaffe: Effects of sex, status, and consequence severity on accounts. *Journal of Personality and Social Psychology*, **58**, 610–621.

Gonzalez, R. (1995). The statistics ritual in psychological research. *Psychological Science*, **5**, 321–326.

Gonzalez, R., & Griffin, D. (1997): On the statistics of interdependence: Treating dyadic data with respect. In S. W. Duck, K. Dindia, W. Ickes, R. Milardo, R. Mills, & B. Sarason (Eds) *Handbook of personal relationships*, 2nd edn (pp. 271–302). Chichester: Wiley.

Gonzalez, R., & Griffin, D. (1998a). *An approximate significance test for the group-level correlation.* University of Michigan and University of Sussex.

Gonzalez, R., & Griffin, D. (1998b). The multiple personalities of the intraclass correlation. University of Michigan and University of Sussex.

Gonzalez, R., & Griffin, D. (in press). The correlational analysis of dyad-level data in the distinguishable case. *Personal Relationships.*

Goodwin, J. S., Hurt, W. C., Key, C. R., & Sarret, J. M. (1987). The effect of marital status on stage, treatment, and survival of cancer patients. *Journal of the American Medical Association,* **258**, 3125–3130.

Gordon, R. A. (1996). Impact of ingratiation on judgments and evaluations: A meta-analytic investigation. *Journal of Personality and Social Psychology,* **71**, 54–70.

Gottman, J. M. (1979). *Marital interaction: Experimental investigations.* New York: Academic Press.

Gottman, J. M., & Levenson, R. W. (1986). Assessing the role of emotion in marriage. *Behavioral Assessment,* **8**, 31–48.

Gottman, J. M., & Parker, J. G. (Eds) (1986). *Conversations of friends.* New York: Cambridge University Press.

Gottman, J. M., Markman, H. J., & Notarius, C. I. (1977). The topography of marital conflict: A sequential analysis of verbal and nonverbal behavior. *Journal of Marriage and the Family,* **39**, 461–478.

Gottman, J. M., Markman, H., & Notarius, C. (1977). The topography of marital conflict: A study of verbal and nonverbal behavior. *Journal of Marriage and the Family,* **39**, 461–477.

Gove, W. R., Hughes, M., & Geerken, M. R. (1980). Playing dumb: A form of impression management with undesirable side effects. *Social Psychology Quarterly,* **43**, 89–102.

Greenberg, L. (1979). Genetic component of bee odor in kin recognition. *Science,* **206**, 1095–1097.

Greenwald, A. G. (1980). The totalitarian ego: Fabrication and revision of personal history. *American Psychologist,* **35**, 603–618.

Griesinger, D. W., & Livingston, J. W. (1973). Toward a model of interpersonal orientation in experimental games. *Behavioral Science,* **18**, 173–188.

Griffin, D., & Gonzalez, R. (1995). The correlational analysis of dyad-level data: Models for the exchangeable case. *Psychological Bulletin,* **118**, 430–439.

Griffin, D., & Gonzalez, R. (1998). *Regression models in dyadic research.* University of Sussex and University of Washington.

Gross, M. (1984). Sunfish, salmon, and the evolution of alternative reproductive strategies and tactics in fishes. In G. Potts & R. Wootton (Eds) *Fish reproduction: Strategies and tactics* (pp. 55–75). New York: Academic Press.

Gubrium, J. F. (1992). *Out of control: Family therapy and domestic disorder.* Newbury Park, CA: Sage.

Gudykunst, W. (1992). *Bridging differences: effective intergroup communication,* 2nd edn. Thousand Oaks, CA: Sage.

Guerrero, L. K. (1997). Nonverbal involvement across interactions with same-sex friends, opposite-sex friends and romantic partners: Consistency or change? *Journal of Social and Personal Relationships*, **14**, 31–58.

Guttentag, M., & Secord, P. F. (1983). *Too many women? The sex ratio question*. Beverly Hills: Sage.

Haggard, E. A. (1958). *Intraclass correlation and the Analysis of Variance*. New York: Dryden Press.

Halberstadt, A. G. (1986). Family socialization of emotional expression and nonverbal communication styles and skills. *Journal of Personality and Social Psychology*, **51**, 827–836.

Hamilton, D. L., & Rose, T. L. (1980). Illusory correlation and the maintenance of stereotypic beliefs. *Journal of Personality and Social Psychology*, **39**, 832–845.

Hamilton, W. D. (1964). The genetical evolution of social behavior. *Journal of Theoretical Biology*, **7**, 1–32.

Harlow, H., & Harlow, M. K. (1962). The effects of rearing conditions on behavior. *Bulletin of the Menniger Clinic*, **26**, 213–224.

Harlow, H., & Harlow, M. K. (1965). The affectional systems. In A. M. Schrier, H. F. Harlow & F. Stollnitz (Eds) *Behavior of nonhuman primates* (Vol. 2). New York: Academic Press.

Harpending, H. (1992). Age differences between mates in southern African pastoralists. *Behavioral and Brain Sciences*, **15**, 102–103.

Harrison, A. A., & Saeed, L. (1977). Let's make a deal: analysis of revelations and stipulations in lonely hearts advertisements. *Journal of Personality and Social Psychology*, **35**, 257–264

Harvey, J. H., Christensen, A., & McClintock, E. (1983). Research methods. In H. H. Kelley, E. Berscheid, A. Christensen, J. H. Harvey, T. L. Huston, G. Levinger, E. McClintock, L. A. Peplau, & D. R. Peterson (Eds) *Close relationships* (pp. 449–485). New York: W. H. Freeman.

Harvey, J. H., Hendrick, S. S., & Tucker, K. (1988). Self-report methods in studying personal relationships. In S. W. Duck, D. E. Hay, S. E. Hobfoll, W. Ickes, & B. M. Montgomery (Eds) *Handbook of personal relationships: Theory, research, and interventions* (pp. 99–113). Chichester: Wiley.

Harvey, J. H., Ickes, W. J., & Kidd, R. F. (1976). A conversation with Fritz Heider. In J. H. Harvey, W. J. Ickes, & R. F. Kidd (Eds) *New directions in attribution research* (Vol. 1, pp. 3–18) Hillsdale, NJ: Erlbaum.

Hatfield, E., Traupmann, J., & Sprecher, S. (1984). Older women's perceptions of their intimate relationships. *Journal of Social and Clinical Psychology*, **2**, 108–124.

Hatfield, E., Walster, G. W., & Berscheid, E. (1978). *Equity: Theory and research*. Boston: Allyn & Bacon.

Hauser, R. M. (1974). Contextual analysis revisited. *Sociological Methods and Research*, **2**, 365–375.

Hayano, D. M. (1980). Communicative competency among poker players. *Journal of Communication*, **30**, 113–20.

Hazan, C., & Shaver, P. R. (1987). Romantic love conceptualized as an attachment process. *Journal of Personality and Social Psychology*, **52**, 511–524.

Hazan, C., & Shaver, P. R. (1990). Love and work: An attachment theoretical perspective. *Journal of Personality and Social Psychology*, **59**, 270–280.

Hazan, C., & Shaver, P. R. (1994a). Attachment as an organizational framework for research on close relationships. *Psychological Inquiry*, **5**, 1–22.

Hazan, C., & Shaver, P. R. (1994b). Deeper into attachment theory. *Psychological Inquiry*, **5**(1), 68–79.

Hazan, C., & Zeifman, D. (1994). Sex and the psychological tether. *Advances in Personal Relationships*, **5**, 151–177.

Hazan, C., Zeifman, D., & Middleton, K. (July, 1994). *Attachment and sexuality.* Paper presented at the International Conference on Personal Relationships, Gottingen, The Netherlands.

Heatherington, L., Daubman, K. A., Bates, C., Ahn, A., Brown, H., & Preston, C. (1993). Two investigations of "female modesty" in achievement situations. *Sex Roles*, **29**, 739–754.

Heider, F. (1958). *The Psychology of Interpersonal Relations.* New York: Wiley.

Heller, K., & Rook, K. S. (1997). Distinguishing the theoretical functions of social ties: Implications of support interventions. In S. W. Duck (Ed.) *Handbook of personal relationships*, 2nd edn (pp. 649–670). Chichester UK: Wiley.

Hendrick, C., & Hendrick, S. S. (1986). A theory and method of love. *Journal of Personality and Social Psychology*, **50**, 392–402.

Hendrick, S. S., & Hendrick, C. (1992). *Liking, loving and relating*, 2nd edn. Pacific Grove, CA: Brooks/Cole.

Hendrick, S. S., & Hendrick, C. (1993). Lovers as friends. *Journal of Social and Personal Relationships*, **10**, 459–466.

Hepburn, J. R., & Crepin, A. E. (1984). Relationship strategies in a coercive institution: A study of dependence among prison guards. *Journal of Social and Personal Relationships*, **1**, 139–158.

Hernton, C. C. (1965/1988). *Sex and racism in America.* New York: Anchor Books.

Higgins, E. T. (1989). Self-discrepancy theory: What patterns of self-beliefs cause people to suffer? In L. Berkowitz (Ed.) *Advances in experimental social psychology* (Vol. 22, pp. 93–136). San Diego: Academic Press.

Hill, C. T., Rubin, Z., & Peplau, L. A. (1976). Breakups before marriage: The end of 103 affairs. *Journal of Social Issues*, **32**, 147–168.

Hill, K., & Hurtado, M. (1989). Hunter-gatherers of the new world. *American Scientist*, **77**, 437–443.

Hill, M. S. (1988). Marital stability and spouses' shared time: A multidisciplinary hypothesis. *Journal of Family Issues*, **9**, 427–451.

Hinde, R. A. (1981). The bases of a science of interpersonal relationships. *Personal relationships 1: Studying personal relationships* (pp. 1–22). London, New York, San Francisco: Academic Press.

Ho, M. K. (1984). *Building a successful intermarriage between religions, social classes, ethnic groups, or races*. St. Meinrad, IN: St. Meinrad Archabbey.

Ho, M. K. (1990). *Intermarried couples in therapy*. Springfield, IL: Thomas.

Hobfoll, S. E., & deVries, M. W. (Eds) (1995). *Extreme stress and communities: Impact and intervention*. Dordrecht: Kluwer.

Hodgins, H. S., Liebeskind, E., & Schwartz, W. (1996). Getting out of hot water: Facework in social predicaments. *Journal of Personality and Social Psychology*, **71**, 300–314.

Hofer, M. A. (1984). Relationships as regulators: A psychobiologic perspective on bereavement. *Psychosomatic Medicine*, **46**, 183–197.

Hofer, M. A. (1987). Early social relationships: A psychobiologist's view. *Child Development*, **58**, 663–647.

Hoffman, M. L. (1976). Empathy, role taking, guilt, and development of altruistic motives. In T. Lickona (Ed.) *Moral development and behavior*. New York: Holt.

Hogan, R. (1982). A socioanalytic theory of personality. In M. Page (Ed.) *Nebraska symposium on motivation* (pp. 55–89). Lincoln, NE: University of Nebraska Press.

Holdaway, S. (1980). The police station. *Urban Life*, **9**, 79–100.

Holman, T. B., & Jacquart, M. (1988). Leisure-activity patterns and marital satisfaction: A further test. *Journal of Marriage and the Family*, **50**, 69–77.

Holmes, J. G. (1981). The exchange process in close relationships: Microbehavior and macromotives. In M. Lerner & S. Lerner (Eds) *The justice motive in social behavior: Adapting to times of scarcity and change* (pp. 261–284). New York: Plenum.

Holmes, J. G., & Murray, S. L. (1996). Conflict in close relationships. In E. T. Higgins & A. W. Kruglanski (Eds) *Social psychology: Handbook of basic principles* (pp. 622–654). New York: Guilford.

Holmes, J. G., & Rempel, J. K. (1989). Trust in close relationships. In C. Hendrick (Ed.) *Review of personality and social psychology* (Vol. 10, pp. 187–220). London: Sage.

Holmes, T. H., & Rahe, R. H. (1967). The social readjustment scale. *Journal of Psychosomatic Research*, **11**, 213–218.

Holmes, W. G., & Sherman, P. W. (1983). Kin recognition in animals. *American Scientist*, **71**, 46–55.

Homans, G. C. (1961). *Social behavior: Its elementary forms*. New York: Harcourt Brace Jovanovich.

Homans, G. C. (1974). *Social behavior: Its elementary forms (revised edn)*. New York: Harcourt Brace Jovanovich.

Honeycutt, J. M. (1993). Memory structures for the rise and fall of personal relationships. *Understanding relationship processes 1: Individuals in relationships* (pp. 60–86). Newbury Park: Sage.

Howitt, D., & Owusu-Bempah, J. (1994). *The racism of psychology: Time for change*. New York: Harvester/Wheatsheaf.

Huesmann, L. R. (1980). Toward a predictive model of romantic behavior. In K. S. Pope *et al.* (Eds) *On love and loving* (pp. 152–171). San Francisco, CA: Jossey-Bass.

Huston, M., & Schwartz, P. (1995). Lesbian and gay male relationships. In J. T. Wood & S. W. Duck (Eds) *Under-studied relationships: Off the beaten track* (pp. 89–121) Thousand Oaks, CA: Sage.

Huston, T. L. (1983). Power. In H. H. Kelley, E. Berscheid, A. Christensen, J. H. Harvey, T. L. Huston, G. Levinger, E. McClintock, L. A. Peplau & D. R. Peterson (Eds) *Close relationships* (pp. 315–359). New York: W. H. Freeman.

Huston, T. L., & Ashmore, R. D. (1986). Women and men in personal relationships. In R. D. Ashmore & F. K. Del Boca (Eds) *The social psychology of female–male relations: A critical analysis of central concepts* (pp. 167–210). Orlando, FL: Academic Press.

Huston, T. L., & Levinger, G. (1978). Interpersonal attraction and relationships. *Annual Review of Psychology*, **29**, 115–156.

Huston, T. L., & Vangelisti, A. L. (1991). Socioemotional behavior and satisfaction in marital relationships: A longitudinal study. *Journal of Personality and Social Psychology*, **61**, 721–733.

Huston, T. L., McHale, S. M., & Crouter, A. C. (1986). When the honeymoon's over: Changes in the marriage relationship over the first year. In R. Gilmour & S. W. Duck (Eds) *The emerging science of personal relationships* (pp. 109–132). Hillsdale, NJ: Lawrence Erlbaum Associates.

Huston, T. L., Robins, E., Atkinson, J., & McHale, S. M. (1987). Surveying the landscape of marital behavior: A behavioral self-report approach to studying marriage. In S. Oskamp (Ed.) *Family processes and problems: Social psychological aspects. Applied Social Psychology Annual*, **7**, 46–71. Newbury Park, CA: Sage.

Huston, T. L., Surra, C. A., Fitzgerald, N. M., & Cate, R. M. (1981). From courtship to marriage: Mate selection as an interpersonal process. *Personal relationships 2: Developing personal relationships* (pp. 53–88). London and New York: Academic Press.

Ickes, W. (1982). A basic paradigm for the study of personality, roles, and social behavior. In W. Ickes & E. S. Knowles (Eds) *Personality, roles, and social behavior* (pp. 305–41). New York: Springer-Verlag.

Ickes, W. (1983). A basic paradigm for the study of unstructured dyadic interaction. In H. T. Reis (Ed.) *New directions for methodology of social and behavioral science: Naturalistic approaches to studying social interaction*, Vo. 15 (pp. 5–21). San Francisco: Jossey-Bass.

Ickes, W. (1984). Compositions in Black and White: Determinants of interaction in interracial dyads. *Journal of Personality and Social Psychology*, **47**, 330–341.

Ickes, W. (1985). Sex-role influences on compatibility in relationships. In W. Ickes (Ed.) *Compatible and incompatible relationships*, (pp. 187–208). New York: Springer-Verlag.

Ickes, W., Bissonnette, V., Garcia, S., & Stinson, L. (1990a). Implementing and using the dyadic interaction paradigm. In C. Hendrick & M. Clark

(Eds) *Review of personality and social psychology*, Vol. 11, (pp. 16–44). Calif.: Sage.

Ickes, W., & Dugosh, J. W. (in press). An intersubjective perspective on social cognition and aging. *Basic and Applied Social Psychology* (special issue on Social Cognition and Aging).

Ickes, W., & Gonzalez, R. (1994). "Social" cognition and *social* cognition: From the subjective to the intersubjective. *Small Group Research*, **25**, 294–315.

Ickes, W., & Gonzalez, R. (1996). "Social" cognition and *social* cognition: From the subjective to the intersubjective. In J. Nye & A. Brower (Eds) *What's so social about social cognition? Social cognition research in small groups*. Newbury Park, CA: Sage.

Ickes, W., Patterson, M. L., Rajecki, D. W., & Tanford, S. (1982). Behavioral and cognitive consequences of reciprocal versus compensatory responses to pre-interaction expectancies. *Social Cognition*, **1**, 160–90.

Ickes, W., Robertson, E., Tooke, W., & Teng, G. (1986). Naturalistic social cognition: Methodology, assessment, and validation. *Journal of Personality and Social Psychology*, **51**, 66–82.

Ickes, W., Stinson, L., Bissonnette, V., & Garcia, S. (1990b). Naturalistic social cognition: Empathic accuracy in mixed-sex dyads. *Journal of Personality and Social Psychology*, **59**, 730–742.

Ickes, W., & Tooke, W. (1988). The observational method: Studying the interaction of minds and bodies. In S. W. Duck, D. E Hay, S. E. Hobfoll W. Ickes, & B. M. Montgomery (Eds) *Handbook of personal relationships: Theory, research and interventions*, (pp. 79–97). Chichester: John Wiley & Sons.

Ickes, W., Tooke, W., Stinson, L., Baker, V., & Bissonnette, V. (1988). Naturalistic social cognition: Intersubjectivity in same-sex dyads. *Journal of Nonverbal Behavior*, **12**, 58–84.

Insko, C. A., Schopler, J., Hoyle, R. H., Dardis, G. J., & Graetz, K. A. (1990). Individual-group discontinuity as a function of fear and greed. *Journal of Personality and Social Psychology*, **58**, 68–79.

Jack, D. C. (1991). *Silencing the self: Women and depression*. Cambridge, MA: Harvard University Press.

Jacobs, J. B. (1974). Participant observation in prison. *Urban Life Culture*, **3**, 221–40.

Jacobson, N. S., & Margolin, G. (1979). *Marital therapy: Strategies based on social learning and behavior exchange principles*. New York: Brunner/Mazel.

James, W. (1890). *The principles of psychology*. New York: Holt.

James, W. (1948). *Psychology*. Cleveland: Fine Editions Press. (Original work published 1890)

Jankowiak, W. R., & Fischer, E. F. (1992). A cross-cultural perspective on romantic love. *Ethnology*, **31**, 149–155.

Janoff-Bulman, R., & Wade, M. B. (1996). The dilemma of self-advocacy for women: Another case of blaming the victim? *Journal of Social and Clinical Psychology*, **15**, 143–152.

Jellison, J. M., & Gentry, K. W. (1978). A self-presentation interpretation of the seeking of approval. *Personality and Social Psychology Bulletin*, **4**, 227–230.

Johnson, D. J. (1992). Developmental pathways: Toward an ecological theoretical formulation of race identity in Black-White biracial children. In M. P. P. Root (Ed.) *Racially mixed people in America* (pp. 37–49). Newbury Park, CA: Sage.

Johnson, D. J., & Rusbult, C. E. (1989). Resisting temptation: Devaluation of alternative partners as a means of maintaining commitment in close relationships. *Journal of Personality and Social Psychology*, **57**, 967–980.

Johnson, M. P. (1989). Commitment to personal relationships. In W. H. Jones & D. W. Perlman (Eds) *Advances in personal relationships* (Vol. 3, pp. 117–143). London: Jessica Kingsley.

Johnson, M. P. (1991a). Commitment to personal relationships. In W. H. Jones & D. Perlman (Eds) *Advances in personal relationships* (Vol. 3, pp. 117–143). London: Kingsley.

Johnson, M. P. (1991b). Reply to Levinger and Rusbult. In W. H. Jones & D. Perlman (Eds) *Advances in personal relationships* (Vol. 3, pp. 171–176). London: Kingsley.

Johnson, M. P., & Ewens, W. (1971). Power relations and affective styles as determinants of confidence in impression formation in a game situation. *Journal of Experimental Social Psychology*, **7**, 98–110.

Johnson, M. P., Huston, T. L., Gaines, S. O. Jr., & Levinger, G. (1992). Patterns of married life among young couples. *Journal of Social and Personal Relationships*, **9**, 343–364.

Jones, E. E. (1964). *Ingratiation*. New York: Appleton-Century-Crofts.

Jones, E. E., & Davis, K. E. (1965). From acts to dispositions: The attribution process in person perception. In L. Berkowitz (Ed.) *Advances in experimental social psychology* (Vol. 2, pp. 283–329). New York: Academic Press.

Jones, E. E., & Goethals, G. R. (1972). Order effects in impression formation. In E. E. Jones *et al.* (Eds) *Attribution: Perceiving the causes of behavior*. Morristown, NJ: General Learning Press.

Jones, E. E., & Nisbett, R. (1971). The actor and the observer: Divergent perceptions of the causes of behavior. In E. E. Jones, D. Kanouse, H. Kelley, R. Nisbett, S. Valins & B. Weiner (Eds) *Attribution: Perceiving the causes of behavior* (pp. 79–94). Morristown, NJ: General Learning Press.

Jones, E. E., & Pittman, T. S. (1982). Toward a general theory of strategic self-presentation. In J. Suls (Ed.) *Psychological perspectives on the self* (Vol. 1, pp. 231–262). Hillsdale, NJ: Erlbaum.

Jones, E. E., Bell, L., & Aronson, E. (1972). The reciprocation of attraction from similar and dissimilar others: A study in person perception and evaluation. In C. G. McClintock (Ed.) *Experimental social psychology* (pp. 142–179). New York: Holt, Rinehart.

Jones, E. E., Gergen, K. J., Gumpert, P., & Thibaut, J. W. (1965). Some conditions affecting the use of ingratiation to influence performance evaluation. *Journal of Personality and Social Psychology*, **1**, 613–625.

Jones, J. M. (1988). Racism in Black and White: a bicultural model of reaction and evaluation. In P. A. Katz & D. A. Taylor (Eds) *Eliminating racism: Profiles in controversy* (pp. 117–135). New York: Plenum.

Jones, R. R., Reid, J. B., & Patterson, G. R. (1975). Naturalistic observations in clinical assessment. In P. McReynolds (Ed.) *Advances in Psychological Assessment* (Vol. 3), San Francisco: Jossey-Bass.

Jones, W. H., & Burdette, M. P. (1994). Betrayal in relationships. In A. L. Weber & J. H. Harvey (Eds) *Perspectives on close relationships* (pp. 243–262). Boston: Allyn & Bacon.

Jourard, S. M. (1971). *Self-disclosure: An experimental analysis of the transparent self*. New York: Wiley Interscience.

Jung, C. G. (1959). Marriage as a psychological relationship. In V. S. De-Laszlo (Ed.) *The basic writings of C. G. Jung* (R. F. C. Hull, Trans.; pp. 531–544). New York: Modern Library. (Original work published 1925).

Kahneman, D., & Tversky, A. (1979). Prospect theory: An analysis of decision under risk. *Econometrica*, **47**, 263–291.

Kahneman, D., & Tversky, A. (1982). The psychology of preferences. *Scientific American*, **246**, 160–173.

Kahneman, D., Slovik, P., & Tversky, A. (1982). *Judgment under uncertainty: Heuristics and biases*. New York: Cambridge University Press.

Kambon, K. K. K., & Hopkins, R. (1993). An African-centred analysis of Penn et al.'s critique of the own-race preference assumption underlying Africentric models of personality. *Journal of Black Psychology*, **19**, 342–349.

Kashy, D. A., & DePaulo, B. M. (1996). Who lies? *Journal of Personality and Social Psychology*, **70**, 1037–1051.

Katz, P. A., & Taylor, D. A. (1988). Introduction. In P. A. Katz & D. A. Taylor (Eds) *Eliminating racism: Profiles in controversy* (pp. 1–16). New York: Plenum.

Keenan, J. M., & Baillet, S. D. (1980). Memory for personally and socially significant events. In R. S. Nickerson (Ed.) *Attention and performance* (Vol. 8, pp. 652–669). Hillsdale, NJ: Erlbaum.

Keenan, J. P., Gallup, G. G., Jr., Goulet, N., Kulkarni, M. (1997). Attributions of deception in human mating strategies. *Journal of Social Behavior and Personality*, **12**, 45–52.

Kelley, H. H. (1972). Attribution in social interaction. In E. E. Jones, D. E. Kanouse, H. H. Kelley, R. E. Nisbett, S. Valins, & B. Weiner (Eds) *Attribution: Perceiving the causes of behavior* (pp. 1–26). Morristown, NJ: General Learning Press.

Kelley, H. H. (1979). *Personal relationships: Their structure and process*. Hillsdale, NJ: Erlbaum.

Kelley, H. H. (1983a). Love and commitment. In H. H. Kelley, E. Berscheid, A. Christensen, J. H. Harvey, T. L. Huston, G. Levinger, E. McClintock, L. A. Peplau & D. R. Peterson (Eds) *Close relationships* (pp. 265–314). New York: W. H. Freeman.

Kelley, H. H. (1983b). The situational origins of human tendencies: A further reason for the formal analysis of structures. *Personality and Social Psychology Bulletin*, **9**, 8–30.

Kelley, H. H. (1984a). Affect in interpersonal relations. In P. Shaver (Ed.) *Review of personality and social psychology* (Vol. 5, pp. 89–115). Newbury Park, CA: Sage.

Kelley, H. H. (1984b). Interdependence theory and its future. *Representative Research in Social Psychology*, **14**, 2–15.

Kelley, H. H. (1984c). The theoretical description of interdependence by means of transition lists. *Journal of Personality and Social Psychology*, **47**, 956–982.

Kelley, H. H. (1991). Lewin, situations, and interdependence. *Journal of Social Issues*, **47**(2), 211–233.

Kelley, H. H. (1997). The "stimulus field for interpersonal phenomena": The source of language and thought about interpersonal events. *Personality and Social Psychology Review*, **1**, 140–169.

Kelley, H. H., & Grzelak, J. L. (1972). Conflict between individual and common interests in an n-person relationship. *Journal of Personality and Social Psychology*, **21**, 190–197.

Kelley, H. H., & Stahelski, A. J., (1970). Social interaction basis of cooperators' and competitors' beliefs about others. *Journal of Personality and Social Psychology*, **16**, 66–91.

Kelley, H. H., & Thibaut, J. W. (1969). Group problem solving. In G. Lindzey & E. Aronson (Eds) *Handbook of social psychology*, 2nd edn (Vol. 4, pp. 1–101). Reading, MA: Addison-Wesley.

Kelley, H. H., & Thibaut, J. W. (1978). *Interpersonal relations: A theory of interdependence*. New York: Wiley.

Kelley, H. H., & Thibaut, J. W. (1985). Self-interest, science, and cynicism. *Journal of Social and Clinical Psychology*, **3**, 26–32.

Kelley, H. H., Berscheid, E., Christensen, A., Harvey, J., Huston, T. L., Levinger, G., McClintock, D., Peplau, L. A., & Peterson, D. (1983). *Close relationships*. San Francisco: Freeman.

Kelly, G. A. (1955). *The psychology of personal constructs* (Vol. 1). New York: Norton.

Kelvin, P. (1977). Predictability, power, and vulnerablity in interpersonal attraction. In S. W. Duck (Ed.) *Theory and practice in interpersonal attraction* (pp. 355–378). London, Academic Press.

Kenny, D. A. (1979). *Correlation and causality*. New York: John Wiley.

Kenny, D. A. (1988). The analysis of data from two-person relationships. In S. W. Duck (Ed.) *Handbook of personal relationships* (pp. 57–77). New York: John Wiley.

Kenny, D. A. (1994). *Interpersonal perception: A social relations analysis*. New York: Guilford Press.

Kenny, D. A. (1995a). Design issues in dyadic research. *Review of Personality and Social Psychology*, **11**, 164–184.

Kenny, D. A. (1995b). The effect of nonindependence on significance testing in dyadic research. *Personal Relationships*, **2**, 67–75.

Kenny, D. A. (1996). Models of non-independence in dyadic research. *Journal of Social and Personal Relationships*, **13**, 279–294.

Kenny, D. A., & La Voie, L. (1984). The social relations model. In L. Berkowitz (Ed.) *Advances in Experimental social psychology* (Vol. 18, pp. 141–182). Orlando: Academic Press.

Kenny, D. A., & La Voie, L. (1985). Separating individual and group effects. *Journal of Personality and Social Psychology*, **48**, 339–348.

Kenny, D. A., & Acitelli, L. K. (1994). Measuring similarity in couples. *Journal of Family Psychology*, **8**, 417–431.

Kenny, D. A., & Albright, L. A. (1987). Accuracy in interpersonal perception: A social relations analysis. *Psychological Bulletin*, **102**, 390–402.

Kenny, D. A., & Judd, C. M. (1986). Consequences of violating the independence assumption in the analysis of variance. *Psychological Bulletin*, **99**, 422–431.

Kenny, D. A., & Judd, C. M. (1996). A general procedure for the estimation of interdependence. *Psychological Bulletin*, **119**, 138–148.

Kenny, D. A., & Kashy, D. A. (1991). Analyzing interdependence in dyads. In B. M. Montgomery & S. W. Duck (Eds) *Studying interpersonal relationships* (pp. 275–285). New York: The Guilford Press.

Kenrick, D. T. (1987). Gender, genes, and the social environment: A biosocial interactionist perspective. In P. Shaver & C. Hendrick (Eds) *Review of personality and social psychology* (Vol. 7, pp. 14–43). Newbury Park, CA: Sage.

Kenrick, D. T. (1994). Evolutionary social psychology: From sexual selection to social cognition. In M. P. Zanna (Ed.) *Advances in experimental social Psychology* (Vol. 26, pp. 75–122). San Diego, CA: Academic Press.

Kenrick, D. T., & Brown, S. (1995). Al Capone, discrete morphs, and complex dynamic systems. *Behavioral and Brain Sciences*, **18**, 560–561.

Kenrick, D. T., & Cialdini, R. B. (1977). Romantic attraction: Misattribution versus reinforcement explanations. *Journal of Personalty and Social Psychology*, **35**, 381–391.

Kenrick, D. T., & Gutierres, S. E. (1980). Contrast effects and judments of physical attractiveness: When beauty becomes a social problem. *Journal of Personality and Social Psychology*, **38**, 131–140.

Kenrick, D. T., & Keefe, R. C. (1992). Age preferences in mates reflect sex differences in reproductive strategies. *Behavioral and Brain Sciences*, **15**, 75–133.

Kenrick, D. T., & Sheets, V. (1994). Homicidal fantasies. *Ethology and Sociobiology*, **14**, 231–246.

Kenrick, D. T., & Trost, M. R. (1987). A biosocial model of relationship formation. In K. Kelley (Ed.) *Females, males and sexuality: Theories and research* (pp. 58–100). Albany: SUNY Press.

Kenrick, D. T., & Trost, M. R. (1989). A reproductive exchange model of heterosexual relationships: Putting proximate economics in ultimate perspective. In C. Hendrick (Ed.) *Review of personality and social psychology: Vol. 10. Close Relationships* (pp. 92–118). Newbury Park: Sage.

Kenrick, D. T., & Trost, M. R. (1993). The evolutionary perspective. In A. E. Beall & R. J. Sternberg (Eds) *Perspectives on the psychology of gender* (pp. 148–172). New York: Guilford.

Kenrick, D. T., & Trost, M. R. (1997). Evolutionary approaches to relationships. In S. W. Duck (Ed.) *Handbook of personal relationships: Theory, research, and interventions*, 2nd edn (pp. 156–177). Chichester: Wiley.

Kenrick, D. T., Dantchik, A., & MacFarlane, S. (1983). Personality, environment, and criminal behavior: An evolutionary perspective. In W. S. Laufer & J. M. Day (Eds) *Personality theory, moral development and criminal behavior* (pp. 201–234). Lexington, Mass.: D. C. Heath & Co.

Kenrick, D. T., Gabrielidis, C., Keefe, R. C., & Cornelius, J. S. (1996). Adolescents' age preferences for dating partners: Support for an evolutionary model of life-history strategies. *Child Development*, **67**, 1499–1511.

Kenrick, D. T., Groth, G. E., Trost, M. R., & Sadalla, E. K. (1993). Integrating evolutionary and social exchange perspectives on relationships: Effects of gender, self-appraisal, and involvement level on mate selection. *Journal of Personality and Social Psychology*, **64**, 951–969.

Kenrick, D. T., Gutierres, S. E., & Goldberg, L. (1989). Influence of popular erotica on judgments of strangers and mates. *Journal of Experimental Social Psychology*, **25**, 159–167.

Kenrick, D. T., Keefe, R. C., Bryan, A., Barr, A., & Brown, S. (1995). Age preferences and mate choice among homosexuals and heterosexuals: A case for modular psychological mechanisms. *Journal of Personality and Social Psychology*, **69**, 1166–1172.

Kenrick, D. T., Neuberg, S. L., Zierk, K. L., & Krones, J. M. (1994). Evolution and social cognition: Contrast effects as a function of sex, dominance, and physical attractiveness. *Personality and Social Psychology Bulletin*, **20**, 210–217.

Kenrick, D. T., Sadalla, E. K., Groth, G., & Trost, M. R. (1990). Evolution, traits, and the stages of human courtship: Qualifying the parental investment model. *Journal of Personality*, **58**, 97–116.

Kenrick, D. T., Sadalla, E. K., & Keefe, R. C. (1998). Evolutionary cognitive psychology: The missing heart of modern cognitive science. In C. Crawford & D. Krebs (Eds) *Handbook of evolutionary psychology* (pp. 485–514). Mahwah, NJ: Lawrence Erlbaum Associates.

Kenrick, D. T., Stringfield, D. O., Wagenhals, W. L., Dahl, R. H., & Ransdell, H. J. (1980). Sex differences, androgyny, and approach responses to erotica: A new variation on the old volunteer problem. *Journal of Personality and Social Psychology*, **38**, 517–524.

Kephart, W. M., & Jedlicka, D. (1988). *The family, society, and the individual*, 6th edn. New York: Harper & Row.

Kerckhoff, A. C. (1974). *Foundations of interpersonal attraction* (pp. 61–77). New York: Academic Press.

Kerckhoff, A. C., & Davis, K. (1962). Value consensus and need complementarity in mate selection. *American Sociological Review*, **27**, 295–303.

Kiecolt-Glaser, J. K., Garner, W., Speicher, C., Penn, G. M., Holliday, J., & Glaser, R. (1984). Psychological modifiers of immunocompetence in medical students. *Psychosomatic Medicine*, **46**, 7–14.

Kiecolt-Glaser, J. K., Ricker, D., George, J., Messick, G., Speicher, G. E., Garner, W., & Glaser, R. (1984). Urinary cortisol levels, cellular immunocompetence, and loneliness in psychiatric inpatients. *Psychosomatic Medicine*, **46**, 15–23.

Kilbourne, B. S., Howell, F., & England, P. (1990). A measurement model for subjective marital solidarity: Invariance across time, gender, and life cycle stage. *Social Science Research*, **19**, 62–81.

Kingston, P. W., & Nock, S. L. (1987). Time together among dual-earner couples. *American Sociological Review*, **52**, 391–400.

Kirkpatrick, L. A., & Davis, K. E. (1993). Attachment style, gender, and relationship stability: A longitudinal analysis. *Journal of Personality and Social Psychology*, **66**, 502–512.

Kirkpatrick, L. A., & Hazan, C. (1994). Attachment styles and close relationships: A four year prospective study. *Journal of Social and Personal Relationships*, **1**, 123–142.

Klein, R., & Johnson, M. (1997). Strategies of couple conflict. *Handbook of personal relationships*, 2nd edn (pp. 469–486). Chichester, UK: Wiley.

Klein, R., & Milardo, R. (1993). Third-party influences on the development and maintenance of personal relationships. In S. W. Duck (Ed.) *Understanding relationship processes:* Vol. 3: *Social contexts of relationships* (pp. 55–77). Newbury Park, CA: Sage Publications.

Kobak, R., & Hazan, C. (1991). Attachment in marriage: The effects of security and accuracy of working models. *Journal of Personality and Social Psychology*, **60**, 861–869.

Köhler, W. (1947). *Gestalt psychology: an introduction to new concepts in modern psychology*. New York: Liveright.

Koocher, G. F. (1977). Bathroom behavior and human dignity. *Journal of Personality and Social Psychology*, **35**, 120–121.

Korolewicz, M., & Korolewicz, A. (1985). Effects of sex and race on interracial dating patterns. *Psychological Reports*, **57**, 1291–1296.

Kotler, T. (1985). Security and autonomy within marriage. *Human Relations*, **38**, 299–321.

Kouri, K. M., & Lasswell, M. (1993). Black–White marriages: Social change and intergenerational mobility. *Marriage and Family Review*, **19**, 241–255.

Kovecses, Z. (1986). *Metaphors of anger, pride, and love: A lexical approach to the structure of concepts*. Amsterdam: John Benjamins.

Kovecses, Z. (1991). A linguists quest for love. *Journal of Personal and Social Relationships*, **8**, 77–98.

Kowalski, R. (1997). Aversive interpersonal behaviors: An overarching framework. In R. Kowalski (Ed.) *Aversive interpersonal behaviors* (pp. 216–234). New York: Plenum.

Kowalski, R. (in press). *The underbelly of social interaction*. Washington: American Psychological Association.

Kowalski, R. M., & Leary, M. R. (1990). Strategic self-presentation and the avoidance of aversive events: Antecedents and consequences of self-enhancement and self-depreciation. *Journal of Experimental Social Psychology*, **26**, 322–336.

Kraemer, H. C., & Jacklin, C. N. (1979). Statistical analysis of dyadic social behavior. *Psychological Bulletin*, **86**, 217–224.

Krebs, D. L., & Miller, D. T. (1985). Altruism and aggression. In G. Lindzey and E. Aronson (Eds) *Handbook of social psychology*, 3rd edn (Vol. 2, pp. 1–71). New York: Random House.

Kreft, I., de Leeuw, J., & van der Leeden, R. (1994). Review of five multilevel analysis programs: Bmdp-5v, genmod, hlm, ml3, varcl. *American Statistician*, **48**, 324–335.

La Gaipa, J. J. (1990). The negative effects of informal support systems. In S. W. Duck, with R. C. Silver (Eds) *Personal relationships and social support* (pp. 122–140). London: Sage.

Lakoff, G. (1987). *Women, fire and dangerous things: What categories reveal about the mind*. Chicago: University of Chicago Press.

Lakoff, G., & Turner, M. (1989). *More than cool reason: A field guide to poetic metaphor*. Chicago: University of Chicago Press.

Lamke, L. K. (1989). Marital adjustment among rural couples: The role of expressiveness. *Sex Roles*, **21**, 579–590.

Lane, J. D., & Wegner, D. M. (1995). The cognitive consequences of secrecy. *Journal of Personality and Social Psychology*, **69**, 237–253.

Langer, S. K. (1948). *Philosophy in a new key: A study of the symbolism of reason, rite, and art*. New York: Mentor.

Larson, D. G., & Chastain, R. L. (1990). Self-concealment: Conceptualization, measurement, and health implications. *Journal of Social and Clinical Psychology*, **9**, 439–455.

Lea, M., & Spears, R. (1995). Love at first byte? Building personal relationships over computer networks. In J. T. Wood & S. W. Duck (Eds) *Understudied relationships: Off the beaten track* (pp. 197–233). Thousand Oaks, CA: Sage.

Leary, M. R. (1995). *Self-presentation: Impression management and interpersonal behavior*. Boulder, CO: Westview Press.

Leary, M. R., & Downs, D. L. (1995). Interpersonal functions of the self-esteem motive: The self-esteem system as a sociometer. In M. Kernis (Ed.) *Efficacy, agency, and self-esteem* (pp. 123–144). New York: Plenum.

Leary, M. R., & Kowalski, R. M. (1990). Impression management: A literature review and two-component model. *Psychological Bulletin*, **107**, 34–47.

Leary, M. R., & Kowalski, R. M. (1995). *Social anxiety*. New York: Guilford.

Leary, M. R., Bednarski, R., Hammon, D., & Duncan, T. (1997). Blowhards, snobs, and narcissists: Interpsonal reactions to excessive egotism. In R. Kowalski (Ed.) *Aversive interpersonal behaviors* (pp. 112–132). New York: Plenum.

Leary, M. R., Landel, J. L., & Patton, K. M. (1996). The motivated expression of embarrassment following a self-presentational predicament. *Journal of Personality*, **64**, 619–636.

Leary, M. R., Nezlek, J. B., Downs, D. L., Radford-Davenport, J., Martin, J., & McMullen, A. (1994). Self-presentation in everyday interactions. *Journal of Personality and Social Psychology*, **67**, 664–673.

Leary, M. R., Tchividjian, L. R., & Kraxberger, B. E. (1994). Self-presentation can be hazardous to your health: Impression management and health risk. *Health Psychology*, **13**, 461– 470.

Lenington, S. (1981). Child abuse: The limits of sociobiology. *Ethology and Sociobiology*, **2**, 17–29.

Leonard, J. L. (1989). Homo sapiens: A good fit to theory, but posing some enigmas. *Behavioral and Brain Sciences*, **12**, 26–27.

LeVay, S. (1993). *The sexual brain*. Cambridge, MA: MIT Press.

Levenson, R. W., & Gottman, J. M. (1983). Marital interaction: Physiological linkage and affective exchange. *Journal of Personality and Social Psychology*, **45**, 587–597.

Levenson, R. W., & Gottman, J. M. (1985). Physiological and affective predictors of change in relationship satisfaction. *Journal of Personality and Social Psychology*, **49**, 85–94.

Leventhal, H., & Sharp, E. (1965). Facial expressions as indicators of distress, In S. S. Tompkin & C. E. Izard (Eds) *Affect, cognition, and personality* (pp. 296–318). New York: Springer.

Levinger, G. (1977). Re-viewing the close relation ship. In G. Levinger & H. L. Raush (Eds) Amherst, MA: University of Massachusetts Press.

Levinger, G. (1979). A social exchange view on the dissolution of pair relationships. In R. L. Burgess & T. L. Huston (Eds) *Social exchange in developing relationships* (pp. 169–193). New York: Academic Press.

Levinger, G. (1991). Commitment vs. cohesiveness: Two complementary perspectives. In W. H. Jones & D. Perlman (Eds) *Advances in personal relationships* (Vol. 3, pp. 145–150). London: Kingsley.

Levinger, G., & Rands, M. (1985). Compatibility in marriage and other close relationships. In W. Ickes (Ed.) *Compatible and incompatible relationships* (pp. 309–331). New York: Springer-Verlag.

Lewin, K. (1936). *Principles of topological psychology*. New York: McGraw-Hill.

Liebowitz, M. (1983). *The chemistry of love*. New York: Berkeley Books.

Liebrand, W. B. G., & Van Run, G. J. (1985). The effects of social motives on behavior in social dilemmas in two cultures. *Journal of Experimental Social Psychology*, **21**, 86–102.

Lind, E. A., & Tyler, T. R. (1988). *The social psychology of procedural justice*. New York: Plenum.

Lindemann, E. (1942). Symptomology and management of acute grief. *American Journal of Psychiatry*, **101**, 141–148.

Littlefield, C. H., & Rushton, J. P. (1986). When a child dies: The sociobiology of bereavement. *Journal of Personality and Social Psychology*, **51**, 797–802.

Livingston, K. R. (1980). Love as a process of reducing uncertainty—Cognitive theory. In K. S. Pope (Ed.) *On love and loving* (pp. 133–151). San Francisco: Jossey-Bass.

Livingstone, M., & Hubel, D. (1988). Segregation of form, color, movement, and depth: Anatomy, physiology, and perception. *Science*, **240**, 740–749.

Lockard, J. S., & Paulhus, D. L. (1988). *Self-deception: An adaptive mechanism?* Englewood Cliffs, NJ: Prentice Hall.

Locke, H. J., & Wallace, K. M. (1959). Short marital adjustment and prediction tests: Their reliability and validity. *Marriage and Family Living*, **21**, 251–255.

Lofland, L. H. (1982). Loss and human connection: An exploration into the nature of the social bond. In W. Ickes & E. S. Knowles (Eds) *Personality, roles, and social behavior* (pp. 219–242). New York: Springer-Verlag.

Lord, C. G. (1980). Schemas and images as memory aids: Two modes of processing social information. *Journal of Personality and Social Psychology*, **38**, 257–269.

Lord, C. G. (1987). Imagining self and others: Reply to Brown, Keenan, and Potts. *Journal of Personality and Social Psychology*, **53**, 445–450.

Lorenz, K. (1970). *Studies in animal and human behavior.* Cambridge, MA: Harvard University Press.

Lumsden, C. J., & Wilson, E. O. (1981). *Genes, mind, and culture: The co-evolutionary process.* Cambridge, MA: Harvard University Press.

Lund, M. (1985). The development of investment and commitment scales for predicting continuity of personal relationships. *Journal of Social and Personal Relationships*, **2**, 3–23.

Lynch, J. J. (1977). *The broken heart: The medical consequences of loneliness.* New York: Basic Books.

Maccoby, E. E. (1990). Gender and relationships: A developmental account. *American Psychologist*, **45**, 513–520.

Major, B., Carrington, P. I., & Carnevale, P. J. D. (1984). Physical attractiveness and self-esteem: Attributions for praise from an other-sex evaluator. *Personality and Social Psychology Bulletin*, **10**, 43–50.

Malamuth, N. M. (1986). Predictors of naturalistic sexual aggression. *Journal of Personality and Social Psychology*, **50**, 953–962.

Mamali, C. (1991). *The dynamic of personal relationships between Dreiser and Mencken: The correspondentogram of a dyadic epistolary space (1907–1945).* Paper presented at the Third Conference of the International Network on Personal Relationships, Normal Bloomington, Illinois.

Mamali, C. (1992). *Correspondence and the reconstruction of social dynamics: The correspondentogram of a nuclear family.* Paper presented at the Workshop on Theoretical Analysis, Department of Sociology, University of Iowa, Iowa City, Iowa.

Mandler, G. (1975). *Mind and emotion.* New York: Wiley.

Mansfield, P., & Collard, J. (1988). *The beginning of the rest of our life: A portrait of newlywed marriage.* London: Macmillan.

Margolin, G., & Wampold, B. E. (1981). Sequential analysis of conflict and accord in distressed and nondistressed marital partners. *Journal of Counseling and Clinical Psychology*, **49**, 554–567.

Markus, H. R. (1977). Self-schemata and processing information about the self. *Journal of Personality and Social Psychology*, **35**, 63–78.

Martin, K. A., & Leary, M. R. (1998) *Self-presentational determinants of health risk behavior among college freshmen.* Manuscript under review, Wake Forest University.

Martin, K., Leary, M. R., & Rejeski, W. J. (in press). Self-presentational concerns in the aged: Implications for health and well-being. *Basic and Applied Social Psychology.*

Martin, R. (1997). "Girls don't talk about garages!": Perceptions of conversation in same- and cross-sex friendships. *Personal Relationships*, **4**, 115–130.

Marx, G. (1987). *The Groucho letters: Letters from and to Groucho Marx*. New York: Fireside.

Maslow, A. H. (1967). A theory of metamotivation: The biological rooting of the value-life. *Journal of Humanistic Psychology*, **7**, 93–127.

McCall, G. J. (1974). A symbolic interactionist approach to attraction. In T. L. Huston (Ed.) *Foundations of interpersonal attraction* (pp. 217–231). New York: Academic Press.

McCall, G. J., & Simmons, J. L. (1991). Levels of analysis: The individual, the dyad, and the larger social group. In B. M. Montgomery & S. W. Duck (Eds) *Studying interpersonal interaction* (pp. 56–81). New York: Guilford.

McClelland, K. E., & Auster, C. J. (1990). Public platitudes and hidden tensions: Racial climates at predominantly White liberal arts colleges. *Journal of Higher Education*, **61**, 607–642.

McClintock, C. G., & Liebrand, W. B. G. (1988). The role of interdependence structure, individual value orientation and other's strategy in social decision making: A transformational analysis. *Journal of Personality and Social Psychology*, **55**, 396–409.

McCornack, S. A., & Levine, T. R. (1990). When lies are uncovered: Emotional and relational outcomes of discovered deception. *Communication Monographs*, **57**, 119–138.

McDougall, W. (1908). *Social psychology: An introduction*. London, Methuen.

McKenna, C. (1989). *Marital satisfaction and sensation seeking in the first ten years of marriage: Self-expansion versus boredom*. Doctoral dissertation, California Graduate School of Family Psychology, San Francisco, CA.

McNeal, J., & Aron, A. (1995, June). *Exciting activities and relationship satisfaction: A comparison of married and dating couples*. Paper presented at the International Network Conference on Personal Relationships, Williamsburg, VA.

Mead, G. H. (1934). *Mind, self, and society*. Chicago: CUP.

Mealey, L. (1995). The sociobiology of psychopathy. *Behavioral and Brain Sciences*, **18**, 523–541.

Mellen, S. L. W. (1981). *The evolution of love*. Oxford, England: W. H. Freeman & Co.

Mencken, H. L. (1991). *The diary of H. L. Mencken*. New York: Vintage Books.

Mendoza, J. L., & Graziano, W. G. (1982). The statistical analysis of dyadic social behavior: A multivariate approach. *Psychological Bulletin*, **92**, 532–540.

Merleau-Ponty, M. (1945). *Phenomenologie de la perception*. Paris: Gallimard.

Messick, D. M., & McClintock, C. G. (1968). Motivational bases of choice in experimental games. *Journal of Experimental Social Psychology*, **4**, 1–25.

Messner, M. A. (1992). Like family: Power, intimacy, and sexuality in male athletes' friendships. In P. Nardi (Ed.), *Men's friendships* (pp. 215–237). Newbury Park, CA: Sage.

Metts, S. (1997). Face and facework: Implications for the study of personal relationships, *Handbook of personal relationships*, 2nd edn (pp. 373–390). Chichester, UK: Wiley.

Middlemist, R. D., Knowles, E. S., & Matter, C. E. (1976). Personal space invasions in the lavatory: Suggestive evidence for arousal. *Journal of Personality and Social Psychology*, **33**, 541–546.

Middlemist, R. D., Knowles, E. S., & Matter, C. E. (1977). What to do and what to report: A reply to Koocher. *Journal of Personality and Social Psychology*, **35**, 122–124.

Miell, D. E. (1987). Remembering relationship development: Constructing a context for interactions In Burnett, R., McPhee, J., & Clarke, D. D. (Eds) *Accounting for relationships* (pp. 60–73). London: Methuen.

Mikula, G. (1983). Justice and fairness in interpersonal relations: Thoughts and suggestions. In H. Tajfel (Ed.) *The social dimension* (pp. 204–227). Cambridge: Cambridge Univ. Press.

Mikulincer, M., & Nachshon, O. (1991). Attachment styles and patterns of self-disclosure. *Journal of Personality and Social Psychology*, **61**, 321–331.

Milardo, R. M. (1984). Theoretical and methodological issues in the identification of the social networks of spouses. *Journal of Marriage and the Family*, **51**, 165–174.

Milardo, R. M., & Wellman, B. (1992). The personal is social. *Journal of Social and Personal Relationships*, **9**, 339–342.

Milardo, R. M., Johnson, M. P., & Huston, T. L. (1983). Developing close relationships: Changing patterns of interaction between pair members and social networks. *Journal of Personality and Social Psychology*, **44**, 964–976.

Miller, G. A., Gallanter, E., & Pribram, K. H. (1960). *Plans and the structure of behavior*. New York: Holt, Rinehart & Winston.

Miller, L. C., & Kenny, D. A. (1986). Reciprocity of self-disclosure at the individual and dyadic levels: A social relations analysis. *Journal of Personality and Social Psychology*, **50**, 713–719.

Miller, L. C., Berg, J. H., & Archer, R. L. (1983). Openers: Individuals who elicit intimate self-disclosure. *Journal of Personality and Social Psychology*, **44**, 1234–1244.

Miller, R. S. (1987). Empathic embarrassment: Situational and personal determinants of reactions to the embarrassment of another. *Journal of Personality and Social Psychology*, **53**, 1061–1069.

Miller, R. S. (1996). *Embarrassment: Poise and peril in everyday life*. New York: Guilford Press.

Miller, R. S. (1997a). Inattentive and contented: Relationship commitment and attention to alternatives. *Journal of Personality and Social Psychology*, **73**, 758–766.

Miller, R. S. (1997b). We always hurt the ones we love: Aversive interactions in close relationships. In R. M. Kowalski (Ed.) *Aversive interpersonal behaviors* (pp. 11–29). New York: Guilford Press.

Mirande, A. (1977). The Chicago family: A reanalysis of conflicting values. *Journal of Marriage and the Family*, **39**, 747–756.

Moghaddam, F. M., Taylor, D. M., & Wright, S. C. (1993). *Social psychology in cross-cultural perspective.* New York: W. H. Freeman.

Molm, L. D. (1985). Relative effects of individual dependencies: Further tests of the relation between power imbalance and power use. *Social Forces,* **63,** 810–837.

Montgomery, B. M. (1986). Interpersonal attraction as a function of open communication and gender. *Communication Research Reports,* **3,** 27–36.

Moore, M. M. (1985). Nonverbal courtship patterns in women. *Ethology and Sociobiology,* **6,** 237–247.

Mori, D., Chaiken, S., & Pliner, P. (1987), "Eating lightly" and the self-presentation of femininity. *Journal of Personality and Social Psychology,* **53,** 693–702.

Morier, D., & Seroy, C. (1994). The effect of interpersonal expectancies on men's self-presentation of gender role attitudes to women. *Sex Roles,* **31,** 493–504.

Morris, D. (1972). *Intimate behavior.* New York: Bantam.

Murphy, B. C. (1989). Lesbian couples and their parents: The effects of perceived parental attitudes on the couple. *Journal of Counseling and Development,* **68,** 46–51.

Murray, S. L. (1995). *Is love blind? Positive illusions, idealization and the construction of satisfaction in close relationships.* Doctoral Dissertation, University of Waterloo.

Murray, S. L., & Holmes, J. G. (1993). Seeing virtues in faults: Negativity and the transformation of interpersonal narratives in close relationships. *Journal of Personality and Social Psychology,* **65,** 707–722.

Murray, S. L., & Holmes, J. G. (1997). A leap of faith? Positive illusions in romantic relationships. *Personality and Social Psychology Bulletin,* **23,** 586–604.

Murray, S. L., Holmes, J. G., & Griffin, D. W. (1996a). The benefits of positive illusions: Idealization and the construction of satisfaction in close relationships. *Journal of Personality and Social Psychology,* **70,** 79–98.

Murray, S. L., Holmes, J. G., & Griffin, D. W. (1996b). The self-fulfilling nature of positive illusions in romantic relationships: Love is not blind, but prescient. *Journal of Personality and Social Psychology,* **71,** 1155–1180.

Murstein, B. I. (1971). Critique of models of dyadic attraction. In B. I. Murstein (Ed.) *Theories of attraction and love* (pp. 1–30). New York: Springer.

Murstein, B. I. (1987). A classification and extension of the SVR theory of dyadic pairing. *Journal of Marriage and the Family,* **42,** 777–792.

Myrdal, G. (1944). *An American dilemma.* New York: Harper & Row.

National Research Council (1989). *A common destiny: Blacks and American society.* Washington, DC: National Academy Press.

Neuberg, S. L., & Fiske, S. T. (1987). Motivational influences on impression formation: Outcome dependency, accuracy-driven attention, and individuating processes. *Journal of Personality and Social Psychology,* **53,** 431–444.

Newcomb, T. M. (1956). The prediction of interpersonal attraction. *American Psychologist,* **11,** 575–586.

Nicholson, J. H. (1998). *Sibling alliances.* Unpublished Ph.D. Thesis, University of Iowa.

Nisbett, R. E., & Ross, L. (1980). *Human inference: Strategies and shortcomings of social judgment.* Englewood Cliffs, NJ: Erlbaum.

Nisbett, R. E., Caputo, C., Legant, P., & Marecek, J. (1973). Behavior as seen by the actor and as seen by the observer. *Journal of Personality and Social Psychology*, **27**, 154–164.

Norman, C., & Aron, A. (1995, June). *The effect of exciting activities on relationships satisfaction: A laboratory experiment.* Paper presented at the International Network Conference on Personal Relationships, Williamsburg, VA.

Olson, D. H. (1977). Insiders' and outsiders' views of relationships: Research studies, *Close relationships: Perspectives on the meaning of intimacy* (pp. 115–135). Amherst: UMass Press.

Olson, D. H., Russell, C. S., & Sprenkle, D. H. (1983). Circumplex model of marital and family systems: VI. Theoretical update. *Family Process*, **22**, 69–83.

Omoto, A. M., & Gunn, D. O. (1994, May). *The effect of relationship closeness on encoding and recall for relationship-irrelevant information.* Paper presented at the May Meeting of the International Network on Personal Relationships, Iowa City, IA.

Orbell, J. M., Van de Kragt, A. J. C., & Dawes, R. M. (1988). Explaining discussion-induced cooperation. *Journal of Personality and Social Psychology*, **54**, 811–819.

Orden, S. R., & Bradburn, N. M. (1968). Dimensions of marriage happiness. *American Journal of Sociology*, **73**, 715–731.

Orpen, C. (1996). The effects of ingratiation and self-promotion tactics on employee career success. *Social Behavior and Personality*, **24**, 213–214.

Orthner, D. K. (1975). Leisure activity patterns and marital satisfaction over the marital career. *Journal of Marriage and the Family*, **37**, 91–101.

Osborne, R. E., & Gilbert, D. T. (1992). The preoccupational hazards of social life. *Journal of Personality and Social Psychology*, **62**, 219–228.

Page, J. R., Stevens, H. B., & Galvin, S. L. (1996). Relationships between depression, self-esteem, and self-silencing behavior. *Journal of Social and Clinical Psychology*, **15**, 381–396.

Panksepp, J., Siviy, S. M., & Normansell, L. A. (1985). Brain opioids and social emotions. In M. Reite & T. Field (Eds) *The psychobiology of attachment and separation* (pp. 3–50). London: Academic Press.

Parham, T. A. (1993). *Psychological storms: The African American struggle for identity.* Chacago: African American Images.

Parkes, C. M., Stevenson-Hinde, J., & Marris, P. (1991). *Attachment across the life cycle.* London: Tavistock/Routledge.

Parks, M. R., & Eggert, L. L. (1991). The role of social context in the dynamics of personal relationships, *Advances in personal relationships* (Vol. 2, pp. 1–34). London: Jessica Kingsley Publishers Ltd.

Parks, M. R., & Floyd, K. (1996). Meanings for closeness and intimacy in friendship. *Journal of Social and Personal Relationships*, **13**, 85–107.

Peeke, H. V. S., & Herz, M. J. (1973). *Habituation*. New York: Academic Press.

Penn, M. L., Gaines, S. O., Jr., & Phillips, L. (1993). On the desirability of own-group preference. *Journal of Black Psychology*, **19**, 303–321.

Pennebaker, J. W. (1997). *Opening up: The healing power of expressing emotions*. New York: Guilford Press.

Peplau, L. A., & Gordon, S. L. (1985). Woman and men in love: Gender differences in close heterosexual relationships. In V. E. O'Leary, R. K. Unger & B. S. Wallston (Eds) *Women, gender, and social psychology* (pp. 257–291). Hillsdale, NJ: Erlbaum.

Perlman, D. (1986, July). *Chance and coincidence in personal relationships*. Paper presented at the Third International Conference on Personal Relationships, Herzlia, Israel.

Perper, T., & Weis, D. L. (1987). Proceptive and rejective strategies of U.S. and Canadian women. *Journal of Sex Research*, **23**, 455–480.

Peterson, D. R. (1983). Conflict. In H. H. Kelley, E. Berscheid, A. Christensen, J. H. Harvey, T. L. Huston, G. Levinger, E. McClintock, L. A. Peplau & D. R. Peterson (Eds) *Close relationships* (pp. 360–396). New York: W. H. Freeman.

Pettigrew, T. F. (1988). Integration and pluralism. In P. A. Katz & D. A. Taylor (Eds) *Eliminating racism: Profiles in controversy* (pp. 19–30). New York: Plenum).

Phillips, L., Penn, M. L., & Gaines, S. O., Jr. (1993). A hermeneutic rejoinder to ourselves and our critics. *Journal of Black Psychology*, **19**, 350–357.

Phinney, J. S. (1995). Ethnic identity and self-esteem: A review and integration. In A. M. Padilla (Ed.) *Hispanic psychology: Critical issues in theory and research* (pp. 57–70). Thousand Oaks, CA: Sage.

Piaget, J. (1963). *The origins of intelligence in children* (M. Cook, Trans.). New York: Norton. (Original work published 1952).

Pinker, S. (1994). *The language instinct*. New York: William Morrow & Co.

Pinkney, A. (1993). *Black Americans*, 4th edn. Englewood Cliffs, NJ: Prentice Hall.

Pipp, S., Shaver, P., Jennings, S., Lamborn, S., & Fischer, K. W. (1985). Adolescents' theories about the development of their relationships with parents. *Journal of Personality and Social Psychology*, **48**, 991–1001.

Planalp, S., & Garvin-Doxas, K. (1994). Using mutual knowledge in conversation: Friends as experts on each other. In S. W. Duck (Ed.) *Dynamics of relationships* (pp. 1–26). Thousand Oaks, CA: Sage.

Plutchik, R. (1967). Marriage as dynamic equilibrium: Implications for research. In H. L. Silverman (Ed.) *Marital counseling: Psychology, ideology, science* (pp. 347–367). Springfield, IL: Charles C. Thomas.

Ponder, E., & Kennedy, W. P. (1927). On the act of blinking. *Quarterly Journal of Experimental Physiology*, **18**, 89–110.

Porterfield, E. (1978). *Black and White mixed marriages*. Chicago: Nelson-Hall.

Prager, K. J. (1995). *The psychology of intimacy*. New York: Guilford.

Prentice, D. A. (1990). Familiarity and differences in self- and other-representations. *Journal of Personality and Social Psychology*, **59**, 369–383.

Presser, H. B. (1975). Age differences between spouses: Trends, patterns, and social implications. *American Behavioral Scientist*, **19**, 190–205.

Pruitt, D. G., & Kimmel, M. J. (1977). Twenty years of experimental gaming: Critique, synthesis, and suggestions for the future. *Annual Review of Psychology*, **28**, 363–392.

Prusank, D., Duran, R., & DeLillo, D. A. (1993). Interpersonal relationships in women's magazines: Dating and relating in the 1970s and 1980s. *Journal of Social and Personal Relationships*, **10**, 307–320.

Quinsey, V. L., Chaplin, T. C., Maguire, A. M., & Upfold, D. (1987). The behavioral treatment of rapists and child molesters. In E. K. Morris & C. J. Braukmann (Eds) *Behavioral approaches to crime and delinquency: Application, research, and theory* (pp. 363–382). New York: Plenum.

Rajecki, D. W. (1985). Predictability and control in relationships: A perspective from animal behavior. In W. Ickes (Ed.) *Compatible and incompatible relationships* (pp. 11–31). New York: Springer-Verlag.

Rajecki, D. W., Bledsoe, S. B., & Rasmussen, J. L. (1991). Successful personal ads: Gender differences and similarities in offers, stipulations, and outcomes. *Basic and Applied Social Psychology*, **12**, 457–469.

Rapoport, A. (1966). *Two-person game theory*. Ann Arbor, MI: Univ. of Michigan.

Reedy, M. N., Birren, J. E., & Schaie, K. W. (1981). Age and sex differences in satisfying love relationships across the adult life span. *Human Development*, **24**, 52–66.

Reik, T. (1944). *A psychologist looks at love*. New York: Farrar & Reinhart.

Reis, H. T. (1998). The science of relationships grows up. *Contemporary Psychology*, **43**, 393–395.

Reis, H. T., & Patrick, B. C. (1996). Attachment and intimacy: Component processes. In E. T. Higgins & A. W. Kruglanski (Eds) *Social psychology: Handbook of basic principles* (pp. 523–563). New York: Guilford.

Reis, H. T., & Shaver, P. (1988). Intimacy as an interpersonal process. In S. W. Duck (Ed.) *Handbook of personal relationships: Theory, research, and interventions* (pp. 367–389). Chichester: Wiley.

Reis, H. T., & Wheeler, L. (1991). Studying social interaction with the Rochester Interaction Record. In *Advances in experimental social psychology*, **24**, 269–318. New York: Academic Press.

Reis, H. T., Nezlek, J., & Wheeler, L. (1980). Physical attractiveness in social interaction. *Journal of Personality and Social Psychology*, **38**, 604–17.

Reis, H. T., Senchak, M., & Solomon, B. (1985). Sex differences in the intimacy of social interaction: Further examination of potential explanations. *Journal of Personality and Social Psychology*, **48**, 1204–1217.

Reissman, C., Aron, A., & Bergen, M. R. (1993). Shared activities and marital satisfaction: Causal direction and self-expansion versus boredom. *Journal of Social and Personal Relationships*, **10**, 243–254.

Rempel, J. K., Holmes, J. G., & Zanna, M. P. (1985). Trust in close relationships. *Journal of Personality and Social Psychology*, **49**, 95–112.

Retzinger, S. M. (1995). Shame and anger in personal relationships. *Relationship challenges: Understanding relationship processes*, **5**, 22–42.

Revenstorf, D., Hahlweg, K., Schindler, L., & Kunert, H. (1984). The use of time series analysis in marriage counseling. In K. Hahlweg & N. S. Jacobson (Eds) *Marital interaction: Analysis and modification* (pp. 199–231). New York: Guilford.

Riesman, D., & Watson, J. (1964). The sociability project: A chronicle of frustration and achievement. In P. E. Hammond (Ed.) *Sociologists at work* (pp. 235–321). New York: Basic Books.

Riggio, R. E. (1986). Assessment of basic social skills. *Journal of Personality and Social Psychology*, **51**, 649–660.

Riordan, C. A., & Tedeschi, J. T. (1983). Attraction in aversive environments: Some evidence for classical conditioning and negative reinforcement. *Journal of Personality and Social Psychology*, **44**, 684–692.

Robertson, J. (1953). Some responses of young children to the loss of maternal care. *Nursing Times*, **49**, 382–386.

Robinson, W. S. (1950). Ecological correlations and the behavior of individuals. *American Sociological Review*, **15**, 351–357.

Robinson, W. S. (1957). The statistical measurement of agreement. *American Sociological Review*, 22, 17–25.

Rogers, C. (1970). *Carl Rogers on encounter groups*. New York: Harper & Row.

Rogers, T. B., Kuiper, N. A., & Kirker, W. S. (1977). Self-reference and the encoding of personal information. *Journal of Personality and Social Psychology*, **35**, 677–688.

Rollins, B., & Feldman, H. (1970). Marriage satisfaction over the family life cycle. *Journal of Marriage and the Family*, **32**, 20–28.

Roloff, M. E., & Cloven, D. H. (1994). When partners transgress: Maintaining violated relationships. In D. J. Canary & L. Stafford (Eds) *Communication and relational maintenance* (pp. 23–43). New York: Academic Press.

Rook, K. S. (1984). The negative side of social interaction: Impact on psychological well-being. *Journal of Personality and Social Psychology*, **46**, 1097–1108.

Rosenblatt, P. C. (1983). *Bitter, bitter tears: Nineteenth-century diarists and twentieth-century grief theorists*. Minneapolis: University of Minnesota Press.

Rosenblatt, P. C., Karis, T. A., & Powell, R. D. (1995). *Multiracial couples: Black and White voices*. Thousand Oaks, CA: Sage.

Rosenfeld, L. B., & Bowen, G. L. (1991). Marital disclosure and marital satisfaction: Direct-effect versus interaction effect models. *Western Journal of Speech Communication*, **55**, 69–84.

Rosner, B. (1982). On the estimation and testing of interclass correlations: The general case of multiple replicates for each variable. *American Journal of Epidemiology*, **116**, 722–730.

Ross, L. (1977). The intuitive psychologist and his shortcomings: Distortions in the attribution process. In L. Berkowitz (Ed.) *Advances in experimental social psychology* (Vol. 10, pp. 173–220). New York: Academic Press.

Rotter, J. B. (1954). *Social learning and clinical psychology*. Englewood Cliffs, NJ: Prentice Hall.

Rowatt, W. C., & Cunningham, M. R. (1997, August). *Impression management for relationship partners: The psychology of other-monitoring*. Paper presented at the meeting of the American Psychological Association, Chicago.

Rubenstein, J. (1973). *City police*. New York: Ferrar, Strauss, & Giroux.

Rubin, L. B. (1985). *Just friends: The role of friendship in our everyday lives*. New York: Harper & Row.

Rudman, L. A. (1998). Self-promotion as a risk factor for women: The costs and benefits of counterstereotypical impression management. *Journal of Personality and Social Psychology*, **74**, 629–645.

Runciman, W. G. (1966). *Relative deprivation and social justice*. Berkeley, CA: University of California Press.

Rusbult, C. E. (1983). A longitudinal test of the investment model: The development (and deterioration) of satisfaction and commitment in heterosexual involvements. *Journal of Personality and Social Psychology*, **45**, 101–117.

Rusbult, C. E. (1991). Comment on Johnson's "Commitment to personal relationships": What's interesting, and what's new? In W. H. Jones & D. Perlman (Eds) *Advances in personal relationships* (Vol. 3, pp. 151–169). London: Kingsley.

Rusbult, C., & Arriaga, X. (1997). Interdependence and personal relationships. In S. W. Duck (Ed.) with K. Dindia, W. Ickes, R. M. Milardo, R. S. L. Mills & B. Sarason, *Handbook of personal relationships*, 2nd edn (pp. 221–250). Chichester, UK: Wiley.

Rusbult, C. E., & Buunk, B. P. (1993). Commitment processes in close relationships: An interdependence analysis. *Journal of Social and Personal Relationships*, **10**, 175–204.

Rusbult, C. E., & Martz, J. M. (1995). Remaining in an abusive relationship: An investment model analysis of nonvoluntary commitment. *Personality and Social Psychology Bulletin*, **21**, 558–571.

Rusbult, C. E., & Van Lange, P. A. M. (1996). Interdependence processes. In E. T. Higgins & A. Kruglanski (Eds) *Social psychology: Handbook of basic principles* (pp. 564–596). New York: Guilford.

Rusbult, C. E., Van Lange, P. A. M., Yovetich, N. A., Wildschut, R. T., & Verette, J. (1999). *A functional analysis of positive illusion in close relationships*. Unpublished manuscript, University of North Carolina at Chapel Hill, Chapel Hill, NC.

Rusbult, C. E., Verette, J., Whitney, G. A., Slovik, L. F., & Lipkus, I. (1991). Accommodation processes in close relationships: Theory and preliminary empirical evidence. *Journal of Personality and Social Psychology*, **60**, 53–78.

Rusbult, C. E., Yovetich, N. A., & Verette, J. (1996). An interdependence analysis of accommodation processes. In G. J. O. Fletcher & J. Fitness (Eds) *Knowledge structures in close relationships: A social psychological approach* (pp. 91–120). Mahwah, NJ: Erlbaum.

Rushton, J. P. (1989a). Genetic similarity, human altruism, and group selection. *Behavioral and Brain Sciences*, **12**, 503–559.

Rushton, J. P. (1989b). Genetic similarity in male friendships. *Ethology and Sociobiology*, **10**, 137–149.

Sabatelli, R. (1984). The marital comparison level index: A measure for assessing outcomes relative to expectations. *Journal of Marriage and the Family*, **46**, 651–661.

Sadalla, E. K., Kenrick, D. T., & Vershure, B. (1987). Dominance and heterosexual attraction. *Journal of Personality and Social Psychology*, **52**, 730–738.

Samovar, L. A., & Porter, R. E. (1995). *Communication between cultures*. Belmont, CA: Wadsworth.

Sande, G. N., Goethals, G. R., & Radloff, C. E. (1988). Perceiving one's own traits and others': The multifaceted self. *Journal of Personality and Social Psychology*, **54**, 13–20.

Sanford, M. D. (1959). *Mollie: The journal of Mollie Dorsey Sanford in Nebraska and Colorado Territories, 1857–1866*. Lincoln: University of Nebraska Press.

Sanjek, R. (1994). Intermarriage and the future of races in the United States. In S. Gregory & R. Sanjek (Eds) *Race* (pp. 103–130). New Brunswick, NJ: Rutgers University Press.

Sarason, B. R., Sarason, I. G., & Gurung, R. A. R. (1997). Close personal relationships and health outcomes: A key to the role of social support. In S. W. Duck (Ed.) *Handbook of personal relationships*, 2nd edn (pp. 547–574). Chichester UK: Wiley.

Satir, V. (1967). *Conjoint family therapy*. Palo Alto, CA: Science and Behaviour Books.

Scanzoni, L. D., & Scanzoni, J. (1981). *Men, women and change*, 2nd edn. New York: McGraw-Hill.

Scheflen, A. E. (1974). *How behavior means*. Garden City, NJ: Anchor.

Schellenberg, J. A. (1978). *Masters of social psychology: Freud, Mead, Lewin, and Skinner*. Oxford: Oxford University Press.

Schlenker, B. R. (1975). Self-presentation: Managing the impression of consistency when reality interferes with self-enhancement. *Journal of Personality and Social Psychology*, **32**, 1030–1037.

Schlenker, B. R. (1980). *Impression management: The self-concept, social identity and interpersonal relations*. Monterey, CA; Brooks/Cole.

Schlenker, B. R. (1985). Identity and self-identification. In B. R. Schlenker (Ed.) *The self and social life* (pp. 65–99). New York: McGraw-Hill.

Schlenker, B. R. (1986). Self-identification: Toward an integration of the private and public self. In R. F. Baumeister (Ed.) *Public self and private self* (pp. 21–62). New York: Springer-Verlag.

Schlenker, B. R., & Leary, M. R. (1982). Audiences' reactions to self-enhancing, self-denigrating, accurate, and modest self-presentations. *Journal of Experimental Social Psychology*, **18**, 89–104.

Schlenker, B. R., & Weigold, M. F. (1992). Interpersonal processes involving impression regulation and management. *Annual Review of Psychology*, **43**, 133–168.

Schlenker, B. R., Dlugolecki, D. W & Doherty, K. (1994). The impact of self-presentations on self-appraisals and behavior: The power of public commitment. *Personality and Social Psychology Bulletin*, **20**, 20–33.

Schneider, D. J. (1969). Tactical self-presentation after success and failure. *Journal of Personality and Social Psychology*, **13**, 262–268.

Schreindorfer, L. S., Leary, M. R., & Keith, J. M. (1998). *In pursuit of acceptance: Interpersonal strategies and consequences of seeking inclusion vs. avoiding exclusion*. Manuscript under review, Wake Forest University.

Schutz, A. (1970). *On phenomenology and social relations*. Chicago: Chicago University Press.

Scott, C. K., Fuhrman, R. W., & Wyer, R. S., Jr. (1991). Information processing in close relationships. In G. J. O. Fletcher & F. D. Fincham (Eds). *Cognition and close relationships* (pp. 37–68). Hillsdale, NJ: Erlbaum.

Secord, P. F. (1983). Imbalanced sex ratios: The social consequences. *Personality and Social Psychology Bulletin*, **9**, 525–543.

Sedikides, C., Campbell, W. K., Reeder, G. D., & Elliot, A. J. (1998). The self-serving bias in relational context. *Journal of Personality and Social Psychology*, **74**, 378–386.

Sedikides, C., Olsen, N., & Reis, H. T. (1993). Relationships as natural categories. *Journal of Personality and Social Psychology*, **64**, 71–82.

Segal, N. (1988). Cooperation, competition, and altruism in human twinships: A sociobiological approach. In K. B. MacDonald (Ed.) *Sociobiological perspectives on human development* (pp. 168–206). New York: Springer-Verlag.

Segrin, C. (in press). Mental health and problematic personal relationships. In K. Dindia & S. W. Duck (Eds) *Communication and personal relationships*. Wiley: Chichester.

Shaffer, D. R., Pegalis, L. J., & Bazzini, D. G. (1996). When boy meets girl (revisited): Gender, gender-role orientation, and prospect of future interaction as determinants of self-disclosure among same- and opposite-sex acquaintances. *Personality and Social Psychology Bulletin*, **22**, 495–506.

Shaver, P. & Rubenstein, C. (1983). Research potential of magazine and newspaper surveys. In H. T. Reis (Ed.) *New directions for methodology of social and behavioral science: Naturalistic approaches to studying social interaction*, **15**, 75–92. San Francisco: Jossey-Bass.

Shaver, P. R., & Hazan, C. (1988). A biased overview of the study of love. *Journal of Social and Personal Relationships*, **5**, 473–501.

Shaver, P. R., & Hazan, C. (1993). Adult romantic attachment: Theory and evidence. In D. Perlman & W. Jones (Eds) *Advances in personal relationships: A research annual* (Vol. 4, pp. 29–70). London: Jessica Kingsley Publishers.

Shaver, P. R., Hazan, C., & Bradshaw, D. (1988). Love as attachment: The integration of three behavioral systems. In R. J. Sternberg & M. L. Barnes (Eds) *The psychology of love* (pp. 68–99). New Haven, CT: Yale University Press.

Shaver, P., Schwartz. J., Kirson, D., O'Connor, C. (1987). Emotion knowledge: Further exploration of a prototype approach. *Journal of Personality and Social Psychology*, **52**, 1061–1086.

Shepher, J. (1971). Mate selection among second generation kibbutz adolescents and adults: Incest avoidance and negative imprinting. *Archives of
Sexual Behavior*, **1**, 293–307.

Short, R. V. (1979). Sexual selection and its component parts: Somatic and
genital selection as illustrated in man and the great apes. *Advances in the
study of behavior*, **9**, 131–155.

Shotter, J. (1992). What is a "personal" relationship? A rhetorical-responsive
account of "unfinished business". In *Attributions, accounts and close relationships* (pp. 19–39). New York: Springer-Verlag.

Shrout, P. E., & Fleiss, J. L. (1979). Intraclass correlations: Uses in assessing
rater reliability. *Psychological Bulletin*, **86**, 420–428.

Sigelman, L., & Welch, S. (1994). *Black Americans' views of racial inequality:
The dream deferred*. Cambridge: Cambridge University Press.

Sillars, A. L., Folwell, A. L., Hill, K. C., Maki, B. K., Hurst, A. P., & Casano,
R. A. (1994). Marital communication and the persistence of misunderstanding. *Journal of Social and Personal Relationships*, **11**, 611–617.

Silver, R. (1978). The parental behavior of ring doves. *American Scientist*, **66**,
209–215.

Simmel, G. (1950). *The sociology of Georg Simmel*. New York: Free Press.

Simon, H. A. (1990). A mechanism for social selection and successful altruism. *Science*, **250**, 1665–1668.

Simpson, G. E., & Yinger, J. M. (1985). *Racial and cultural minorities: An
analysis of prejudice and discrimination*, 5th edn. New York: Plenum.

Simpson, J. A. (1987). The dissolution of romantic relationships: Factors involved in relationship stability and emotional distress. *Journal of Personality and Social Psychology*, **53**, 683–692.

Simpson, J. A. (1990). The influence of attachment styles on romantic relationships. *Journal of Personality and Social Psychology*, **59**, 971–980.

Simpson, J. A., & Gangestad, S. W. (1991). Individual differences in sociosexuality: Evidence for convergent and discriminant validity *Journal of Personality and Social Psychology*, **60**, 870–883.

Simpson, J. A., & Gangestad, S. W. (1992). Sociosexuality and romantic partner choice. *Journal of Personality*, **60**, 31–51.

Simpson, J. A., Gangestad, S. W., & Lerma, M. (1990). Perception of physical
attractiveness: Mechanisms involved in the maintenance of romantic relationships. *Journal of Personality and Social Psychology*, **59**, 1192–1201.

Simpson, J. A., Rholes, W. S., & Nelligan, J. S. (1992). Support seeking and
support giving within couples in an anxiety-provoking situation: The role of
attachment styles. *Journal of Personality and Social Psychology*, **62**, 434–
446.

Singh, D. (1993). Adaptive significance of female physical attractiveness: Role
of waist-to-hip ratio. *Journal of Personality and Social Psychology*, **65**, 293–
307.

Sivadas, E., & Machleit, K. A. (1994). A scale to determine the extent of
object incorporation in the extended self. *American Marketing Association*,
5, 143–149.

Smith, E., & Henry, S. (1996). An in-group becomes part of the self: Response time evaluation. *Personality and Social Psychology Bulletin*, **22**, 635–642.

Smith, J. L., Berry, N. J., & Whiteley, P. (1997). The effect of interviewer guise upon gender self-report responses as a function of interviewee's self-monitoring position. *European Journal of Social Psychology*, **27**, 237–243.

Snyder, M. (1984). When belief creates reality. In L. Berkowitz (Ed.) *Advances in experimental social psychology* (Vol. 18, pp. 247–305). New York: Academic Press.

Snyder, M., & Ickes, W. (1985). Personality and social behavior. In G. Lindzey & E. Aronson (Eds) *The handbook of social psychology*, 3rd edn (Vol. 2, pp. 883–947). New York: Random House.

Snyder, M., & Simpson, J. A. (1984). Self-monitoring and dating relationships. *Journal of Personality and Social Psychology*, **47**, 1281–1291.

Snyder, M., Tanke, E., & Berscheid, E. (1977). Social perception and interpersonal behavior: On the self-fulfilling nature of social stereotypes. *Journal of Personality and Social Psychology*, **35**, 656–666.

Solomon, R. L. (1980). The opponent-process theory of acquired motivation: The costs of pleasure and the benefits of pain. *American Psychologist*, **35**, 691–712.

Sorrentino, R. M., Holmes, J. G., Hanna, S. E., & Sharp, A. (1995). Uncertainty orientation and trust in close relationships: Individual differences in cognitive styles. *Journal of Personality and Social Psychology*, **68**, 314–327.

Spanier, G. (1976). Measuring dyadic adjustment: New scales for assessing the quality of marriage and similar dyads. *Journal of Marriage and the Family*, **38**, 15–28.

Spence, J., Helmreich, R., & Stapp, J. (1975). Ratings of self and peers on sex role attributes and their relation to self-esteem and conceptions of masculinity and femininity. *Journal of Personality and Social Psychology*, **32**, 29–39.

Spickard, P. R. (1989). *Mixed blood: Intermarriage and ethnic identity in twentieth-century America*. Madison, WI: University of Wisconsin Press.

Spigner, C. C. (1994). Black/White interracial marriages: A brief overview of U.S. Census data, 1980–1987. In R. Staples (Ed.) *The Black family: Essays and studies*, 5th edn (pp. 149–152). Belmont, CA: Wadsworth.

Spitz, R. A. (1946). Anaclitic depression. *Psychoanalytic Study of the Child*, **2**, 313–342.

Sprecher, S. (1985). Sex differences in bases of power in dating relationships. *Sex Roles*, **12**, 449–462.

Sprecher, S., & Metts, S. (1989). Development of the "Romantic Beliefs Scale" and examination of the effects of gender and gender-role orientation. *Journal of Social and Personal Relationships*, **6**, 387–411.

Sprecher, S., Aron, A., Hatfield, E., Cortese, A., Potapova, E., & Levitskaya, A. (1994). Love: American style, Russian style, and Japanese style. *Personal Relationships*, **1**, 349–369.

Sroufe, L. A., & Fleeson, J. (1986). Attachment and the construction of relationships. In W. W. Hartup & Z. Rubin (Eds) *Relationships and development* (pp. 51–72). Hillsdale, NJ: Lawrence Erlbaum Associates.

Sroufe, L. A., & Waters, E. (1977). Attachment as an organizational construct. *Child Development*, **48**, 1184–1199.

Stack, S. (1980). The effects of marital dissolution on suicide. *Journal of Marriage and the Family*, **42**, 83–91.

Stack, S. (1981). Divorce and suicide: A time series analysis, 1933–1970. *Journal of Family Issues*, **2**, 77–90.

Stack, S. (1989). The impact of divorce on suicide in Norway, 1951–1980. *Journal of Marriage and the Family*, **51**, 229–238.

Stafford, L., & Canary, D. J. (1991). Maintenance strategies and romantic relationship type, gender, and relational characteristics. *Journal of Social and Personal Relationships*, **8**, 263–275.

Staples, R. (1994). Interracial relationships: A convergence of desire and opportunity. In R. Staples (Ed.) *The Black family: Essays and studies*, 5th edn (pp. 142–149). Belmont, CA: Wadsworth.

Staples, R., & Mirande, A. (1980). Racial and cultural variations among American families: A decennial review of the literature. *Journal of Marriage and the Family*, **42**, 887–903.

Stein, C. H. (1993). Felt obligation in adult family relationships. In S. W. Duck (Ed.) *Understanding relationship processes 3: Social contexts of relationships* (pp. 78–99). Thousand Oaks: Sage.

Stein, C. H., Bush, E. G., Ross, R. R., & Ward, M. (1992). Mine, yours, and ours: A configural analysis of the networks of married couples in relation to marital satisfaction and individual well-being. *Journal of Social and Personal Relationships*, **9**, 365–383.

Stein, J. (1982). *Edie: An American biography*. New York: Dell.

Steiner, I. D. (1974). Whatever happened to the group in social psychology? *Journal of Experimental Social Psychology*, **10**, 94–108.

Steiner, I. D. (1986). Paradigms and groups. In L. Berkowitz (Ed.) *Advances in experimental social psychology* (Vol. 19, pp. 251–289). New York: Academic Press.

Stephan, W. G. (1985). Intergroup relations. In G. Lindzey & E. Aronson (Eds) *Handbook of social psychology*, 3rd edn (Vol. 2, pp. 599–638). New York: Random House.

Stern, D. N. (1977). *The first relationship: Mother and infant*. Cambridge, MA: Harvard University Press.

Sternberg, R. J., & Barnes, M. L. (1985). Real and ideal others in romantic relationships: Is four a crowd? *Journal of Personality and Social Psychology*, **49**, 1586–1608.

Stevens, C. K., & Kristof, A. L. (1995). Making the right impression: A field study of applicant impression management during job interviews. *Journal of Applied Psychology*, **80**, 587– 606.

Stinson, L., & Ickes, W. (1992). Empathic accuracy in the interactions of male friends versus male strangers. *Journal of Personality and Social Psychology*, **62**, 787–797.

Stires, L. D., & Jones, E. E. (1969). Modesty vs. self-enhancement as alternative forms of ingratiation. *Journal of Experimental Social Psychology*, **5**, 172–188.

Stone, L. (1988). Passionate attachments in the West in historical perspective. In W. Gaylin & E. Person (Eds) *Passionate attachments* (pp. 15–26). New York: Free Press.

Strachan, C. E., & Dutton, D. G. (1992). The role of power and gender in anger responses to sexual jealousy. *Journal of Applied Social Psychology*, **22**, 1721–1740.

Strahan, R. (1974). Situational dimensions of self-reported nervousness. *Journal of Personality Assessment*, **38**, 341–352.

Stroebe, W. (1980). Process loss in social psychology: Failure to exploit? In R. Gilmour & S. W. Duck (Eds) *The development of social psychology* (pp. 181–208). London: Academic Press.

Strube, M. J. (1988). The decision to leave an abusive relationship: Empirical evidence and theoretical issues. *Psychological Bulletin*, **104**, 236–250.

Studd, M. V., & Gattiker, U. E. (1991). The evolutionary psychology of sexual harassment in organizations. *Ethology and Sociobiology*, **12**, 247–290.

Suls, J. (1977). Gossip as social comparison. *Journal of Communication*, **27**, 164–168.

Suomi, S. J. (1982). Sibling relationships in nonhuman primates. In M. E. Lamb & B. Sutton-Smith (Eds) *Sibling relationships*. Hillsdale, NJ: Erlbaum.

Surra, C. A. (1987). Reasons for changes in committment: Variations by courtship type. *Journal of Social and Personal Relationships*, **4**, 17–33.

Surra, C. A., & Longstreth, M. (1990). Similarity of outcomes, interdependence, and conflict in dating relationships. *Journal of Personality and Social Psychology*, **59**, 501–516.

Surra, C. A., & Ridley, C. A. (1991). Multiple perspectives on interaction: Participants, peers, and observers. In B. M. Montgomery & S. W. Duck (Eds) *Studying interpersonal interaction* (pp. 35–55). New York: Guilford.

Surra, C. A., Arizzi, P., & Asmussen, L. (1988). The association between reasons for commitment and the development and outcome of marital relationships. *Journal of Social and Personal Relationships*, **5**, 47–63.

Swann, W. B., Jr. (1983). Self-aggrandisement: Bringing social reality into harmony with the self. In J. Suls & A. G. Greenwald (Eds) *Social psychology perspectives* (Vol 2, pp. 33–66). Hillsdale, NJ: Erlbaum.

Swann, W. B., Jr., De La Ronde, C., & Hixon, J. G. (1994). Authenticity and positivity strivings in marriage and courtship. *Journal of Personality and Social Psychology*, **66**, 857–869.

Swann, W. B., Jr., Stein-Seroussi, A., & Giesler, R. B. (1992). Why people self-verify. *Journal of Personality and Social Psychology*, **62**, 392–401.

Symons, D. (1979). *The evolution of human sexuality*. New York: Oxford University Press.

Tajfel, H. (1979). Individuals and groups in social psychology. *British Journal of Social Psychology*, **18**, 183–190.

Tajfel, H., & Turner, J. C. (1979). An integrative theory of intergroup conflict. In W. G. Austin & S. Worchel (Eds) *The social psychology of intergroup relations* (pp. 33–47). Monterey, CA: Brooks/Cole.

Tangney, J. P., & Fischer, K. W. (Eds) (1995). *Self-conscious emotions*. New York: Guilford.

Tangney, J. P., Miller, R. S., Flicker, L., & Barlow, D. H. (1996). Are shame, guilt, and embarrassment distinct emotions? *Journal of Personality and Social Psychology*, **70**, 1256–1264.

Tardy, C. H., & Hosman, L. A. (1991). Experimentation. In B. M. Montgomery & S. W. Duck (Eds) *Studying interpersonal relationships* (pp. 219–35). New York: Guilford Press.

Taylor, D. A., & Altman, I. (1987). Communication in interpersonal relationships: Social penetration processes. In M. Roloff & G. Miller (Eds) *Interpersonal processes: New directions in communication research* (pp. 257–277). Newbury Park, CA: Sage.

Taylor, D. A., & Katz, P. A. (1988). Conclusion. In P. A. Katz & D. A. Taylor (Eds) *Eliminating racism: Profiles in controversy* (pp. 359–369). New York: Plenum.

Taylor, D. A., Altman, I., & Wheeler, L. (1972). Self-disclosure in isolated groups. *Journal of Personality and Social Psychology*, **26**, 39–47.

Taylor, D. M., & Moghaddam, F. M. (1994). *Theories of intergroup relations: International social psychological perspectives*, 2nd edn. Westport, CT: Praeger.

Taylor, S. (1998). The social being in social psychology. In D. T. Gilbert, S. F. Fiske & G. Lindzey (Eds) *The handbook of social psychology*, 4th edn (Vol. 1, pp. 58–95). Boston: McGraw-Hill.

Taylor, S. E. (1991). Asymmetrical effects of positive and negative events: The mobilization-minimization hypothesis. *Psychological Bulletin*, **110**, 67–85.

Taylor, S. E., & Brown, J. D. (1988). Illusion and well-being: A social psychological perspective on mental health. *Psychological Bulletin*, **103**, 193–210.

Teger, A. I. (1980). *Too much invested to quit*. New York: Pergamon.

Tennov, D. (1979). *Love and limerence: The experience of being in love*. New York: Stein & Day.

Terkel, S. (1991). *Race: How Blacks and Whites think and feel about the American obsession*. New York: Anchor Books.

Tesser, A. (1988). Toward a self-evaluation maintenance model of social behavior. In L. Berkowitz (Ed.) *Advances in experimental social psychology* (Vol. 11, pp. 288–338). San Diego, CA: Academic Press.

Thibaut, J. W., & Kelley, H. H. (1959). *The social psychology of groups*. New York: Wiley.

Thibaut, J., & Faucheux, C. (1965). The development of contractual norms in a bargaining situation under two types of stress. *Journal of Experimental Social Psychology*, **1**, 89–102.

Thibaut, J., & Gruder, C. L. (1969). Formation of contractual agreements between parties of unequal power. *Journal of Personality and Social Psychology*, **11**, 59–65.

Thibaut, J., & Walker, L. (1975). *Procedural justice: A psychological analysis*. New York: Wiley.

Thiessen, D., Young, R. K., & Burroughs, R. (1993). Lonely hearts advertisments reflect sexually dimorphic mating strategies. *Ethology and Sociobiology*, **14**, 209–229.

Thomas, G., Fletcher, G. J. O., & Lange, C. (1997). On-line empathic accuracy in marital interaction. *Journal of Personality and Social Psychology*, **72**, 839–850.

Thompson, J. M. (1995). Silencing the self: Depressive symptomatology and close relationships. *Psychology of Women Quarterly*, **19**, 337–353.

Thornhill, R., & Gangestad, S. W. (1994). Human fluctuating asymmetry and sexual behavior. *Psychological Science*, **5**, 297–302.

Thornhill, R., & Thornhill, N. W. (1989). The evolution of psychological pain. In R. W. Bell & N. J. Bell (Eds) *Sociobiology and the social sciences* (pp. 73–103). Lubbock: Texas Tech University Press.

Tice, D. M., Butler, J. L., Muraven, M. B., & Stillwell, A. M. (1995). When modesty prevails: Differential favorability of self-presentation to friends and strangers. *Journal of Personality and Social Psychology*, **69**, 1120–1138.

Timmer, S. G., Veroff, J., & Hatchett, S. (1996). Family ties and marital happiness: the different marital experiences of black and white newlywed couples. *Journal of Social and Personal Relationships*, **13**, 335–359.

Tjosvold, D. (1981). Unequal power relationships within a cooperative or competitive context. *Journal of Applied Social Psychology*, **11**, 137–150.

Todd, J., McKinney, J. L., Harris, R., Chadderton, R., & Small, L. (1992). Attitudes toward interracial dating: Effects of age, sex, and race. *Journal of Multicultural Counseling and Development*, **20**, 202–208.

Tooby, J., & Cosmides, L. (1992). The psychological foundations of culture. In J. H. Barkow, L. Cosmides & J. Tooby (Eds) *The adapted mind: Evolutionary psychology and the generation of culture* (pp. 19–136). New York: Oxford University Press.

Tooke, W., & Camire, L. (1991). Patterns of deception in intersexual and intrasexual mating strategies. *Ethology and Sociobiology*, **12**, 345–364.

Townsend, J. M. (1993). Sexuality and partner selection: Sex differences among college students. *Ethology and Sociobiology*, **14**, 305–330.

Traupmann, J., & Hatfield, E. (1981). Love and its effect on mental and physical health. In J. March, S. Kiesler, R. Fogel, E. Hatfield & E. Shana (Eds) *Aging: Stability and change in the family* (pp. 253–274). New York: Academic Press.

Trevarthen, C. (1979). Communication and cooperation in early infancy: a description of primary intersubjectivity. In M. Bullowa (Ed.), *Before Speech: The Beginnings of Human Communication.* Cambridge: Cambridge University Press.

Triandis, H. C. (1988). The future of pluralism revisited. In P. A. Katz & D. A. Taylor (Eds) *Eliminating racism: Profiles in controversy* (pp. 31–50). New York: Plenum.

Triandis, H. C. (1990). Cross-cultural studies of individualism and collectivism. *Nebraska symposium on motivation*, **39**, 41–133.

Trivers, R. L. (1972). Parental investment and sexual selection. In B. Campbell (Ed.) *Sexual selection and the descent of man 1871–1971* (pp. 136–179). Chicago: Aldine.

Trivers, R. L. (1985). *Social evolution.* Menlo Park, CA: Benjamin/Cummings Publishing.

Trovato, E. (1986). The relation between marital dissolution and suicide: The Canadian case. *Journal of Marriage and the Family,* **48**, 341–348.

Trovato, E. (1987). A longitudinal analysis of divorce and suicide in Canada. *Journal of Marriage and the Family,* **49**, 193–203.

Trovato, E., & Lauris, G. (1989). Marital status and mortality in Canada: 1951–1981. *Journal of Marriage and the Family,* **51**, 907–922.

Tucker, M. B., & Mitchell-Kernan, C. (1995). Social structural and psychological correlates of interethnic dating. *Journal of Social and Personal Relationships,* **12**, 341–361.

Tucker, P., & Aron, A. (1993). Passionate love and marital satisfaction at key transition points in the family life cycle. *Journal of Social and Clinical Psychology,* **12**, 135–147.

U.S. Bureau of the Census (1994). *Statistical abstract of the United States: 1994.* Washington, DC: U.S. Department of Commerce.

van Dijk, T. A. (1993). *Elite discourse and racism.* Newbury Park, CA. Sage.

Van Lange, P. A. M., & Rusbult, C. E. (1995). My relationship is better than—and not as bad as—yours is: The perception of superiority in close relationships. *Personality and Social Psychology Bulletin,* **21**, 32–44.

Van Lange, P. A. M., Agnew, C. R., Harinck, F., & Steemers, G. E. M. (1997). From game theory to real life: How social value orientation affects willingness to sacrifice in ongoing close relationships. *Journal of Personality and Social Psychology,* **73**, 1330–1344.

Van Lange, P. A. M., Rusbult, C. E., Drigotas, S. M., Arriaga, X. B., Witcher, B. S., & Cox, C. L. (1997). Willingness to sacrifice in close relationships. *Journal of Personality and Social Psychology,* **72**, 1373–1395.

Veith, J. L., Buck, M., Getzlaf, S., Van Dalfsen, P., & Slade, S. (1983). Exposure to men influences the occurrence of ovulation in women. *Physiology and Behavior,* **31**, 313–315.

Villanova, P., & Bernardin, H. J. (1989). Impression management in the context of performance appraisal. In R. A. Giacalone & P. Rosenfeld (Eds) *Impression management in the organization* (pp. 299–313). Hillsdale, NJ: Lawrence Erlbaum Associates.

von Baeyer, C. L., Sherk, D. L., & Zanna, M. P. (1981). Impression management in the job interview: When the female applicant meets the male (chauvinist) interviewer. *Personality and Social Psychology Bulletin,* **7**, 45–51.

Vorauer, J. D., & Miller, D. T. (1997). Failure to recognize the effect of implicit social influence on the presentation of self. *Journal of Personality and Social Psychology,* **73**, 281–295.

Vormbrock, J. K. (1993). Attachment theory as applied to war-time and job-related marital separation. *Psychological Bulletin,* **114**, 122–144.

Vuorenkowski, V., Wasz-Hockert, O., Koivisto, E., & Lind, J. (1969). The effect of cry stimulus on the lactating breast of primipara: A thermographic study. *Experientia,* **25**, 1286–1287.

Wallach, M. A., & Wallach, L. (1983). *Psychology's sanction for selfishness: The error of egoism in theory and therapy*. San Francisco: W. H. Freeman.

Waller, W. (1938). *The family: A dynamic interpretation*. New York: Dryden.

Walster, E. (1965). The effect of self-esteem on romantic liking. *Journal of Personality and Social Psychology*, **1**, 184–197.

Walster, E., & Walster, G. W. (1963). Effect of expecting to be liked on choice of associates. *Journal of Personality and Social Psychology*, **67**, 402–404.

Walster, E., Berscheid, E., & Walster, G. W. (1976). New directions in equity research. In L. Berkowitz & E. Walster (Eds) *Advances in experimental social psychology* (Vol. 9, pp. 1–42). New York: Academic Press.

Walster, E., Walster, G. W., Piliavin, J., & Schmidt, L. (1973). "Playing hard to get": Understanding an elusive phenomenon. *Journal of Personality and Social Psychology*, **26**, 113–121.

Walters, R. W. (1993). *Pan Africanism in the African Diaspora: An analysis of modern Afrocentric political movements*. Detroit: Wayne State University Press.

Warner, R. R. (1984). Mating behavior and hermaphroditism in coral reef fishes. *American Scientist*, **72**, 128–134.

Watzlawick, P., Beavin, J., & Jackson, D. (1967). *Pragmatics of human communication: A study of interactional patterns, pathologies and paradoxes*. New York: Norton.

Wegner, D. M. (1980). The self in prosocial action. In D. M. Wegner & R. R. Vallacher (Eds) *The self in social psychology* (pp. 131–157). New York: Oxford University Press.

Wegner, D. M., & Gold, D. B. (1995). Fanning old flames: Emotional and cognitive effects of suppressing thoughts of a past relationship. *Journal of Personality and Social Psychology*, **68**, 782–792.

Wegner, D. M., & Lane, J. D. (1995). From secrecy to psychopathology. In J. W. Pennebaker (Ed.) *Emotion, disclosure and health* (pp. 25–46). Washington, DC: American Psychological Association.

Wegner, D. M., Giuliano, T., & Hertel, P. T. (1985). Cognitive interdependence in close relationships. *Compatible and incompatible relationships* (pp. 253–276). New York: Springer-Verlag.

Wegner, D. M., Lane, J. D., & Dimitri, S. (1994). The allure of secret relationships. *Journal of Personality and Social Psychology*, **66**, 287–300.

Weick, K. (1968). Systematic observational methods. In G. Lindzey & E. Aronson (Eds) *The handbook of social psychology*, 2nd edn (Vol. 11, pp 357–451). Reading, MA: Addison-Wesley.

Weiner, B. (1986). *An attributional theory of motivation and emotion*. New York: Springer-Verlag.

Weiss, R. S. (1973). *Loneliness: The experience of emotional and social isolation*. Cambridge, MA: MIT Press.

Weiss, R. S. (1975). *Marital separation*. New York: Basic Books.

Weiss, R. S. (1982). Attachment in adult life. In C. M. Parkes & J. Stevenson-Hinde (Eds) *The place of attachment in human behavior* (pp. 171–184). New York: Basic Books.

Weiss, R. S. (1988). Loss and recovery. *Journal of Social Issues*, **44**, 37–52.

Wellman, B. (1985). Domestic work, paid work and net work. In S. W. Duck & D. Perlman (Eds) *Understanding personal relationships*. Beverly Hills: Sage.

Werking, K. (1997). *Just good friends: Cross-sex friendships*. New York: Guilford Press.

Werner, C., Altman, I., Brown, B., & Ginat, J. (1993). Celebrations in personal relationships: A transactional/dialectical perspective. *Social contexts of relationships* [*Understanding Relationship Processes*], **3**, 109–138.

West, C. (1993). *Race Matters*. Boston: Beacon.

Weston, K. (1991). *Families we choose*. New York: Columbia University Press.

Wetzel, C. G., & Insko, C. A. (1982). The similarity-attraction relationship: Is there an ideal one? *Journal of Experimental Social Psychology*, **18**, 253–276.

Wheeler, L., & Miyake, K. (1992). Social comparison in everyday life. *Journal of Personality and Social Psychology*, **62**, 760–773.

Wheeler, L., & Nezlek, J. (1977). Sex differences in social participation. *Journal of Personality and Social Psychology*, **35**, 742–754.

Wheeler, L., & Reis, H. T. (1991). Self-recording of everyday life events: Origins, types, and uses. *Journal of Personality*, **59**, 339–354.

Wheeler, L., Reis, H. T., & Nezlek, J. (1983). Loneliness, social interaction, and sex roles. *Journal of Personality and Social Psychology*, **45**, 943–953.

Whitam, F. L., Diamond, M., & Martin, J. (1993). Homosexual orientation in twins: A report on 61 pairs and three triplet sets. *Archives of Sexual Behavior*, **22**, 187–206.

Whitbeck, L. B., & Hoyt, D. R. (1994). Social prestige and assortative mating: A comparison of students from 1956 and 1988. *Journal of Social and Personal Relationships*, **11**, 137–145.

White, G. L. (1980). Inducing jealousy: A power perspective. *Personality and Social Psychology Bulletin*, **6**, 222–227.

White, G. L., & Kight, T. D. (1984). Misattribution of arousal and attraction: Effects of salience of explanations of arousal. *Journal of Experimental Social Psychology*, **20**, 55–64.

White, G. L., & Mullen, P. E. (1989). *Jealousy: Theory, research, and clinical strategies*. New York: Guilford.

White, G. L., Fishbein, S., & Rutstein, J. (1981). Passionate love and misattribution of arousal. *Journal of Personality and Social Psychology*, **41**, 56–62.

White, J. L., & Parham, T. A. (1990). *The psychology of Blacks: An African-American perspective*, 2nd edn. Englewood Cliffs, NJ: Prentice Hall.

White, L. K. (1983). Determinants of spousal interaction: marital structure or marital happiness. *Journal of Marriage and the Family*, **45**, 511–519.

White, R. W. (1959). Motivation reconsidered: The concept of competence. *Psychological Review*, **66**, 297–333.

Wiederman, M. W. (1993). Evolved gender differences in mate preferences: Evidence from personal advertisements. *Ethology and Sociobiology*, **14**, 331–352.

Wiederman, M. W., & Allgeier, E. R. (1993). Gender differences in sexual jealousy: Adaptionist or social learning explanation? *Ethology and Sociobiology*, **14**, 115–140.

Wieselquist, J., Rusbult, C. E., Foster, C. A., & Agnew, C. R. (in press). Commitment, pro-relationship behavior, and trust in close relationships. *Journal of Personality and Social Psychology*.

Wilkinson, G. S. (1988). Reciprocal altruism in bats and other mammals. *Ethology and Sociobiology*, **9**, 85–100.

Wilkinson, G. S. (1990). Food sharing in vampire bats. *Scientific American*, February, 76–82.

Williams, J. E., & Best, D. L. (1990). *Sex and psyche: Gender and self viewed cross- culturally*. Newbury Park, CA: Sage.

Williams, K. D. (1997). Social ostracism. In R. Kowalski (Ed.) *Aversive interpersonal behaviors* (pp. 133–171). New York: Plenum.

Wilson, E. O. (1975). *Sociobiology: The new synthesis*. Cambridge, MA: Harvard University Press.

Wilson, M., & Daly, M. (1985). Competitiveness, risk taking, and violence: The young male syndrome. *Ethology and Sociobiology*, **6**, 59–73.

Wiseman, J. P. (1986). Friendship: Bonds and binds in a voluntary relationship. *Journal of Social and Personal Relationships*, **3**, 191–211.

Wish, M., Deutsch, M., & Kaplan, S. J. (1976). Perceived dimensions of interpersonal relations. *Journal of Personality and Social Psychology*, **33**, 409–420.

Wolfgang, M. E. (1958). *Patterns in criminal homicide*. Philadelphia: University of Pennsylvania Press.

Wong, M. M., & Csikszentmihalyi, M. (1991). Affiliation motivation and daily experience: Some issues on gender differences. *Journal of Personality and Social Psychology*, **60**, 154–164.

Wood, J. T. (1993). Engendered relationships: Interaction, caring, power, and responsibility in intimacy, *Understanding relationship processes 3: Social contexts of relationships* (pp. 27–53). Newbury Park: Sage.

Wood, J. T. (1995a). Feminist scholarship and the study of relationships. *Journal of Social and Personal Relationships*, **12**, 103–120.

Wood, J. T. (1995b). *Relational communication: Continuity and change in personal relationships*. Belmont, CA: Wadsworth.

Wood, J. T., & Cox, J. R. (1993). Rethinking critical voice: materiality and situated knowledge. *Western Journal of Communication*, **57**, 278–287.

Wood, J. T., Dendy, L. L., Dordek, E., Germany, M., & Varallo, S. M. (1994). Dialectic of difference: A thematic analysis of intimates' meanings for difference. In K. Carter & M. Presnell (Eds) *Interpretive approaches to interpersonal communication* (pp. 115–136). New York: SUNY Press.

Wright, R. A., & Contrada, R. J. (1986). Dating selectivity and interpersonal attraction: Toward a better understanding of the "elusive phenomenon." *Journal of Social and Personal Relationships*, **3**, 131–148.

Yee, A. H., Fairchild, H. H., Weizmann, F., & Wyatt, G. E. (1993). Addressing psychology's problems with race. *American Psychologist*, **48**, 1132–1140.

Yinger, J. M. (1994). *Ethnicity: Source of strength? Source of conflict?* Albany, NY: SUNY Press.

Yovetich, N. A., & Rusbult, C. E. (1994). Accommodative behavior in close relationships: Exploring transformation of motivation. *Journal of Experimental Social Psychology*, **30**, 138–164.

Zack, N. (1993). *Race and mixed race.* Philadelphia: Temple University Press.

Zajonc, R. B. (1968). Attitudinal effects of mere exposure. *Journal of Personality and Social Psychology Monograph Supplement*, **9** (2, Pt. 2), 1–27.

Zanna, M. P., & Pack, S. J. (1975). On the self-fulfilling nature of apparent sex differences in behavior. *Journal of Experimental Social Psychology*, **11**, 583–591.

Zimbardo, P. G. (1977). *Shyness.* New York: Jove.

Zorn, T. (1995). Bosses and buddies: Constructing and performing simultaneous hierarchical and close friendship relationships. In J. T. Wood & S. W. Duck (Eds) *Under-studied relationships: Off the beaten track* (pp. 122–147). Thousand Oaks, CA: Sage.

Zweigenhaft, R. L., & Domhoff, G. W. (1991). *Blacks in the White establishment? A study of race and class in America.* New Haven, CT: Yale University Press.

AUTHOR INDEX

Abbey, A., 85, 166
Acitelli, L. K., 2, 8, 153, 217, 219, 222, 224, 226
Adams, J. S., 3
Adams, R. G., 56
Agnew, C. R., 87, 100–102, 106, 122, 127, 137
Agyei, Y., 33, 34
Ahn, A., 148
Ahuvia, A., 120
Ainsworth, M. D. S., 42, 45, 50, 51
Albright, L. A., 213
Alcock, J., 15
Aldridge, D. P., 66, 70, 71
Alger, C. E ., 169
Allan, G. A., 218, 222, 223, 224
Allen, J. B., 118, 126
Allgeier, E. R., 25
Allport, G. W., 57, 61, 62, 67, 70, 71, 75, 76
Altman, I., 45, 46, 114, 132, 216, 218, 224
Ames, M. A., 33
Andersen, P. A., 74, 219
Anderson, J. L., 11
Angleitner, A., 25
Antill, J. K., 164
Apsler, R., 140
Archer, R. L., 164
Argyle, M., 216, 218
Aron, A., 45, 71, 79, 98, 110, 111, 113–119, 121–127, 134, 137, 150
Aron, E. N., 45, 79, 98, 110, 111, 113, 115–127, 134, 137, 150
Aronson, E., 114, 125
Arriaga, X. B., 103, 104
Asante, M., 74
Asch, S, 134
Asher, S, J., 43
Ashmore, R. D., 72
Atkinson, J., 167, 176, 177
Auster, C. J., 70
Axelrod, R., 26, 89, 95, 97

Back, K. W., 222
Backman, C. W., 45
Bailey, J. M., 33, 34
Baillet, S. D., 124
Baker, V., 120,
Baldwin, M. W., 79, 106, 131
Bandura, A., 6, 110
Barbee, A. P., 22, 220, 225
Barker, R. G., 169
Barkow, J. H., 31
Barlow, D. H., 136
Barnes, L. C., 148
Barnes, M. F., 14, 24, 83
Barr, A., 33–35
Barrett, K., 51
Bartholomew, K., 38
Bassin, E., 83
Bates, C., 148
Bateson, G., 219
Bator, R. J., 134
Batson, C. D., 99
Baum, A., 178
Baumeister, R. F., 105, 130, 131, 133, 135, 136, 139, 140, 148, 149
Baxter, L. A., 116, 146, 153, 220
Bazzini, D. G., 134
Beach, F.A., 19
Beach, S. R. H., 149
Beall, A., 223
Beavin, J., 225
Becker, H. S., 87
Bednarski, R., 225
Belk, R. W., 120
Bell, K. L., 136
Bell, L., 125
Belsky, J., 31
Bendtschneider, L., 221
Berg, J. H., 45, 132, 148, 164
Bergen, M. R., 118
Berger, C. R., 114, 219
Berger, P., 218
Bergler, E., 115

Bergmann, J. R., 225
Berkowitz, L., 89
Berlyne, D. E., 68, 116
Bern, S. L., 164
Bernardin, H. J., 135
Bernstein, I. S., 61
Bernston, G. C., 220
Berry, N. J., 142
Berscheid, E., 2, 3, 43, 50, 69, 92, 102,
     105, 215–217, 219–221, 223
Best, D. L., 148
Betzig, L., 21, 25
Birren, J. E., 48
Bissonnette, V. L., 2, 103, 120, 169, 177
Blackstone, T., 73, 76
Blau, P. M., 3, 87,
Bledsoe, S. B., 22
Blehar, M. C., 42, 45, 50, 51
Blieszner, R., 56
Blood, R. O., 114
Bloom, B. L., 43
Blumstein, P., 90
Bock, R. D., 197
Bolger, N., 219
Bolig, R., 22
Bombar, M. L., 149
Bond, M. H., 148
Bowen, G. L., 148
Bower, G. H., 124
Bowlby, J., 5, 38–42, 81, 100
Bradburn, N. M., 116, 117
Bradbury, T. N., 106, 140, 219, 223
Bradshaw, D., 43
Braito, R., 144
Brake, S., 51
Brehm, S. S., 22, 48, 115
Brennan, K. A., 53
Brewer, M. B., 72, 120
Brickman, P., 85
Briggs, S., 169
Britt, T. W., 152
Britton, B., 144
Britton, S. D., 142
Brockner, J., 87
Broude, G. J., 23
Brown, B. B., 114, 216, 218, 224
Brown, D. E., 16
Brown, H., 148
Brown, J. D., 85
Brown, R., 72
Brown, S., 14, 33–35
Bryan, A., 33–35
Bryk, A. S., 19
Buber, M., 120
Buck, M., 51

Buller, D. B., 145
Burdette, M. P., 140
Burgoon, J. K., 29, 145
Burnett, R., 165
Burnstein, E., 17
Burroughs, R., 22
Bush, E. G., 220, 221
Buss, D. M., 11, 14–16, 20, 22, 24, 25,
     33–35
Butler, J. L., 132, 149
Buunk, A. P., 25, 86, 87, 102, 140
Byers, J. A., 26
Byers, K. Z., 26
Byrne, D., 69, 125, 222

Cacioppo, J. T., 178,
Cameron, C., 22
Camire, L., 26, 143
Campbell, A., 85
Campbell, D. T., 102
Campbell, W. K., 137
Campos, J., 51
Canary, D. J., 88, 134
Caputo, C., 122
Carnevale, P. J. D., 139, 142
Carrington, P. I., 139
Carter, C. S., 46
Casano, R. A., 130, 136
Cate, R. M., 219
Chadderton, R., 56, 61
Chaiken, S., 138
Chao, P., 71
Chaplin, T. C., 171
Chapman, J. P., 63
Chapman, L. J., 63
Chastain, R. L., 144
Cherlin, A., 70
Chrisman, S. M., 144
Christensen, A., 176
Cialdini, R. B., 118, 152
Clance, P. R., 144
Clark, M. E., 22
Clark, M. S., 17, 103, 171
Clark, R. D., 20
Clark, R. E., 169
Cloven, D. H., 136, 138
Clulow, C., 70
Cohen, C. L., 223
Collard, J., 165
Collins, N. L., 38
Connor, C., 105
Contrada, R. J., 134, 143
Converse, P. E., 85
Cook, W. L., 86
Cornelius, J. S., 23

Cortese, A., 71, 126
Cosmides, L., 11, 16, 26, 27, 31, 33, 34, 93
Cox, J. R., 224
Cox, V C., 178
Cozby, P. C., 132
Crandall, C., 17
Crawford, C. B., 11
Crepin, A. E., 223
Crittenden, P. M., 53
Crosby, F., 83
Crouter, A. C., 85, 137, 218
Csikszentmihalyi, M., 167
Cunningham, M. R., 22, 152, 225
Cupach, W. R., 140, 219
Curtis, R. C., 45
Cutler, W. B., 51

Dainton, M., 142
Daly, M., 13–15, 20, 21, 25, 27–29, 31, 32, 136, 165
Daniels, L. R., 89
Dantchik, A., 14
Dardis, G. J., 90
Darley, J. M., 146
Darwin, C., 10, 19, 24
Daubman, K. A., 148
Davidson, J. R., 66, 71
Davies, J. C., 83
Davis, D. M., 148
Davis, K. E., 38, 72, 105
Davis, M. H., 103
Dawes, R. M., 89
Dawkins, R., 14
De La Ronde, C., 150
de Leeuw, J., 197
Dean, D. G., 144
Deci, E. L., 6, 110
DeFazio, V. J., 169
Dehue, F. M. J., 97
Dendy, L. L., 219
DeNicholas, M. E., 152
Denzin, N. K., 45
DePaulo, B. M., 105, 136, 144, 145
Derlega, V. J., 132, 148, 219
Deutsch, F. M., 22
Deutsch, M., 86, 103
deVries, M. W., 3
deWaal, F., 17, 18
Diamond, M., 33
Dimitri, S., 145
Dindia, K., 116, 148, 219
Dixson, M. D., 224
Dlugolecki, D. W, 131
Doherty, K., 131
Doherty, R. W.,71

Dollard, J., 113
Domhoff, G. W., 56, 57, 71
Donner, A., 185, 191
Dordek, E., 219
Downs, D. L., 132, 136, 139, 140, 144
Draper, P., 31
Drigotas, S. M., 83, 88
Druen, P. B., 22, 225
Du Bois, W. E. B., 61, 69, 75
Duck, S. W., 2, 3, 8, 58, 59, 67, 75, 107, 111, 112, 132, 161, 162, 165, 166, 176, 215, 216, 218–224, 226
Duckitt, J., 70
Dugosh, J.W., 2, 216, 217, 218, 226
Duncan, S., 204, 205, 209
Duncan, T., 225
Dunkel-Schetter, C., 85
Durodoye, B., 70
Dutton, D. G., 45, 87, 118, 119, 126

Early, G., 75
Eggert, L. L., 218, 224
Eibl-Eibesfeldt, I., 19, 43, 44
Ekman, P., 19
Eliasziw, M., 191
Elliot, A. J., 137
Ellis, B. J., 20
Ellis, L., 33
England, P., 116
Epstein, J. A., 144
Erikson, E. H., 113
Essed, P., 71
Ewens, W., 88

Fairchild, H. H., 69
Faucheux, C., 89
Feeney, J., 38
Fehr, B., 219
Feldman, H., 114
Felmlee, D. H., 83, 87, 136, 220
Festinger, L., 83, 222
Fiala, S. E., 148
Finch, J. F., 152
Fincham, F. D., 3, 106, 140, 219
Fine, M. A., 74
Fischer, E. F., 21
Fischer, K. W., 3, 122
Fishbein, S., 118
Fisher, R. A., 48, 185
Fiske, D. W., 204, 205, 209
Fiske, S. T., 62, 88, 94, 104
Fitness, J., 219
Fitzgerald, N. M., 219
Fleiss, J. L., 185
Fleming, J. H., 146

Fletcher, G. J. O., 3, 106, 137, 219
Flicker, L., 136
Floyd, F., 166
Floyd, K., 134
Folwell, A. L., 130, 136
Form, W. H., 29
Foster, C. A., 101, 106
Frable, D. E. S., 73, 76
Freeman, D., 20
French, M., 70
Fried, M. L., 169
Friesen, W. V., 19
Frijda, N. H., 85, 104, 105
Fuhrman, R. W., 94
Funderberg, L., 67
Furman, W., 56
Furnham, A., 216, 218

Gabrielidis, C., 23
Gaines, S. O. Jr., 61, 68–71, 73–75, 78, 216
Gallanter, E., 41
Gallup, G. G., Jr., 139, 143
Galvin, S. L., 138, 144
Gangestad, S. W., 14, 15, 53, 85, 163
Garcia, C. R., 51
Garcia, S., 2, 103, 169
Garner, W., 43
Garvin-Doxas, K., 137
Gattiker, U. E., 20
Gaulin, S., 33, 34
Geary, D. G., 24
Gecas, V., 6, 110
Geerken, M. R., 144
Geisler, R. B., 150
Gelles, R. J., 27, 84
Gentry, K. W., 143
Gergen, K. J., 135
Germany, M., 219
Getzlaf, S., 51
Gilbert, D. T., 66, 137
Gilligan, S. G., 124
Ginat, J., 218, 224
Ginsberg, D., 169
Ginsburg, G. P., 224
Giuliano, T. A., 2, 148
Givens, D. B., 19
Gladue, B. A., 33, 34
Glaser, R., 43
Glenn, N. D., 114
Gliekauf-Hughes, C., 144
Goethals, G. R., 122, 134
Goffman, E., 57, 63, 73, 76, 77, 132, 140, 141, 153, 154
Gold, D. B., 145
Goldberg, L., 33

Goldsmith, H., 51, 197
Gonzales, M. H., 140
Gonzalez, R., 2, 188, 191, 195, 202, 206, 208, 212, 215–217
Goodwin, J. S., 43
Gordon, R. A., 139
Gordon, S. L., 224
Gottman, J. M., 90, 95, 169, 171, 172
Goulet, N., 139, 143
Gove, W. R., 144
Graetz, K. A., 90
Graham, J., 216, 218
Graziano, W. G., 43, 211
Greenberg, L., 29
Greenwald, A. G., 29
Griesinger, D. W., 95
Griffin, D., 2, 86, 130, 140, 188, 191, 195, 202, 203, 206, 208, 209, 220
Gross, M., 11
Groth, G. E., 13, 14, 33
Gruder, C. L., 89
Grzelak, J. L., 90
Gubrium, J. F., 145
Gudykunst, W., 72, 221
Guerrero, L. K., 136, 137
Gump, R V., 169
Gumpert, P., 135
Gunn, D. O., 124
Gurung, R. A. R., 3, 221, 226
Gutierres, S. E., 33
Guttentag, M., 88

Haggard, E. A., 185, 186
Hahlweg, K., 166
Halberstadt, A. G., 100
Halford, L. J., 169
Hamilton, D. L., 63
Hamilton, W. D., 12, 26
Hammon, D., 225
Hanna, S. E., 103
Harinck, F., 87, 100, 101
Harlow, H., 44
Harlow, M. K., 44
Harpending, H., 23
Harris, R., 56, 61
Harrison, A. A., 22
Harvey, J. H., 66, 163, 165, 176, 179
Hatchett, S., 220
Hatfield, E., 3, 19, 20, 48, 71, 115, 126
Hause, K. S., 134
Hauser, R. M., 197
Hazan, C., 38, 43, 45, 49, 51, 53, 79, 100, 127
Heatherington, L., 148
Heider, F., 3, 62, 64, 120

Heller, K., 226
Helms-Erickson, H., 218
Hendrick, C., 163, 169, 223
Hendrick, S. S., 163, 165, 169, 176, 179, 223
Henry, S., 124
Hepburn, J. R., 223
Hernton, C. C., 66, 70–72, 74, 76
Hertel, P. T., 2
Herz, M. J., 114
Higgins, E. T., 83
Hill, C. T., 47
Hill, K., 17
Hill, M. S., 117
Hilton, J. L., 146
Hinde, R. A., 226
Hixon, J. G., 150
Ho, M. K., 57, 70
Hobfoll, S. E., 3
Hodgins, H. S., 136
Hofer, M. A., 50, 51
Hoffman, M. L., 119
Hogan, R., 31
Hogg, E., 136
Holdaway, S., 169
Holland, C. L., 144
Holliday, J., 43
Holman, T. B., 117
Holmes, J. G., 29, 31, 86, 87, 90, 101, 103, 104, 106, 130, 136, 140, 151, 195, 203, 209, 220
Homans, G. C., 3
Honeycutt, J. M., 219
Horowitz, L. M., 38
Hosman, L. A., 178
Howell, F., 116
Howitt, D., 69
Hoyle, R. H., 90
Hoyt, D. R., 222
Hubel, D., 34
Huesmann, L. R., 114
Huggins, G. R., 51
Hughes, M., 144
Hupka, R. B., 25
Hurst, A. P., 130, 136
Hurst, M., 226
Hurt, W. C., 43
Hurtado, M., 17
Huston, M., 48, 71, 72, 77, 85, 87, 98, 134, 137, 167, 176, 177, 219, 221, 222
Huston, T. L., 75, 165
Hutton, D. G., 148

Ickes, W. J., 2, 66, 70, 103, 120, 143, 168, 169, 170, 172, 175, 178, 182, 184, 196, 199, 203, 212, 215–218, 226

Insko, C. A., 83, 90
Iverson, A., 45, 118, 126

Jack, D. C., 144
Jacklin, C. N., 210, 211
Jackson, D., 225
Jacobson, N. S., 114
Jacquart, M., 117
James, W., 10, 120
Jankowiak, W. R., 21
Janoff-Bulman, R., 148
Jedlicka, D., 72
Jellison, J. M., 143
Jennings, S., 122
Johnson, D. J., 72, 85, 87, 101
Johnson, M. P., 74, 75, 88, 101, 165, 221
Jones, E. E., 105, 122, 125, 132, 134, 135, 140, 143, 149
Jones, J. M., 75
Jones, W. H., 140
Jourard, S. M., 132
Judd, C. M., 185, 190
Jung, C. G., 115, 120

Kahneman, D., 65, 66, 85, 145
Kambon, K. K., 74
Kaplan, S. J., 86
Karis, T. A., 61, 67, 68, 70, 71, 75, 77
Karney, B. R., 223
Kashy, D. A., 144, 145, 177
Katz, P. A., 72
Keefe, R. C., 23, 31, 33–35
Keenan, J. M., 124
Keenan, J. P., 139, 143
Keith, J. M., 145
Kelleher, S., 219
Kelley, H. H., 3, 59, 65, 67, 80, 81, 83, 85, 86, 90, 91, 93, 95, 98–107, 208, 215, 216, 218, 219.
Kelly, G. A., 63, 220
Kelvin, P., 225
Kennedy, W. P., 169
Kenny, D. A., 2, 98, 148, 177, 182, 183, 185, 186, 188, 190, 197, 210, 211, 213, 216, 217, 222
Kenrick, D. T., 13–16, 20, 21, 23, 24, 27, 28, 31–35, 79, 118
Kephart, W. M., 72
Kerckhoff, A. C., 72, 222
Key, C. R., 43
Kidd, R. F., 66
Kiecolt-Glaser, J. K., 43
Kight, T. D., 118
Kilbourne, B. S., 116
Kimmel, M. J., 97

Kingston, P. W., 116, 117
Kirkendol, S. E., 144
Kirker, W. S., 123
Kirkpatrick, L. A., 38, 53
Kirson, D., 105
Kitayama, S., 17
Klein, R., 221
Knowles, E. S., 177
Kobak, R., 38
Köhler, W., 62
Koivisto, E., 51
Kojetin, B. A., 146
Koocher, G. F., 177
Korolewicz, A., 70
Korolewicz, M., 70
Kotler, T., 48
Kouri, K. M., 67, 71
Koval, J. J., 185
Kovecses, Z., 111
Kowalski, R. M., 105, 133, 135, 139, 142,
    219
Kraemer, H. C., 210, 211
Kraxberger, B. E., 141
Krebs, D. L., 60
Kreft, I., 197
Kristof, A. L., 148
Krones, J. M., 33
Krull, D. S., 66
Kuiper, N. A., 123
Kulkarni, M., 139, 143
Kunert, H., 166

La Gaipa, J. J., 219
La Voie, L., 196, 197, 213
Lakoff, G., 111, 112
Lamb, M., 51
Lamborn, S., 122
Lamke, L. K., 163, 164
Landel, J. L., 140
Lane, J. D., 145
Lange, C., 137
Langer, S. K., 111
Langston, C. A., 102, 137
Larsen, R., 25
Larson, D. G., 144
Lasswell, M., 67, 71
Lauris, G., 169
Lea, M., 149
Leary, M. R., 105, 115, 130–133, 135, 136,
    139–142, 144, 149, 225
Leatham, G., 166
Legant, P., 122
Leibowitz, M., 46, 47, 48
Lenington, S., 28
Leonard, J. L., 23

Lerma, M., 85
LeVay, S., 33
Levenson, R. W., 171, 172
Leventhal, H., 169
Levine, T. R., 145
Levinger, G., 56–59, 74, 101, 134
Levitskaya, A., 71, 126
Lewin, K., 86
Liebeskind, E., 136
Liebrand, W. B. G., 97, 100
Lind, E. A., 103
Lind, J., 51
Lindemann, E., 51
Linder, D. E., 114, 118
Littig, L. W., Jr., 149
Littlefield, C. H., 29
Livingston, J. W., 95
Livingston, K. R., 114
Livingstone, M., 34
Lockard, J. S., 18
Locke, H. J., 114
Lofland, L. H., 42
Longstreth, M., 40, 219
Lord, C. G., 123
Lorenz, K., 44
Lumsden, C. J., 11, 15, 16, 18, 31
Lund, M., 164
Lynch, J. J., 43

Maccoby, E. E., 224
MacFarlane, S., 14
Machleit, K. A., 120
Maguire, A. M., 171
Major, B., 139
Maki, B. K., 130, 136
Malamuth, N. M., 171
Mamali, C., 167
Mandler, G., 104
Manning, D. J., 140
Mansfield, P, 165
Marecek, J., 122
Margolin, G., 95, 114
Margulis, S. T., 132, 219
Markman, H. J., 95, 166, 169
Markus, H. R., 123
Marris, P., 38
Martin, J., 33, 132, 136, 144
Martin, K., 144
Martin, R., 147
Martz, J. M., 84
Marx, G., 167
Maslow, A. H., 121
Matter, C. E., 177
Mazanec, M., 146, 220
McCain, G., 178

McCall, G. J., 67, 75, 121
McCall, M. A., 118
McClelland, K. E., 70
McClintock, C. G., 97, 100
McClintock, E., 176
McCornack, S. A., 145
McDonald, R. P., 197
McDougall, W., 10
McHale, S. M., 85, 137, 167, 176, 177
McKenna, C., 117
McKenry, P. C., 22
McKinney, J. L., 56, 61
McMullen, A., 132, 136, 144
McNeal, J., 117
Mead, G. H., 4
Mealey, L., 14
Melinat, E., 134
Mellen, S. L. W., 16, 21
Mencken, H. L., 164
Mendoza, J. L., 211
Merleau-Ponty, M., 120
Messick, D. M., 100
Messner, M. A., 70
Metts, S., 132, 140, 164, 219, 225
Middlemist, R. D., 177
Middleton, K., 53
Miell, D. E., 107, 226
Mikula, G., 12
Mikulincer, M., 38, 53
Milardo, R. M., 165, 221, 224
Miller, D. T., 60, 142
Miller, G. A., 41
Miller, K., 45
Miller, L. C., 98, 164
Miller, N. E., 113
Miller, N., 72
Miller, R. S., 85, 136, 137, 139–141, 143,
   151, 152, 219, 225
Mills, J., 17, 103, 171
Mirande, A. 74
Mitchell-Kernan, C., 70
Miyake, K., 149
Moghaddam, F. M., 17, 72
Molm, L. D., 88
Montgomery, B. M., 45
Moore, M. M., 19
Mori, D., 138
Morier, D., 138
Morris, D., 16
Mullen, P. E., 25, 87
Muraven, M. B., 132, 149
Murphy, B. C., 222
Murray, S. L., 86, 87, 90, 130, 136, 140,
   151, 195, 203, 209, 220
Murstein, B. I., 125, 136, 222

Myrdal, G., 70

Nachshon, O., 38, 53
National Research Council, 63, 70
Nelligan, J. S., 100
Nelson, G., 122, 123, 124
Neuberg, S. L., 33, 94
Newcomb, T. M., 125
Nezlek, J. B., 132, 136, 144, 165
Nicholson, J. H., 146, 220
Nisbett, R. E., 122
Nisbett, R. E., 65, 66, 122
Nock, S. L., 116, 117
Noller, P., 38
Norman, C., 119
Normansell, L. A., 48
Nosow, S., 29
Notariu., 95, 169

Oathout, H. A., 103
Olsen, N., 121, 150
Olson, D. H., 59, 67, 75, 113, 224
Omoto, A. M., 124
Orbell, J. M., 89
Orden, S. R., 116, 117
Orpen, C., 148
Orthner, D. K., 116, 117
Osborne, R. E., 137
Oskamp, S., 22
Oubaid, V., 25
Owusu-Bempah, J., 69

Pack, S. J., 138
Page, J. R., 144
Panksepp, J., 48
Parham, T. A., 69, 74
Paris, M., 127
Parkes, C. M., 38
Parks, M. R., 134, 218, 224
Patrick, B. C., 100
Patterson, M. L., 170, 175
Patton, K. M., 140
Paulhus, D. L., 18
Paulus, P. B., 178
Pederson, J. H., 140
Peeke, H. V. S., 114
Pegalis, L. J., 134
Pelham, B. W., 66
Penn, G. M., 43
Penn, M. L., 68–70, 73, 74
Pennebaker, J. W., 132
Peplau, L. A., 47, 224
Perper, T., 19
Peterson, D. R., 90
Petronio, S., 132, 219

Pettigrew, T. F., 70, 72
Petty, R. E., 178
Phillips, L., 68–70, 73, 74
Phinney, J. S., 72
Piaget, J., 111
Pieper, W. A., 144
Piliavin, J., 143
Pillard, R. C., 33
Pinker, S., 11
Pinkney, A., 63
Pipp, S., 122
Pittman, G., 146, 220
Pittman, T. S., 143
Planalp, S., 137
Pliner, P., 138
Plutchik, R., 114
Pond, K., 166
Ponder, E., 169
Porterfield, E., 62, 67, 71, 74–77
Potapova, E., 71, 126
Powell, M. C., 98
Powell, R. D., 61, 67, 68, 70, 71, 75, 77
Powers, E. A., 144
Prager, K. J., 219
Prentice, D. A., 122, 124
Presser, H. B., 22
Preston, C., 148
Preti, G., 51
Pribram, K. H., 41
Pruitt, D. G., 97, 142

Quinsey, V. L., 171

Radford-Davenport, J., 132, 136, 144
Radloff, C. E., 122
Rahe, R. H., 31
Rajecki, D. W., 22, 59, 60–62, 170, 175
Rands, M., 56–59
Rapoport, A., 90
Rasmussen, J. L., 22
Raudenbush, S. W., 197
Read, S. J., 38
Reed, E. S., 61, 70, 75
Reeder, G. D., 137
Reedy, M. N., 48
Reik, T., 115, 120
Reis, H. T., 3, 100, 119, 121, 139, 150, 165, 166, 176, 177, 215–217, 219, 220, 223
Reissman, C., 118
Rejeski, W. J., 144
Rempel, J. K., 101, 106
Retzinger, S. M., 219
Revenstorf, D., 166
Rholes, W. S., 100

Ridley, C. A., 59, 67, 75, 220, 224
Riesman, D., 169
Riggio, R. E., 142
Riordan, C. A., 118
Robertson, E., 212
Robertson, J., 40
Robins, E., 167, 176, 177
Robinson, W. S., 183, 185, 197
Rodgers, W. L., 85
Rodriguez, G., 126
Rogers, C., 132
Rogers, T. B., 123
Rollins, B., 114
Roloff, M. E., 136, 138
Rook, K. S., 219, 226
Rose, T. L., 63
Rosenblatt, P. C., 61, 62, 67, 68, 70, 71, 75, 77, 164
Rosenfeld, L. B., 148
Rosner, B., 191
Ross, L., 65, 66
Ross, R. R., 220, 221
Rotter, J. B., 125
Rowatt, W. C., 152
Rubenstein, C., 163
Rubin, J. Z., 87
Rubin, L. B., 76
Rubin, Z., 47
Rudman, L. A., 146, 148, 153
Runciman, W. G., 120
Rusbult, C. E., 74, 83–88, 98, 99, 101–104, 106, 107, 122, 128, 130, 137, 138, 216
Rushton, J. P., 28, 29
Russell, C. S., 113
Rutstein, J., 118
Rutt, D. J., 226

Sabatelli, R., 83
Sacks, D., 136
Sadalla, E. K., 13, 14, 33
Saeed, L., 22
Sande, G. N., 122
Sanford, M. D., 164
Sanjek, R., 56, 67, 72
Sants, H. K. A., 59, 67, 176, 224
Sarason, B. R., 3, 221, 226
Sarason, I. G., 3, 221, 226
Sarret, J. M., 43
Satir, V., 146
Scanzoni, J., 88
Scanzoni, L. D., 88
Schachter, S., 222
Schaie, K. W., 48
Scherbaum, C., 73, 76
Schindler, L., 166

Schlenker, B. R., 130–133, 138, 149–151
Schmidt, L., 143
Schmitt, D. P., 15, 20, 33
Schneider, D. J., 135
Schopler, J., 90
Schreindorfer, L. S., 145
Schutz, A., 4
Schwartz, J., 105
Schwartz, P., 71, 77, 90, 221, 222
Schwartz, W., 136
Scott, C. K., 94
Secord, P. F., 45, 88
Sedikides, C., 121, 137, 150
Segal, N., 29
Segrin, C., 225
Semmelroth, J., 25
Senchak, M., 139
Seroy, C., 138
Shaffer, D. R., 134
Shair, H., 51
Sharp, A., 103
Sharp, E., 169
Shaver, P. R., 38, 43, 51, 53, 79, 100, 105,
     119, 122, 127, 219, 163
Sheets, V., 28
Shepher, J., 34
Sherk, D. L., 142
Sherman, P. W., 29
Short, R. V., 43
Shotter, J., 217
Shrout, P. E., 185
Sigelman, L., 73
Sillars, A. L., 130, 136
Silver, R., 50
Simmel, G., 223
Simmons, J. L., 67, 75
Simon, H. A., 102
Simpson, G. E., 74
Simpson, J. A., 14, 38, 53, 83, 85, 87, 100,
     142, 163
Singh, D., 14
Sivadas, E., 120
Siviy, S. M., 48
Slade, S., 51
Slovik, P., 65, 66, 145
Small, L., 56, 61
Smith, E., 124
Smith, J. L., 142
Smith, K., 146, 220
Smith, M., 136
Smollan, D., 113, 121
Snyder, M., 92, 101, 142, 178
Solomon, B., 139
Solomon, R. L., 85
Sorrentino, R. M., 103

Spanier, G., 163, 164
Sparks, W., 22
Spears, R., 149
Speicher, C., 43
Spickard, P. R., 67, 71, 72
Spigner, C. C., 72
Spitz, R. A., 40
Spitzberg, B. H., 219
Sprecher, S., 48, 71, 83, 88, 126, 164
Sprenkle, D. H., 113
Sroufe, L. A., 42
Stack, S.170
Stafford, L., 88, 134, 142
Stahelski, A. J., 100, 101
Staples, R., 67, 71, 74
Steemers, G. E. M., 87, 100, 101
Stein, C. H., 220, 221
Stein, J., 168, 219
Stein, P. J., 22
Stein-Seroussi, A., 150
Steinberg, L., 31
Stenberg, C., 51
Stephan, W. G., 63, 70
Stern, D. N., 45
Sternberg, R. J., 83, 223
Stevens, C. K., 148
Stevens, H. B., 144
Stevenson-Hinde, J., 38
Stillwell, A. M., 132, 149
Stinson, L., 2, 103, 120, 169, 182, 184,
     196, 199, 203
Stires, L. D., 135
Stone, L., 21
Strachan, C. E., 87
Strahan, R., 135
Straus, M. A., 27
Strejc, H., 226
Stroebe, W., 4
Strongman, K, 219
Strube, M. J., 84
Studd, M. V., 20
Suls, J., 225
Suomi, S. J., 29
Surra, C. A., 40, 59, 67, 75, 219, 220, 224
Swann, W. B., Jr., 3, 111, 150
Symons, D., 14, 20, 22

Tajfel, H., 72, 120
Tanford, S., 170, 175
Tangney, J. P., 3, 136
Tanke, E., 92
Tardy, C. H., 178
Taylor, D. A., 45, 72
Taylor, D. M., 17, 72
Taylor, D., 46, 132,

Taylor, S. E., 62, 85
Taylor, S., 216
Tchividjian, L. R., 141
Tedeschi, J. T., 118
Teger, A. I., 87
Teng, G., 212
Tennov, D., 46
Terkel, S., 67
Tesser, A., 110, 120, 149
Thibaut, J. W., 3, 80, 81, 83, 86, 89, 93,
    95, 98, 99, 102, 103, 106, 135, 208
Thiessen, D., 22
Thomas, G., 137
Thompson, J. M., 188
Thompson, K., 71
Thornhill, N. W., 31
Thornhill, R., 14, 15, 31
Tice, D. M., 132, 148, 149
Timmer, S. G., 220
Tjosvold, D., 89
Tobey, A. E., 53
Todd, J., 56, 61
Tooby, J., 11, 16, 26, 27, 31, 33, 34, 93
Tooke, W., 26, 120, 143, 168, 172, 212
Traupmann, J., 48, 115
Trevarthan, C., 41
Triandis, H. C., 66, 71
Trivers, R. L., 12, 13, 15, 18, 24, 26
Trost, M. R., 13, 14, 16, 21, 27, 33, 35, 79
Trovato, E., 169
Tucker, K., 163, 165, 176, 179
Tucker, M. B., 70
Tucker, P., 114–116
Tudor, M., 122, 123, 124
Turner, J. C., 120
Turner, M., 111
Tversky, A., 65, 66, 85, 145
Tyler, T. R., 103

U. S. Bureau of the Census, 56
Upfold, D., 171

Vallone, R. D., 134
Van Dalfsen, P., 51
Van de Kragt, A. J. C., 89
van der Leeden, R., 197
van Dijk, T. A., 69
Van Lange, P. A. M., 86, 87, 99–102, 107,
    130, 122, 137
Van Run, G. J., 100
Van Yperen, N. W., 86
Vangelisti, A. L., 98
Varallo, S. M., 219
Veith, J. L., 51
Verette, J., 87, 88, 98, 101, 103, 138

Veroff, J., 220
Vershure, B., 14
Villanova, P., 135
Vinsel, A., 114, 216
von Baeyer, C. L., 142
Vorauer, J. D., 142
Vormbrock, J. K., 50
Vuorenkowski, V., 51

Wade, M. B., 148
Walker, L., 103
Wall, S., 42, 45, 50, 51
Wallace, K. M., 114
Wallace, L. A., 134
Wallach, L., 98
Wallach, M. A., 98
Waller, W., 88
Walster, E., 102, 125, 139, 143
Walster, G. W., 3, 102, 125, 143
Walters, R. W., 75
Wampold, B. E., 95
Ward, M., 220, 221
Warner, R. R., 11
Wasz-Hockert, O., 51
Waters, E., 42, 45, 50, 51
Watson, J., 169
Watzlawick, P., 225
Weghorst, S. J., 25
Wegner, D. M., 2, 119, 145
Weick, K., 169
Weigold, M. F., 150
Weiner, B., 104
Weis, D. L., 19
Weiss, R. S., 42, 47
Weizmann, F., 69
Welch, S., 73
Wellman, B., 221, 224
Werking, K., 221
Werner, C., 218, 224
West, L., 8, 146, 220
Westen, D., 25
Weston, K., 221
Wetter, D. W., 140
Wetzel, C. G., 83
Wheeler, L., 45, 149, 165, 166, 176, 177
Whitam, F. L., 33
Whitbeck, L. B., 222
White, G. L., 6, 25, 87, 118
White, J. L., 69, 74
White, L. K., 116
White, R. W., 110
White, S. W., 43
Whiteley, P., 142
Widenmann, S., 153
Wiederman, M. W., 22, 25

Wieselquist, J., 101, 106
Wilkinson, G. S., 17
Williams, J. E., 148
Williams, K. D., 143, 20
Wilson, E. O., 10, 11, 15, 16, 18, 31, 81
Wilson, M. I., 13–15, 20, 21, 25, 27, 29, 32, 165
Wilson, M., 28, 31
Wiseman, J. P., 219
Wish, M., 86
Wishnov, V. B., 135
Wolfe, D.W., 114
Wolfgang, M. E., 27
Wong, M. M., 167
Wood, J. T., 131, 219, 220, 224, 226,
Wright, R. A., 134, 143
Wright, S. C., 17

Wyatt, G. E., 69
Wyer, M. M., 144
Wyer, R. S., Jr., 94

Yee, A. H., 69
Yinger, J. M., 57, 74
Young, A.M., 224
Young, R. K., 22
Yovetich, N. A., 98, 138

Zalenski, C. M., 22
Zanna, M. P., 101, 138, 142
Zeifman, D., 38, 45, 49, 53
Zierk, K. L., 33
Zimring, L., 136
Zorn, T., 146
Zweigenhaft, R. L., 56, 57, 71

SUBJECT INDEX

Adaptation, 15
Altruism, 28, 216
Arousal, 118
Attachment, 38–44, 46, 49, 51, 52
Attraction, 118, 125
Audience, 146, 218
Augmentation, 64, 65

Basis for dependence, 89
Behavior Control (BC), 86

Choice, 217, 218, 223
Closeness, 121
Communication, 19
Comparison Level (CL), 83
Comparison Level for Alternatives (CL-alt), 83
Contexts, 218
Correspondence of outcomes, 86, 89
Cuckolds, 28
Culture, 31, 148, 221

Daily hassles, 219
Dark side, 219
Deception, 26
Decline of relationships, 115
Degree of dependence, 83, 86
Desired self, 150
Diary and account studies, 164
Dominance, 18
Drinks, 37
Dyadic data analysis, 183, 188, 190, 196, 203
Dyads, 181, 188, 190, 196, 205

Economic factors, 222
Embarrassment, 140, 219, 225
Emotional bonds, 10, 43, 46
Epistolary studies, 167
Ethical questions, 160
Ethnicity, 57
Everyday lives, 165, 166

Evolutionary psychology, 9–11, 15, 19, 29, 32
Exchange, 3, 4
Excuses, 140
Experimental methods, 170, 178

Fate Control (FC), 86
Flirting, 44, 45
Friendship, 17, 28

Gays, 76, 221
Genetics, 11
Given matrix vs. Effective matrix, 92
Gossip, 225
Group identification, 221

Hamlet, 1, 2

Impostor phenomenon, 144
Impressions, 13, 134, 137, 147, 152, 153
Impression management, 130, 136, 138, 148
Inclusive fitness, 12, 25
Ingratiation, 133, 139
Insiders, 55, 56, 66, 67, 70, 71, 73, 76, 216, 224
Interaction matrix, 81, 82
Interaction record studies, 165
Interdependence, 80, 92, 98, 127, 182, 184, 216
Interpersonal attraction, 47, 72
Interpersonal interaction, 209
Interpersonal relations, 208, 209
Interracial relationships, 56, 62, 66, 70, 74, 76
Interview studies, 164
Intimacy, 47, 50, 53
Intraclass correlation, 185, 187, 188, 190

Jealousy, 24
Jury decision-making, 216, 225

Kin selection, 12, 16, 21, 98, 31

Language, 11, 225
Lesbians, 76, 221
Lethargy, 49
Level of analysis, 159
Life-event archival methods, 169, 177
Love, 46, 47, 114

Marital satisfaction, 115, 117
Marriages, 20, 223
Mate selection, 12, 13, 20, 22, 23, 26, 33
Meaning analysis, 103, 104
Metaphors, 111, 112
Multiple audience problem, 146
Mutuality of dependence, 88

Need to belong, 135
Neighbors, 217
Norms, 142, 146, 148

Observational methods, 168, 177
Obtrusive methods, 159
Outsiders, 55, 58, 59, 62, 64, 67, 73, 221, 224
Ox, one's neighbor's, 217

Parental investment, 13
Peer report methods, 167, 177
Personal relationships, 113–115, 221
Perspectives, 159
Philosophy of method, 161
Physical contact, 50, 53
Physiological methods, 171, 178
Prejudice, 57, 63, 76, 77
Protest, 39
Psychological congruence, 225
Pubs, 224

Questionnaire studies, 163

Reflexive Control (RC), 86
Rejection, 145
Relational interest, 136, 142, 143, 152
Relational processes, 136, 152, 153, 220, 223
Relationship development, 49, 50

Relationship phases, 54
Research design, 203
Roles, 146, 147
Romantic relationships, 13, 16, 20, 21

Satisfaction vs. Dependence, 83–85
Self, 111, 119, 121, 123, 124, 141, 150
Self-disclosure, 131, 132, 134, 219, 225
Self-efficacy, 110
Self-expansion, 110–112, 115, 122
Self-presentation, 130–132, 140, 141, 144, 145, 147, 152
Self-report methods, 162, 176
Self-silencing, 138, 143, 144, 149
Separation distress, 40, 41, 48
Sex, 48, 50, 140, 226
Sexual selection, 12, 19, 20, 24
Shame, 149, 150
Similarity, 61, 69, 222
Sleep, 42, see also Lethargy
Social cognition, 222
Social comparison, 222
Social contexts, 222
Social identity, 68, 72, 73, 152
Socio-economic factors, 222
Statistical correlation, 195
Stereotypes, 63, 216
Stigma, 63
Sugar, 18

Talk, 225
Trade-off problem, 158, 159, 175, 179
solutions to, 161, 179
Transformation of motivation, 92–94, 96, 97, 99
Transition lists, 90, 95
Turning points, 220

Unobtrusive methods, 159
Unrequited love, 126

Violence, 27
Voluntary vs. nonvoluntary dependence, 84

Xenophobia, 58, 59, 61, 67

Related titles of interest...

European Journal of Social Psychology

Edited by FRITZ STRACK
In its six issues each year, this innovative journal publishes original research in all areas of social psychology, and is dedicated to fostering scientific communication within Europe and between European and other social psychologists.
ISSN: 0046 2772

European Review of Social Psychology

Edited by WOLFGANG STROEBE and MILES HEWSTONE
This annual series reflects the dynamism of social psychology in Europe and the attention now being paid to European ideas and research. The volumes in this series form an indispensable reference resource for all social psychologists. The series

- Provides readers with broad coverage through its geographical spread and theoretical diversity of authors
- Presents carefully edited chapters to give consistency and accessibility to an international exchange of information
- Encompasses the most up-to-date, authoritative view of contemporary social psychology today - an indispensable reference text for all social psychologists

Volume 10 0471 608130   Dec 1999   Hardback
0471 899682   Dec 1999   Paperback